W9-CHE-584

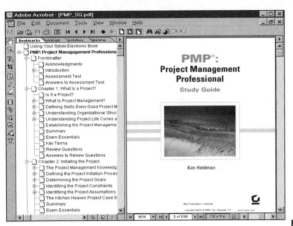

Search through the complete book in PDF!

- Access the entire *PMP: Project Management Professional Study Guide,* complete with figures and tables, in electronic format.

- Search the *PMP: Project Management Professional Study Guide* chapters to find information on any topic in seconds.

- Use Adobe Acrobat Reader (included on the CD-ROM) to view the electronic book.

Use the Electronic Flashcards for PCs or Palm devices to jog your memory and prep last minute for the exam!

- In addition to the Bonus Exams, we've included 100 Flashcard questions to ensure your knowledge of vital project management practices.

- Reinforce your understanding of key concepts with these hardcore flashcard-style questions.

Prepare for the PMP exam on the go with your handheld device!

- While you're waiting for your next meeting to begin, or riding to work on the train, make the most of your downtime by reviewing Flashcard questions on your handheld device.

- Download the Flashcards to your Palm device and take them with you. Now you can study for the exam anytime, anywhere.

SYBEX

PMP®: Project Management Professional Study Guide

Project Management Professional Exam Objectives

OBJECTIVE	CHAPTER
Project Initiation	
Determine Project Goals	2
Determine Deliverables	2
Determine Process Outputs	2
Document Constraints	2
Document Assumptions	2
Define Strategy	3
Identify Performance Criteria	3
Determine Resource Requirements	3
Define Budget	3
Produce Formal Documentation	3
Project Planning	
Refine Project	4
Create WBS	4
Develop Resource Management Plan	5
Refine Time and Cost Estimates	5
Establish Project Controls	6, 7
Develop Project Plan	7
Obtain Plan Approval	7
Project Execution	
Commit Resources	8
Implement Resources	8
Manage Progress	8, 9
Communicate Progress	8
Implement Quality Assurance Procedures	9

SYBEX

Exam objectives and content are subject to change at any time without prior notice and at the Project Management Institute's sole discretion. Please visit PMI®'s website (www.pmi.org) for the most current information of their exam content.

SYBEX

PMP:
Project Management Professional

Study Guide

PMP®:
Project Management Professional
Study Guide

Kim Heldman, PMP

San Francisco • London

Associate Publisher: Neil Edde
Acquisitions and Developmental Editor: Elizabeth Hurley
Editor: Ronn Jost
Production Editor: Kylie Johnston
Technical Editors: Claudia M. Baca, Patti Jansen
Book Designer: Bill Gibson
Graphic Illustrator: Tony Jonick
Electronic Publishing Specialist: Judy Fung
Proofreaders: Dave Nash, Laurie O'Connell, Yariv Rabinovitch, Nancy Riddiough
Indexer: Nancy Guenther
CD Coordinator: Dan Mummert
CD Technician: Kevin Ly
Cover Designer: Archer Design
Cover Illustrator/Photographer: Natural Selection

Library of Congress Card Number: 2002100063

ISBN: 0-7821-4106-4

Manufactured in the United States of America

10 9 8 7 6 5 4 3

SYBEX

To Our Valued Readers:

Sybex® is excited to be publishing the *PMP: Project Management Professional Study Guide*, the first of its kind for the increasingly critical business area of project management. The "soft skills" covered are certainly different from the technical topics one usually finds in Sybex® Study Guides, but the relevance of such skills to the world of IT and beyond will be immediately evident to all who peruse this invaluable book.

Just as the Project Management Institute is committed to establishing measurable standards for certifying project management professionals, Sybex is committed to providing those professionals with the skills and knowledge needed to meet those standards. Our author and editors have worked hard to ensure that this *PMP: Project Management Professional Study Guide* is comprehensive, in-depth, and pedagogically sound. We're confident that this book will meet and exceed the demanding standards of the certification marketplace and help you, the PMP exam candidate, succeed in your endeavors.

Good luck in pursuit of your PMP certification!

Neil Edde
Associate Publisher—Certification
Sybex, Inc.

To BB for your ever continuing encouragement and support.

—Kim Heldman

Acknowledgments

Thank you to the terrific team at Sybex for their dedication, encouragement, and diligence in producing this book. Thanks especially to Kylie Johnston, production editor, for answering all my questions. I cannot say enough good things about my great experiences working with the team at Sybex. They are all wonderful. And thanks to all the rest of the behind-the-scenes team including Judy Fung, Tony Jonick, Kevin Ly, Dan Mummert, Dave Nash, Laurie O'Connell, Yariv Rabinovitch, and Nancy Riddiough.

A very special thank you to Elizabeth Hurley for taking a chance on this book and for giving me the opportunity to write it. Elizabeth, you're the best!

Thank you to Ronn Jost for the excellent editing job and for never losing patience with me when I accidentally changed official titles and terms throughout the manuscript. He kept me straight and caught anomalies I never would have seen.

Thanks as well to the technical editors, Claudia Baca and Patti Jansen, for their sharp eye and good suggestions.

None of this would have been possible without the continued suggestions, support, and encouragement from my best friend in the whole world, BB. Thanks to Bob and Terri for your prayers—they're always coveted and pulled me through when I had doubts. Thanks to Jill and John for your cheerleading behind the scenes and to mom and dad for giving me the love of reading. And thanks also to Jason, Leah, Noelle, Amanda, Matt, Kate, and Juliette for understanding my limited availability and for your encouragement and enthusiasm.

Contents at a Glance

Contents

Introduction

This book was designed for anyone thinking of taking the Project Management Professional (PMP®) exam sponsored by the Project Management Institute (PMI®). This certification is growing in popularity and demand in all areas of business. PMI has experienced explosive growth in membership over the last few years, and more organizations are recognizing the importance of PMP certification.

This book assumes you have knowledge of general project management practices, but not necessarily specific *Guide to the Project Management Body of Knowledge (PMBOK)* practices. It's written so that you can skim through areas you are already familiar with, picking up the specific *Guide to the PMBOK* terminology where needed to pass the exam. Those of you with no formal training in project management but lots of experience will find the project management processes and techniques defined in such a way that you'll recognize things you've always done and be able to identify them with *Guide to the PMBOK* process names or methodologies.

PMI offers the most recognized certification in the field of project management, and this book deals exclusively with their procedures and methods. There are many methods of project management, each with its own terminology, tools, and procedures. If you are familiar with another organized project management methodology, don't assume you already know the *Guide to the PMBOK* processes. I strongly recommend you learn all of the processes—their key inputs, tools and techniques, and outputs. Take time to memorize the Key Terms found at the end of every chapter as well. Sometimes just understanding the definition of a term will help you answer a question. It might be that you've always done that particular thing or used the methodology described but called it by another name. Know the name of each process and its primary purpose.

An Exam Essentials section appears at the end of every chapter to highlight the topics you'll most likely find on the exam and help you focus on the most important material covered in the chapter so that you'll have a solid understanding of those concepts. However, it isn't possible to predict what questions will be covered on your particular exam, so be sure to study everything in the chapter.

Like the exam itself, this study guide is organized in terms of process groups and the natural sequence of events a project goes through in its life cycle. By contrast, other study guides organize their material by knowledge area—human resource management, communications management, and so on—and it can be confusing when studying for the exam to map the processes in each knowledge area to process groups.

Review Questions are provided at the end of every chapter. You can use these to gauge your understanding of the subject matter before reading the chapter and to point out the areas where you need to concentrate your study time. If you can answer at least 80 percent of the Review Questions, you can probably feel comfortable moving on to the next chapter. If you can't answer that many correctly, reread the chapter, or the section that seems to be giving you trouble, and try the questions again.

Don't rely on studying the Review Questions exclusively as your study method. The questions you'll see on the exam will be different than the questions presented in the book. There are 200 randomly generated questions on the PMP exam, so it isn't possible to cover every potential exam question in the Review Questions section of each chapter. Make sure you understand the concepts behind the material presented in each chapter and memorize all the formulas as well.

What Is the PMP Certification?

PMI was founded in 1969 and first started offering the Project Management Professional certification exam in 1984. They are accredited as an American National Standards Institute (ANSI) standards developer and also have the distinction of being the first organization to have their certification program attain International Organization for Standardization (ISO) 9001 recognition.

PMI boasts a worldwide membership of 86,000, with members from 125 different countries. Local PMI chapters meet regularly and allow project managers to exchange information and learn about new tools and techniques of project management or new ways to use established techniques. I encourage you to join a local chapter and get to know other professionals in your field.

PMI is the leader in project management practices and is the most widely recognized organization and certification in the field. PMI strives to maintain and promote standards and ethics in this field and offers publications, training, seminars, chapters, special interest groups, and colleges to further the project management discipline.

Why Become PMP Certified?

The following benefits are associated with becoming PMP certified:

- It demonstrates proof of professional achievement.

- It increases your marketability.

- It provides greater opportunity for advancement in your field.

- It raises customer confidence in you and your company's services.

Demonstrates Proof of Professional Achievement

PMP certification is a rigorous process that documents your achievements in the field of project management. The exam tests your knowledge of the disciplined approaches, methodologies, and project management practices as described in the *Guide to the PMBOK* published by the Project Management Institute.

You are required to have several years of experience in project management before sitting for the exam, as well as 35 hours of formal project management education. Your certification assures employers and customers that you are well grounded in project management practices and disciplines. It shows that you've got the hands-on experience, as well as a mastery of the processes and disciplines, to manage projects effectively and motivate teams to produce successful results.

Increases Your Marketability

Many industries are realizing the importance of project management and its role in the organization. They are also seeing that simply proclaiming a head technician to be "project manager" does not make it so. Project management, just like engineering, information technology, and a host of other trades, has its own specific qualifications and skills. Certification tells potential employers you've got the skills, experience, and knowledge to drive successful projects and ultimately improve the company's bottom line.

Certification will always make you stand out over the competition. If you are certified and are competing against a project manager without certification, chances are you will come out as the top pick. As a hiring manager, all things being equal, I will always opt for the candidate who has certification over the candidate who doesn't have it. Certification tells potential employers you have gone the extra mile. You've spent time studying techniques and methods as well as employing them in practice. It shows dedication to your own professional growth and enhancement, and to adhering to and advancing professional standards.

Provides Opportunity for Advancement

PMP certification displays your willingness to pursue growth in your professional career and shows that you're not afraid of a little hard work to get what you want. Potential employers will interpret your pursuit of this certification as a high-energy, success-driven, can-do attitude on your part. They will see that you're likely to display these same characteristics on the job, which will help make the company successful. Your certification displays a success-oriented, motivated attitude that will open up opportunities for future career advancements in your current field as well as new areas you might want to explore.

Raises Customer Confidence

Just as the PMP certification assures employers that you've got the background and experience to handle project management, customers are also assured they have a competent, experienced project manager at the helm. Certification will help your organization sell customers on your abilities to manage their projects. Customers, like potential employers, want the reassurance that those working for them have the knowledge and skills necessary to carry out the duties of the position and that professionalism and personal integrity are of utmost importance. Individuals who hold these ideals will translate their ethics and professionalism to their work. This enhances the trust customers will have in you, which in turn will give you the ability to influence them on important project issues.

How to Become PMP Certified

There are several requirements you'll need to fulfill in order to sit for the PMP exam. PMI has detailed the certification process quite extensively at their website. Go to www.pmi.org and click the Certification tab to get the latest information on certification procedures and requirements.

As of the date of this publication, you are required to fill out an application to sit for the PMP exam. You can submit this application online at http://certificationapp.pmi.org. You will also need to document 35 hours of formal project management education. This might include college classes, seminars, workshops, or training sessions. Be prepared to list the class titles, location, date, and content.

In addition to filling out the application and documenting your formal project management training, there is one additional set of criteria you'll need to meet to sit for the exam. These criteria fall into two categories. You need to meet the requirements for only one of these categories.

- Category 1 is for those who hold a baccalaureate degree. You'll need to provide proof, via transcripts, of your degree with your application. In addition, you'll need to complete verification forms, found at the PMI website, that show 4500 hours of project management experience that spans a minimum of three years and no more than six years.

- Category 2 is for those who do not hold a baccalaureate degree but do hold a high-school diploma or equivalent. You will need to complete verification forms documenting 7500 hours of project management experience that spans a minimum of five years and no more than eight years.

The exam fee at the time of this publication is $405 for PMI members and $555 for non-PMI members. Testing is conducted at Prometric centers. You can find a center near you at the PMI website. You have six months from the time PMI receives and approves your completed application to take the exam. You'll need to bring a form of identification such as a driver's license with you to the Prometric center on the test day. You will not be allowed to take anything with you into the testing center. You will be given a calculator, pencils, and scrap paper by the center. You will turn in all scrap paper, including the notes and squiggles you've jotted during the test, to the center upon completion of the exam.

The exam is scored immediately, so you will know if you've passed at the conclusion of the test. You're given four hours to complete the exam, which consists of 200 randomly generated questions that cover the following process groups and areas: Initiation, Planning, Executing, Controlling, Closing, and Professional Responsibility. All unanswered questions are scored as wrong answers, so it benefits you to guess at an answer if you are stumped on a question.

After you've received your certification, you'll be required to earn 60 professional development units (PDUs) every three years to maintain certification. Approximately one hour of structured learning translates to one PDU. The PMI website details what activities constitute a PDU, how many PDUs each activity earns, and how to register your PDUs with PMI to maintain your certification. As an example, attendance at a local chapter meeting earns one PDU.

Who Should Buy This Book?

If you are serious about passing the PMP exam, you should buy this book and use it to study for the exam. This book is unique in that it walks you through the project processes from beginning to end, just as projects are performed in practice. You will benefit from reading this book by learning specific *Guide to the PMBOK* processes and techniques coupled with real-life scenarios that describe how project managers in different situations handle problems and the various issues all project managers are bound to encounter during their career. This study guide describes in detail the exam objective topics in each chapter and has attempted to cover all of the important project management concepts.

How to Use This Book and CD

We've included several testing features both in the book and on the companion CD-ROM. Following this Introduction is an Assessment Test that you can use to check your readiness for the actual exam. Take this test before you start reading the book. It will help you determine the areas you may need to brush up on. The answers to the Assessment Test appear after the last question of the test. Each answer includes an explanation and a note telling you in which chapter this material appears.

As mentioned, to test your knowledge as you progress through the book, there are Review Questions at the end of each chapter. As you finish each chapter, answer the Review Questions and then check to see if your answers are right—the correct answers appear on the pages following the last question. You can go back to reread the section that deals with each question you got wrong to ensure that you answer the question correctly the next time you are tested on the material. You'll also find 180+ flashcard questions on the CD for on-the-go review. Download them right onto your Palm device for quick and convenient reviewing.

In addition to the Assessment Test and the Review Questions, you'll find a Practice Exam in the book and a Bonus Exam on the CD. Take these practice exams just as if you were actually taking the exam (i.e., without any reference material). When you have finished the first exam, move on to the next exam to solidify your test-taking skills. If you get more than 90 percent of the answers correct, you're ready to go ahead and take the real exam.

Additionally, if you are going to travel but still need to study for the PMP exam, and you have a laptop with a CD-ROM drive, you can take this entire book with you just by taking the CD. This book is in PDF (Adobe Acrobat) format so it can be easily read on any computer.

The Exam Objectives

Behind every certification exam, you can be sure to find exam objectives—the broad topics in which the exam developers want to ensure your competency. The official PMP exam objectives are listed here.

 Exam objectives are subject to change at any time without prior notice and at PMI's sole discretion. Please visit the Certification page of PMI's website, www.pmi.org, for the most current listing of exam objectives.

Domain 1.0: Initiation

The objectives for this domain are as follows:

1. Determine Project Goals.

2. Determine Deliverables.

3. Determine Process Outputs.

4. Document Project Constraints.

5. Document Project Assumptions.

6. Define Strategy.

7. Identify Performance Criteria.

8. Determine Resource Requirements.

9. Define Budget.

10. Produce Formal Documentation.

Domain 2.0: Planning

The objectives for this domain are as follows:

1. Refine Project.

2. Create WBS.

3. Develop Resource Management Plan.

4. Refine Time and Cost Estimates.

5. Establish Project Controls.

6. Develop Project Plan.

7. Obtain Plan Approval.

Domain 3.0: Execution

The objectives for this domain are as follows:

1. Commit Resources.

2. Implement Resources.

3. Manage Progress.

4. Communicate Progress.

5. Implement Quality Assurance Procedures.

Domain 4.0: Control

The objectives for this domain are as follows:

1. Measure Performance.

2. Refine Control Limits.

3. Take Corrective Action.

4. Evaluate Effectiveness of Corrective Action.

5. Ensure Plan Compliance.

6. Reassess Control Plans.

7. Respond to Risk Event Triggers.

8. Monitor Project Activity.

Domain 5.0: Closing

The objectives for this domain are as follows:

1. Obtain Acceptance of Deliverables.

2. Document Lessons Learned.

3. Facilitate Closure.

4. Preserve Product Records and Tools.

5. Release Resources.

Domain 6.0: Professional Responsibility

The objectives for this domain are as follows:

1. Ensure Integrity.

2. Contribute to Knowledge Base.

3. Apply Professional Knowledge.

4. Balance Stakeholder Interests.

5. Respect Differences.

Tips for Taking the PMP Exam

Here are some general tips for taking your exam successfully:

- Get to the exam center early so that you can relax and review your study materials.

- Read the exam questions very carefully. Make sure you know exactly what the question is asking and don't be tempted to answer too quickly.

- Unanswered questions score as wrong answers. It's better to guess than leave a question unanswered.

- If you're not sure of an answer, use a process of elimination to identify the obvious incorrect answers first. Narrow the remaining choices down by referring back to the question, looking for key words that might tip off the answer.

- Visit the PMI website at `www.pmi.org` for the latest information regarding certification and to find a testing site nearest you.

Assessment Test

1. Which performance measurement tells us how much more of the budget is required to finish the project?

    A. ETC

    B. EV

    C. AC

    D. EAC

2. Which of the following compression techniques increases risk?

    A. Crashing

    B. Resource leveling

    C. Fast tracking

    D. Lead and lag

3. You are a project manager for Waterways Houseboats, Inc. You've been asked to perform a benefit/cost analysis for two proposed projects. Project A costs $2.4 million with potential benefits of $12 million and future operating costs of $3 million. Project B costs $2.8 million with potential benefits of $14 million and future operating costs of $2 million. Which project should you recommend?

    A. Project A because the cost to implement is cheaper than Project B

    B. Project A because the potential benefits plus the future operating costs are less in value than the same calculation for Project B

    C. Project B because the potential benefits minus the implementation and future operating costs are greater in value than the same calculation for Project A

    D. Project B because the potential benefits minus the costs to implement are greater in value than the same calculation for Project A

4. These diagrams rank order factors for corrective action by frequency of occurrence. They are also a type of histogram:

    A. Control charts

    B. Process flowcharts

    C. Scatter diagrams

    D. Pareto diagrams

5. You've been assigned as a project manager on a research and development project for a new dental procedure. You've published the scope statement and are working on the scope management plan. What is the purpose of the scope management plan?

    A. It describes and documents a scope baseline to help make future project decisions.

    B. It decomposes project deliverables.

    C. It describes how project scope changes will be incorporated into the project and how project scope will be managed.

    D. It describes how cost and time estimates can be composed for project scope changes.

6. What is one of the most important skills a project manager can have?

    A. Negotiation skills

    B. Influencing skills

    C. Communication skills

    D. Problem-solving skills

7. The project manager has the greatest influence over quality during which process?

    A. Quality Planning

    B. Quality Assurance

    C. Quality Control

    D. Quality Change Control

8. Project managers have the highest level of authority and the most power in which type of organizational structure?

    A. Projectized

    B. Strong matrix

    C. Functional

    D. Balanced matrix

9. You are the project manager for Heartthrobs by the Numbers Dating Services. You're working on an updated Internet site that will display pictures as well as short bios of prospective heartbreakers. You have your activity list and resource requirements in hand and are planning on using qualitatively based durations and reserve time to determine activity durations. Which of the following is true?

    A. You are using inputs of the Activity Duration Estimating process.

    B. You are using tools and techniques of the Cost Estimating process.

    C. You are using tools and techniques of the Activity Duration Estimating process.

    D. You are using inputs of the Cost Estimating process.

10. You are a project manager who has recently held a project team kick-off meeting where all the team members were formally introduced to each other. Some of the team members know each other from other projects and have been working with you for the past 3 weeks during the Planning processes. Which of the following is true?

    A. Team building begins once all the members of the team are identified and introduced to each other. This team is in the storming stage of Team Development.

    B. Team building begins at the Planning process. This team is in the storming stage of Team Development.

    C. Team building begins once all the members of the team are identified and introduced to each other. This team is in the forming stage of Team Development.

    D. Team building begins at the Planning process. This team is in the forming stage of Team Development.

11. Project managers spend what percentage of their time communicating?

  A. 90

  B. 85

  C. 75

  D. 50

12. All of the following are true regarding configuration management except:

  A. Requires all acceptance decisions to be made through the CCB

  B. Serves as a change control system

  C. Describes the physical characteristics of the product of the project

  D. Controls changes to the characteristics of an item

13. Which of the following project-scheduling techniques allows for conditional and probabilistic treatment?

  A. GERT

  B. CPM

  C. PERT

  D. CPM and PERT

14. Which of the following contracts should you use for projects that have a degree of uncertainty and require a large investment early in the project life cycle?

  A. Fixed price

  B. Cost reimbursable

  C. Lump sum

  D. Unit price

15. You are the project manager for Lucky Stars Candies. You've identified the deliverables and requirements and documented them where?

A. In the scope statement, which will be used as in input to the Scope Definition process

B. In the scope definition document, which is used as an input to the Scope Planning process

C. In the WBS, which is an output of the Scope Planning process

D. In the WBS, which is a tool and technique of the Scope Definition process

16. All of the following are true regarding Ishikawa diagrams in the Quality Planning process except:

A. They are also called cause-and-effect diagrams.

B. They are also called fishbone diagrams.

C. They are a tool and technique of this process.

D. They are an output of this process.

17. The primary function of the Closing process is to:

A. Formalize lessons learned and distribute this information to project participants

B. Perform audits to verify the project results against the project requirements

C. Formalize project completion and disseminate this information to project participants

D. Perform post-implementation audits to document project successes and failures

18. What is the purpose of the project charter?

    A. To recognize and acknowledge the project sponsor

    B. To recognize and acknowledge the existence of the project and commit organizational resources to the project

    C. To acknowledge the existence of the project team, project manager, and project sponsor

    D. To describe the selection methods used to choose this project over its competitors

19. Which performance measurement tells us what the projected total cost of the project will be at completion?

    A. ETC

    B. CPI

    C. SPI

    D. EAC

20. People are motivated by the need for achievement, power, or affiliation according to which theory?

    A. Expectancy theory

    B. Achievement theory

    C. Contingency theory

    D. Theory X

21. You are a project manager working in a foreign country. You observe that some of your project team members are having a difficult time adjusting to the new culture. You provided them training on cultural differences and the customs of this country before arriving, but they still seem uncomfortable and disoriented. Which of the following is true?

A. This is the result of working with teams of people from two different countries.

B. This condition is known as culture shock.

C. This is the result of jet lag and travel fatigue.

D. This condition is known as global culturalism.

22. The Project Management Knowledge Areas:

    A. Include Initiation, Planning, Executing, Controlling, and Closing

    B. Consist of nine different areas that bring together processes that have things in common

    C. Consist of five different processes that bring together phases of projects that have things in common

    D. Include Planning, Executing, and Controlling processes as these three processes are commonly interlinked

23. You are the project manager for a construction company that is building a new city and county office building in your city. You recently looked over the construction site to determine if the work to date was conforming to the requirements and quality standards. Which tool and technique of Quality Control are you using?

    A. Performance measurements

    B. Inspection

    C. Sampling

    D. Prevention

24. Which of the following is true regarding Administrative Closure?

    A. It occurs at the end of a project phase and at the end of the project.

    B. It occurs at the end of the project phase only.

    C. It occurs at the end of the project only.

    D. It is performed prior to Contract Closeout.

25. You are the project manager for Heart of Texas casual clothing company. Your project involves installing a new human resources system. You've identified the risks associated with this project and are ready for the next step. What is the next step?

A. You will evaluate the risks and assign probabilities and impacts using Qualitative and/or Quantitative Risk Analysis.

B. You will use the Delphi technique to confirm the risks you've detailed and identify others you may have missed.

C. You must evaluate the risks and assign probabilities and impacts using both Qualitative Risk Analysis, which comes first, then Quantitative Risk Analysis.

D. You will define the steps to take to respond to the risks and detail them in the risk response plan.

26. The project sponsor has approached you with a dilemma. The CEO announced at the annual stockholders meeting that the project you're managing will be completed by the end of this year. The problem is that this is six months prior to the scheduled completion date. It's too late to go back and correct her mistake, and stockholders are expecting implementation by the announced date. You must speed up the delivery date of this project. Your primary constraint before this occurred was the budget. What actions can you take to help speed up the project?

A. Hire more resources to get the work completed faster.

B. Ask for more money so that you can contract out one of the phases you had planned to do with in-house resources.

C. Utilize negotiation and influencing skills to convince the project sponsor to speak with the CEO and make a correction to her announcement.

D. Examine the project plan to see if there are any phases that can be fast tracked, and then revise the project plan to reflect the compression of the schedule.

27. During your project meeting, a problem was discussed and a resolution to the problem was reached. During the meeting, the participants started wondering why they thought the problem was such a big issue. Sometime after the meeting, you received an e-mail from one of the meeting members saying they've changed their mind about the solution reached in the meeting and need to resurface the problem. The solution reached during the initial project meeting is an example of which of the following conflict resolution techniques?

    A. Confrontation

    B. Forcing

    C. Smoothing

    D. Storming

28. You are the project manager for Heartthrobs by the Numbers Dating Services. You're working on an updated Internet site that will display pictures as well as short bios of prospective heartbreakers. You've just completed your project staff assignments and published the project team directory. Which process are you in?

    A. Resource Planning

    B. Organizational Planning

    C. Project Development Planning

    D. Staff Acquisition

29. Which of the following describes the Executing process?

    A. Project plans are put into action.

    B. Project performance measurements are taken and analyzed.

    C. Project plans are developed.

    D. Project plans are published.

30. Each of the following describes an element of the Scope Definition process except:

   A. Breaking down the major deliverables of the project into smaller, manageable components

   B. Supporting detail

   C. Decomposition

   D. Improving the accuracy of time and cost estimates

31. Which of the following are tools and techniques of the Initiation process?

   A. Project selection methods and expert judgment

   B. Project selection criteria and expert judgment

   C. Constraints and assumptions and expert judgment

   D. Expert judgment and project charter

32. Your project involves the research and development of a new food additive. You're ready to release the product to your customer when you discover that a minor reaction might occur in people with certain conditions. The reactions to date have been very minor, and no known long-lasting side effects have been noted. As project manager you should:

   A. Do nothing because the reactions are so minor that very few people will be affected.

   B. Inform the customer that you've discovered this condition and tell them you'll research it further to determine the impacts.

   C. Inform your customer that there is no problem with the additive except for an extremely small percentage of the population and release the product to them.

   D. Tell the customer you'll correct the reaction problems in the next batch but you'll release the first batch of product to them now to begin using.

33. According to the *Guide to the PMBOK*, the project manager is identified and assigned during which process?

    A. As an input to the Initiation process

    B. As an input to the Planning process

    C. As an output of the Initiation process

    D. As an output of the Scope Planning process

34. All of the following are true regarding the ADM method except:

    A. It's a tool and technique of Activity Sequencing.

    B. It uses one time estimate to determine durations.

    C. It's also called AOA.

    D. It's rarely used today.

35. You have been assigned to a project that will allow job seekers to fill out applications and submit them via the company website. You report to the VP of human resources. You are also responsible for screening applications for the information technology division and setting up interviews. The project coordinator has asked for the latest version of your changes to the online application page for his review. Which organizational structure do you work in?

    A. Functional organization

    B. Weak matrix organization

    C. Projectized organization

    D. Balanced matrix organization

36. What type of organization experiences the least amount of stress during project closeout?

    A. Projectized

    B. Functional

    C. Weak matrix

    D. Strong matrix

37. You work for a company that writes billing software programs for the communication industry. You've just been assigned a new project. The customer is located in a distant country that limits the number of foreigners allowed into the country. You identify this risk in your risk management plan. The critical point during the project is installation and setup. You might do which of the following given these circumstances?

   A. Use a design of experiments technique to develop a contingency plan.

   B. Develop a cause-and-effect diagram that identifies the contract type you should use for a project like this.

   C. Use sensitivity analysis to assist you in developing the appropriate risk response for this situation.

   D. Develop a contingency plan for installation.

38. You are working on a project that will upgrade the phone system in your customer service center. You have used bottom-up estimating techniques to assign costs to the project activities and have determined the cost baseline. Which of the following is true?

   A. You have completed the Cost Estimating process and now need to complete the Cost Budgeting process to determine the project's baseline.

   B. You have completed the Project Plan Development process and established a project baseline to measure future project performance against.

   C. You have completed the Cost Estimating process and now need to complete the Project Plan Development process to establish a project baseline to measure future project performance against.

   D. You have completed the Cost Budgeting process, and the cost baseline will be used to measure future project performance.

39. You know that PV = 470, AC = 430, EV = 480, EAC = 500, and BAC = 525. What is VAC?

   A. 70

   B. 20

   C. 25

   D. 30

40. All of the following are characteristics of the project Closing processes except:

   A. Probability for success is greatest here.

   B. The project manager's influence is greatest here.

   C. The stakeholders' influence is least here.

   D. Risk is greatest here.

41. You are refining the product description for your company's new line of ski boots. Which of the following is true?

   A. You are in the Initiation process of your project and know that the product description will contain more detail in this stage and that a decreasing amount of detail will be added to it as the project progresses.

   B. You are in the Planning process of your project and know that the product description will contain less detail in this stage and greater detail as the project progresses.

   C. You are in the Initiation process of your project and know that the product description should contain the most detail possible at this stage as this is critical information for the Planning process.

   D. You are in the Initiation process of your project and know that the product description will contain less detail in this stage and greater detail as the project progresses.

42. This process applies evaluation criteria to the bids and proposals received from potential vendors:

   A. Solicitation

   B. Contract Administration

   C. Source Selection

   D. Quality Assurance

43. All of the following are tools and techniques of the Integrated Change Control process except:

A. Configuration management

B. Performance measurements

C. Change requests

D. Additional planning

44. You need to convey some very complex, detailed information to the project stakeholders. The best method of communicating this kind of information is?

A. Verbal

B. Vertical

C. Horizontal

D. Written

45. You have just prepared an RFP for release. Your project involves a substantial amount of contract work detailed in the RFP. Your favorite vendor drops by and offers to give you and your spouse the use of their company condo for your upcoming vacation. It's located in a beautiful resort community that happens to be one of your favorite places to go for a get away. What is the most appropriate response?

A. Thank the vendor but decline the offer as you know this could be considered a conflict of interest.

B. Thank the vendor and accept. This vendor is always offering you incentives like this, so this offer does not likely have anything to do with the recent RFP release.

C. Thank the vendor, accept the offer, and immediately tell your project sponsor so they're aware of what you're doing.

D. Thank the vendor but decline the offer because you've already made another arrangement for this vacation. Ask them if you can take a rain check and arrange another time to use the condo.

46. PERT is:

    A. The longest path

    B. A weighted average technique

    C. A simulation technique

    D. Widely used in practice to determine schedule durations

47. What are the Scope Planning process tools and techniques?

    A. Benefit/cost analysis, work breakdown structure templates, expert judgment, and supporting detail

    B. Product analysis, benefit/cost analysis, alternatives identification, and expert judgment

    C. Product analysis, work breakdown structure templates, supporting detail, and expert judgment

    D. Benefit/cost analysis, alternatives identification, supporting detail, and expert judgement

48. You are a project manager for Swirling Seas Cruises food division. You're considering two different projects regarding food services on the cruise lines. The initial cost of Project Fish'n for Chips will be $800,000 with expected cash inflows of $300,000 per quarter. Project Picnic's payback period is six months. Which project should you recommend?

    A. Project Fish'n for Chips because its payback period is two months shorter than Project Picnic's

    B. Project Fish'n for Chips because the costs on Project Picnic are unknown

    C. Project Picnic because Project Fish'n for Chips' payback period is four months longer than Project Picnic's

    D. Project Picnic because Project Fish'n for Chips' payback period is two months longer than Project Picnic's

49. You are the project manger for Xylophone Phonics. They produce children's software programs that teach basic reading and math skills. You're performing cost estimates for your project and don't have a lot of details yet. You will use which of the following techniques?

A. Analogous estimating techniques, because this is a form of expert judgment that uses historical information from similar projects

B. Bottom-up estimating techniques because this is a form of expert judgment that uses historical information from similar projects

C. Monte Carlo Analysis, because this is a modeling technique that uses simulation to determine estimates

D. Parametric modeling, because this is a form of simulation used to determine estimates

50. As a PMP, one of your responsibilities is to ensure integrity on the project. When your personal interests are put above the interests of the project or when you use your influence to cause others to make decisions in your favor without regard for the project outcome, this is considered:

A. Conflict of interest

B. Using professional knowledge inappropriately

C. Culturally unacceptable

D. Personal conflict issue

51. Your project is in the Scope Definition process. You've just completed the WBS. Which of the following is true?

A. The WBS breaks the project deliverables down to a level where alternatives identification can be used to determine how level two assignments should be made.

B. The WBS breaks the project deliverables down to a level where project constraints and assumptions can be easily identified.

C. The WBS breaks the project deliverables down to the work package level where product analysis can be documented.

D. The WBS breaks the project deliverables down to the work package level where cost and time estimates can be easily determined and quality control measurements can be determined.

52. The product description, strategic plan, project selection criteria, and historical information are considered:

    A. Inputs to the project Planning process

    B. Inputs to the project Overview process

    C. Inputs to the project Initiation process

    D. Inputs to the project Execution process

53. What are decision models?

    A. Project selection criteria

    B. Project selection methods

    C. Project selection committees

    D. Project resource and budget selection criteria

54. Performance reporting tools and techniques include all of the following except:

    A. Earned value analysis

    B. Statistical sampling

    C. Variance analysis

    D. Performance reviews

55. Which of the following is true regarding constraints and assumptions?

    A. Constraints restrict the actions of the project team, and assumptions are considered true for planning purposes.

    B. Constraints are considered true for planning purposes, and assumptions limit the options of the project team.

    C. Constraints consider vendor availability and resource availability to be true for planning purposes. Assumptions limit the project team to work within predefined budgets or time lines.

    D. Constraints and assumptions are inputs to the Initiation process. They should be documented, as they will be used throughout the project Planning process.

56. You are the project manager for a construction company that is building a new city and county office building in your city. Your CCB recently approved a scope change. You know that scope change might come about as a result of all of the following except:

   A. Schedule revisions

   B. Product scope change

   C. Changes to the agreed-upon WBS

   D. Changes to the project requirements

57. What are the tools and techniques of the Quantitative Risk Analysis process?

   A. Checklists, flowcharting, interviewing

   B. Interviewing, sensitivity analysis, decision tree analysis, simulation

   C. Checklists, sensitivity analysis, decision tree analysis, information-gathering techniques

   D. Interviewing, checklists, assumptions analysis, risk probability impact

58. Name the ethical code you'll be required to adhere to as a PMP.

   A. *Project Management Policy and Ethics Guide*

   B. *Project Management Professional Standards and Ethics*

   C. *Project Management Code of Professional Ethics*

   D. *Project Management Professional Code of Professional Conduct*

59. You are the project manger for Xylophone Phonics. They produce children's software programs that teach basic reading and math skills. You are ready to assign project roles, responsibilities, and reporting relationships. Which project Planning process are you working on?

   A. Resource Planning

   B. Organizational Planning

   C. Staff Acquisition

   D. Human Resource Acquisition

60. Critical path tasks are those tasks that:

A. Have equal pessimistic, optimistic, and most likely estimated times

B. Have a float time of zero

C. Have the same start date

D. Have multiple early start dates and early finish dates

Answers to Assessment Test

1. A. Estimate to completion calculates how much more of the budget is needed to complete the project if everything continues at the current level of performance. For more information, please see Chapter 9.

2. C. Fast tracking is a compression technique that increases risk and potentially causes rework. Fast tracking is starting two projects previously scheduled to start one after the other at the same time. For more information, please see Chapter 7.

3. C. Project B's benefit/cost analysis is a $9.2 million benefit to the company compared to $6.6 million for Project A. Benefit/cost analysis takes into consideration the initial costs to implement and future operating costs. For more information, please see Chapter 3.

4. D. Pareto diagrams rank order important factors for corrective action by frequency of occurrence. For more information, please see Chapter 10.

5. C. The scope management plan outlines how project scope will be managed and how changes will be incorporated into the project. For more information, please see Chapter 4.

6. C. Negotiation, influencing, and problem-solving skills are all important for a project manager to possess; however, good communication skills are the most important skills a project manager can have. For more information, please see Chapter 1.

7. B. Quality Assurance is the process where project managers have the greatest amount of influence over quality. For more information, please see Chapter 9.

8. A. Project managers have the highest level of power and authority in a projectized organization. They also have high levels of power and authority in a strong matrix; however, a matrix organization is a blend of functional and projectized organizations, and therefore, the project manager does not have quite the same level of authority as they would in a projectized organization. For more information, please see Chapter 1.

9. C. Qualitatively based durations and reserve time are two of the tools and techniques of the Activity Duration Estimating process. The other tools are expert judgment and analogous estimating. For more information, please see Chapter 5.

10. D. Team building begins at the Planning process of your project. In this question, the team members have just been formally introduced to each other, so they are still in the forming stage of Team Development. For more information, please see Chapter 8.

11. A. Project managers spend about 90 percent of their time communicating through status meetings, team meetings, e-mail, verbal communications, and so on. For more information, please see Chapter 8.

12. A. Configuration management serves as a change control system; it describes the physical characteristics of the product; and it controls changes to the characteristics of the product or item. It tracks the changes requested and made and their status. For more information, please see Chapter 10.

13. A. GERT is the only technique that allows for conditional branching and looping and probabilistic treatment. For more information, please see Chapter 7.

14. B. Cost reimbursable contracts are used when the degree of uncertainty is high and when the project requires a large investment prior to completion of the project. For more information, please see Chapter 6.

15. A. The scope statement contains an exhaustive list of the project deliverables, their requirements, and measurable criteria used to determine project completion. The scope statement is an input to the Scope Definition process and is used to create the WBS. For more information, please see Chapter 4.

16. D. Cause-and-effect diagrams, also called Ishikawa or fishbone diagrams, show the relationship between the effects of quality problems and their causes. Cause-and-effect diagrams were developed by Kaoru Ishikawa. For more information, please see Chapter 6.

17. C.   The primary function of the Closing process is to formalize project completion and disseminate this information to the project participants. For more information, please see Chapter 11.

18. B.   The purpose of a project charter is to recognize and acknowledge the existence of a project and commit resources to the project. The charter names the project manager and project sponsor, but that's not its primary purpose. For more information, please see Chapter 3.

19. D.   Estimate at completion estimates the total cost of the project at completion based on the performance of the project to date. For more information, please see Chapter 9.

20. B.   Achievement theory conjectures that people are motivated by the need for achievement, power, or affiliation. For more information, please see Chapter 8.

21. B.   When people work in unfamiliar environments, culture shock can occur. Training and researching information about the country you'll be working in can help counteract this. For more information, please see Chapter 12.

22. B.   The Project Management Knowledge Areas bring processes together that have commonalities. For example, Project Integration Management consists of the Project Plan Development, Project Plan Execution, and Integrated Change Control processes. For more information, please see Chapter 2.

23. B.   Inspection involves physically looking at, measuring, or testing results to determine if they conform to your quality standards. Performance measurements are not part of the Quality Control process, and prevention is not an identified tool and technique of Quality Control. For more information, please see Chapter 10.

24. A.   Administrative Closure occurs at the end of the project phase and at the end of the project itself. Administrative Closure is performed after Contract Closeout. It is the last process performed on your project. For more information, please see Chapter 11.

25. A. Since you've identified the risks, you've completed the Risk Identification process. The Delphi technique is a tool and technique of the Risk Identification process, so answer B is not correct. You will proceed to assign probabilities and impacts using Qualitative or Quantitative Risk Analysis, or both. You can use either process or both processes. They are not both required, therefore answer C is incorrect. For more information, please see Chapter 6.

26. D. Fast tracking is the best answer in this scenario. Budget was the original constraint on this project, so it's highly unlikely the project manager would get more resources to assist with the project. The next best thing is to compress phases to shorten the project duration. For more information, please see Chapter 1.

27. C. The smoothing technique does not usually result in a permanent solution. The problem is downplayed to make it seem less important than it is, which makes the problem tend to resurface later. For more information, please see Chapter 8.

28. D. The Staff Acquisition outputs are the assignment of project staff and project team directory. For more information, please see Chapter 5.

29. A. The Executing process takes published project plans and turns them into actions to accomplish the goals of the project. For more information, please see Chapter 1.

30. B. Supporting detail is an output of the Scope Planning process. For more information, please see Chapter 4.

31. A. Project Initiation has two tools and techniques: project selection methods and expert judgment. For more information, please see Chapter 3.

32. B. Honesty and truthful reporting are required of PMPs. In this situation, you would inform the customer of everything you know regarding the problem and work to find alternative solutions. For more information, please see Chapter 12.

33. C. According to the *Guide to the PMBOK*, the project manager is identified and assigned as an output of the Initiation process. In practice, project managers are very often assigned at the beginning of this process. For more information, please see Chapter 2.

34. B. The arrow diagramming method (ADM), also called activity on arrow (AOA), uses more than one time estimate to determine project duration. For more information, please see Chapter 5.

35. B. Functional managers who have lots of authority and power working with project coordinators who have minimal authority and power characterizes a weak matrix organization. Project managers in weak matrix organizations are sometimes called project coordinators, project leaders, or project expeditors. For more information, please see Chapter 1.

36. C. Weak matrix organizational structures tend to experience the least amount of stress during the project closeout processes. For more information, please see Chapter 11.

37. D. You will develop a contingency plan that might include contracting with a vendor in the customer's country to perform the installation and setup should your team be unable to enter the country. Cause-and-effect diagrams are used during the Quality Planning process to map out problems and their causes. For more information, please see Chapter 6.

38. D. The Cost Estimating and Cost Budgeting processes include bottom-up estimating techniques as well as analogous estimating, parametric modeling, and computerized tools. However, answer D is correct because the cost baseline is an output of the Cost Budgeting process and is used to measure and track the project throughout the remaining process groups. For more information, please see Chapter 7.

39. C. VAC is calculated this way: BAC – EAC. Therefore, $525 - 500 = 25$. For more information, please see Chapter 9.

40. D. Risk is lowest during the Closing processes as you've completed the work of the project at this point. For more information, please see Chapter 11.

41. D. Product descriptions are input to the Initiation process and contain less detail now and more detail as the project progresses. For more information, please see Chapter 2.

42. C. Source Selection receives bids and proposals from potential vendors and applies evaluation criteria to them to make a selection. For more information, please see Chapter 9.

43. C. Change requests are in input to the Integrated Change Control process. The other tools and techniques of this process are change control system and project management information system. For more information, please see Chapter 10.

44. D. Information that is complex and detailed is best conveyed in writing. A verbal follow-up would be good to answer questions and clarify information. Vertical and horizontal are ways of communicating within the organization. For more information, please see Chapter 8.

45. A. The best response is to decline the offer. This is a conflict of interest, and accepting the offer puts your own integrity and the contract award process in jeopardy. For more information, please see Chapter 12.

46. B. PERT is the Program Evaluation and Review Technique that uses weighted average and standard deviation to determine project durations. It is used for large, highly complex projects. For more information, please see Chapter 7.

47. B. The tools and techniques of the Scope Planning process include product analysis, benefit/cost analysis, alternatives identification, and expert judgment. For more information, please see Chapter 4.

48. D. The payback period for Project Fish'n for Chips is eight months. This project will receive $300,000 every three months, or $100,000 per month. The $800,000 will be paid back in eight months. For more information, please see Chapter 3.

49. A. Analogous estimating, also called top-down estimating, is a form of expert judgment. Analogous estimating can be used to estimate cost or time and considers historical information from previous, similar projects. For more information, please see Chapter 5.

50. A. A conflict of interest is any situation that compromises the outcome of the project or ignores the impact to the project to benefit yourself or others. For more information, please see Chapter 12.

51. D. The work package level is the lowest level in the WBS. Time and cost estimation is easily determined at this level as are resource assignments. Quality control measurements can be determined at this level as well. For more information, please see Chapter 4.

52. C. Initiation process inputs include the product description, which describes the characteristics of the product; the strategic plan, which outlines the vision of the company; project selection criteria, which help determine how projects will be selected; and historical information regarding past projects of a similar nature. For more information, please see Chapter 2.

53. B. Decision models are project selection methods used as tools and techniques in Initiation. Decision models include benefit measurement methods and constrained optimization methods. For more information, please see Chapter 3.

54. B. Statistical sampling is a tool and technique of the Quality Control process. For more information, please see Chapter 9.

55. A. Constraints limit the options of the project team by restricting action or dictating action. Budget, time, and quality are the three most common constraints. Assumptions are presumed to be true for planning purposes. Always validate your assumptions. For more information, please see Chapter 2.

56. A. Scope changes will cause schedule revisions, but schedule revisions do not change the project scope. Project requirements are part of the scope statement, and therefore D is one of the correct responses. For more information, please see Chapter 10.

57. B.   The Quantitative Risk Analysis process has four tools and techniques: interviewing, sensitivity analysis, decision tree analysis, and simulation. For more information, please see Chapter 6.

58. D.   The *Project Management Professional Code of Professional Conduct* is published by PMI, and all PMPs are expected to adhere to its standards. For more information, please see Chapter 12.

59. B.   The Organizational Planning process identifies project resources, documents roles and responsibilities of project team members and stakeholders, and documents reporting relationships. For more information, please see Chapter 5.

60. B.   Critical path tasks are those tasks with zero float time. Float time, or slack time, is the amount of time between an activity's early start date and late start date. For more information, please see Chapter 7.

Chapter

1

What Is a Project?

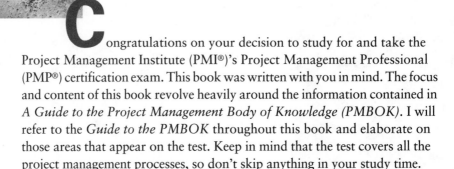

Congratulations on your decision to study for and take the Project Management Institute (PMI®)'s Project Management Professional (PMP®) certification exam. This book was written with you in mind. The focus and content of this book revolve heavily around the information contained in *A Guide to the Project Management Body of Knowledge (PMBOK)*. I will refer to the *Guide to the PMBOK* throughout this book and elaborate on those areas that appear on the test. Keep in mind that the test covers all the project management processes, so don't skip anything in your study time.

When possible, I'll pass on hints and study tips that I collected while studying for the exam myself. Your first tip is to familiarize yourself with the terminology used in the *Guide to the PMBOK*. PMI has worked hard to develop and define standard project management terms, and these terms are used interchangeably among industries. For example, *resource planning* means the same thing to someone working in construction, information technology, or telecommunications. You'll find *Guide to the PMBOK* terms explained throughout this book. Even if you are an experienced project manager, you might find that PMI uses specific terms for things that you call by another name. So, step one is to get familiar with the terminology.

This chapter lays the foundation for building and managing your project. We'll address project and project management definitions as well as organizational structures. Good luck!

Is It a Project?

The VP of marketing approaches you with a fabulous idea. "Fabulous" because he's the big boss and because he thought it up. He wants to set up kiosks in local grocery stores as mini offices. These offices will offer customers the ability to sign up for new wireless phone services, make their wireless phone bill payments, and purchase equipment and accessories. He believes that the exposure in grocery stores will increase awareness of the company's offerings. After all, everyone has to eat, right? He told you that the board of directors has already cleared the project and he'll dedicate as many resources to this as he can. He wants the new kiosks in place in 12 stores by the end of next year. The best news is he's assigned you to head up this project.

Your first question should be, "Is it a project?" This may seem elementary, but confusing projects with ongoing operations happens often. According to the *Guide to the PMBOK,* page 4, "…a project is a temporary endeavor undertaken to create a unique product, service or result."

Quotations from the *Guide to the PMBOK* are cited in the text with the following abbreviation: *Guide to the PMBOK:* Project Management Institute, *A Guide to the Project Management Body of Knowledge (PMBOK® Guide)* 2000 Edition, Project Management Institute, Inc., 2000.

Projects are temporary in nature, while operations are ongoing. Projects have definitive start dates and definitive end dates. The project is completed when the goals and objectives of the project are accomplished. Sometimes projects end when it's determined that the goals and objectives cannot be accomplished and the project is canceled. Operations involve work that is continuous without an ending date and often repeat the same process.

Projects exist to bring about a product or service that hasn't existed before. In this sense, a project is unique. However, don't get confused by the term *unique*. For example, Ford Motor Company is in the business of designing and assembling cars. Each model that Ford designs and produces can be considered a project. The models differ from each other in their features and are marketed to people with various needs. An SUV serves a different purpose and clientele than a luxury model. The design and marketing of these two models are unique projects. The actual assembly of the cars can be considered an operation—a repetitive process that is followed for most makes and models.

Determining the characteristics and features of the different car models is carried out through what the *Guide to the PMBOK* terms as *progressive elaboration.* This means throughout the project, specific incremental steps are taken to examine the needs and requirements of the product of the project (the SUV, for example) and to fulfill the objectives. These needs are examined in detail and continually monitored and updated throughout the project.

A project is successful when it meets or exceeds the expectations of the stakeholders. *Stakeholders* are those folks with a vested interest in your project. They are the people who have something to either gain or lose as a result of the project. The *project sponsor*, generally an executive in the organization with the authority to assign resources and enforce decisions regarding the project, is a stakeholder. The customer is a stakeholder as are contractors and suppliers. The project manager and the managers from other departments in the organization are stakeholders as well. It's important to identify all the stakeholders in your project up front. If you leave out an important stakeholder or their department's function and don't discover the error until well into the project, it could be a project killer.

Figure 1.1 shows a sample listing of the kinds of stakeholders involved on a typical project.

FIGURE 1.1   Project stakeholders

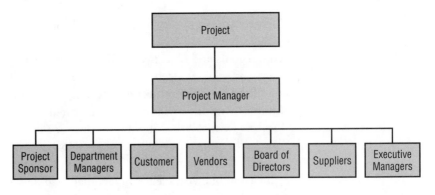

Many times, stakeholders have conflicting interests. It's the project manager's responsibility to understand these conflicts, and try to resolve them. Be certain to identify and meet with all key stakeholders early in the project to understand all their needs and constraints. When in doubt, stakeholder conflicts should always be resolved in favor of the customer.

We've just learned that a project has several characteristics:

- Projects are unique.

- Projects are temporary in nature and have a definite beginning and ending date.

- Projects are completed when the project goals are achieved.

- A successful project is one that meets or exceeds the expectations of your stakeholders.

Using these criteria, let's examine the assignment from the VP of marketing to determine if it is a project:

Is it unique?   Yes, because the kiosks don't exist in the local grocery stores. This is a new way of offering the company's services to its customer base. While the service the company is offering isn't new, the way they are presenting their services is.

Does the project have a limited time frame?   Yes, the start date of this project is today, and the end date is the end of next year. It is a temporary endeavor.

Is there a way to determine when the project is completed?   Yes, the kiosks will be installed, and services will be offered from them. Once all of the kiosks are intact and operating, the project will come to a close.

Is there a way to determine stakeholder satisfaction?   Yes, the expectations of the stakeholders will be documented in the form of requirements during the planning processes. These requirements will be compared to the finished product to determine if it meets the expectations of the stakeholder.

Houston, we have a project.

What Is Project Management?

You've determined that you indeed have a project. What now? The notes you scratched out on the back of a napkin at coffee break might get you started, but that's not exactly good project management practice.

We have all witnessed this scenario—an assignment is made and the project team jumps directly into the project, busying themselves with building the product or service requested. Often, careful thought is not given to the project-planning process. I'm sure you've heard co-workers toss around statements like, "That would be a waste of valuable time" or "Why plan when you can just start building?" Project progress is rarely measured against the customer requirements. In the end, the delivered product or service doesn't meet the expectations of the customer! This is a frustrating experience for all those involved. Unfortunately, many projects follow this poorly constructed path.

Project management is a process that involves several things including planning, putting the project plan into action, and measuring progress and performance. Planning is one of the most important functions you'll perform during the course of a project. It sets the standard for the rest of the project's life and is used to track future project performance. Before we begin the planning process, we'll need to look at some of the skills needed to perform project management functions and some of the constraints found on all projects.

Project Constraints

In my organization, and I'm sure the same is true in yours, there are far more project requests than we have resources to work on them. In this case, resources are a constraint. You'll find a similar phenomenon occurs on individual projects as well. Every project must work within the triple constraint combination of time, money, and quality. One or two of the triple constraints, sometimes all three, are limited. You might work on projects where you have an almost unlimited budget (don't we wish), but time is the limitation. You can have all the money and people you need to accomplish your project, but you need to complete the project in 24 months. The computer-programming changes required for the year 2000 are an example of a time-constrained project because moving the date wasn't an option.

Other projects might present the opposite scenario. You have all the time you need to complete the project, but the budget is fixed. Still other projects may incorporate two or three of the constraints. Government agencies are notorious for starting projects that have at least two and sometimes all three constraints. For example, new tax law legislation is passed that impacts the computer programming, requiring new programs to calculate and track the tax changes. Typically, a due date is given when the tax law takes effect, and the organization responsible is required to implement the changes with no additions to budget or staff. In other words, they are told to use existing resources to accomplish the goals of the project. The specific requirements of the project are such that quality cannot be fudged to try to meet the time deadline.

As a project manager, one of your biggest jobs is to balance the triple constraints while meeting or exceeding the expectations of your stakeholders. In most projects, you will usually be faced with balancing only one or two of the triple constraints. For example, if the project goal is a high-quality product, the saying goes, "I can give it to you fast or I can give to you cheap, but I can't give it to you fast and cheap."

Tools and Techniques

Project management brings together a set of tools and techniques, performed by people, to describe, organize, and monitor the work of project activities. *Project managers* are the people responsible for managing the project processes and applying the tools and techniques used to carry out the project activities. There are many advantages to organizing projects and teams who utilize these techniques. We'll be examining these advantages in-depth throughout the remainder of this book.

Programs are groups of projects that are managed using the same techniques in a coordinated fashion. Sometimes, programs include aspects of ongoing operations as well. This would be the case where a very large program exists with many subprojects under it—for example, building a new shopping mall. Many subprojects exist underneath this program such as excavation, construction, interior design, store placement, marketing, facilities management, etc. Each of the subprojects is really a project unto itself. Each has its own project manager, who reports to a project manager with responsibility over several of the areas, who in turn reports to the head project manager over the entire program. After the structure itself is built, the management of the facility is considered the ongoing operations part of this program.

Project management involves many skills and techniques. According to the *Guide to the PMBOK,* page 6, "Project management is the application of knowledge, skills, tools, and techniques to project activities to meet project requirements." It is the responsibility of the project manager to ensure project management techniques are applied and followed.

Defining Skills Every Good Project Manager Needs

Many times, organizations will knight their technical experts as project managers. The skill and expertise that made them stars in their technical fields are mistakenly thought to translate into project management skills. This is not necessarily so.

Project managers are generalists with many skills in their repertoire. They are problem solvers who wear many hats. Project managers might indeed possess technical skills, but technical skills are not a prerequisite to project management. Your project team will have technical experts, and they are the people whom the project manager will rely on for technical details. I have seen project managers with many years experience in the construction industry successfully manage multi-million dollar information technology projects. This is because project management techniques apply across industries and across projects. Understanding and applying good project management techniques, along with a solid understanding of general management skills, are career builders for all aspiring project managers.

Project Manager's Tool Bag

Project managers have been likened to small-business owners. They need to know a little bit about every aspect of management. The various skills in a project manager's tool bag can be broken out in a more or less declining scale of importance. Let's discuss each of the skills in a bit more detail.

Communication Skills

One of the single most important characteristics of a first-rate project manager is excellent communication skills. Written and oral communications are the backbone of all successful projects. Many forms of communication will exist during the life of your project. As the creator or manager of most of the project communication (project documents, meeting updates, status reports, etc.), it's your job to ensure that the information is explicit, clear, and complete so that your audience will have no trouble understanding what has been communicated. Once the information has been distributed, it is the responsibility of the person receiving the information to make sure they understand it.

There are many forms of communication and communication styles, which we will cover in more depth in Chapter 8, "Developing the Project Team."

Organizational Skills

Organizational and planning skills are probably the second most important skills a project manager can possess. Organization takes on many forms. As project manager, you'll have project documentation, requirements information, memos, project reports, personnel records, vendor quotes, contracts, and much more to track and be able to locate in a moment's notice. You will also have to organize meetings, put together teams, and perhaps manage and organize media release schedules depending on your project.

Closely associated with organizational skills are time management skills. Take some time to attend a time management class if you've never attended one. They have some great tips and techniques to help you prioritize problems and interruptions, prioritize your day, and manage your time.

Planning is discussed extensively throughout the course of this book. There isn't any aspect of project management that doesn't first involve planning. Planning skills go hand in hand with organizational skills. Combining these two with excellent communication skills is almost a sure guarantee of your success in the project management field.

Budgeting Skills

Project managers establish and manage budgets and therefore need some knowledge of finance and accounting principles. Especially important in this skill area is the ability to perform cost estimates for project budgeting. There are different methods available to determine the project costs. They range from estimating individual activities and rolling the estimates up, to estimating the project's cost in one big chunk. These methods will be discussed more fully in later chapters.

After a budget is determined, you can start spending. This sounds more exciting than it actually is. Reading and understanding vendor quotes, preparing or overseeing purchase orders, and reconciling invoices are budgeting skills that will be used by the project manager on most projects. These costs will be linked back to project activities and expense items in the project's budget.

Problem Solving

Show me a project and I'll show you problems. All projects, in fact much of everyday life, have some problems. Isn't that what they say builds character? But I digress.

Problem solving is really a twofold process. First, you must define the problem. Often when defining problems, we end up just describing the symptoms instead of really getting to the heart of what the problem is. To avoid that, ask yourself questions like, "Is it an internal or external problem?" or "Is it a technical problem?" or "Are there interpersonal problems between team members? Is it managerial?" These kinds of questions will help you to get to the meat of the problem.

Next, after the problem has been defined, you have some decisions to make. It will take a little time to examine and analyze the problem, the situation causing it, and the solution alternatives available. After this analysis, the project manager will determine the best course of action to take and implement the decision.

Negotiation and Influencing

Effective problem solving requires negotiation and influencing skills. We all utilize negotiation skills in one form or another every day. For example, on a nightly basis I am asked, "Honey, what do you want for dinner?" Then the negotiations begin, and the fried chicken versus swordfish discussion commences. Simply put, negotiating is working with others to come to agreement. Negotiation on projects will be necessary in almost every area from scope definition, to budgets, contracts, resource assignments, and more.

Influencing is really convincing the other party that swordfish is a better choice than fried chicken even if that is what they want. In other words, it's the ability to get people to do things they wouldn't do otherwise. It's also the ability to change minds and the course of events, and to influence outcomes.

These skills will be utilized in all areas of project management. Start practicing now because, guaranteed, you'll need these skills on your next project.

Leading

Leadership and *management* are not synonymous terms. Leaders impart vision, gain consensus for strategic goals, establish direction, and inspire and motivate others. Managers focus on results and are concerned with getting the job done according to the requirements. Even though leaders and managers are not the same, project managers must exhibit the characteristics of both during different times on the project. Understanding when to switch from leadership to management and then back again is a finely tuned and necessary talent.

Team Building and Human Resources

Project managers will rely heavily on team building and human resource management skills. Teams are often formed with people from different parts of the organization. These people may or may not have worked together before—so there may be some component of team-building groundwork that will involve the project manager. The project manager will set the tone for the project team and will help them work through the various team-forming stages to become fully functional. The project manager may take on a variety of roles during this initial team-building process.

An interesting caveat to the team-building role is that project managers many times are responsible for motivating team members who are not their direct reports. This has its own set of challenges and dilemmas. One way to help this situation is to ask the functional manager to allow you to participate in your project team members' performance reviews. Use the negotiation and influencing skills I talked about earlier to make sure you're part of this process.

A Mile Wide and an Inch Deep

Project managers are an interesting bunch. They know a little bit about a lot of things and are excellent communicators. Or, as one person said, he's "a mile wide and an inch deep." They have the ability to motivate people, even those who have no reason to be loyal to the project, and they can make the hard-line calls when necessary. Project managers can get caught in sticky situations that occasionally require making decisions that are good for the company (or the customer) but aren't good for certain stakeholders. These offended stakeholders will then drag their feet, and the project manager has to play the heavy in order to motivate and gain their cooperation again. Some organizations hire contract project managers to run their large, company-altering projects just because they don't want to burn out a key employee in this role. Fortunately, that doesn't happen often.

Now that you've been properly introduced to some of the skills you need in your tool kit, you'll know to be prepared to communicate, solve problems, lead, and negotiate your way through your next project.

Understanding Organizational Structures

Just as projects are unique, so are the organizations in which they're carried out. The key to determining the type of organization you work in is by measuring how much authority senior management is willing to delegate to project managers. While uniqueness abounds in business cultures, all organizations are structured in one of three ways: functional, projectized, or matrix. Variations and combinations exist among these three structures, such as a projectized structure within a functional organization, and weak matrix, balanced matrix, and strong matrix organizations.

It pays to know and understand the organizational structure and the culture of the entity you're working with. Companies with aggressive cultures that are comfortable in a leading-edge position within their industry are highly likely to take on risky projects. Project managers who are willing to suggest new ideas and projects that have never been undertaken before are likely to receive a warm reception in this kind of environment. Conversely, organizational cultures that are risk averse and prefer the follow-the-leader position within their industry are highly unlikely to take on risky endeavors. Project managers with risk-inclined, aggressive styles are likely to receive a cool reception in a culture like this.

The level of authority the project manager enjoys is denoted by the organizational structure. For example, a project manager within a functional organization has little to no formal authority. And their title may not be project manager, but instead they're called a project leader, project coordinator, or perhaps project expeditor.

Let's take a look at each of these organizations individually to better understand how the project management role works in each one.

Functional Organizations

The most common type of organization is the *functional organization*. Chances are you work in this type of organization. This is probably the oldest style of organization and is therefore known as the traditional approach to organizing businesses.

Functional organizations are centered on specialties and grouped by function; hence the term *functional organization*. As an example, the organization might have a human resources department, finance department, marketing department, etc. The work in these departments is specialized and requires people who have the skills sets and experiences in these specialized functions to perform specific duties for the department. Figure 1.2 shows a typical org chart for a functional organization.

FIGURE 1.2   Functional org chart

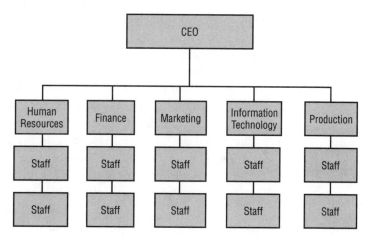

You can see that this type of organization is set up to be a hierarchy. Staff personnel report to managers who report to department heads who report to vice presidents who report to the CEO. In other words, each employee reports to only one manager, and ultimately, one person at the top is in charge. Many companies today, as well as governmental agencies, are structured in a hierarchical fashion. In organizations like this, be aware of the chain of command. A strict chain of command may exist, and the corporate culture might dictate that you follow it. Roughly translated: *Don't talk to the big boss without first talking to your boss who talks to their boss who talks to the big boss.* Wise project managers should determine if there is a chain of command, how strictly it's enforced, and how the chain is linked before venturing outside of it.

Each department or group in a functional organization is managed independently and has a limited span of control. Marketing doesn't run the finance department or their projects, for example. The marketing department is concerned with their own functions and projects. If it were necessary for the marketing department to get input from the finance department on a project, the marketing team members would follow the chain of command. A marketing manager would speak to a manager in finance to get the needed information and then pass it back down to the project team.

Commonalities exist among the personnel assigned to the various departments in a functional organization. In theory, people with similar skills and experiences are easier to manage as a group. Instead of scattering them throughout the organization, it is more efficient to keep them functioning together. Work assignments are easily distributed to those who are best suited for the task when everyone with the same skill works together. Along these lines, workers in functional organizations specialize in an area of expertise—finance, for instance—and then become very good at their specialty. Usually, the supervisors and managers of these workers are experienced in the area they supervise and are able to recommend training and career enrichment activities for their employees.

There is a clear upward career path for people in a functional organization. An assistant budget analyst may be promoted to a budget analyst and then eventually to a department manager over many budget analysts.

Functional organizations have their disadvantages. If this is the kind of organization you work in, you probably have experienced some of them.

One of the greatest disadvantages for the project manager is that they have little to no formal authority. This does not mean that project managers in functional organizations are doomed to failure. Many projects are undertaken and successfully completed within this type of organization. Good communication, interpersonal, and influencing skills on the part of the project manager are required to bring about a successful project under this structure.

In a functional organization, the vice president or senior department manager is usually the one responsible for projects. The title of project manager denotes authority, and in a functional structure, that authority rests with the VP.

Projects are typically undertaken in a divided approach in a functional organization. For example, the marketing department will work on their portion of the project and then hand it off to the manufacturing department to complete their part of the project and so on. The work the marketing department does is considered a marketing project, while the work the manufacturing department does is considered a manufacturing project.

Some projects require project team members from different departments to work together at the same time on various aspects of the project. Project team members in this structure will more than likely remain loyal to their functional manager. The functional manager is responsible for their performance reviews, and their career opportunities lie within the functional department—not within the project team. Exhibiting leadership skills by forming a common vision regarding the project and the ability to motivate people to work toward that vision are great skills to exercise in this situation. As previously mentioned, it also doesn't hurt to have the project manager work with the functional manager in contributing to the employee's performance review.

Competition for resources and project priorities can become fierce when multiple projects are undertaken within a functional organization. For example, in my organization, it's common to have competing project requests from three or more departments all vying for the same resources. Thrown into the heap is the requirement to make mandated tax law changes, which automatically usurps all other priorities. This sometimes causes frustration and political infighting. One department thinks their project is more important than another and will do anything to get that project pushed ahead of the others. Again, it takes great skill and diplomatic abilities to keep projects on track and functioning smoothly. In a later chapter, we'll discuss the importance of gaining stakeholder buy-in, prioritization, and communication distribution to avert some of these problems.

Functional organizations are the most common form of organization. Project managers have little authority in these organizations, but with the right skills, they can successfully accomplish many projects. Table 1.1 highlights the advantages and disadvantages of this type of organization.

TABLE 1.1 Functional Organizations

Advantages	Disadvantages
Enduring organizational structure.	Project manager has little to no formal authority.
Clear career path with separation of functions allowing specialty skills to flourish.	Multiple projects compete for limited resources and priority.
Employees have one supervisor with a clear chain of command.	Project team members are loyal to the functional manager.

Projectized Organizations

Projectized organizations are nearly the opposite of functional organizations. The focus of this type of organization is the project itself. The idea behind a projectized organization is to develop loyalty to the project, not to a functional manager.

Figure 1.3 shows a typical org chart for a projectized organization.

FIGURE 1.3   Projectized org chart

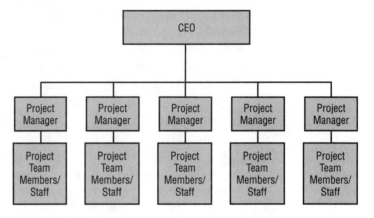

Organizational resources are dedicated to projects and project work in purely projectized organizations. Project managers almost always have ultimate authority over the project in this structure and report directly to the CEO. In a purely projectized organization, supporting departments like human resources and accounting might report directly to the project manager as well. Project managers are responsible for making decisions regarding the project and acquiring and assigning resources. They have the authority to choose and assign resources from other areas in the organization or to hire them from outside if needed. However, project managers in all organizational structures are limited by the triple constraints. For example, if the budget doesn't exist to hire additional resources, the project manager will have to come up with alternatives to solve this problem.

Teams are formed and often *collocated,* which means that team members physically work at the same location. Project team members report to the project manager, not a functional or departmental manager. One obvious drawback to a projectized organization is that project team members may find themselves out of work at the end of the project. An example of this might be a consultant who works on a project until completion and then is put on the bench or let go at the end of the project. Some inefficiency exists in this kind of organization when it comes to resource utilization. If you have a situation where you need a highly specialized skill at certain times throughout the project, the resource you're using to perform this function might be idle during other times in the project.

 Real World Scenario

The Projectized Graphic Artist

You've been appointed project manager for your company's website design and implementation. You're working in a projectized organization, so you have the authority to acquire and assign resources. You put together your team including programmers, technical writers, testers, and business analysts. Debbie, a highly qualified graphic arts designer, is also part of your team. Debbie's specialized graphic arts skills are needed only at certain times throughout the project. When she has completed the graphics design portion of the screen she's working on, there isn't anything else for her to do until the next page is ready. Depending on how involved the project is and how the work is structured, days or weeks might pass before Debbie's skills are needed. This is where the inefficiency occurs in a purely projectized organization. The project manager will have to find other duties that Debbie can perform during these downtimes. It's not practical to let her go and then hire her back when she's needed again.

In this situation, you might assign Debbie to other project duties when she's not working on graphics design. Perhaps she can edit the text for the web pages or assist with the design of the upcoming marketing campaign. You might also share Debbie's time with another project manager in the organization.

During the planning process, you will discover the skills and abilities of all your team members so that you can plan their schedule accordingly and eliminate idle time.

Projectized structures can coexist within functional organizations. In the case of a high-profile, critical project, for instance, the functional organization might appoint a special project team to work only on that project. The team is structured outside the bounds of the functional organization, and the project manager has ultimate authority for the project. This is a workable project management approach and ensures open communication between project manager and team members. At the end of the project, the project team is dissolved, and the project members return to their functional areas to resume their usual duties.

In summary, projectized organizations are identified several ways:

- Project managers have ultimate authority over the project.

- The focus of the organization is the project.

- The organization's resources are focused on projects and project work.

- Team members are collocated.

- Loyalties are formed to the project, not to a functional manager.

Matrix Organizations

Matrix organizations came about to minimize the differences between, and take advantage of, the strengths and weaknesses of functional and projectized organizations. The idea at play here is that the best of both organizational structures can be realized by combining them into one. The project objectives are fulfilled, and good project management techniques are utilized while still maintaining a hierarchical structure in the organization.

Employees in a matrix organization report to one functional manager and at least one project manager. It's possible that employees could report to multiple project managers if they are working on multiple projects at one time. Functional managers pick up the administrative portion of the duties and assign employees to projects. They also monitor the work of their employees on the various projects. Project managers are responsible for executing the project and giving out work assignments based on project activities. Project managers and functional managers share the responsibility of performance reviews for the employee. In a nutshell, functional managers assign employees to projects, while project managers assign tasks associated with the project.

Matrix organizations allow project managers to focus on the project and project work just like in a projectized organization. The project team is free to focus on the project objectives without distractions from the functional department.

Project managers should take care when working up activity and project estimates for the project in a matrix organization. The estimates should be given to the functional managers for input before publishing. The functional manager is the one in charge of assigning or freeing up resources to work on projects. If the project manager is counting on a certain employee to work on the project at a certain time, the project manager should determine their availability up front with the functional manager. Project estimates might have to be modified if it's discovered that the employee they were counting on is not available when needed.

As we've discussed, a lot of communication and negotiation takes place between the project manager and the functional manager. This calls for a balance of power between the two, or one will dominate the other.

In a strong matrix organization, the balance of power rests with the project manager. They have the ability to strong-arm the functional managers into giving up their best resources for projects. Sometimes, more resources than necessary are assembled for the project, and then project managers negotiate these resources among themselves, cutting out the functional manager altogether, as you can see in Figure 1.4.

FIGURE 1.4   Strong matrix org chart

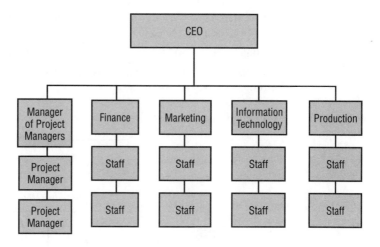

On the other end of the spectrum is the weak matrix (see Figure 1.5). As you would suspect, the functional managers have all the power in this structure. Project managers are really project coordinators or expeditors with part-time responsibilities on projects in a weak matrix organization. Project managers have little to no authority, just like in the functional organization. On the other hand, the functional managers have a lot of authority and make all the work assignments. The project manager simply expedites the project.

FIGURE 1.5   Weak matrix org chart

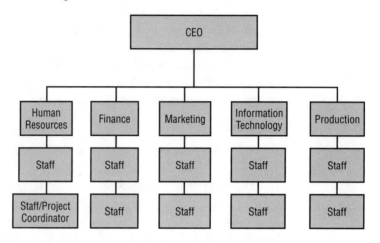

In between the weak matrix and the strong matrix is an organizational structure called the balanced matrix (see Figure 1.6). The features of the balanced matrix are what we've been discussing throughout this section. The power is balanced between project managers and functional managers. Each manager has responsibility for their parts of the project or organization, and employees get assigned to projects based on the needs of the project, not the strength or weakness of the manager's position.

FIGURE 1.6   Balanced matrix org chart

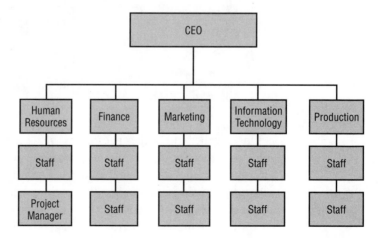

Matrix organizations have subtle differences, and it's important to understand their differences for the exam. The easiest way to remember them is that the weak matrix has many of the same characteristics as the functional organization, while the strong matrix has many of the same characteristics as the projectized organization. The balanced matrix is exactly that—a balance between weak and strong where the project manager shares authority and responsibility with the functional manager. Table 1.2 compares all three structures.

TABLE 1.2 Comparing Matrix Structures

	Weak Matrix	**Balanced Matrix**	**Strong Matrix**
Project Manager's Title:	Project coordinator, project leader, or project expeditor	Project manager	Project manager
Project Manager's Focus:	Split focus between project and functional responsibilities	Projects and project work	Projects and project work
Project Manager's Power:	Minimal authority and power	Balance of authority and power	Full authority and power
Project Manager's Time:	Part time on projects	Full time on projects	Full time on projects
Organization Style:	Most like functional organization	Blend of both weak and strong matrix	Most like a projectized organization
Project Manager Reports to:	Functional manager	A functional manager, but shares authority and power	Manager of project managers

Most organizations today use some combination of the organizational structures described here. It's rare that an organization would be purely functional or purely projectized. For example, the functional organization will often use a projectized environment for critical projects, while keeping the hierarchical activities of the organization intact.

Organizations are unique, as are the projects they undertake. Understanding the organizational structure will help you, as a project manager, with the cultural influences and communication avenues that exist in the organization to gain cooperation and successfully bring your projects to a close.

Understanding Project Life Cycles and Project Management Processes

Project life cycles are similar to the life cycle that parents experience raising their children to adulthood. Children start out as infants and generate lots of excitement wherever they go. However, not much is known about them at first. So we study them as they grow and assess their needs. Over time, they mature and grow (and cost a lot of money in the process), until one day the parents' job is done.

Projects start out just like this and progress along a similar path. Someone comes up with a great idea for a project and actively solicits support for the project. The project, after being approved, progresses through the intermediate phases to the ending phase, where the project is completed and closed out.

Project Life Cycles and Phases

All projects are divided into phases, and all projects, large or small, have a similar life cycle structure. At a minimum, a project will have a beginning or initiation phase, an intermediate phase or phases, and an ending phase. The number of phases depends on the project complexity and its industry. All the collective phases the project progresses through in concert are called the *project life cycle*.

The end of each phase allows the project manager, stakeholders, and project sponsor the opportunity to determine if the project should continue to the next phase. Project phases evolve through the life cycle in a series of "hand-offs." The end of one phase typically marks the beginning of the next. For example, in the construction industry, feasibility studies often take place in the beginning phase of a project. The purpose of the feasibility study might be to determine if the project is worth undertaking and whether the project will be profitable for the construction company. The completion and approval of the feasibility study trigger the beginning of the planning and design phase.

You will recognize phase completion because each phase has a specific *deliverable*, or multiple deliverables, that marks the end of the phase. A deliverable is an output that must be produced to bring the phase or project to completion. Deliverables are tangible and can be measured and easily proved. For instance, a hypothetical deliverable produced in the beginning phase of our construction industry example would be the feasibility study. Deliverables might also include things like design documents, project budgets, blueprints, project schedules, prototypes, etc. This analysis allows those involved the opportunity to determine if the project should continue to the next phase. The feasibility study might show that environmental impacts of an enormous nature would result if the construction project were undertaken at the proposed location. Based on this information, a go or no-go decision can be made at the end of this phase. The end of a phase also gives the project manager the ability to discover, address, and take corrective action against errors discovered during the phase.

There are times when phases are overlapped to shorten or compress the project schedule. The *Guide to the PMBOK* terms this *fast tracking*. Fast tracking means that a later phase is started prior to completing and approving the phase, or phases, that come before it.

All projects follow the life cycle pattern and, as a result, have the following things in common. In the beginning phase, which is where the Initiation process occurs, costs are low, and there are few team members assigned to the project. As the project progresses, costs and staffing increases and then tapers off at the closing phase. The potential that the project will come to a successful ending is lowest at the beginning of the project with an increasing chance for success as the project progresses through the life cycle stages. Risk is highest at the beginning of the project and gradually decreases the closer the project comes to completion. And stakeholders have the greatest chance of influencing the project in the beginning phases and less and less influence as the project progresses.

To give you a better idea of when certain characteristics influence a project, refer to Table 1.3. A recap of the impacts in the beginning life cycle phase is shown here.

TABLE 1.3 Characteristics of the Initiation Process

Low Impact/Probability	High Impact/Probability
Costs	Risk
Staffing levels	Stakeholder influence
Chance for successful completion	

Project Management Processes

Project management processes, according to the *Guide to the PMBOK*, organize and describe the work of the project. These processes are performed by people and, much like the project phases, are interrelated and dependent on one another. For example, it would be difficult to identify specific project activities without first having an understanding of the project requirements.

PMI Process Groups

The *Guide to the PMBOK* documents five process groups in the project management process: Initiation, Planning, Executing, Controlling, and Closing. We'll look at an overview of each process here and go into more detail in later chapters.

Initiation

The Initiation process, as its name implies, occurs at the beginning of the project or phase. Initiation acknowledges that a project, or the next project phase, should begin. Initiation grants the approval to commit the organization's resources to working on the project or phase.

Planning

Planning is the process of formulating and revising planning documents to be used throughout the remainder of the project. This process group is where the project requirements are fleshed out and stakeholders are identified. Planning has more processes than any of the other project management processes. The Executing, Controlling, and Closing process groups all rely on the Planning process group and the documentation produced during the Planning processes in order to carry out their functions. Project managers will perform frequent iterations of the Planning processes prior to project completion. Projects are unique, and as such have never been done before.

Therefore, Planning must encompass all areas of project management and consider budgets, activity definition, scope planning, schedule development, risk identification, staff acquisition, procurement planning, and more. The greatest conflicts a project manger will encounter in this process group are project prioritization issues.

Executing

The Executing process group involves putting the project plans into action. It's here that the project manager will coordinate and direct project resources to meet the objectives of the project plan. The Executing process keeps the project plan on track and ensures that future execution of project plans stays in line with project objectives. The Executing process group will utilize the most project time and resources. Costs are usually highest during the Executing process. Project managers will experience the greatest conflicts over schedules in this phase.

Controlling

The Controlling process group is where project performance measurements are taken and analyzed to determine if the project is staying true to the project plan. If it's discovered that variances exist, corrective action is taken to get the project activities aligned with the project plan. This might require additional passes through the Planning process to realign to the project objectives.

Closing

The Closing process group is probably the most often skipped process in project management. Once the project objectives have been met, most of us are ready to move on to the next project. However, Closing is important as all the project information is gathered now and stored for future reference. The documentation collected during Closing processes can be reviewed and utilized to avert potential problems on future projects. Contract closeout occurs here, and formal acceptance and approval are obtained from project stakeholders.

The Process Flow

The five process groups are *iterative* and should not be thought of as one-time processes. These processes will be revisited throughout the project life cycle several times as the project is refined. PMI calls this process of going back through the process groups an *iterative process*. The completion of each process allows the project manager and stakeholders to reexamine the business needs of the project and determine if the project is satisfying those needs. And it is another opportunity to make a go or no-go decision.

Figure 1.7 shows the five process groups in a typical project life cycle. Keep in mind that during phases of a project, the Closing phase can provide input to the Initiation phase. For example, once the feasibility study we discussed earlier is accepted or closed, it becomes input to the Initiation phase of design and planning.

FIGURE 1.7   Project management process groups

It's important to understand the flow of these processes for the exam. If you remember the processes and their inputs and outputs, it will help you when you're trying to decipher an exam question. Sometimes just understanding which process the question is asking about will help you determine the answer. One trick you could use to memorize these processes is to remember syrup of ipecac. (You probably have some of this poison antidote in your medicine cabinet at home.) When you sound out the first initial of each of the processes, it sounds like "ipecac"—IPECC (Initiation, Planning, Executing, Controlling, and Closing).

Processes exist within most of the process groups. For example, the Closing life cycle process group consists of two processes, Contract Closeout and Administrative Closure. Each process takes inputs and uses them in conjunction with various tools and techniques to produce outputs. It's outside the scope of this book to list all the inputs, tools and techniques, and outputs for each process in each life cycle phase. You'll find these detailed in the

Guide to the PMBOK, and I highly recommend you get familiar with them. There are test questions regarding inputs, tools and techniques, and outputs. One way to keep them all straight is to remember tools and techniques usually require action of some sort, be it measuring, applying some skill or technique, planning, or using expert judgment. Outputs are usually in the form of a deliverable. Remember that a deliverable is characterized with results or outcomes that can be measured, are tangible, and are provable. Last but not least, outputs from one process sometimes serve as inputs to another process.

Establishing the Project Management Office

The concept of a *project management office*, sometimes referred to as the PMO, has been around for several years. You won't need to know anything about PMOs for the exam. However, in practice, you'll find many organizations are establishing PMOs in many different forms. The purposes of establishing a PMO, and its benefits, are many. The most common reason a company starts a project management office is to establish and maintain procedures and standards for project management methodologies to be used throughout the organization. In some organizations, project managers might work directly for the PMO and are assigned from this office to projects as they are initiated. The PMO, depending on its size and function, sometimes has experts available that assist project managers in project planning, estimating, and business assumption verification tasks. They serve as mentors to junior-level project managers and act as consultants to the senior project managers.

The PMO takes responsibility for maintaining and archiving project documentation. All project documentation and information is collected and tracked by the PMO for future reference. This office compares project goals with project progress and gives feedback to the project teams. This office also measures the project performance of active projects and suggests corrective actions. The PMO evaluates completed projects for their adherence to the triple constraints and asks the following: Did the project meet the time frames established, did it stay within budget, and was the quality acceptable?

Project management offices are becoming more common in organizations today, if for no other reason, simply to serve as a collection point for project documentation. Some PMOs are fairly sophisticated and prescribe the standards and methodologies to be used in all project phases across the enterprise. Still others provide all these functions and also offer project management consulting services. However, the establishment of a PMO is not required in order for you to apply good project management practices to your next project.

Summary

Phew, we covered a lot of ground in this chapter. We learned that projects exist to bring about a unique product or service. Projects are temporary in nature and have definite beginning and ending dates.

Stakeholders are those people or organizations that have a vested interest in the outcome of the project. Stakeholders include people like the project sponsor, the customer, key management personnel, the project manager, contractors, suppliers, and more. Projects are considered complete when the project meets or exceeds the expectations of the stakeholders.

Project management is a discipline that brings together a set of tools and techniques to describe, organize, and monitor the work of project activities. Project managers are the ones responsible for carrying out these activities.

Every project must work within constraints. The primary constraints that will affect all projects are the triple constraints of budget, time, and quality.

Project managers have a wide variety of skills. Not only should they be versed in the field they're working in, but in general management skills as well. Communication is the most important skill a project manager will use in the course of a project.

Organizational structures come in variations of three forms: functional, projectized, and matrix organizations. Functional organizations are traditional with hierarchical reporting structures. Project managers have little to no authority in this organization. Projectized organizations are structured around project work, and staff personnel report to project managers. Project managers have full authority in this organizational structure. Matrix organizations are a combination of the functional and projectized. A project manager's authority varies depending on the structure of the matrix, be it a weak matrix, balanced matrix, or strong matrix.

Projects progress along a life cycle path. The life cycle consists of phases, and the *Guide to the PMBOK* process groups are performed throughout the project's life cycle. The *Guide to the PMBOK* process groups are Initiation, Planning, Executing, Controlling, and Closing.

Project management offices are a way to organize and establish standards for project management techniques within an organization. They can also serve as a project library, housing project documentation for future reference.

Exam Essentials

Be able to describe the difference between projects and operations.   A project is temporary in nature with a definite beginning and ending date. Operations are ongoing.

Be able to denote some of the skills every good project manager should possess.   Communication, budgeting, organizational, problem solving, negotiation and influencing, leading, and team building.

Be able to differentiate the different organizational structures.   Organizations are usually structured in some combination of the following: functional, projectized, and matrix (including weak matrix, balanced matrix, and strong matrix).

Be able to name the five project management processes.   Initiation, Planning, Executing, Controlling, and Closing.

Key Terms

We've learned a lot of new key words in this chapter. PMI has worked hard to develop and define standard project management terms that apply across industries. Here is a list of some of the terms we came across in this chapter:

collocation	project life cycle
deliverable	project management
fast tracking	project management office (PMO)
functional organization	project manager
iterative	project sponsor
matrix organization	projectized organization
program	project
progressive elaboration	stakeholder

Review Questions

1. Which organization has set the de facto standards for project management techniques?

   A. PMBOK

   B. PMO

   C. PMI

   D. PMA

2. The VP of marketing approaches you and requests that you change the visitor logon screen on the company's website to include a username with at least six characters. This is considered:

   A. Project initiation

   B. Ongoing operations

   C. A project

   D. Project execution

3. Your company manufactures small kitchen appliances. They are introducing a new product line of appliances in designer colors with distinctive features for kitchens in small spaces. These new products will be offered indefinitely starting with the spring catalog release. Which of the following is true?

   A. This is a project because this new product line has never been manufactured and sold by this company before.

   B. This is an ongoing operation because the company is in the business of manufacturing kitchen appliances. Introducing designer colors and features is simply a new twist on an existing process.

   C. This is an ongoing operation because the new product line will be sold indefinitely. It's not temporary.

   D. This is not a project or an ongoing operation. This is a new product introduction not affecting ongoing operations.

4. Your company manufactures small kitchen appliances. They are introducing a new product line of appliances in designer colors with distinctive features for kitchens in small spaces. These new products will be offered indefinitely starting with the spring catalog release. In order to determine the characteristics and features of the new product line, you will have to perform which of the following?

   A. Fast tracking

   B. Consulting with the stakeholders

   C. Planning the project life cycle

   D. Progressive elaboration

5. A project is considered successful when:

   A. The product of the project has been manufactured.

   B. The project sponsor announces the completion of the project.

   C. The product of the project is turned over to the operations area to handle the ongoing aspects of the project.

   D. The project meets or exceeds the expectations of the stakeholders.

6. The VP of customer service has expressed concern over a project you're involved in. His specific concern is that if the project is implemented as planned, he'll have to purchase additional equipment to staff his customer service center. The cost is substantial and was not taken into consideration in the project budget. The project sponsor insists that the project must go forward as originally planned or the customer will suffer. Which of the following is true?

   A. The VP of customer service is correct. Since the cost was not taken into account at the beginning of the project, the project should not go forward as planned. Project initiation should be revisited to examine the project plan and determine how changes can be made to accommodate customer service.

   B. The conflict should be resolved in favor of the customer.

   C. The conflict should be resolved in favor of the project sponsor.

   D. The conflict should be resolved in favor of the VP of customer service.

7. Which of the following brings together a set of tools and techniques used to describe, organize, and monitor the work of project activities?

   A. Project managers

   B. *Guide to the PMBOK*

   C. Project management

   D. Stakeholders

8. What are the triple constraints?

   A. Time, schedules, and quality

   B. Time, availability, and quality

   C. Time, money, and schedules

   D. Time, money, and quality

9. You are the project manager for a large construction project. The project objective is to construct a set of outbuildings to house the Olympic support team that will be arriving in your city 18 months from the project start date. You've been given a budget of $12 million to complete this project. Resources are easily attained. Which of the triple constraints is the primary constraint for this project?

   A. Time, because the date cannot be moved

   B. Money, because the budget is set at $12 million

   C. Resources, because they're not fixed

   D. Quality, because the buildings have to be functional and safe

10. You are the project manager for a large construction project. The project objective is to construct a set of outbuildings to house the Olympic support team that will be arriving in your city 18 months from the project start date. Resources are not readily available as they are currently assigned to other projects. Jack, an expert crane operator, is needed for this project two months from today. Which of the following skills will you use to get Jack assigned to your project?

A. Negotiation and influencing skills

B. Communication and organizational skills

C. Communication skills

D. Problem-solving skills

11. You are a project manager with technical expertise in the pharmaceutical industry. You've decided to try your hand at project management in the entertainment industry. Which of the following is true?

A. You will likely be successful because communication skills are your strong suit. You anticipate having technical experts on your project team to address industry specifics that you're not familiar with.

B. You will likely be successful because your organizational skills are excellent. You anticipate having technical experts on your project team to address industry specifics that you're not familiar with.

C. You will probably be successful because you have a friend in the entertainment industry that has briefed you on all the important aspects of this project that you'll need to know. You anticipate having technical experts on your project team to address industry specifics that you're not familiar with.

D. You will probably not be successful because you have little knowledge of the entertainment industry even though you anticipate having technical experts on your project team to address industry specifics that you're not familiar with.

12. You are managing a project to install a new postage software system that will automatically print labels and administer postage for certified mailings, overnight packages, and other special mailing needs. You've attempted to gain the cooperation of the business analyst working on this project and need some answers. She is elusive and tells you that this project is not her top priority. To avoid situations like this in the future, you should:

    A. Establish the business analyst's duties well ahead of due dates and tell her you'll be reporting on her performance to her functional manager.

    B. Establish the business analyst's duties well ahead of due dates and tell her you are expecting her to meet these expectations because the customer is counting on the project meeting due dates to save significant costs on their annual mailings.

    C. Negotiate with the business analyst's functional manager during the planning process to establish expectations and request to participate in the business analyst's annual performance review.

    D. Negotiate with the business analyst's functional manager during the planning process to establish expectations and inform the functional manager of the requirements of the project. Agreement from the functional manager will assure the cooperation of the business analyst.

13. The amount of authority a project manager possesses can be related to:

    A. The project manager's communication skills

    B. The organizational structure

    C. The amount of authority the manager of the project manager possesses

    D. The project manager's influencing skills

14. What is one of the advantages of a functional structure?

A. All employees report to one manager and have a clear chain of command.

B. All employees report to two or more managers, but project team members show loyalty to functional managers.

C. The organization is focused on projects and project work.

D. Teams are collocated.

15. You have been assigned to a project in which the objectives are to direct customer calls to an Interactive Voice Response system before being connected to a live agent. You are in charge of the media communications for this project. You report to the project manager in charge of this project and the VP of marketing, who share responsibility for this project. Which organizational structure do you work in?

A. Functional organization

B. Weak matrix organization

C. Projectized organization

D. Balanced matrix organization

16. You have been assigned to a project in which the objectives are to expand three miles of the north-south highway through your city by two lanes in each direction. You are in charge of the demolition phase of this project, and you report to the project manager in charge of this project. You have been hired on contract and will be released at the completion of the demolition phase. What type of organizational structure does this represent?

A. Functional organization

B. Weak matrix organization

C. Projectized organization

D. Balanced matrix organization

17. What are the five project management process groups, in order?

    A. Initiation, Executing, Planning, Controlling, and Closing

    B. Initiation, Controlling, Planning, Executing, and Closing

    C. Initiation, Planning, Controlling, Executing, and Closing

    D. Initiation, Planning, Executing, Controlling, and Closing

18. You have been assigned to a project in which the objectives are to expand three miles of the north-south highway through your city by two lanes in each direction. You are interested in implementing a new project process called design-build in order to speed up the project schedule. The idea is that the construction team will work on the first mile of the highway reconstruction at the same time the design team is coming up with plans for the third mile of the reconstruction rather than completing all design before any construction begins. This is an example of:

    A. Managing the projects as a program

    B. Fast tracking

    C. Progressive elaboration

    D. Collocation

19. During which project management process are risk and stakeholder's ability to influence project outcomes the highest at the beginning of the process?

    A. Planning

    B. Executing

    C. Initiation

    D. Controlling

20. You are a project manager working on gathering requirements and establishing estimates for the project. Which process group are you in?

    A. Planning

    B. Executing

    C. Initiation

    D. Controlling

Answers to Review Questions

1. **C.** The Project Management Institute (PMI) is the industry-recognized standard for project management practices.

2. **B.** Projects exist to create a unique product or service. The logon screen in this question is not a unique product. A minor change has been requested, indicating this is an ongoing operation function. Some of the criteria for projects are that they are unique, temporary with definitive start and end dates, and considered complete when the project goals are achieved.

3. **A.** This is a project. The product line is new, which implies this is a unique product—it hasn't been done before. We can discern a definite start and end date by the fact that the new appliances must be ready by the spring catalog release.

4. **D.** Progressive elaboration is the process of determining the characteristics and features of the product of the project. Progressive elaboration is carried out in steps in detailed fashion.

5. **D.** A project is considered successful when stakeholder needs and expectations are met or exceeded.

6. **B.** Conflicts between stakeholders should always be resolved in favor of the customer. This question emphasizes the importance of identifying your stakeholders and their needs as early as possible in the project. We'll discuss this more in later chapters.

7. **C.** Project management brings together a set of tools and techniques to organize project activities. Project managers are the ones responsible for managing the project processes.

8. **D.** The triple constraints that drive all projects are time, money, and quality.

9. A. The primary constraint on this project is time because the date absolutely cannot move. The Olympics are scheduled to begin on a certain date, and this can't be changed. The budget is also a constraint because it's set at $12 million, but in this example, it would be a secondary constraint. It's important that the project manager understands the priority of the constraints and manages to them.

10. A. Negotiation and influencing skills are needed to convince Jack's boss and come to agreement concerning his assignment.

11. A. Project management processes span industries. A project manager can take these skills across industries and apply them successfully. Technical experience in the industry doesn't hurt, but it's not required. The most important skill any project manager can have is communication skills. Poor communication skills might lead to an unsuccessful conclusion no matter how strong the project manager's other skills are.

12. C. Negotiate with the functional manager to participate in the business analyst's annual performance review.

13. B. The level of authority the project manager has is determined by the organizational structure. For instance, in a functional organization, the project manager has little to no authority, but in a projectized structure, the project manager has full authority.

14. A. An advantage for employees in a functional organization is that they have only one supervisor and a clear chain of command exists.

15. D. Employees in a balanced matrix often report to two or more managers. Functional managers and project managers share authority and responsibility for projects. There is a balance of power between the functional managers and project managers.

16. C. Projectized organizations are focused on the project itself. One issue with this type of structure is determining what to do with project team members when they are not actively involved on the project. One alternative is to release them when they are no longer needed.

17. D. Remember the acronym that sounds like syrup of ipecac: IPECC.

18. B. Fast tracking is starting a new phase before the phase you're working on is completed. This compresses the project schedule, and the project is completed sooner as a result.

19. C. The Initiation process is where stakeholders have the greatest ability to influence outcomes of the project. Risk is highest during this stage because of the high degree of unknown factors.

20. A. The Planning process is where requirements are fleshed out, stakeholders are identified, and estimates on project costs and time are made.

Chapter

2

Initiating the Project

PMP EXAM CONTENT FROM THE PROJECT INITIATION PERFORMANCE DOMAIN COVERED IN THIS CHAPTER:

- ✓ 1. Determine Project Goals.
- ✓ 2. Determine Deliverables.
- ✓ 3. Determine Process Outputs.
- ✓ 4. Document Constraints.
- ✓ 5. Document Assumptions.

Now that you're fully armed with a detailed overview of project management, you can easily determine if your next assignment really is a project or an ongoing operation. You've also learned some of the basics of good project management techniques and the knowledge areas where you might need specific expertise. We're going to start putting those techniques into practice in the Initiation process. And, as you've probably already guessed, we'll be using some of the general management skills we outlined in Chapter 1 also.

One of the first skills you are going to put to use will be your communication skills. Are you surprised? Of course you're not. It all starts with communication. You can't start defining the project until you've first talked to the project sponsor, key stakeholders, and management personnel. All good project managers have honed their communication skills to a nice sharp edge.

You'll remember from Chapter 1 that project Initiation is the first process in a project life cycle. You can think of it as the official project kickoff. Initiation acknowledges that the project, or the next phase in an active project, should begin. Initiation then culminates in the publication of a project charter. We'll discuss project charters in Chapter 3 in more depth. But we've got work to do before we're ready to produce the project charter, so we'll wrap up this chapter with a discussion of the preliminary elements of a charter document.

We will also talk about project Initiation and introduce some of the things that make up this process. But before we dive into Initiation, we'll first take a look at what PMI calls the Project Management Knowledge Areas. Knowledge areas are a collection of processes that share similar themes and, therefore, benefit from the expertise of specific knowledge and skills in each of these areas.

At the end of this chapter, we'll introduce a case study that will illustrate the main points of the chapter. We'll take this case study with us from chapter to chapter and begin building a project from each of things we learned.

The Project Management Knowledge Areas

According to the *Guide to the PMBOK*, project Initiation, as we've discussed, is the first project management process group in the life cycle of a project. In addition to the project process groups, the *Guide to the PMBOK* classifies the processes that make up each project management process group into nine *Project Management Knowledge Areas*. These groupings, or knowledge areas, bring together processes that have things in common. For example, Project Cost Management involves all aspects of the budgeting process, as you would suspect, such as Resource Planning, Cost Estimating, Cost Budgeting, and Cost Control. These processes belong to different project management process groups, but because they all involve costs and budgeting, they share many aspects in common.

Understanding the Project Management Knowledge Areas

Let's take a closer look at each area so we really understand how their role works with the process groups. Included in each of the following subsections is a figure that illustrates the knowledge area, the processes that make up each knowledge area, and the project management process groups that each process belongs to. This will help you to see the big picture in terms of process groups versus knowledge areas. We will be discussing each of the processes in the various knowledge areas throughout the book, but for now, let's take a high-level look at each of them.

Project Integration Management

Project Integration Management (see Figure 2.1) is comprised of three processes: Project Plan Development, Project Plan Execution, and Integrated Change Control.

The Project Integration knowledge area is concerned with coordinating all aspects of the project plan and is highly interactive. Project planning, project execution, and change control occur throughout the project and are repeated continuously while working on the project. Project planning and execution involve weighing the objectives of the project against alternatives to bring the project to a successful completion. Change control impacts the project plan, which in turn impacts execution, so you can see that these three processes are very tightly linked. The processes in this area also interact with other processes in the remaining knowledge areas.

FIGURE 2.1 Project Integration Management

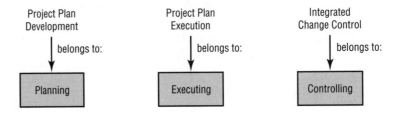

Project Integration Management

Project Scope Management

Project Scope Management (see Figure 2.2) has five processes: Initiation, Scope Planning, Scope Definition, Scope Verification, and Scope Change Control.

Project Scope Management is concerned with the work of the project. All of the processes involved with the work of the project, and only the work that is required to complete the project, are found in this knowledge area. We'll talk about Initiation in more detail in the remainder of this chapter. Scope Planning, Scope Definition, Scope Verification, and Scope Change Control involve detailing the requirements of the product of the project and the activities that will eventually comprise the project plan, verifying those details using measurement techniques, and controlling changes to these processes.

FIGURE 2.2 Project Scope Management

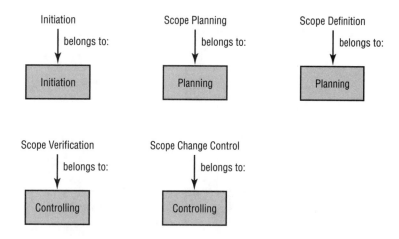

Project Time Management

The *Project Time Management* knowledge area (see Figure 2.3) also has five processes: Activity Definition, Activity Sequencing, Activity Duration Estimating, Schedule Development, and Schedule Control.

This knowledge area is concerned with estimating the duration of the project plan activities, devising a project schedule, and monitoring and controlling deviations from the schedule. Collectively, this knowledge area deals with completing the project in a timely manner.

In many cases, all of the activity processes described here along with schedule development are completed as one activity. Sometimes, only one person is needed to complete these five processes, and they're all worked on at the same time. Time management is an important aspect of project management as it concerns keeping the project activities on track and monitoring those activities against the project plan to assure the project is completed on time.

FIGURE 2.3 Project Time Management

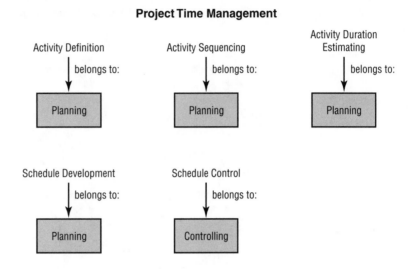

Project Time Management

Project Cost Management
========================

As its name implies, the *Project Cost Management* knowledge area (see Figure 2.4) centers around costs and budgets. The processes that make up this knowledge area are as follows: Resource Planning, Cost Estimating, Cost Budgeting, and Cost Control.

The activities in the Project Cost Management knowledge area establish estimates for costs and resources and keep watch over those costs to ensure that the project stays within the approved budget. Depending on the complexity of the project, these processes might need the involvement of more than one person. For example, the finance person might not have expertise in the Resource Planning area, so the project manager will need to bring in a staff member with those skills to complete the Resource Planning process.

FIGURE 2.4 Project Cost Management

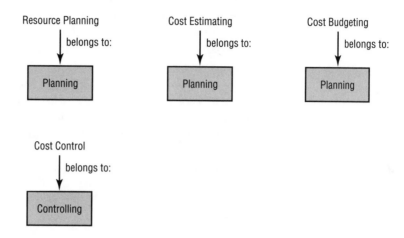

Project Cost Management

Project Quality Management

The *Project Quality Management* knowledge area (see Figure 2.5) assures that the project meets the requirements that the project was undertaken to produce. These processes measure overall performance, and monitor project results and compare them to the quality standards set out in the project-planning process to assure that the customer will receive the product or service they thought they purchased.

Project Quality Management is composed of the following three processes: Quality Planning, Quality Assurance, and Quality Control.

FIGURE 2.5 Project Quality Management

Project Quality Management

Project Human Resource Management

Project Human Resource Management (see Figure 2.6) involves all aspects of people management and personal interaction including leading, coaching, dealing with conflict, and more. Some of the project participants whom you'll get to practice these skills on include stakeholders, team members, and customers. Each requires the use of different communication styles, leadership skills, and team-building skills. A good project manager knows when to enact certain skills and communication styles based on the situation.

The Project Human Resource knowledge area contains the following processes: Organizational Planning, Staff Acquisition, and Team Development.

FIGURE 2.6 Project Human Resource Management

Project Communications Management

The processes that make up the *Project Communications Management* knowledge area (see Figure 2.7) are as follows: Communications Planning, Information Distribution, Performance Reporting, and Administrative Closure.

The processes in the Project Communications knowledge area are related to general communication skills but aren't the same thing. Communication skills are considered general management skills that the project manager utilizes on a daily basis. The processes in the Communications knowledge area seek to ensure that all project information including project plans, risk assessments, meeting notes, and more is collected and documented. These processes also ensure information is distributed and shared with appropriate stakeholders and project members. At project close, the information is archived and used as a reference for future projects. This is referred to as *historical information* in several project processes.

FIGURE 2.7   Project Communications Management

Project Communications Management

Communications Planning	Information Distribution	Performance Reporting
belongs to:	belongs to:	belongs to:
Planning	Executing	Controlling

Administrative Closure
belongs to:
Closing

Project Risk Management

Project Risk Management (see Figure 2.8) contains six processes: Risk Management Planning, Risk Identification, Qualitative Risk Analysis, Quantitative Risk Analysis, Risk Response Planning, and Risk Monitoring and Control.

As the name of this knowledge area implies, these processes are concerned with identifying and planning for potential risks that may impact the project. Organizations will often combine several of these processes into one step. For example, Risk Identification, Qualitative Risk Analysis, and Quantitative Risk Analysis might be performed at the same time. The important thing about this process is that you should strive to identify all the risks and develop responses for those with the greatest consequences to the project objectives.

FIGURE 2.8 Project Risk Management

Project Risk Management

Risk Management Planning → belongs to: → Planning

Risk Identification → belongs to: → Planning

Qualitative Risk Analysis → belongs to: → Planning

Quantitative Risk Analysis → belongs to: → Planning

Risk Response Planning → belongs to: → Planning

Risk Monitoring and Control → belongs to: → Controlling

Project Procurement Management

The *Project Procurement Management* knowledge area (see Figure 2.9) includes the processes involved with purchasing goods or services from external vendors, contractors, and suppliers. When discussing the Procurement Management processes, it's assumed that the discussion is taking place from the perspective of the buyer. As the project manager, you would be the buyer purchasing the goods or services from a supplier or contractor, so these processes should be examined from that perspective.

The processes in the Project Procurement Management knowledge area are as follows: Procurement Planning, Solicitation Planning, Solicitation, Source Selection, Contract Administration, and Contract Closeout.

The PMP exam will most likely have a question or two regarding the processes that make up a knowledge area. Remember that knowledge areas bring together processes by commonalities, so thinking about the knowledge area itself should tip you off to the processes that belong to it. Projects are executed in process group order, but the knowledge areas allow a project manager to think about groups of processes that require specific skills. This makes the job of assigning resources easier because team members with specific skills might be able to work on and complete several processes at once.

FIGURE 2.9 Project Procurement Management

Project Procurement Management

Procurement Planning	Solicitation Planning	Solicitation
belongs to:	belongs to:	belongs to:
Planning	Planning	Executing

Source Selection	Contract Administration	Contract Closeout
belongs to:	belongs to:	belongs to:
Executing	Executing	Closing

The remainder of this book will deal with processes and process groups as they occur in life cycle order (i.e., Initiation, Planning, Executing, Controlling, and Closing) as this is the way you will encounter and manage them during a project.

Defining the Project Initiation Process

Your company's quarterly meeting is scheduled for today. You take your seat, and each of the department heads gets up and starts giving their usual "ain't this great" rah-rah speech one after the other. You barely notice that the CEO takes the stage. He starts out his part of the program pretty much the same way the department heads did. Suddenly, your daydreaming trance is shattered when you hear the CEO say, "…and the new phone system will be installed by Thanksgiving."

Wait a minute. You work in the telecom department and haven't heard a word about this project until today. You also have a funny feeling that you've been elected to manage this project. It's amazing how good communication skills are so important for project managers but not…well, we won't go there.

Project Initiation

Project *Initiation* is the formal recognition that a project should begin and resources should be committed to the project. Unfortunately, many projects are initiated the way our CEO did in this example. Each of us, at one time or another, has experienced being handed a project with little to no information and told to "make it happen." The new phone system scenario is an excellent example of how *not* to initiate a project.

Taking one step back from Initiation leads us to ask, "How do projects come about in the first place? Do CEOs just make them up like in this example?" Even though our CEO announced this new project at the company meeting with no forewarning, there is no doubt it came about as a result of a legitimate need. Believe it or not, CEOs don't just dream projects up to give us all something to do. They're concerned about the future of the company and the needs of the business and its customers.

The business itself might drive the need for a project, customers might demand changes to products, or legal requirements may create the need for a new project. According to the *Guide to the PMBOK*, projects come about as a result of one of six needs or demands.

Needs and Demands

Organizations exist to generate profits or serve the public. To stay competitive, organizations are always examining new ways of creating business, better ways of gaining efficiencies, or better ways to serve their customers. Sometimes laws are passed to force organizations to make their products safer or to protect the environment. Projects result from all of these needs. Most projects will fit one of the six needs or demands described below. It is those needs and/or demands that dictate the germination of a project. In the following sections, let's take a closer look at each of these areas.

Marketing Demand

The demands of the marketplace can drive the need for a project. For example, a bank initiates a project to offer customers the ability to apply for mortgage loans over the Internet due to a drop in interest rates and an increase in demand for refinances and new home loans.

Business Need

The new phone system we talked about earlier that was announced at the quarterly meeting came about as a result of a business need. The CEO, on advice from his staff, was advised that call volumes were maxed on the existing system. Without a new system, customer service response times would suffer, and that would eventually affect the bottom line.

Customer Request

Customer requests run the gamut. Generally speaking, most companies have customers, and their requests can drive new projects. Customers can be internal or external to the organization. Government agencies don't have external customers per se (we're captive customers at any rate), but there are internal customers within departments and across agencies.

Perhaps you work for a company that sells remittance-processing equipment and you've just landed a contract with a local utility company. This project is driven by the need of the utility company to automate their process, or upgrade their existing process. The utility company's request to purchase your equipment and consulting services is the project driver.

Technological Advance

Do you happen to own one of those electronic personal digital assistants? They keep names and addresses handy and usually come with a calendar and a to-do list of some kind. I couldn't live without mine. However, there is always a newer, better version coming to market. The introduction of satellite communications now allows these little devices to connect to the Web or get e-mail almost anywhere in the world. The introduction of the satellite communications ability is an example of a technological advance. Due to this introduction, electronics manufacturers revamped their products to take advantage of this new technology.

Legal Requirement

Private industry as well as government agencies generate new projects as a result of laws passed every legislative season. For example, new sales tax laws might require modifications or new programming to the existing sales tax system. The requirement that food labels appear on every package describing the ingredients and the recommended daily allowances of certain vitamins is another example of a project driven by legal requirements.

Social Need

The last need is a result of social demands. For example, perhaps a developing country is experiencing a fast-spreading disease that's infecting large portions of the population. Medical supplies and facilities are needed to vaccinate and cure those infected with the disease. Another example might include cleaning up waste products from the water supply of manufacturing plants prior to putting the water back into a local river or stream to prevent contamination.

Project Initiation Process

Initiation is part of the Project Scope Management knowledge area. As we've learned, this knowledge area deals with identifying a project, the stakeholders, and the project requirements. The Initiation process lays the groundwork for the Planning process group that follows Initiation. A high percentage of projects fail due to poor planning or no planning. Properly planning your project up front dramatically increases the project's chance for success. Since Initiation is the foundation of Planning, the importance of Initiation is self evident.

The project Initiation process has several inputs: product description, strategic plan, project selection criteria, and historical information. Each of these inputs is processed using tools and techniques to produce the final outputs, one of which is the project charter. Now, we'll examine each of these inputs in a bit more detail.

Product Description

As you might deduce, the product description describes the product. The product description should be documented and should clearly outline the characteristics of the product or service. This description should also include the business need that's driving the reason for the project.

Product descriptions contain less detail in the early phases of a project and more detail as the project progresses. Product details are progressively elaborated to come up with the final product description. It will contain the greatest amount of detail at the project Execution process.

When a project is performed under contract, typically the buyer of the product or service will provide the product description to the vendor or contractor. The product description serves as a statement of work when the project is contracted to a vendor. A statement of work describes the product or service in enough detail so that the vendor can accurately price the contract and satisfactorily fulfill the requirements of the project. The statement of work is covered in more detail in Chapter 6.

Strategic Plan

Part of the responsibility of a project manager during the Initiation process is to take into consideration the company's strategic plan. Perhaps the strategic plan states that one of the company goals is to build 15 new stores by the end of the fiscal year. If the project your company is considering undertaking is to install a new human resources software system, it would make sense to write the requirements for your project with the 15 new stores in mind. Your management team will refer to the strategic plan when choosing which new projects to initiate and which ones to drop depending on their relationship to the strategic vision of the company.

Project Selection Criteria

Project selection involves making determinations regarding which projects to accept or reject based on criteria such as financial data, sales potential in the marketplace, etc. This subject will be dealt with more thoroughly in Chapter 3.

Historical Information

Historical information can be very useful to project managers and to stakeholders. When you're evaluating new projects, historical information about previous projects of a similar nature can be very handy in determining if the new project should be accepted and initiated. Historical information on an active project gathered and documented during the project can be examined to assist in determining whether the project should proceed to the next phase. Historical information will help you in determining project goals, with estimating activities, and during the project-planning processes. You'll find that historical information is an input to several processes .

Developing a Project Overview

One of the first steps a project manager will take in the Initiation process is to develop a project overview. Some organizations call this a project concept document. The four inputs described in the last section will help to outline the project overview and will be used again when formulating the final project charter.

It should be noted that the *Guide to the PMBOK* holds the view that a project manager is identified and assigned at the completion of the Initiation process. While sometimes that's true, in practice it's common that the project manager is involved at the beginning of the Initiation process and assists with the project overview and information-gathering tasks.

At the completion of the Initiation process, the organization has committed to fund the project and provide the necessary resources to carry it out, or has killed the project. The project has the lowest probability of succeeding during Initiation. That's because no action has been taken regarding project activities. In other words, you haven't actually begun to produce the product of the project. Quite a bit of work will have gone into the project at this stage, but most of it regards the overview of the project and the business justification for the project. The stakeholders have greatest ability to influence project outcome at this stage because nothing has been cast in stone yet. There is still time for them to negotiate requirements and deliverables. Risk is highest during Initiation because any number of things can happen between now and the time the project is completed. The project might not be approved, the funding might not be approved, the strategic direction of the company could change and the project no longer fits in with the new vision, the customer could change her mind, etc. This list could become quite lengthy.

Project failure can be controlled and minimized by accurately applying project management techniques to your project and by proper planning.

 Real World Scenario

The Diet-Cola Marketing Opportunity

Elizabeth is the project manager for a large soft drink beverage company located in Tallahassee, Florida. One sunny morning, Roger Bruist, the marketing vice president, pays her a visit.

"I asked your boss if it was okay to directly talk to you about this project—she said it would be fine," he starts. "As you've probably heard, we're test marketing a new diet-cola opportunity that we thought would be a big seller. Long story short, I had lunch the other day with a friend of mine from the club. He ordered his usual diet cola but requested three slices of lemon with it. I stared at him while he squeezed those lemons into his diet and dunked the last rind into the mix. Well, I have to tell you the taste is fabulous!

"We've toyed around with the exact lemon-to-cola mixture in the lab and have come up with what we think is the optimum mix that results in the tastiness factor we're looking for.

"We've worked together, and I know your work is top-notch. What we'd like for you to do is put together a project that test markets our new soda in three test areas. We want to target markets that utilize a lot of diet soda. We think the best places to target would be Denver, Las Vegas, and the Seattle area.

"We want a project plan that details the distributors we'll send the soda to and how we'll obtain the demographics we're looking for. My department will supply you with the marketing profiles and plans you need to implement in your project plan. We'd also like a page added to the company's website that talks about the new beverage. The project should also include key players from the National Soft Drink Association and have a large, splashy intro on their website as well. You can visit their site at www.nsda.org."

As a project manager, you will often have projects presented to you that are barely past the big-picture stage. Roger has a good idea of how he wants to test market this new product, but many other processes must come into play here such as planning, budgeting, risk assessment, reporting, and so on. A lot of energy is focused on the vision of the project and the wants and needs of the stakeholders. It's your job to take the vision, examine the needs of all the stakeholders including Roger's, and bring the vision to fruition.

Determining the Project Goals

Several terms are tossed about and sometimes used interchangeably when talking about projects. They are words such as goals (sometimes called objectives), requirements, and deliverables. Their meanings are sometimes blurred together, but there is some differentiation between these terms. Goals and objectives are the purpose for undertaking the project, and they describe the final result of the project. "Increase warehouse space to house the new product line for distribution" or "provide faster turnaround times on loan application services" are both examples of goals. In other words, the purpose for the project is to do something or accomplish something—a goal.

Project Goals

Goals describe the *what* it is you're trying to do, accomplish, or produce. Goals and objectives should be stated in tangible terms. If your goal is to increase warehouse space, it would be better to say the goal is to build four new warehouses. Describing the number of new warehouses to be built is specific and tangible. For that reason, we'll know the project is completed when this goal is met. The goal of offering faster loan approvals might be better stated that the company will provide loan applications over the Internet to speed the application process.

There's no hard and fast rule here. Goals and objectives can be combined and simply called *goals*. What's important is that you come away understanding what the end purpose of the project is and how to identify when it's been accomplished.

You've probably seen this acronym regarding goal setting a dozen times, but it's worth repeating. Goals should follow the SMART rule:

S—Specific   Goals should be specific and written in clear, concise, understandable terms.

M—Measurable   Goals should be measurable.

A—Accurate   Goals should be accurate and should describe precisely what's required.

R—Realistic and tangible   Goals that are impossible to accomplish are not realistic and not attainable. Goals must be centered in reality. It's not likely you and I will be sending up rocket ships full of chocolate candies to sell to tourists visiting the moon anytime soon.

T—Time bound   Goals should have a time frame with an end date assigned to them.

Hmm, this all sounds familiar. It seems there are some similarities between goal setting and how we describe and document projects. Let's look at that acronym again from a project perspective:

S—Specific   The project goals are specific and stated in clear, concise, understandable terms and are documented in the project charter and scope statement. Projects exist to bring about a unique, specific product or service that hasn't existed before.

M—Measurable   The deliverables of the project or project phase are measurable against verifiable outcomes or results.

A—Accurate The verification and measurement of requirements and deliverables are used to determine accuracy and also to ascertain if the project is on track according to the project plan.

R—Realistic and tangible Projects are unique and produce tangible products or services. The triple constraints of any project help to define realistic goals and realistic requirements based on the limitations the constraints put on the project.

T—Time bound Projects are performed in specific time frames with a definite beginning and definite end date.

Project Requirements

Requirements are not the same as goals and objectives. Requirements are specifications of the goal or deliverables. Requirements help answer the question, "How will we know it's successful?" Requirements are the specifications or necessary prerequisites that make up the product or service you're producing. Let's say you're building those four warehouses. Some of the requirements might be the square footage of each building, the number of loading docks, the location of the warehouses, etc.

Project Deliverables

Deliverables are measurable outcomes, measurable results, or specific items that must be produced to consider the project or project phase completed. Deliverables, like goals, must be specific and verifiable. A manufacturing unit that is part of a larger project might be required to produce widgets with a 3-inch diameter. These will in turn be assembled into the final product. This deliverable is specific and measurable. However, if the deliverable was not documented or not communicated to the manager responsible for the manufacturing unit, there could be a disaster waiting to happen. If they deliver 2-inch widgets instead of the required 3-inch version, it would throw the entire project off schedule or, perhaps, cause the project to fail. This could be a career-limiting move for the project manager because it's the project manager's responsibility to document deliverables and monitor the progress of those deliverables throughout the project or project phase.

A project phase can have multiple deliverables. As in the example above, if you are assembling a new product with many parts, each of the parts could be considered independent deliverables.

The bottom line is this: No matter how well you apply your project skills, if the wrong deliverables are produced or the project is managed to the wrong goals, you will have an unsuccessful project on your hands.

Stakeholders

Now we're ready to identify and talk to those stakeholders about the project and get more specifics regarding the goals and deliverables of the project. Our objective at this point is to compile a project overview, or project definition. The overview will have enough information to describe the project, the business requirements, the project's objectives, and how we'll recognize when the project is successfully completed.

Think of stakeholders and project participants as a highly polished orchestra. Each participant has a part to play. Some play more than others. And alas, some play their parts better than others. An integral part of project management is getting to know your stakeholders and the parts they play. You'll remember from Chapter 1 that stakeholders are those people or organizations who have a vested interest in the outcome of the project. They have something to either gain or lose as a result of the project. According to the *Guide to the PMBOK*, stakeholders are officially identified in the Planning process. In practice, key stakeholders will have to be contacted early on to get their input for the project overview, goals, and deliverables.

Identifying key stakeholders at this point should be fairly easy. Stakeholders might include the project sponsor, the customer (who might be one in the same as the project sponsor), the project manager, project team members, management personnel, contractors, suppliers, etc. Stakeholders can be internal or external to the organization. One way to uncover stakeholders whom you might not have thought about right at the start is to ask known stakeholders if they're aware of anyone else that might be impacted by this project. Ask team members if they're aware of stakeholders who haven't been identified. Stakeholders might come to the forefront once you start uncovering some of the goals and deliverables of the project also.

Don't forget important stakeholders. That could be a project killer. Leaving out an important stakeholder, or one whose business processes weren't considered during project Initiation and Planning, could spell disaster for your project. Not to mention it could be another one of those career-limiting moves for the project manager.

It's important for the project manager to understand each stakeholder's role in the project and their role in the organization. Get to know them and their interests. Determine the relationship structure among the various stakeholders. Start cultivating partnerships with these stakeholders now as it's going to get pretty cozy during the course of your project. If you establish good working relationships up front and learn a little about their business concerns and needs, it might be easier to negotiate or motivate them later on when you have a pressing issue that needs action. Knowing which stakeholders work well together and which don't can also help you in the future. One stakeholder may have the authority or influence to twist the arm of another, figuratively speaking of course. Or conversely, you might know of two stakeholders who act like oil and water when put into the same room together. This can be valuable information to keep under your hat for future reference.

Communicating with Stakeholders

Now those finely honed communication skills are going to come in handy. In order to determine the specific goals of your project, you'll want to meet with each of the key stakeholders and document their ideas of the project goals. It's also a good idea at this point to gain an understanding of their needs and concerns regarding the project. Ask them why the project is needed. Ask what business process the project will change, enhance, or replace. Perhaps the existing business processes, and the systems that support them, are so old that little documentation exists for them. Determine if there is a critical business need for this project or if it's a "nice to have" as we say around our office. What will be the result of this project? Will customer service be improved, or sales increased? Find out what prevents the stakeholders today from achieving the results they hope the project will accomplish. Ask about the deliverables and how they can be verified and measured. And always ask the stakeholder how they will know that the project was completed successfully.

Remember that the definition of a successful project is one that meets or exceeds stakeholders' expectations. Understand and document those expectations and you're off to a good start. We'll talk about managing to those expectations in a later chapter.

One way to help identify project goals is to talk about what is not included in a project. For example, let's say you're working on a highway project to create a new on-ramp from a downtown city street. The goal of this project is to have a new on-ramp constructed and ready for traffic in 18 months from the project start date. Specifically excluded from this project is the demolition of a deteriorating bridge adjacent to the new on-ramp. Make sure you state this in the project overview.

The Project Overview Document

The project overview document is a high-level look at the project goals and deliverables. It serves the purpose of capturing the intended outcome of the project and its deliverables. It will provide a brief background of the project and describe the business opportunity the company is attempting to capitalize on. It will also describe the business objectives the project should meet. The overview lays the groundwork for future consensus on deliverables and project expectations.

Some organizations will require a feasibility study at this point in the project. *Feasibility studies* are undertaken for several reasons. One is to determine if the project is a viable project. They'll also determine the probability of the project succeeding. Feasibility studies can also examine the viability of the product of the project. For example, the study might ask, "Will the new lemon-flavored soda be a hit? Or, is it marketable?" The study might also look at the technical issues related to the project and determine if the technology proposed is feasible, reliable, and easily assimilated into the organization's existing technology structure.

The group of people conducting the feasibility study should not be the same ones who will work on the project. Project team members may have built-in biases toward the project and will tend to influence the feasibility outcome toward those biases.

 Real World Scenario

The Interactive Voice Response Tax-Filing System

Jason, Sam, and Kate are web programmers working for the Department of Revenue in the State of Bliss. Ron, their manager, approaches them one day with an idea.

"Team, business unit managers are thinking it would be a great idea to offer taxpayers the ability to file their income tax over the telephone. We already offer them the ability to file on the Internet, thanks to all your efforts on that project last year. It's been a fabulous success. No other state has had the success that Bliss has had with our Internet system.

"Kate, I know you've had previous experience with IVR technology, but I'm not sure about you guys, so this is new territory for us. I'd like to hear what each of you thinks about this project."

Jason speaks up first. "I think it's a great idea. You know me, I'm always up for learning new things, especially when it comes to programming. When can we start?"

Sam echoes Jason's comments.

"This technology is pretty sophisticated," Kate says. "Jason and Sam are excellent coders and could work on the programming side of things, but I would have to pick up the telephony piece on my own. After we're up and running, we could go over the telephony portions step by step so Jason and Sam can help me support it going forward. I'd really like to take on this project. It would be good for the team and good for the department."

Ron thinks for a minute. "I think a feasibility study is in order. The senior director over the tax business unit doesn't know if this project is cost justified and has some concerns about its life span. Looks like we might have some technical issues to deal with on our side, and I don't want Kate going it alone without first examining all the impacts."

Now that we've fleshed out the project goals and have a high-level view of the deliverables, it's time for the next step. But never fear, we'll be reviewing goals and refining deliverables over the next few chapters. We'll also be using them to help formulate requirements and project estimates. But we're getting ahead of ourselves. We need to constrain this chapter to the topic at hand. Which brings up the next topic—project constraints.

Identifying the Project Constraints

We introduced the triple constraints in Chapter 1. They are time, budget, and quality. All project managers have to deal with these constraints in all projects. No project manager I know has ever been given unlimited funding and unlimited time to produce a perfect product. In reality, if we were given unlimited funding and unlimited time, some of us probably wouldn't accomplish much. This is especially true for all of you out there who are the perfectionist types. Just tweak this and then tweak that, it will be perfect next iteration...I know because I'm one of you!

Constraints are one of the outputs of the Initiation process. Constraints are anything that either restricts the actions of the project team or dictates the actions of the project team. Constraints put you in a box. (I hope you're not claustrophobic.) As a project manager, you have to manage *to* the project constraints, which sometimes requires creativity. Like most disciplines, project management is as much art as it is science.

Types of Constraints

As I said, time can be a project constraint. This usually comes in the form of an enforced deadline, commonly known as the "make it happen now" scenario. If you are in charge of the company's holiday bash scheduled for December 10, your project is time constrained. Once the invitations are out and the hall has been rented, you can't move the date. All activities on this project are driven by the due date.

Budgets are another one of the triple constraints. Budgets limit the project team's ability to obtain resources and might potentially limit the scope of the project. For example, component X cannot be part of this project because the budget doesn't support it.

Quality would typically be restricted by the specifications of the product or service. Those 3-inch widgets we talked about earlier could be considered a quality constraint. Most of the time, if quality is a constraint, one of the other constraints—time or budget—has to have some give. You can't produce high quality on a restricted budget and within a tightly restricted time schedule. Of course, there are exceptions, but only in the movies.

Schedule constraints can cause interesting dilemmas for the project manager. For example, say you're the project manager in charge of building a new football stadium in your city. The construction of the stadium will require the use of cranes—and crane operators—at certain times during the project. If crane operators are not available when your project plan calls for them, you'll have to make schedule adjustments so that the crane operators can come in at the right time.

Technology is a marvelous thing. In fact, how did humans survive prior to the invention of computers and cell phones? Technology certainly can be marvelous, but it can also be a project constraint. For example, your project might require the use of brand-new technology that is still so new it's not been released on a wide-scale basis. One impact might be that the project will take an additional six months because existing technologies need to be used instead of the new technology.

Directives from management can be constraints as well. If you've never experienced a directive from management, you're not working in the real world. And, when performing work on contract, the provisions of the contract can be constraints.

Managing Constraints

Constraints, particularly the triple constraints, can be used to help drive out the goals of the project. If it's difficult to discern which constraint is the primary constraint, ask the project sponsor something like this, "Ms. Sponsor, if you could only have one of these two alternatives, which would you choose? The project is delivered on the date you've stated, or the quality is manufactured to the exact specifications you've given." If Ms. Sponsor replies with the quality response, you know your primary constraint is quality. If push comes to shove during the project Planning process, time might have to give because quality cannot.

Be sure to document your constraints. Constraints and assumptions, which we'll talk about in the next section, are used as inputs to other project processes.

You'll want to understand what the primary constraint is on the project. If you assume the primary constraint is budget when in actuality the primary constraint is time, in the immortal words of two-year-olds worldwide, "Uh-oh." Understanding the constraints and which one carries the most importance will help you out later on in the project Planning process with things like scope planning, scheduling, estimating, and project plan development. That's assuming your project gets to the project Planning process. Which brings us to the next topic, project assumptions.

Identifying the Project Assumptions

You've probably heard the old saying about the word *assume*...something about what it makes out of "u" and "me." In the case of project management, however, throw this old saying out the window because it's not true.

It's essential to understand and document the assumptions you're making, and your stakeholders are making, about the project. It's also important to find out as many of the assumptions as you can up front. Projects can fail, sometimes after lots of progress has been made on the project, because an important assumption was forgotten or the assumption was incorrect.

Assumptions are an output of the Initiation process and will be used as inputs to other processes later in the project.

Documenting Your Assumptions

Let's say you make plans to meet your buddy for lunch on Friday at 11:30 at your favorite spot. When Friday rolls around, you assume he's going to show up, barring any catastrophes between the office and the restaurant. Project assumptions work the same way. For planning purposes, you presume the event or thing you've made the assumptions about is true, real, or certain. For example, you might assume that key resources will be available when needed on the project. Document that assumption. If Nancy is the one and only resource who can perform a specific task at a certain point in the project, document your assumption that Nancy will be available and run it by her manager. If Nancy happens to be on a plane for Helsinki at the time you thought she was going to be working on the project, you could have a real problem on your hands.

Other assumptions could be things such as vendor delivery times, product availability, contractor availability, the accuracy of the project plan, the assumption that key project members will perform adequately, contract signing dates, project start dates, and project phase start dates. This is not an exhaustive list but should get you thinking in the right direction. As you interview your stakeholders, ask them about their assumptions and document them. Use brainstorming exercises with your team and other project participants to come up with additional assumptions.

Try to validate your assumptions whenever possible. When discussing assumptions with vendors, make them put it in writing. In fact, if the services or goods you're expecting to be delivered by your suppliers are critical to the project, include a clause in the contract to assure a contingency plan in case they fail to perform. For example, if you're expecting 200 PCs to be delivered, configured, and installed by a certain date, require the vendor to pay the cost of rental equipment in the event they can't deliver on the promised due date.

Remember, when assumptions are incorrect or not documented, it could cause problems halfway through the project and might even be a project killer.

The Kitchen Heaven Project Case Study

This chapter will introduce a case study that we'll follow throughout the remainder of the book. You'll find an updated case study closing out every chapter. They're designed to show you how a project manager might apply the material covered in the chapter to a real-life project. As happens in real life, not every detail of every process is followed during all projects. Remember that the processes from the *Guide to the PMBOK* that we'll cover in the remaining chapters are project management guidelines. You will often combine processes during your projects, which allows you to perform several steps at once. The case studies will present situations or processes that you might find during your projects and describe how one project manager resolves them.

Project Case Study: New Kitchen Heaven Retail Store

You are a project manager for Kitchen Heaven, a chain of retail stores specializing in kitchen utensils, cookware, dishes, small appliances, and some gourmet food stuffs such as bottled sauces and spices. You're fairly new to the position, having been hired to replace a PM who recently retired.

Kitchen Heaven currently owns 49 stores in 34 states and Canada. The world headquarters for Kitchen Heaven is in Denver, Colorado. Counting full-time and part-time employees, the company employs 1500 people, 200 of whom work in the headquarters office.

The company has yearly earnings of $200 million with average profits on earnings of $30 million. The company is publicly held under the KHVN ticker, and stock is currently at $17.50/share with a price-to-earnings ratio of 15.8.

The company's mission statement reads this way: "Great gadgets for people interested in great food."

Recently the vice president of marketing came to pay you a visit. Dirk Perrier is a very nice man, well dressed, with the formal air that you would suspect a person in his capacity might have. He shakes your hand and gives you a fresh, toothy smile.

"You may not have heard, but we've decided to go forward with our 50th store opening! Sales are up, and our new line of ceramic cookware is a hot seller, no pun intended. I don't know if you're familiar with our store philosophy, so let me take a moment to explain it. We like to place our stores in neighborhoods that are somewhat affluent. We don't seek out the wealthy shoppers, nor do we place our shops in areas where only the wealthy travel. But the plain fact is that most of our shoppers have incomes of over $50,000 a year. We make an effort to place our stores in areas where those folks normally shop.

"Also, unlike some of our competitors who like to maintain a *hoity-toity* store persona, we're more interested in targeting the nongourmet customer, one who's interested in cooking but won't be making Peking duck. So, the stores are upbeat, and convey a little bit of country ambiance—kind of a laid-back feel, if you will.

"Our next store is going to be right here in our home area—Colorado Springs. We have a store in Boulder and one in Denver in the Cherry Creek area, but none down south. Because this is going to be our 50th store, we plan on having a 50th grand-opening celebration with the kind of surprises and activities you might expect for such a notable opening.

"Our stores generally occupy from 2000 to 4000 square feet of retail space, and we typically use local contractors for the build-out. A store build-out usually takes 120 days from the date the property has been procured until the doors open to the public. I can give you our last opening's project plan so you have a feel for what happens. Your job will be to procure the property, negotiate the lease, procure the shelving and associated store furnishings, get a contractor on the job, and prepare the 50th store festivities. My marketing folks will assist you with that last part.

"You have six months to complete the project. Any questions?"

You take in a deep breath and collect your thoughts. Dirk has just given you a lot of information with hardly a pause in between thoughts. A few initial things drift through your head while you're reaching for your notebook.

You work in a functional organization with a separate projectized department responsible for carrying out projects of this nature. You've been with the company long enough to know that Dirk is high up there in the executive ranks and carries the authority and the power to make things happen. Therefore, Dirk is the perfect candidate for project sponsor.

You grab your notebook and start documenting some of the things Dirk talked about, clarifying with him as you write:

- The project goal is to open a new store in Colorado Springs six months from today.

- The store should be located in an affluent area.

- The store will carry the full line of products from utensils to gourmet food items.

- The grand opening will be accompanied by lots of fanfare because this is the 50th store opening.

You have a question or two for Dirk. The first is, "Who are some of the other key stakeholders whom I should speak with?"

"There's Jake Peterson over facilities. He's in charge of store furnishings, shelving, things like that. Any supplies for the stores that aren't retail products. He can help out with store build-outs, too. He supervised our last eight stores and did a terrific job.

"Ricardo Ramirez heads up our information technology area. Don't tell him I said this, but I'm not very technical myself and don't really know what you're going to need from Ricardo. I do know he takes care of wiring and installing the point-of-sale terminals, but you'll have to get with Ricardo for all the other details."

"Anyone else?" you ask.

"You should also talk to Jill Overstreet, the director in charge of retail products. She can help with the initial store stocking, and once the store is open, her group will take over the ongoing operations. All the district managers report to Jill. "

"Great, thanks. Now another question," you say. "Is time the driver on this project? Is there a special reason it has to open...let's see I'm coming up with the date of February 1st?"

"Yes, we want the store open the first week in February. Early February is when the Garden and Home Show conference hits the Springs area. We'll have a trade show booth there. We know from experience in other areas that our stores generally see a surge in sales during this month as a result of the trade show. It's a great way to get a lot of advertising out there and let folks know where we're located."

"Tell me, Dirk, is there a budget set for this project yet?"

"We haven't set a hard figure," Dirk replies. "But again, from past experience we know it takes anywhere from $1.5 to $2 million to open a new store. And we don't want to forget the big bash at grand opening."

You thank Dirk and tell him you're going to contact Jake, Ricardo, and Jill to ask them a few questions about the project goals.

Dirk concludes with, "Feel free to come to me with questions or concerns at any time."

You document what you've learned so far in your project overview document. You decide to e-mail a summary of your notes to Jake, Ricardo, and Jill for their review before meeting with them personally.

Project Case Study Checklist

Project Goal: To open a new store in Colorado Springs six months from today.

Demand: Company data concludes that the Kitchen Heaven consumers have incomes of over $50,000 a year. The Colorado Springs area is home to a large number of people with that income. Currently, there is not a Kitchen Heaven there, but there appears to be a demand for one.

Project Sponsor: Dirk Perrier, VP of marketing.

Stakeholders: Jake Peterson, Ricardo Ramirez, and Jill Overstreet.

Organizational Structure: Functional organization with a separate projectized department.

Constraints: Time.

Assumptions:

- A store build-out usually takes 120 days.

- Jill Overstreet will help with the initial store stocking.

- Jake Peterson will supervise over facilities and store build-outs as well.

- Ricardo Ramirez will provide IT details.

- The budget for the project will be anywhere from $1.5 to $2 million.

Summary

We started out this chapter with a discussion of the nine Project Management Knowledge Areas from the *Guide to the PMBOK*. Knowledge areas bring together the project processes that have things in common. This allows the project manager the opportunity to assign resources with specific skills to multiple project processes. Sometimes these resources might be able to combine project processes and perform them as one activity.

Projects come about as a result of one of six needs or demands, according to the *Guide to the PMBOK*: marketing demand, business need, customer requests, technological advances, legal requirements, and social needs.

Project Initiation is the first process in a project's life cycle. Initiation is the formal recognition that a project, or project phase, should begin and commits the organization to dedicate resources to the project.

The Initiation process has four inputs: product description, strategic plan, project selection criteria, and historical information. These inputs are developed using tools and techniques of the Initiation process to produce the final outputs.

Project managers, according to the *Guide to the PMBOK*, are not identified and assigned until the completion of the Initiation process. In reality, project managers usually are identified at the beginning of the Initiation process.

The project goal is the purpose for undertaking the project. Goals should be SMART: specific, measurable, accurate, realistic, and time bound. Projects can also be defined using the SMART acronym. Interview stakeholders to determine project goals and begin to understand deliverables of the project.

Get to know your stakeholders so that you understand the parts they play and how much authority they have. It doesn't hurt to also get familiar with their position in the organization, how much power they have, and how they interact with other stakeholders.

Constraints can restrict or dictate the actions of the project team. Constraints usually involve time, budget, and quality but can also include schedules, technology, and more. Document your constraints as they'll be used as inputs to future project processes.

Throw out that old saying about assumptions and document these as well.

Exam Essentials

Be able to name the nine Project Management Knowledge Areas. Project Integration Management, Project Scope Management, Project Time Management, Project Cost Management, Project Quality Management, Project Human Resource Management, Project Communications Management, Project Risk Management, and Project Procurement Management.

Be able to distinguish between the six needs or demands that bring about project creation. Marketing demand, business need, customer requests, technological advances, legal requirements, and social needs.

Be able to denote the project Initiation inputs. Product description, strategic plan, project selection criteria, and historical information.

Be able to identify the purpose for the project Initiation process. To recognize the existence of a new project or project phase, and to commit resources to begin the project or project phase.

Be able to define project constraints and assumptions. Project constraints limit the options of the project team and restrict their actions. Sometimes constraints dictate actions. Time, budget, and quality are the most common constraints. Assumptions are conditions that are presumed to be true or real.

Key Terms

Before you take the exam, be certain you are familiar with the following terms:

assumption

constraint

feasibility study

Initiation

Project Communications Management

Project Cost Management

Project Human Resource Management

Project Integration Management

Project Management Knowledge Areas

Project Procurement Management

Project Quality Management

Project Risk Management

Project Scope Management

Project Time Management

requirement

Review Questions

1. The Project Integration Management knowledge area is made up of which of the following processes?

   A. Initiation, Project Plan Development, and Integrated Change Control

   B. Project Plan Development, Project Plan Execution, and Integrated Change Control

   C. Project Plan Development, Initiation, and Scope Planning

   D. Initiation, Scope Planning, and Integrated Change Control

2. When a project is being performed under contract, the product description is provided by which of the following?

   A. The buyer

   B. The project sponsor

   C. The project manager

   D. The contractor

3. You are the project manager for Fun Days vacation packages. Your new project assignment is to head up the Fun Days resort opening in Austin, Texas. You are estimating the duration of the project plan activities, devising the project schedule, and monitoring and controlling deviations from the schedule. Which of the Project Management Knowledge Areas are you working in?

   A. Project Scope

   B. Project Quality

   C. Project Integration

   D. Project Time

4. The Project Human Resource Management knowledge area contains which of the following processes?

A. Staff Acquisition, Team Development, and Resource Planning

B. Staff Acquisition, Team Development, and Performance Reporting

C. Organizational Planning, Staff Acquisition, and Team Development

D. Organization Planning, Team Development, and Resource Planning

5. Your company is going to introduce a new service called Phone Home. This service will allow you to speak the name of the person you want to call into your cellular phone. To call home, you would simply speak the word *home* into the phone, and it will dial that number for you. Your company is taking advantage of the progress that has been made recently with voice recognition software. Initial projections show that market demand is very high for this product. This project came about as a result of which of the following?

A. Marketing demand

B. Customer request

C. Business need

D. Technological advance

6. You are a project manager for the information technology division of a local satellite TV broadcasting company. This spring, the chief information officer for your company gave you the project to convert and upgrade all the PCs in the department to the latest release of a specific desktop application. Prior to this conversion, all manner of desktop software existed on machines throughout the company and had caused increasing problems with sharing files and information across the company. A lot of unproductive hours were spent typing information into several formats. This project came about as a result of which of the following?

A. Technological advance

B. Business need

C. Customer request

D. Legal requirement

7. What are the inputs to the Initiation process?

    A. Product description, strategic plan, project selection criteria, and historical information

    B. Product description, strategic plan, project overview document, and historical information

    C. Strategic plan, project overview document, feasibility study, and historical information

    D. Product description, strategic plan, constraints, and assumptions

8. You work for a large manufacturing plant. You're working on a new project for an overseas product release. This is the company's first experience in the overseas market, and they hope to make a big splash with the introduction of this product. The project entails producing your product in a concentrated formula and packaging it in smaller containers than the U.S. product uses. A new machine is needed in order to mix the first set of ingredients in the concentrated formula. Which of the following is true?

    A. The new machine, the concentrated formula, and the smaller package are each project constraints.

    B. The new machine, the concentrated formula, and the smaller package description must be incorporated into the product description document.

    C. The new machine, the concentrated formula, and the smaller package are each project assumptions.

    D. The new machine, the concentrated formula, and the smaller package are each considered deliverables.

9. You work for a large manufacturing plant. You're in the Initiation process of a new project for an overseas product release. This is the company's first experience in the overseas market, and they hope to make a big splash with the introduction of this product. The project entails producing your product in a concentrated formula and packaging it in smaller containers than the U.S. product uses. A new machine is needed in order to mix the first set of ingredients in the concentrated formula. Which of the following actions should the project manager take?

    A. The project manager should document the project's goals and known deliverables in a high-level overview document and recommend the project proceed.

    B. The project manager should document the project's goals and known deliverables in a high-level overview document and assume the project is a go.

    C. The project manager should document the project's goals and known deliverables in a high-level overview document and recommend a feasibility study be performed.

    D. The project manager should document the project's goals and known deliverables in a high-level overview document and deliver it to the stakeholders.

10. What are the Initiation process outputs?

    A. Project charter, identification and assignment of project manager, constraints, and project overview documents

    B. Project charter, project overview, feasibility study, and constraints

    C. Project charter, identification and assignment of project manager, constraints, and assumptions

    D. Identification and assignment of project manager, project overview, constraints, and assumptions

11. The purpose of the Initiation process is to:

   A. Formally recognize the existence of a project or project phase

   B. Formally recognize the need that brought about the project be it marketing demand, customer requests, business need, technological advances, or legal requirements

   C. Formally recognize the stakeholders of the project and identify them in the project charter

   D. Formally recognize the project sponsor and document his or her project goals

12. Your nonprofit organization is preparing to host its first annual 5K run/walk in City Park. You worked on a similar project for the organization two years ago when it co-hosted the 10K run through Overland Pass. Which of the Initiation process inputs might be helpful to you on your new project?

   A. The strategic plan, because you'll want to make sure the project reflects the overall strategic direction of the organization.

   B. Historical information on the 10K run project. You might be able to gather helpful project information since this new project is similar in nature.

   C. The product description, which would describe all the details of the run/walk program.

   D. Historical information from the recent blood drive project.

13. Which of the following is true regarding product descriptions?

A. The product description is an output of the Initiation process. It describes the characteristics of the product or service.

B. The product description is an output of the Initiation process. It describes the characteristics of the product or service and contains less detail in the early phases of the project.

C. The product description is an input of the Initiation process. It describes the characteristics of the product or service and contains a lot of detail in the early phases of the project.

D. The product description is an input of the Initiation process. It describes the characteristics of the product or service.

14. Deliverables can be described as:

A. The purpose for undertaking the project

B. The verifiable results of products or services that must be produced to consider the project complete

C. The specifications regarding the goals of the project that must be produced to consider the project complete

D. The measurable outcomes of the project goals

15. You are a project manager working on a new software product your company plans to market to businesses. The project sponsor told you that the project must be completed by September 1. The company plans to demo the new software product at a trade show in late September and therefore needs the project completed in time for the trade show. However, the sponsor has also told you that the budget is fixed at $85,000 and cannot be increased by even $10 due to overall budget cuts this year. You must complete the project within the given time frame and budget. Which of the following is the primary constraint for this project?

A. Budget

B. Quality

C. Time

D. Schedule

16. You are a project manager for a documentary film company. In light of a recent national tragedy, the company president wants to get a new documentary on the rescue efforts of the heroic firefighters to air as soon as possible. She's looking to you to make this documentary the best that's ever been produced in the history of this company. She guarantees you free rein to use whatever resources you need to get this project done quickly. However, the best photographer in the company is currently working on another assignment. Which of the following is true?

    A. The primary constraint is time because the president wants the film done quickly. She told you to get it to air as soon as possible.

    B. Resources are the primary constraint. Even though the president has given you free rein on resource use, you assume she didn't mean those actively assigned to projects.

    C. The schedule is the primary constraint. Even though the president has given you free rein on resource use, you assume she didn't mean those actively assigned to projects. The photographer won't be finished for another three weeks on his current assignment, so schedule adjustments will have to be made.

    D. The primary constraint is quality because the president wants this to be the best film ever produced by this company. She's given you free rein to use whatever resources needed to get the job done.

17. What limits the options of the project team?

    A. Technology

    B. Constraints

    C. Deliverables

    D. Assumptions

18. Your project depends on a key deliverable from a vendor you've used several times before with great success. You're counting on the delivery to arrive on June 1. This is an example of:

    A. Constraint

    B. Objective

    C. Assumption

    D. Goal

19. Halloween is approaching fast. Your market research shows that the little yellow chicks and pink bunny marshmallow candies are the best-selling candy at Easter time, outselling all other types of candies. This prompts the company to introduce a new version of marshmallow candies with Halloween themes this season. Which of the following is true?

A. This project came about due to customer request, and the primary constraint is time.

B. This project came about due to market demand, and the primary constraint is time.

C. This project came about due to market demand, and the primary constraint is quality.

D. This project came about due to customer request, and the primary constraint is quality.

20. Your company provides answering services for several major catalog retailers. The number of calls coming into the service center per month has continued to increase over the past 18 months. The phone system is approaching the maximum load limits and needs to be upgraded. You've been assigned to head up the upgrade project. Based on the company's experience with the vendor who worked on the last phone upgrade project, you're confident they'll be able to assist you with this project as well. Which of the following is true?

A. You've made an assumption about vendor availability and expertise. The project came about due to a business need.

B. Vendor availability and expertise are constraints. The project came about due to a business need.

C. You've made an assumption about vendor availability and expertise. The project came about due to a marketing demand.

D. Vendor availability and expertise are constraints. The project came about due to a marketing demand.

Answers to Review Questions

1. B. Project Integration is made up of Project Plan Development, Project Plan Execution, and Integrated Change Control

2. A. The buyer provides product descriptions when projects are performed under contract.

3. D. Project Time Management involves the following processes: Activity Definition, Activity Sequencing, Activity Duration Estimating, Schedule Development, and Schedule Control.

4. C. The Human Resources knowledge area involves managing people and relationships. It includes Organizational Planning, Staff Acquisition, and Team Development. Remember that Resource Planning is part of the Project Cost Management Knowledge area, not Human Resource Management.

5. D. The correct answer is technological advance. Marketing demand is high for the service, but the service did not come about as a result of customers asking for it; rather, it came to market because of the advances in technology.

6. B. This came about due to a business need. Staff members were spending unproductive hours producing the same information, thus causing the company a loss. The time the employees spent retyping information that was already written could have been spent doing something more productive.

7. A. Initiation has four process inputs. Constraints and assumptions are outputs of the Initiation process.

8. D. Deliverables are tangible, verifiable outcomes or items that must be produced in order to complete the project or project phase. These items wouldn't be considered goals because the goal of the project is to break into the overseas market with a successful product revamped for that audience.

9. C. The most correct answer is to perform a feasibility study. Since this project is taking the company into a new, unknown market, there's lots of potential for error and failure. A feasibility study would help the stakeholders determine if the project is viable and cost effective, and whether it has a high potential for success.

10. C. Project Initiation outputs are the project charter, identification and assignment of the project manager, constraints, and assumptions. Remember for the test that project managers aren't officially assigned until the end of Initiation (as an output) but in reality are often times assigned at the beginning of the Initiation process.

11. A. Initiation formally recognizes the existence of a project. Stakeholders might be identified in the Initiation process but according to the *Guide to the PMBOK* are officially identified during the Planning process.

12. B. Historical information on projects of a similar nature can be very helpful when initiating new projects. They can help in formulating project deliverables and identifying constraints and assumptions, and will be helpful further on in the project Planning process as well.

13. D. Product descriptions are inputs to Initiation and contain less detail in the beginning phases of a project and more detail as the project progresses.

14. B. Deliverables are measurable or verifiable results or specific items that must be produced in order to consider the project complete.

15. C. The primary constraint is time. Since the trade show demos depend on project completion and the trade show is in late September, the date cannot be moved. The budget is the secondary constraint in this example.

16. D. The primary constraint is quality. If you made the assumption as stated in selection B, you assumed incorrectly. Clarify these assumptions with your stakeholders and project sponsors. This applies to option C as well.

17. B. Constraints restrict the actions of the project team.

18. C. This is an example of an assumption. You've used this vendor before and not had any problems. You're assuming there will be no problems with this delivery based on your past experience.

19. B. Market research shows the demand for the candies is extremely high during the Easter season. It's highly likely sales would be high during the Halloween season as well. Time is the constraint as Halloween is driven by a hard date.

20. A. The project came about due to a business need. The phones have to be answered as that's the core business. Upgrading the system to handle more volume is a business need. An assumption has been made regarding vendor availability. Always validate your assumptions.

Chapter

3

Creating a Project Charter

PMP EXAM CONTENT FROM THE PROJECT INITIATION PERFORMANCE DOMAIN COVERED IN THIS CHAPTER:

- ✓ 6. Define Strategy.
- ✓ 7. Identify Performance Criteria.
- ✓ 8. Determine Resource Requirements.
- ✓ 9. Define Budget.
- ✓ 10. Produce Formal Documentation.

The second half of Chapter 2 started us on the journey into the project life cycle processes with an introduction to project Initiation. We've already learned how to identify and document the goals of the project. And we talked about project deliverables, constraints, and assumptions. This chapter formally recognizes the launching of the project with the creation of a project charter.

We'll conclude the project Initiation process with this chapter and begin the Planning process in Chapter 4. We'll discuss one more input to the Initiation process and the tools and techniques of project Initiation, and then finish up the chapter with documenting the project charter. The primary goal of the Initiation process is to produce the project charter.

Using Project Selection Methodologies

Project selection methodologies will vary depending on the company, the people serving on the selection committee, the criteria used, and the project. Sometimes selection criteria and methodologies will be purely financial, sometimes purely marketing, and sometimes they'll be based on public perception or political perception, or some combination of all of these and more. We'll look at project selection criteria, which is how projects are selected and prioritized. Then we'll finish up with project selection methods, which calculate measurable differences between projects and determine the tangible benefits to the company of choosing or not choosing the project.

Defining Project Selection Criteria

Most organizations have a formal, or at least semiformal, process to select and prioritize projects. In my organization, a steering committee is responsible for project review, selection, and prioritization. A steering committee is a group of folks comprised of senior managers and sometimes midlevel managers who represent each of the functional areas in the organization.

Here's how our process works. The steering committee requests project ideas from the business staff prior to the beginning of the fiscal year. These project ideas need to be developed into a project overview, or project concept document, like we discussed in Chapter 1. These project overview documents contain the project goals, a description of the deliverables, the business justification for the project, a desired implementation date, what the organization stands to gain from implementing the project, a list of the functional business areas affected by the project, and if applicable a benefit/cost analysis (we'll talk about that in a bit).

A special steering committee meeting is called to review the projects, and a determination is made on each project as to whether it will be included on the upcoming list of projects for the new year. Once the no-go projects have been weeded out, the remaining projects are prioritized according to their importance and benefit to the organization. The projects are documented on an official project list, and progress is reported on the active projects at the regular monthly steering committee meetings.

In theory, it's a great idea. In practice, it works only moderately well. Priorities can and do change throughout the year. New projects come up that weren't originally submitted during the call for projects that must be added to the list. Reprioritization begins anew, and resource alignment and assignments are shuffled. But again, we're getting ahead of ourselves. Just be aware that organizations usually have a process to recognize and screen project requests, accept or reject those requests based on some selection criteria, and prioritize the projects based on some criteria.

Large, complex projects may be subject to further review via a feasibility study before a decision can be made to accept the project. You will recall that feasibility studies determine the viability of the project and help the company determine if the product or service of the project is marketable, profitable, safe, and doable.

What's the criteria? Funny you should ask. Project selection criteria is an input to the project Initiation process. According to the *Guide to the PMBOK*, project selection criteria is concerned with the product of the project. In other words, selection criteria is concerned with what the product or service of the project will produce and how it will benefit the company. Selection criteria concerns every area of business from marketing to finance to information technology to human resources. It can be subjective or objective. Criteria for judging project selection could include financial measurements. For example, the selection criteria might dictate that projects must increase profits by a certain percentage in order to be considered. Equally, project selection criteria might include the criteria that an increase in market share or an increase in the public awareness of the company or product will be enjoyed as a result of this project. There aren't any rules for project selection as the components of selection criteria are up to the company, steering committee, or project review committee to determine.

Predetermined selection criteria, such as mentioned above, is one aspect of project selection, but so is the individual opinion, and power, of selection committee members. Don't underestimate the importance of the authority, political standing, and individual aspirations of selection committee members. Those committee members who happen to carry a lot of weight in company circles, so to speak, are likely to get their projects approved just on the fact that they are who they are. This is sometimes how project selection works in my organization. How about yours?

Describing Project Selection Methods

Project selection criteria, as we just discussed, is an input to the Initiation process. Project selection methods are a technique used during the Initiation process to pick one project over another or to measure one particular project's benefit to the organization. Selection criteria differs from selection methods in that selection criteria is concerned with the product of the project and selection methods measure the benefits of the project, or they compare the measurable benefits of one project against another.

According to the *Guide to the PMBOK*, there are two categories of selection methods: benefit measurement methods and constrained optimization methods. We'll discuss constrained optimization methods first.

For the purposes of the exam, all you need to understand about constrained optimization methods is they are mathematical models that use linear, dynamic, integer, nonlinear, and/or multiobjective programming in the form of algorithms—or in other words, a specific set of steps to solve a particular problem. These are complicated mathematical formulas and algorithms that are beyond the scope of this book and require an engineering, statistical, or mathematical background to fully understand. Projects of enormous complexity would use techniques such as these to make decisions regarding projects. The vast majority of project selection techniques will use the benefit measurement methods to make project selection decisions.

Benefit measurement methods employ various forms of analysis and comparative approaches to make project selections. One common form of analysis is the benefit/cost analysis. This compares the financial benefits to the company of performing the project to the costs of implementing the project. Obviously, a sound project choice is one where the costs to implement or produce the product of the project are less than the financial benefits. How much less is an individual decision. Some companies are comfortable with a small margin, others with a much larger margin between the two figures.

When examining costs for the benefit/cost analysis, include the costs to produce the product or service, costs to take the product to market, and ongoing operational support costs. For example, let's say your company is considering writing and marketing a database software product that will allow banks to dissect their customer base, determine which types of customers buy which types of products, and then market more effectively to those customers. Some of the costs you will take into account are the costs to develop the software such as programmer costs, hardware costs, testing costs, etc; marketing costs such as advertising, traveling costs to perform demos at potential customer sites, etc.; and ongoing costs such as having a customer support staff available during business hours to assist customers with product questions and problems.

Let's say the cost to produce this software plus the ongoing support costs total $5 million. Initial projections look like demand for this product is high. Over a 3-year period, the potential life of the software in its proposed form, projected revenues are $12 million. Taking only the financial information into account, the benefits outweigh the costs of this project. This project should receive a go recommendation.

Projects of significant cost or complexity usually take into account more than one benefit measurement method when making go or no-go decisions, or deciding on one project over another. Keep in mind that selection methods can take subjective matter into account as well—the project is a go because it's the new CEO's pet project; nothing else needs to be said.

Another project selection technique in the benefit measurement category is a scoring model, or weighted scoring model. My organization uses weighted scoring models to not only choose between projects, but also as a method to choose between competing bids on outsourced projects.

Weighted scoring models are quite simple. The project selection committee should decide on the criteria that will be used on the scoring model—for example, profit potential, marketability of the product or service, the ability of the company to quickly and easily produce the product or service, and so on. Each of these criteria is assigned a weight, depending on the importance of the criteria to the project committee. More important criteria should carry a higher weight than the less important criteria.

Then, each project is rated on a scale from 1 to 5 (or some such assignment) with the higher number being the more desirable outcome to the company and the lower number having the opposite effect. This rating is then multiplied by the weight of the criteria factor and added to other weighted criteria scores for a total weighted score. Let's look at an example that brings this together (see Table 3.1).

TABLE 3.1 Weighted Scoring Model

Criteria	Weight	Project A Score*	Project B Score*	Project C Score*
Profit potential	5	5	5	3
Marketability	3	4	3	4
Ease to produce/ support	1	4	3	2
Weighted score	—	41	37	29

*5 = highest.

In this example, Project A is the obvious choice.

The remaining benefit measurement methods involve a variety of cash flow analysis techniques including payback period, discounted cash flows, net present value, and internal rate of return. We'll look at each of these techniques individually and provide you with a crash course on their meanings and calculations.

Payback Period

The *payback period* is the length of time it takes the company to recoup the initial costs of producing the product or service of the project. This method compares the initial investment to the cash inflows expected over the life of the product or service. For example, say the initial investment on our project is $200,000 with expected cash inflows of $25,000 per quarter every quarter for the first 2 years, and $50,000 per quarter from thereon. The payback period is 2 years and can be calculated as follows:

Cash inflows = $25,000 × 4 (quarters in a year) = $100,000/year total inflow

Year 1 inflows = $100,000

Year 2 inflows = $100,000

Total = $200,000

Payback is reached in 2 years.

The fact that inflows are $50,000 per quarter starting in year 3 makes no difference as payback is reached in 2 years.

Payback period is the least precise of all the cash flow calculations. That's because payback period does not consider the value of the cash inflows made in later years, commonly called the *time value of money*. For example, if you had a project with a 5-year payback period, the cash inflows in year 5 would be worth less than they would be were we to receive them today. The next section will explain this idea more fully.

Discounted Cash Flows

As I just stated, money received in the future is worth less than money received today. The reason for that is the time value of money. If I borrowed $2000 from you today and promised to pay it back in 3 years, you would expect me to pay interest in addition to the original amount borrowed. Okay, if you were a family member or really close friend maybe you wouldn't, but ordinarily this is the way it works. You would have had the use of the $2000 had you not lent it to me. If you had invested the money (Does this bring back memories of your mom telling you to save your money?), you'd receive a return on that money. Therefore, the future value of the $2000 you lent me today is $2315.25 in 3 years from now at 5 percent interest per year. Here's the formula for future value calculations:

$$FV = PV (1 + i)^n$$

In English, this formula says the future value (FV) of the investment equals the present value (PV) times (1 plus the interest rate) times the number of time periods the interest is paid. Let's plug in our numbers:

$FV = 2000\ (1.05)^3$

$FV = 2000\ (1.157625)$

$FV = \$2315.25$

The *discounted cash flow* technique compares the value of the future cash flows of the project to today's dollars. In order to calculate discounted cash flows, we need to know the value of the investment in today's terms, or the present value (PV). PV is calculated as follows:

$PV = FV \div (1 + i)^n$

This is the reverse of the FV formula we talked about earlier. So, if we asked the question what is $2315.25 in 3 years from now worth today given a 5 percent interest rate, we'd used the formula above. Let's try it.

$PV = \$2315.25 \div (1 + .05)^3$

$PV = \$2315.25 \div 1.157625$

$PV = 2000$

$2315.25 in 3 years from now is worth $2000 today.

Discounted cash flow is calculated just like this for the projects you're comparing for selection purposes. Apply the PV formula to the projects you're considering and then compare the discounted cash flows of all the projects against each other to make a selection. Here is an example comparison of two projects using this technique:

Project A is expected to make $100,000 in 2 years.

Project B is expected to make $120,000 in 3 years.

If the cost of capital is 12 percent, which project should you choose?

Using the PV formula above, calculate each project's worth.

The PV of Project A = $79,719.

The PV of Project B = $85,414.

Project B is the project that will return the highest investment to the company and should be chosen over Project A.

Net Present Value

Projects generally begin with a company investing some amount of money into the project to complete and accomplish its goals. In return, the company expects to receive revenues, or cash inflows, from the resulting project. *Net present value (NPV)* allows you to calculate an accurate value for the project. The mathematical formula for NPV is complicated, and you do not need to memorize it in that form for the test. However, you do need to know how to calculate NPV for the exam. I've given you some examples of a less complicated way to perform this calculation in Tables 3.2 and 3.3 using the formulas you've already seen.

Net present value works like discounted cash flows in that you bring the value of future monies received into today's dollars. With NPV, you evaluate the cash inflows using the discounted cash flow technique applied to each period the inflows are expected instead of in one sum. The total present value of the cash flows is then deducted from your initial investment to determine NPV. NPV assumes that cash inflows are reinvested at the cost of capital.

Here's the rule, if the NPV calculation is greater than zero, accept the project. If the NPV calculation is less than zero, reject the project.

Look at the example below of two projects (see Tables 3.2 and 3.3). Project A and Project B have total cash inflows that are the same at the end of the project, but the amount of inflows at each period differs for each project. We'll stick with a 12 percent cost of capital. Note that the PV calculations were rounded to two decimal places.

TABLE 3.2 Project A

Year	Inflows	PV
1	10,000	8,929
2	15,000	11,962
3	5,000	3,559
Total	30,000	24,450
Less investment	—	24,000
NPV	—	**450**

TABLE 3.3 Project B

Year	Inflows	PV
1	7,000	6,250
2	13,000	10,367
3	10,000	7,118
Total	30,000	23,735
Less investment	—	24,000
NPV	—	**<265>**

Project A has an NPV greater than zero and should be accepted. Project B has an NPV less than zero and should be rejected. When you get a positive value for NPV, it means that the project will earn a return at least equal to or greater than the cost of capital.

Another note on NPV calculations: Projects with high returns early in the project are better projects than projects with lower returns early in the project. In our example above, Project A fits this criteria also.

Internal Rate of Return

The *internal rate of return (IRR)* is the most difficult equation of all the cash flow techniques we've discussed. It is a complicated formula and should be performed on a financial calculator or computer. IRR can be figured manually, but it's a trial-and-error approach to get to the answer.

Technically speaking, IRR is the discount rate when the present value of the cash inflows equals the original investment. Projects with higher IRR values are generally considered better than projects with low IRR values.

For the exam, you need to know that IRR is the discount rate when NPV equals zero, IRR assumes that cash inflows are reinvested at the IRR value, and you should choose projects with the highest IRR value.

Project Selection Methods

One, two, or several of these methods can be used alone or in combination to come up with a selection decision. Remember that payback period is the least precise, NPV is the most conservative approach, and NPV and IRR will generally bring you to the same accept/reject conclusion.

Project selection methods, and particularly the benefit measurement methods, can be used to evaluate multiple projects or a single project. You might be weighing one project against another, or simply considering if the project you're proposing is worth doing. Constrained optimization methods and benefit measurement methods are often called decision models. For the exam, remember that decision models are used as project selection methods (tools and techniques) not as project selection criteria (input). Also note that the financial benefit measurement methods and the benefit/cost methods can be used for project justification, which we will discuss in Chapter 4. I'll refer you back to this section to review these methods when we get to project justification in the next chapter.

Expert judgment is the last tool and technique in the Initiation process. The concept behind expert judgment is to rely on individuals, or groups of people, who have training, specialized knowledge, or skills in the areas you're assessing. In the case of project Initiation, expert judgment would be helpful in assessing the inputs to the Initiation process—i.e., product descriptions, strategic plan, project selection criteria, and historical information. For example, as the project manager, you might rely on the expertise of your executive committee to determine how the proposed project gels with the strategic plan. Or, you might rely on team members who have participated on similar projects in the past to make recommendations regarding the proposed project.

Expert judgment is a tool and technique used in many other planning processes as well. According to the *Guide to the PMBOK*, experts might be found in other departments within the organization, external or internal consultants, professional and technical associations, or industry groups.

 Real World Scenario

Fun Days Vacation Resorts

Jerry is project manager for Fun Days Vacation Resorts. He is working on three different project proposals to present to the executive steering committee for review. As part of the information-gathering process, Jerry attends the various resorts pretending to be a guest. This gives him a feel for what Fun Days guests experience on their vacations, and it better prepares him to present project particulars and alternatives.

Jerry has prepared the project overviews for three projects and called upon the experts in marketing to help him out with the projected revenue figures. He works up the numbers and finds the following:

- Project A—payback period = 5 years; IRR = 38 percent

- Project B—payback period = 3.5 years; IRR = 23 percent

- Project C—payback period = 2 years; IRR = 23 percent

Funding exists for only one of the projects. Jerry recommends Project A and predicts this is the project the steering committee will choose since the projects are mutually exclusive.

Jerry's turn to present comes up at the steering committee. Let's listen in on the action.

"And, on top of all the benefits I've just described, Project A provides an IRR of 38 percent, a full 15 percent higher than the other two projects we discussed. I recommend the committee choose Project A."

"Thank you Jerry," Colleen says. "Good presentation." Colleen is the executive chairperson of the steering committee and has the authority to break ties or make final decisions when the committee can't seem to agree.

"However, here at Fun Days we like to have our fun sooner rather than later." Chuckles ensue from the steering committee. They've all heard this before. "I do agree that a 38 percent IRR is a terrific return, but the payback is just too far out into the future. There are too many risks and unknowns for us to take on a project with a payback period this long. As you know, our industry is directly impacted by the health of the economy. Anything can happen in 5 years' time. I think we're much better off going with Project C. I recommend we accept Project C. Committee members, do you have anything to add?"

Identifying the Project's Initial Requirements

We're close to wrapping up the Initiation phase with the publication of the project charter. But we've got one more stop to make before we get to the project charter. This section covers project requirements—not like the requirements of the product of the project we talked about in

Chapter 2. These requirements are resource requirements and budget requirements needed to perform the work of the project. This is the last piece of information you'll gather before writing the project charter.

Most selection committees will want to have some feel for the impact the project will have on the organization in terms of resources and costs. We will delve much deeper into these two topics in Chapter 5, where we'll talk at length about estimation techniques. For now, let's do an overview of each of these areas.

For more information on estimation techniques, please see Chapter 5, "Resource Planning and Estimating."

Defining Resource Requirements

It's forecasted to be a great summer day, one of those perfect hiking or biking kind of days. You and a couple of friends decide a hike is just what you need and think it'd be fun to bring along a light lunch. First, you dig out those old hiking boots you've had since college from the depths of the closet and blow the dust off them. Your feet are protected, now what about that lunch? You poke through the fridge and pull out some aged cheese, a fat bunch of red grapes, a loaf of crusty baguette, and a good bottle of Shiraz. You'll need glasses and a wine opener too. Next, you pull out that daypack you ordered from that outdoorsy catalog because it looked so cool and you knew it would come in handy one day. Sunscreen and maybe some chocolate sandwich cookies for your friends top off the loaded daypack. You're all set. All you need now is to meet up with the friends, pile into the car, and drive to the trailhead.

If we think of the hike as our project—I'm using the term loosely in this case—the resources can be considered the boots, food, glasses, wine opener, sunscreen, and daypack. Add your friends in the mix and the car to drive you to the trailhead and you've identified all the resources you're going to need for this project. Oh, a trail map might be handy too.

This is exactly how resource identification works on projects. After you've identified the project goals and the project deliverables, you should have a fairly easy time of identifying the kinds of resources you're going to need to complete the project. These will vary from project to project. One known resource entity is human resources. All projects will need some human effort and intervention to carry out the project. Also consider things like equipment, materials, hardware, software, telephones, office space, travel arrangements, contractors, desks, network connections, etc.

Some of these things may sound trivial, but consider the overall impact to the organization when determining what resources are needed. For example, if you're working on a large construction project and need to temporarily house the design team, they will need office furniture, telephones, PCs, design software, and network connections. Telephones and network connections might require new lines, which take time and money to install.

My organization once engaged contractors to work on a project without considering office space, telephone lines, or network connections. The contractors showed up for work as planned and had no place to sit. We set up tables in the hallway for them and had the network team run long cables taped down to the floor out to their PCs on the tables until the project was over. And, they used their own cell phones for telephones. The project manager didn't do an adequate job of determining resource needs for this project. Unfortunately for this project manager, the contractor office space turned out to be the least important of the resource requirements he "didn't think about."

You will also want to detail the type of human resources you're going to need for your project. Does your project require specific skills? If so, note the skills needed. If they cannot be obtained internally, you will have to consider contractor help and factor that into the project costs. Does your project require the help of staff from other areas of the organization? Again, if so, document this. Briefly describe the roles and responsibilities of the key project team members, or key resources needed for the project. Include this information in the project charter.

At this stage, you don't need every nitty-gritty detail. You're looking for the big hitters that will take time, money, or people with specialized skills to implement. These are the kinds of resources the selection committee will want to know about.

Determining the Initial Budget

Identifying the initial budget is a lot like identifying the initial resource requirements. Again, the selection committee is looking for the major impacts to the organization regarding the costs of performing the project and purchasing necessary equipment or services to carry out project activities. A project budget needs to be established once the project is initiated so that project costs can be attributed directly to it.

Breaking Down Project Costs

Project costs can be broken down into roughly three areas. Human resource costs, resource or project costs, and administrative costs. The responsibility for determining these costs rests on either the project manager or a finance manager in a functional organization. Sometimes the budget is predetermined by the executive management staff and you're told what it is and have to work with what you're given.

When you are the one responsible for determining the initial budget, there are a couple of places you can look that will help you with estimating project costs. One of the first places to consider is previous projects that are similar in scope to your project. Review the project documents from similar projects and use their total costs to give you a starting place. From there, you can make adjustments to your new budget according to the differences in scope and detail of the new project versus the one you're using as a reference.

You can also talk with key team members, key stakeholders, or others with experience on similar projects and ask them what projects of this type have cost in the past. They're also good folks to run your initial budget figures by before making them public. We'll talk more about cost-estimating techniques in Chapter 5.

Human Resource Costs

Human resource, or personnel costs, can be one of your biggest expenses depending on the kind of project you're working on. Any project that is labor intensive, or requires highly specialized skills or knowledge, will likely have high personnel costs.

Resource or Project Costs

The project itself will have resource expenses directly related to the project. These are costs that are specific to the project, not the day-to-day operation expenses that we'll cover in a minute. These resource costs might be things like travel expense related to the project, long-distance phone bills, specialized talent hired for certain portions of the project, vendor fees, equipment purchases, hardware purchases, etc. Again, depending on the kind of project you're working on, resource expenses can be quite high as well. The construction of a new theme hotel on the Las Vegas strip, for example, could run into the tens of millions of dollars in material resources alone, let alone the human resource costs to design, construct, and build the hotel.

Administrative Costs

Administrative costs are the day-to-day type costs that keep the organization running, but are not directly related to the project. For example, office equipment, local phone charges, leases (unless office space or building space was leased specifically to house project members, in which case this expense would be a resource expense charged against the project), heat and lights, support personnel, etc.

The project manager will want to identify the major expenses of the project and have some general thoughts about project costs to share with the selection committee. The project budget will be further defined once adequate estimating can be completed, and at that time, the final project budget can be submitted for approval.

Formalizing and Publishing the Project Charter

We've covered a lot of material before finally getting to this point, formalizing and publishing the project charter. That's because as you've seen, a lot of information goes into the project charter. This document is the foundation for the remaining project activity planning, execution, and control processes. Keep in mind if your project is performed under contract, the contract itself can serve as the project charter.

The *project charter* is the official, written acknowledgment and recognition that a project exists. It's issued by senior management and gives the project manager authority to assign organizational resources to the work of the project. It is usually the first official document of the project once acceptance of the project has been granted. Good project charters that are well documented will address many of the questions your stakeholders are likely to have up front. If your charter is good, you'll avoid a lot of issues early on.

Pulling the Project Charter Together

In order to create a useful and well-documented project charter, you will start with including a staple group of components. The project charter should include an overview of the project, its goals and objectives, the project deliverables, the business case or need for the project, resource and cost estimates, and a feasibility study if one was performed. The charter should describe the preliminary roles and responsibilities of the project manager, project staff, project sponsor, and executive management. We have covered most of these items in depth. Creating the project charter is a matter of incorporating all the information we've gathered so far, as outlined above, and putting it in the document. However, we've only touched on roles and responsibilities of key project members, so let's take a closer look at this area and then wrap up with some final notes on project charters.

Project Manager

The project manager is the person who will assume responsibility for the success of the project. The project manager's primary responsibilities are project planning and then executing and managing the project plan. The oversight of the project charter and project plan assures the project manager that everyone knows and understands what's expected of them and what constitutes a successful project. The project charter and project plan provide for smooth problem resolution as the project goals and objectives, deliverables, and tasks are detailed in these documents.

The project charter identifies the project manager and describes the authority the project manager has in carrying out the project.

Project managers will be responsible for setting the standards and policies for the projects they work on. As a project manager, it is your job to establish and communicate the project procedures to the project team and stakeholders.

Project managers will identify activities and tasks, resource requirements, project costs, project requirements, performance measures, and more. Communication and documentation must become the project manager's best friends. Keeping stakeholders, the project sponsor, the project team, and all other interested parties informed is "job one," as the famous car manufacturer's ads say.

Project Sponsor

Have you ever attended a conference or event that was put on by a sponsor? In the information technology field, conferences and seminars are often sponsored by software development companies. The sponsor pays for the event, the facilities, and the goodies, and provides an opportunity for vendors to display their wares. In return, the sponsor comes out looking like a winner—because they really are footing the bill for all this fun, the sponsor gets to call the shots on conference content, and they get the prime spots for discussing their particular software solutions. And last but not least, they usually are the keynote speaker and get to present their information to a captive audience.

Project sponsors are similar to this in that they rally support from stakeholders and the executive management team for the project. The project sponsor is usually an executive in the organization who has the power and authority to make decisions and settle disputes or conflicts regarding the project. The sponsor takes the project to the limelight, so to speak, and gets to call the shots regarding project outcomes.

Sponsors are actively involved in the Initiation and Planning phases of the project and tend to have less involvement during the Execution and Controlling phases. It's up to the project manager to keep the project sponsor informed of all project activities, project progress, and any conflicts or issues that arise. The sponsor is the one with the authority to resolve conflict and set priorities when these things can't be dealt with any other way.

Project Champion

The project champion is another strong project supporter. Unlike the sponsor, the project champion doesn't necessarily have a lot of authority or executive powers. The champion helps focus attention on the project from a technical perspective. The project champion is usually someone with a great deal of technical expertise or industry knowledge regarding the project. They can lend credibility to the viability of the project and to the skills and abilities of the key project team members to carry out project activities. Sometimes, the project manager may act as project champion.

Functional Managers

We covered functional managers in Chapter 2. As a reminder, we'll mention them here again briefly as project managers must work with and gain the support of functional managers in order to complete the project. Functional managers fulfill the administrative duties of the organization, provide and assign staff members to projects, and conduct performance reviews for their staff.

The *Guide to the PMBOK* states that a manager who is external to the project should publish the charter. In practice, my experience has been that the project charter is published under the name of the project sponsor. The charter can be written by the project manager in either case, and usually is, but the project manager's name is not the name on the project charter document. For the exam, remember that the charter is published by a manager external to the project.

Project Charter Sign-Off

The project charter isn't complete until you've received sign-off from the project sponsor, senior management, and key stakeholders. Sign-off indicates that the document has been read by those signing it (let's hope so anyway) and that they agree with its contents and are on board with the project. It also involves the major players right from the beginning and hopefully wins their continued participation in the project going forward. This is important because the charter states the project goals and deliverables, and the time, resources, and costs needed to meet those goals. If someone has a problem with them, now is the time to raise the red flag. Signing the project charter document is the equivalent of agreeing to and endorsing the project. This doesn't mean that the project charter is set in stone, however. Project charters will change throughout the course of the project. As more details are uncovered and outlined and as the Planning process begins, more project issues will come to light. This is part of the iterative process of project management and is to be expected. The charter will occasionally be revised to reflect these new details, project plans will be revised, and project execution will change to incorporate the new information or direction.

According to the *Guide to the PMBOK*, the project manager is assigned to the project as an output of the Initiation process. The project charter usually names the project manager. And the signed project charter gives the project manager the authority to assign resources to the project and move on to the Planning process.

Everyone mentioned here—the project manager, the project sponsor, the project champion, the functional managers, the stakeholders, the clients, and anyone else impacted by the project—should receive a copy of the written project charter. If you've done a good job with the project charter, and it's been agreed to and signed off by the project sponsor and stakeholders, you've made your job of producing a scope statement, covered in Chapter 4, much easier.

Project Case Study: New Kitchen Heaven Retail Store

You review your notes and reread the project charter you've prepared for the Kitchen Heaven retail store one last time before looking for Dirk. When you saw him last, he pointed you in the direction of three of the project stakeholders: Jake Peterson, Jill Overstreet, and Ricardo Ramirez. After your meetings with Jake and then Jill, you were better able to refine the project overview and deliverables.

You finally run across Dirk in a hallway near the executive washroom.

"Dirk, I'm glad I caught you. I'd like to go over the project charter with you before the kick-off meeting tomorrow. Do you have a few minutes?"

"Sure," Dirk says to you. "Let's have it."

"The project charter states the project goal, which of course is to open the 50th Kitchen Heaven store in Colorado Springs. I also documented the deliverables, many of which we talked about last time we met.

"When I met with Jake, he confirmed it takes 120 days to do the store build-out. That includes having the shelves set up and in place, ready to stock with inventory."

Dirk asks if Jake told you about his store location idea.

"Yes, Jake gave me a contact name, and I've left her a voice mail. The sooner we can get that lease signed the better. It takes Jake 120 days to do the build-out, and Jill said she needs 2 weeks lead time to order the initial inventory and stock the shelves. That puts us pretty close to our February 1st deadline counting the time to get the lease papers signed."

"Sounds good so far," Dirk replies. "What else?"

"I included an updated description of the products and services the new store will offer, based on the documentation that was written from the last store opening. Jill reviewed the updates to the description, so we should be in the clear there. The store will include some new lines that we've decided to take on—cookware from famous chefs, that kind of thing.

"The project charter also outlines your role as the project sponsor, my role as project manager, and our expectations of the project staff. Jake has already made contact with a general contractor in the Springs, and he is ready to roll once we've signed the lease."

You add, "I'm using your estimate of $2 million as our initial budget request. Based on projected inflows, I've calculated a payback period of 16 months with an IRR of 22 percent."

"That's impressive," replies Dirk. "Even better than our Phoenix store. If I recall, the payback period there was just over 2 years. Let's hope those numbers hold true."

"I think they're reliable figures. Jill showed me her data based on recent store openings in similar-sized cities. And we factored in the economic conditions of the Colorado Springs area. Since they're on a growth pattern, we think the timing is perfect.

"One more thing, Dirk. Since we're including the big bash at grand opening as part of the deliverables, I talked to some of your folks in marketing to get some ideas. They are thinking we should have some great giveaways as door prizes and that we will want to cater in the food. They also thought having some live cooking demonstrations with some local chefs would be a good attraction."

"So what's next?" Dirk asks.

"As you know, the project kickoff is scheduled for tomorrow. What I'll need then is for you to talk about the project and the goals, the commitment you'll need from the management team to support this project, and introduce me as the project manager. I've already forwarded a copy of the project charter to the meeting attendees so that they can review it before the meeting. And, I included a list of the assumptions we've made so far as an appendix to the charter. Lastly, I'll need you to ask everyone present to sign a copy of the project charter."

"Sounds like you've covered everything," Dirk says. "I don't anticipate any problems tomorrow as everyone is looking forward to this store opening."

Project Case Study Checklist

Payback period calculated at 16 months

IRR calculated at 22 percent

Met with stakeholders to determine high-level list of deliverables:

- Project store opening on Feb 1

- Build-out of storefront

- Retail product line delivered 2 weeks prior to grand opening

- Grand-opening party with cooking demos

Created project charter, which contains:

- Overview of project goals and objectives

- List of deliverables

- Business case for the project

- Initial completion date of Feb 1

- Initial budget of $2 million

- Definition of roles of project sponsor and project manager

Kickoff meeting set up to discuss charter and obtain sign-off

---

Summary

We're well on our way to a successful project. We've finished up the Initiation process in this chapter and will begin the Planning process in the next chapter.

We learned about one more input to the Initiation process, which is project selection criteria. Selection criteria is defined by a selection committee, or steering committee, to make determinations as to how projects get selected and prioritized.

Project selection methods, on the other hand, are a tool and technique in the Initiation process. Selection methods include decision models in the form of benefit measurement methods and constrained optimization methods. The constrained optimization methods utilize mathematical models. Benefit measurement methods come in the form of benefit/cost analyses, scoring models, and economic analyses. These are primarily comparative approaches. Besides benefit/cost analysis, the most commonly used form of benefit measurement methods is cash flow analysis.

Analysis of cash flows includes payback period, discounted cash flows, net present value (NPV), and internal rate of return (IRR). These last three methods are concerned with the time value of money—or in other words, converting future dollars into today's value. Generally, projects with a shorter payback period are desired over longer payback periods. Projects that have an NPV greater than zero should be accepted. And projects with the highest IRR value are considered a better benefit to the organization than projects with low IRR values.

Expert judgment is considered a tool and technique of Initiation. Experts usually have specialized knowledge or skills and could include staff from other departments in the company, external or internal consultants, and members of professional and technical associations or industry groups.

Initial project requirements should be included in the project charter. Resources, personnel, budgets, and costs should be outlined to give the selection committee some overall idea of project costs.

The project charter is the official acknowledgment and recognition that the project exists. It appoints the project manager and outlines their authority. It contains an overview of the project, and the project's goals and objectives. The charter should be signed by the project sponsor, stakeholders, and other key management members and then published and distributed to all interested parties.

The case study project charter will include all the elements talked about in this chapter. It's a formalized document that represents the things you've mentioned here to Dirk. Recall that a charter is the document that authorizes the project to go forward. As such, it has to be comprehensive and include details such as the project goals and deliverables, resource needs, the business need for the product of the project, the project sponsor, roles and responsibilities of other project members, projected budget, and other items that are relevant to managers who must authorize and endorse the project.

Exam Essentials

Be able to define decision models.   Decision models are project selection methods that are a tool and technique in the Initiation process. Decision models include benefit measurement methods and constrained optimization methods.

Be able to describe and calculate payback period.   Payback period is the amount of time it will take the company to recoup its initial investment in the product of the project. It's calculated by adding up the expected cash inflows and comparing them to the initial investment to determine how many periods it takes for the cash inflows to equal the initial investment.

Be able to denote the decision criteria for NPV and IRR.   Projects with an NPV greater than zero should be accepted, and those with an NPV less than zero should be rejected. Projects with high IRR values should be accepted over projects with lower IRR values. IRR is the discount rate when NPV is equal to zero, and IRR assumes reinvestment at the IRR rate.

Be able to describe the importance of the project charter.   The project charter is the document that officially recognizes and acknowledges that a project exists. It dedicates the organization's resources to the project, names the project manager, and describes the goals and deliverables of the project.

Be able to describe the importance of sign-off of the project charter. Sign-off assures all parties have read the charter, agree to its contents, and endorse the project. Participation early on by the key stakeholders will likely ensure their participation in the project as it progresses.

Key Terms

Before you take the exam, be certain you are familiar with the following terms:

discounted cash flow	payback period
internal rate of return (IRR)	project charter
net present value (NPV)	

Review Questions

1. What are the tools and techniques used in the Initiation process?

   A. Project selection criteria, historical information, expert judgment

   B. Project selection methods, historical information, expert judgment

   C. Project selection criteria, expert judgment

   D. Project selection methods, expert judgment

2. Comparative methods, scoring methods, and economic and cash flow analysis are all part of which of the following?

   A. Benefit measurement methods, which are a tool and technique in Initiation

   B. Constrained optimization methods, which are a tool and technique in Initiation

   C. Benefit measurement methods, which are an input to Initiation

   D. Decision models, which are an output of Initiation

3. You are the project manager for the Late Night Smooth Jazz Club chain, with stores in 12 states. Smooth Jazz is considering opening a new club in Arizona or Nevada. You have derived the following information:

   Project Arizona: Payback period is 18 months, and the NPV is <250>.

   Project Nevada: Payback period is 24 months, and the NPV is 300.

   Which project would you recommend to the selection committee?

   A. Project Arizona because the payback period is shorter than Project Nevada

   B. Project Nevada because the NPV is a positive number

   C. Project Arizona because the NPV is a negative number

   D. Project Nevada because the NPV is a higher number than Project Arizona's NPV

4. You are the project manager for the Late Night Smooth Jazz Club chain, with stores in 12 states. Smooth Jazz is considering opening a new club in Kansas City or Spokane. You have derived the following information:

   Project Kansas City: The payback period is 27 months, and the IRR is 35 percent.

   Project Spokane: The payback period is 25 months, and the IRR is 32 percent.

   Which project should you recommend to the selection committee?

   A. Project Spokane because the payback period is shortest

   B. Project Kansas City because the IRR is highest

   C. Project Spokane because the IRR is lowest

   D. Project Kansas City because the payback period is longest

5. Which of the following is true regarding NPV?

   A. NPV assumes reinvestment at the cost of capital.

   B. NPV decisions should be made based on the highest value for all of the selections.

   C. NPV assumes reinvestment at the prevailing rate.

   D. NPV assumes reinvestment at the NPV rate.

6. You are the project manager for Insomniacs International. Since you don't sleep much, you get a lot of project work done. You're considering recommending a project that costs $575,000, and expected inflows are $25,000 per quarter for the first 2 years, and then $75,000 per quarter thereafter. What is the payback period?

   A. 40 months

   B. 38 months

   C. 39 months

   D. 41 months

7. Which of the following is true regarding IRR?

   A. IRR assumes reinvestment at the cost of capital.

   B. IRR is the discount rate when NPV is greater than zero.

   C. IRR is a constrained optimization method.

   D. IRR is the discount rate when NPV is equal to zero.

8. Mathematical models using linear, dynamic, integer, or algorithm models are considered:

   A. Project selection criteria

   B. A form of expert judgment

   C. Project selection methods

   D. A form of historical information

9. You are the newly appointed project manager for a pharmaceutical company. Your company has asked you to head up a project to research a new children's medication. You've identified the lab equipment you'll need, the software needed to perform analysis and measurements, and the skill level and types of the technicians and researchers for this project. Which of the following is true?

   A. The project manager and resources have been identified as part of the outputs of the Initiation process, and this information can be found in the project charter.

   B. The resources and project manager have been identified as an input to the project Initiation phase. Further information is needed to produce the project charter, which will include the resources and project manager.

   C. The project manager and resources have been identified as part of the project selection process. The selection committee requires resource information to make a final decision.

   D. The resources and project manager have been identified as a result of a tool and technique in the Initiation process.

10. Your selection committee meets on a semiannual basis. They've determined that projects must meet or exceed a specific profit limit in order to be accepted and prioritized on the project list. Which of the following is true?

    A. The selection committee has defined project selection criteria, which is a tool and technique of Initiation.

    B. The selection committee has defined project selection methods, which is a tool and technique of Initiation.

    C. The selection committee has defined project selection methods, which are an input to Initiation.

    D. The selection committee has defined project selection criteria, which is an input to Initiation.

11. What are the Initiation process outputs?

    A. Project charter, historical information, and project manager identification and assignment

    B. Project charter, project manager identification and assignment, constraints, and assumptions

    C. Project charter, historical information, constraints, and assumptions

    D. Project charter, constraints, and assumptions

12. Ruby is an administrative assistant with another department. Her manager has agreed to loan Ruby's services to you on a part-time basis during your current project. Ruby is putting together the cost projections you've gathered so far. You want to include these costs in the project charter. Ruby is formatting this information for you into a spreadsheet package and is printing copies. Which of the following is true?

    A. All of the costs, including Ruby's time, are charged to the project.

    B. All of the costs Ruby is typing into the spreadsheet are project costs. Ruby's time is not directly related to the project and should not be included.

    C. The project costs, including Ruby's time, should be included in the project charter.

    D. The project costs, excluding Ruby's time, should be considered project constraints.

13. Your project selection committee used a weighted scoring model and found that Project B, with a score of 54, should be chosen over the other competing projects. Which of the following is true?

    A. Weighted scoring models are a benefit measurement method, which is a tool and technique in the Initiation process.

    B. Weighted scoring models are a constrained optimization method, which is an output of the Initiation process.

    C. Weighted scoring models are a constrained optimization method, which is a tool and technique in the Initiation process.

    D. Weighted scoring models are a benefit measurement method, which is an output of the Initiation process.

14. Your selection committee is debating between two projects. Project A has a payback period of 18 months. Project B has a cost of $125,000 with expected cash inflows of $50,000 the first year and $25,000 per quarter after that. Which project should you recommend?

    A. Either Project A or Project B because the payback periods are equal

    B. Project A because Project B's payback period is 21 months

    C. Project A because Project B's payback period is 24 months

    D. Project A because Project B's payback period is 20 months

15. Which of the following is true?

    A. Discounted cash flow analysis is the least precise of the cash flow techniques as it does not consider the time value of money.

    B. NPV is the least precise of the cash flow analysis techniques as it assumes reinvestment at the discount rate.

    C. Payback period is the least precise of the cash flow analysis techniques as it does not consider the time value of money.

    D. IRR is the least precise of the cash flow analysis techniques because it assumes reinvestment at the cost of capital.

16. Project selection criteria might include:

A. Benefit measurement methods

B. Constrained optimization analysis

C. NPV calculations

D. Potential market share or increased public perception

17. You are a project manager for Zippy Tees. Your selection committee has just chosen a project you recommended for implementation. Your project is to manufacture a line of miniature stuffed bears that will be attached to your company's trendy T-shirts. The bears will be wearing the same T-shirt design as the shirt they're attached to. Your project sponsor thinks you've really impressed the big boss and wants you to skip to the manufacturing process right away. What is your response?

A. To agree with the project sponsor because they are your boss, and they have a lot of authority and power in the company.

B. To require that a preliminary budget be established and a resource list be put together to alert other managers of the requirements of this project. This should be published and signed by the other managers who are impacted by this project.

C. To require a project charter be published and signed off on by all stakeholders before proceeding.

D. To require a project charter be written to include the resources needed, budget, and project manager's authority. The project manager is the only one who needs to see this document as other documents will be distributed later that contain the same detail as the charter.

18. Which of the following is true regarding the project charter?

A. The project charter should be published under the name of a manager external to the project.

B. The project charter should be published under the project sponsor's name.

C. The project charter should be published under the name of the project manager.

D. The project charter should be published under the name of the project champion.

19. You are the project manager for Zippy Tees. Your company has decided to outsource the manufacturing of miniature bears to be attached to your trendy T-shirts. Which of the following is true?

    A. A good product description is all that's required. The project manager will supply this to the vendor.

    B. The contract can serve as the project charter. The product description will be included in the contract.

    C. The project manager should write the project charter because the project manager will be managing the vendor portion of this project as well.

    D. The vendor should write the project charter as they are responsible for manufacturing the bears.

20. The project charter:

    A. Includes a product description, describes the business need of the project, and is published by the project manager

    B. Includes a product description, describes the business need of the project, and is published by the project sponsor

    C. Includes the contract when the project is performed by a vendor and is published by a manager external to the project

    D. Includes a product description, describes the business need of the project, and is published by a manager external to the project

Answers to Review Questions

1. D. The tools and techniques in the Initiation process are project selection methods and expert judgment.

2. A. Benefit measurement methods include comparative methods, scoring models, and cash flow analysis, which are all part of the project selection method tools and techniques in Initiation.

3. B. Projects with NPV greater than zero should be given an accept recommendation.

4. B. Projects with the highest IRR value are favored over projects with lower IRR values.

5. A. Net present value assumes reinvestment is made at the cost of capital.

6. C. Year 1 and 2 inflows are each $100,000 for a total of $200,000. Year 3 inflows are an additional $300,000. Add one more quarter to this total and the $575,000 is reached in 3 years and 3 months, or 39 months.

7. D. IRR assumes reinvestment at the IRR rate and is the discount rate when NPV is equal to zero.

8. C. Mathematical models are part of the constrained optimization methods used as a project selection method technique.

9. A. Initiation outputs include the project charter and identification and assignment of the project manager. Resource needs are detailed in the project charter.

10. D. Project selection criteria can be objective or subjective. Selection criteria is an input to the Initiation process. Project selection methods use decision models to assist with project selection and are a tool and technique of the Initiation process.

11. B. Outputs to Initiation include the project charter, project manager identification and assignment (even though this might be stated in the charter, this is still a specific output of Initiation), constraints, and assumptions.

12. B. Project costs are those costs directly related to the project. Ruby is part time on the project and works for the organization, not the project manager. Therefore, her time is not counted in the initial budget projections.

13. A. Benefit measurement methods include comparative methods and scoring models, among others, to make project selections.

14. B. Project B has a payback period of 21 months. $50,000 is received in the first 12 months with another $75,000 coming in over each of the next 3 quarters, or 9 months.

15. C. Payback period does not consider the time value of money and is therefore the least precise of all the cash flow analysis techniques.

16. D. Project selection criteria includes subjective information such as potential market share. Objective material can be considered in project selection criteria, but the other answers listed here are specific project selection methods.

17. C. The project should be kicked off with a project charter outlining the project goals, deliverables, resources, budget, and roles and responsibilities of the project team. This assures everyone is working from the same assumptions and with the same goals in mind.

18. A. According to the *Guide to the PMBOK*, the project charter should be published by a manager external to the project but with sufficient power and authority to carry it off.

19. B. When a project is performed under contract, the contract can serve as the project charter. Project charters always include product descriptions.

20. D. Project charters, according the *Guide to the PMBOK*, must at least include the product description and the business need for the product or service of the project. Charters are published by managers external to the project according to the *Guide to the PMBOK* but in practice are often published by the project sponsor.

Chapter

4

Creating the Scope Statement and WBS

PMP EXAM CONTENT FROM THE PROJECT PLANNING PERFORMANCE DOMAIN COVERED IN THIS CHAPTER:

✓ 1. Refine Project.

✓ 2. Create WBS.

Great job! You've successfully completed the project Initiation process and published the project charter. The project is officially under way. Stakeholders have been informed, there is management buy-in on the project, the project manager has been assigned, and the project goals and deliverables have been identified. A solid foundation for the Planning process is in place.

This chapter will begin the Planning process of the project. We will continue discussing the Planning processes through Chapter 7. Planning is a significant activity in any project and, if done correctly, will go a long way toward ensuring project success.

We will begin this chapter by taking one more look at project goals and deliverables. Requirements definition will be derived from these and documented in the scope statement. We'll discuss the scope management plan and all it entails, and then begin the schedule-planning activities by describing the WBS. The WBS is not a new World Baseball Series as some would hope; rather it's the work breakdown structure.

This chapter will wrap up with a short discussion of the Communications Planning process. We've talked a lot about documentation so far, and we will discuss it more in this chapter. Documentation is something you will do throughout the remainder of the project, and the Communications Planning process details how to collect information, how to store it, and when and how to distribute it to stakeholders.

Scoping Out the Project

S*cope Planning* is the first process in the Planning process group. The scope statement, which is an output of Scope Planning, will become an input into the second Planning process, which is Scope Definition. We'll get to Scope Definition later in this chapter.

You've most likely discovered by now that we've done a lot of documentation. Well, the documentation exercises don't stop with the project charter. Documentation should become the mantra of all good project managers. "Is that documented?" should be an ever present question on the mind of the project manager. Documentation can save your bacon, so to speak, later in the project. Now you've probably guessed that we're going to move into another area of documentation, and you're right. But first, let's talk about some of the elements of Scope Planning before we get to the documenting part.

Scope Planning, like all other processes, has inputs, tools and techniques, and outputs. The primary purpose of Scope Planning is twofold: to produce the scope statement and the scope management plan. We'll deal with each of these documents in more detail after we look at the inputs and tools and techniques used to produce these two documents.

The inputs to Scope Planning are items you are already familiar with: the product description, project charter, project constraints, and project assumptions. If you've read the previous chapters, you're up to speed on these elements.

We also have already discussed two of the tools and techniques of Scope Planning: benefit/cost analysis and expert judgment. You'll remember from Chapter 3 that benefit/cost analysis (also called cost benefit analysis) is comparing the costs of the project to the expected benefits of the project. Benefit/cost might include cash flow analysis and economic analysis. These techniques determine a project's profitability and viability and may also be used as selection criteria. Expert judgment is relying on people or groups with specific skills, knowledge, or training to help assess the process inputs.

Two techniques remain for the Scope Planning process: product analysis and alternatives identification.

Product analysis goes hand in hand with the product description. Product analysis is simply a deeper understanding of the product or service of the project. According to the *Guide to the PMBOK*, this goes further than product description in that product analysis might include performing value analysis, function analysis, systems-engineering techniques, or value-engineering techniques to further define the product or service. It's beyond the scope of this book to go into these analysis techniques. For exam purposes, you just need to know that product analysis is a tool and technique of Scope Planning.

Alternatives identification is a technique used to discover different methods or ways of accomplishing the project. For example, brainstorming might be used to discover alternative ways of implementing one of the project objectives. Perhaps the project's budget doesn't allow for a portion of the project that the stakeholders really think needs to be included. Brainstorming might uncover an alternative that would allow the needed portion to be accomplished.

We have our inputs at hand and have used the tools and techniques described to analyze these inputs. Now we're ready to document them in the scope statement.

Writing the Scope Statement

One of the project manager's primary goals is to accurately document the deliverables and requirements of the project, and then manage the project so that they are produced according to the agreed-upon criteria. Deliverables describe the components of the goals and objectives in a quantifiable way.

Objectives and deliverables are sometimes referred to as critical success factors. Critical success factors are those elements that must be completed in order for the project to be considered complete. For example, if you're building a bridge, one of the deliverables might be to produce a specific number of trusses that will be used to help support the bridge. Without the trusses, the bridge couldn't be completed; in fact, the bridge might not stand without them. The trusses, in this case, are a critical success factor. Not all deliverables are necessarily critical success factors, but many of them will fall into this category and should be documented as such.

At this point, the project manager needs to discover and document all of the requirements of the project. Requirements describe the characteristics of the deliverable. Some of the requirements of the deliverable from our bridge example might be that the trusses are constructed of a specific kind of steel, or steel cable, or they must be a certain color and of a certain height or curvature, etc.

Again the project manager needs to pull those communications skills out of her tool bag and use them to interview stakeholders and business process owners about the project requirements. Business process owners are those people who are experts in their particular area of the business. They are invaluable resources to the project manager. They are usually the midlevel managers and line managers who still have their fingers in the day-to-day portion of the business. For example, it takes many experts in various areas to produce and market a great bottle of beer. There are machinists whose specialty is regulating and keeping the stainless steel and copper drums in top working order. There are chemists who sometimes daily check and adjust the secret formulas brewing in the vats. Graphic artists must develop colorful and interesting labels and cartons to attract the attention of those thirsty patrons. And of course, those great TV commercials advertising the tasty brew are produced by yet another set of business experts. These are the kinds of people you'll want to interview. Sometimes getting the business process owners and stakeholders (who could be one and the same depending on the project) together in a meeting room and brainstorming the requirements will produce terrific results. Depending on the size of the project, this isn't always possible, but the idea holds true. Interview your stakeholders and business experts to get at the requirements and then document them in the scope statement.

Why Do You Need a Scope Statement?

The purpose of the *scope statement* is to document the project goals, deliverables, and requirements so that they can be used as a baseline for future project decisions. A lot of work regarding the scope statement has already been accomplished by producing the project charter. The charter is used as an input to the scope statement and already contains the project goals and major project deliverables. If the project charter was written well, it's simply a matter of transferring the goals and deliverables information from the charter to the scope statement.

The scope statement is the baseline for the project, as mentioned above. This means if questions arise or changes are proposed later in the project, they can be compared to what's documented in the scope statement. In this way, the scope statement establishes a common understanding among the stakeholders and project team members regarding project requirements and deliverables. The criteria outlined in the scope statement will also be used to determine if the project was completed successfully.

Scope Statement Components

According to the *Guide to the PMBOK*, the scope statement should include all of the following: project justification, project product, project deliverables, and project objectives. If details surrounding these are spelled out in other documents, you don't have to re-enter all the information into the scope statement. Simply reference the other document in the scope statement so readers know where to find it. Let's do a quick recap of each of the elements in the project scope.

Project Justification

This describes the business need of the project. If the business need, or business case, was written as part of the project charter, reference it in the scope statement. Project justification also includes the cost benefit and cash flow analysis used to determine the projected profitability of the project. See Chapter 3 for details on these techniques.

Project Product

This is the product description we talked about in Chapter 3. If the product description is contained in the project charter, just reference the project charter in the scope statement.

If you think you might need a refresher on product description, take a minute to jog your memory by reviewing the relevant section in Chapter 3.

Project Deliverables

The *Guide to the PMBOK* describes these as the major deliverables of a project and all the subcomponents that make up the deliverables. The completion of these deliverables signals project completion. For example, our project goal or objective might be to produce a new bottle of beer for the holidays. One major deliverable is the holiday cartons to hold the bottles. The subcomponents to produce this major deliverable might be the carton design, photographs, color choices, and so on.

Project Objectives

Objectives always involve the triple constraints: time, cost, and quality. In the case of goals and objectives, the triple constraints are used as measurements to determine project satisfaction and completion.

You'll remember from Chapter 3 that objectives, or goals, are specific, measurable, and timely. Continuing with our holiday beer example, the objective of this project would be properly stated this way according to the *Guide to the PMBOK:* Beer Buddies, Inc. will produce two million cases of holiday beer to be shipped to our distributors by October 30 at a cost of $1.5 million or less.

The objective criteria are clearly stated, and fulfillment of the project objective, or goal, is easily measured. Stakeholders will know the objective is met when the two million cases are produced and shipped by the due date within the budget constraint.

The *Guide to the PMBOK* states that objectives are sometimes called critical success factors. In practice, deliverables are sometimes referred to as critical success factors as well.

Being Clear and Concise

It's important that the project objectives, deliverables, and requirements are clearly and concisely stated in the scope statement so there are no misunderstandings later on. "Producing a special run of holiday beer" is not the same as "producing two million cases of holiday beer by October 30." The former statement can be interpreted different ways by the project sponsor and project manager. You'd have to put real effort into misunderstanding the latter statement.

The scope statement should contain a comprehensive listing of all the project requirements. This is important because this document forms the basis for agreement between the stakeholders and project team from this point forward. You'll want to be certain you have not missed anything when writing the scope statement. Run the draft by some of the key stakeholders and project team members before publishing it to see if they think anything is missing. You're going to use this document to determine if the project has been successfully completed by comparing what's been delivered to what's described here, so you want to be sure you've covered everything.

Just like the project charter, the scope statement should be published and distributed to the stakeholders, key management personnel, and project team members. You will also want a formal sign-off procedure for the scope statement. When stakeholders sign off and agree to the scope statement, they're agreeing to the deliverables and requirements of the project. And, as with the project charter, their agreement and endorsement of the project requirements and deliverables will likely sustain their participation and cooperation throughout the rest of the project. That doesn't mean they'll agree to everything as the project progresses, but it does mean the stakeholders are informed and will likely remain active project participants.

The following may seem obvious, but we'll note it anyway: Objectives, deliverables, and requirements not specifically included in the scope statement are explicitly excluded from the project. Your scope statement could have a section for exclusions so that everyone knows in advance what isn't going to be included in the project.

Supporting detail is an output of the Scope Planning process and directly references the information you've assembled for the scope statement. Supporting detail should be documented and should include the project constraints, assumptions, and any other information not specifically documented in the scope statement. You could list the deliverables and requirements that are excluded from the project here, unless they were already noted in the scope statement. This document, like the scope statement, will be referenced in future Planning processes, so keep it handy.

We're making progress. We've covered two of the three Scope Planning process outputs: the scope statement and supporting detail. All the deliverables and requirements have now been documented along with measurable or quantifiable criteria for each. Stakeholders have approved and signed off on them, and the scope statement has been published and distributed. However, like other project-planning documents, the scope statement is not cast in stone. The scope statement can and probably will change as the project progresses. Changes to the project scope should be noted and the scope statement modified to incorporate these changes. Changes are managed according to the scope management plan, which we'll discuss in the next section.

 Real World Scenario

Mountain Streams Services

Maria Sanchez is the CEO of Mountain Streams Services. She recently accepted a prestigious industry award on behalf of the company. Maria knows that without the dedication and support of her employees, Mountain Streams Services wouldn't have achieved this great milestone.

Maria wants to host a reception for the employees and their guests in recognition of all their hard work and contributions to the company. Maria has appointed you to arrange the reception.

The reception is scheduled for April 12, and Maria has given you a budget of $125 per person. The company employs 200 people. The reception should be semiformal.

You've documented the deliverables as follows:

- Location selection

- Food and beverage menu

- Invitations

- Entertainment

- Insurance coverage

- Decorations

- Photographer

- Agenda

In addition to the deliverables, you want to go over the following requirements with Maria to be certain you both are in agreement:

- The location should be somewhere in the downtown area.

- Employees are encouraged to bring one guest, but no children.

- There will be an open bar paid for by Maria.

- The agenda will include a speech by Maria followed by the distribution of bonus checks to every employee—this is to be kept secret until the reception.

- The decorations should include gold-trimmed fountain pens with the company logo at every place setting for the attendees to keep.

Once you've documented all the particulars, you ask to speak with Maria to go over this scope statement and get her agreement before proceeding with the project plan and task assignments.

Publishing the Scope Management Plan

Change is inevitable. One thing you and I know for certain is that changes are going to occur on your next project. Change isn't something to be dreaded, but it is something to be managed. The *scope management plan* helps the project manager do just that. This plan is an important supplementary document to the project plan as it describes how changes to the project scope will be incorporated into the project. It also defines the process of how to go about requesting a change.

The scope management plan should be written and distributed at roughly the same time the scope statement is published. If you get the scope management plan in the hands of the stakeholders early on, it will hopefully eliminate questions about scope changes later in the project.

The purpose of the scope management plan, according to the *Guide to the PMBOK*, is to analyze the reliability and stability of the project scope. In other words, it examines the likelihood that scope change will occur (meaning changes to goals, deliverables, or requirements). The plan answers the questions, "Are a lot of changes expected?" and "How dramatic will the changes be?" This is determined by the complexity of the project you're working on. The example of the employee reception at the end of the last section probably won't have a lot of change because the project is small and the deliverables and requirements are simple and very clear.

The Scope Management Change Process

According to the *Guide to the PMBOK*, the scope management change process can be formal or informal. I would agree that for small, uncomplicated projects with one or two stakeholders, an informal process will work well. Large or complex projects should always have a scope management plan. In either case, it's been my experience whether the process is formal or informal, all change requests should be put in writing. Stakeholders and project managers can sometimes have foggy memories. And what you think you said might not be what the stakeholder heard and vice versa. Documenting the change request eliminates these issues.

Hmm, have we talked about documentation?

All changes should be requested in writing on a formal change request form, and the impact of the changes noted. Changes will usually impact one, if not all, of the triple constraints. But for now, all we need to know is the kind of change requested and have a high-level understanding of its impact on time, cost, or quality. These changes should be logged and tracked throughout the course of the project. Some changes will not be approved but might need to be incorporated into the next product release or project. If you log and file these change requests with the project information, they will help you define the requirements for the next project. In a later chapter, we'll discuss the process for change approval and communication of the change.

For the exam, remember that the scope management plan is a document that identifies how project scope will be managed and how those changes will be incorporated into the project. It assesses the probability of scope changes, their frequency, and their impact. Formalizing this process for large or complex projects is highly recommended.

Formulating the Scope Definition

Now we're getting to the meat of the project Planning process. We've identified and documented all the project deliverables and requirements, and we're ready to further break these down into project work. In the *Scope Definition* process, the project deliverables are broken down into smaller, manageable components so that we can plan project tasks and activities. This subdividing of deliverables into smaller components is the purpose of the Scope Definition process. The *Guide to the PMBOK* calls this *decomposition*. We can take this one step further by breaking the smaller components down even further into what the *Guide to the PMBOK* terms work packages. We'll cover work packages in a later section.

This breaking-down process will accomplish several things for us, one of which is improving estimates. It's easier to estimate the costs, time, and resources needed for individual work components than it is to estimate them for a whole body of work or deliverable. Using smaller components also makes it easier to assign performance measures and controls. These give us a baseline to compare against throughout the project or phase. And finally, assigning resources and responsibility for the components of work makes better sense as several resources with different skills might be needed to complete one deliverable. Breaking them down assures that assignment, and the responsibility for that assignment, goes to the proper parties.

The Scope Definition process has five inputs that we've already covered elsewhere. They are the scope statement, project constraints, assumptions, other Planning process outputs, and historical information.

The tools and techniques of Scope Definition are the work breakdown structure templates and decomposition. These tools work together to create the work breakdown structure (WBS), which we'll look at next.

Creating the Work Breakdown Structure

Have you ever mapped out a family tree? A *work breakdown structure* is very similar to a family tree. It maps out the deliverables of the project with subdeliverables and activities stemming from each major deliverable in a tree format. The *Guide to the PMBOK*, pages 59 and 60, describes a WBS this way: "A WBS is a deliverable-oriented grouping of project components that organizes and defines the total scope of the project; work not included in the WBS is outside the scope of the project." Simply put, a WBS is a deliverables-oriented hierarchy that defines the work of the project.

The WBS will be used throughout many of the remaining Planning processes and is an important part of project planning. As you probably have concluded, everything we've done so far builds on the previous step. The project charter outlines the project goals and major deliverables. The scope statement further refines these deliverables into an exhaustive list. Now, that comprehensive list of deliverables is going to be used to build the framework of the WBS.

The importance and accuracy of the work you've done up to this point can't be stressed enough. Your WBS will only be as accurate as your list of deliverables. The deliverables will become the groupings that will form the higher levels of the WBS from which activities will be derived.

The WBS should detail the full scope of work needed to complete the project. This breakdown will smooth the way for estimating project cost and time, scheduling resources, and determining quality controls later in the Planning process. Project progress will be based on the estimates and measurements assigned to the WBS segments. So again, accuracy and completeness are required when composing your WBS.

Constructing the WBS

There is no "right" way to construct a WBS. In practice, the tree structure is used quite often. (This structure also resembles an organization chart.) But a WBS could be composed in outline form as well—the choice is yours. The organization of the content in the WBS is consistent no matter which form you use. Its content is defined by a series of levels. These levels are often in sequential order, but they don't have to be. The WBS defines the work that needs to be done. The sequential ordering of those tasks takes place in a later step, although in practice, you'll probably combine these steps. We'll look at the WBS content next.

Understanding the Various WBS Levels

Although the project manager is free to determine the number of levels in the WBS based on the complexity of the project, the highest level of the WBS, level one, is considered the project itself. This is followed by the deliverables, which might be followed by more deliverables followed by activities and so on. Each of these breakouts is called a level in the WBS with the project itself as level one, the deliverables as level two, and so on. The easiest way to describe this process is with an example. Let's suppose you work for a software company that publishes children's games. You're the project manager for the new Billy Bob's Bassoon game, which teaches children about music, musical rhythm, and beginning sight reading. The first level of our WBS is the project name; it appears at the top of the WBS, as shown in Figure 4.1.

The next level should describe the major deliverables for the project. In our example, some of the deliverables might be requirements definition, design specifications, and programming. This isn't an exhaustive list of deliverables; in practice, you would go on to place all of your major deliverables into the WBS as level two content. For illustration purposes, we'll just look at a slice of the WBS for this project. Figure 4.1 shows the WBS with level one and level two detail added.

FIGURE 4.1 WBS levels one and two

Level three content might be deliverables that are further broken out from the major deliverables of level two, or it might be activities that contribute to the deliverable. Our software example shows further deliverables as level three content. See Figure 4.2 for an illustration of the WBS so far.

FIGURE 4.2   WBS levels one, two, and three

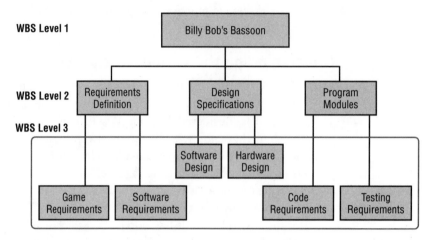

The goal here is to eventually break the work out to the point where responsibility and accountability can be assigned to a specific person or team of people for each unit of work. The higher levels of the WBS contain the deliverables and use nouns as their descriptors. Reaching way back to my grade school English, I recall that a noun is a person, place, or thing. In our example, the deliverables in level two and three are described using nouns. The activity level, level four in our example in Figure 4.3, is described using verbs, or action words. Some of the verbs used in level four are *define*, *design*, *determine*, etc. There are many more activities that would go with these deliverables, but for the sake of illustration, we've listed just a few for each deliverable to give you an idea of how the WBS is constructed.

You can see from our illustrations how a poor scope definition, or inadequate list of deliverables, will lead to a poorly constructed WBS. Not only will this make the WBS look sickly, but the project itself will suffer and might even succumb to the dreaded premature project demise. The final cost of the project will be higher than estimated, and lots of rework (translate as late nights and weekends) will be needed to account for the missing work not listed on the WBS. You can construct a good WBS and maintain a healthy project by taking the time to document all the deliverables during the Scope Planning process.

FIGURE 4.3   WBS levels one, two, three, and four

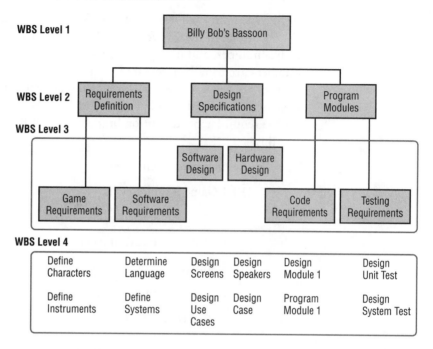

Work breakdown structures can be constructed using WBS templates or the WBS from a similar completed project. A bit earlier, we mentioned that WBS templates are a tool and technique in the Scope Definition process. While every project is unique, many companies repeat the same kind of projects over and over. The deliverables are similar from project to project, and they generally follow a consistent path. The WBS templates can be used in a case like this as a tool to simplify the WBS process, saving the project manager time.

We also mentioned that decomposition is a tool and technique of the Scope Definition process. This is the breaking down of the deliverables into smaller, manageable components, as our illustrations have shown.

Large, complex projects are often composed of several subprojects that collectively make up the main project. The WBS for a project such as this would show the subprojects as level two detail. These subprojects would then list their major deliverables as level three content, perhaps more deliverables as level four, and activities as level five and so on.

Unique WBS Identifiers

Each element at each level of the WBS should be assigned a unique identifier according to the *Guide to the PMBOK*. This unique identifier is typically a number, and it's used to track the cost of the WBS element. These numbers are usually associated with the corporation's financial system chart of accounts. Collectively, these numeric identifiers are known as the *code of accounts*, also called a chart of accounts. The numbering scheme for the requirements definition branch of the WBS might look something like this:

10 Requirements Definition

    10-1 Game Requirements

        10-1-1 Define Characters

        10-1-2 Define Instruments

    10-2 Software Requirements

        10-2-1 Determine Language

        10-2-2 Define Systems

 Real World Scenario

The Lincoln Street Office Building

Flagship International has just purchased a new building to house their growing staff. They consider themselves very lucky to have won the bid on the property located in a prime section of the downtown area. The building is a historic building and is in need of some repairs and upgrades to make it suitable for office space. Constructing the renovations will require special handling and care as outlined in the *Historical Society Building Revisions Guide*.

Alfredo Magginetti is the project manager assigned to the renovation project. Alfredo has already gathered the deliverables for this project. In so doing, he's discovered that he will not be able to manage all the work himself. He will need several subproject managers working on individual deliverables all reporting to him. Alfredo calls a meeting with the other project managers to deliver the WBS. Let's eavesdrop on the meeting.

"As you all know, we're planning to move into the Lincoln Street building by November 1st. There is quite a bit of work to do between now and then, and I'm enlisting each of you to manage a segment of this project. Take a look at this WBS."

A portion of the WBS Alfredo constructed looks like this:

Lincoln Street Building Renovation

1.0 Facility Safety

    1.1 Sprinkler System

    1.2 Elevators

    1.3 Emergency Evacuation Plans

2.0 Asbestos Abatement

    2.1 Inspection and Identification

    2.2 Plans for Removal

3.0 Office Space

    3.1 Building Floor Plans

    3.2 Plans for Office Space Allocation

    3.3 Plans for Break Room Facilities

    3.4 Plans for Employee Workout Room

Alfredo continues, "I'm going to manage the Facility Safety project. Adrian, I'd like you to take the Asbestos Abatement project, and Orlando, you're responsible for the Office Space project."

"Alfredo," Adrian says. "Asbestos abatement is going to take contractors and specialized equipment. We don't have staff to do these tasks."

"I understand. You'll need to take charge of securing the contractor to handle this. You're responsibility will be to manage the contractor and keep them on schedule," Alfredo answers.

> Orlando reminds Alfredo that he's missed a deliverable on the WBS. "Part of the Office Space project needs to include the network communications and telecommunications equipment rooms. I don't see that on here."
>
> "Good point, Orlando," Alfredo says. "The level three and four elements of this WBS are not complete. Each of you has been assigned to the subproject level, or level two. Your first assignment is to meet back here in 2 weeks with your WBS broken down to the activity level for each of your projects. And I'd like to see some ideas about the staff assignments you'd make at the activity level and how long you think these activities will take. We'll refine those after we meet next."

Defining Work Packages

As mentioned, the project manager is free to determine the number of levels in the WBS based on the complexity of the project. You need to include enough levels to accurately estimate project time and costs but not so many levels that it's difficult to distinguish between the activities. Regardless of the number of levels in a WBS, the lowest level in a WBS is called a *work package*.

Work packages are the tasks that can be easily assigned to one person, or team of people, with clear accountability and responsibility for completing the assignment. Assignments are easily made at the work package level; however, assignments can be made at any level in the WBS as in the Historical Building scenario. The work package level is where time estimates, cost estimates, and resource estimates are determined.

Including Activities

There is some controversy among project managers over whether activities should be listed on the WBS. There isn't a rule in the *Guide to the PMBOK* regarding this; it's up to the project manager to determine how far to break the deliverables down and whether to include activities. In practice, I often include activities on my work breakdown structure as it facilitates other Planning processes later on. In this case, the activities are the work package level. However, you should realize that large, complex projects will not likely list activities on the WBS. Large projects made up of a series of smaller subprojects will likely break the project down to a work package level. In this case, the work package is a collection of related tasks. The work packages can then be assigned to individual managers who will in turn break them down into activities during the Activity Definition process later in the Planning process.

This may seem self-evident, but work elements not shown on the WBS are not included in the project. The same holds true for the scope statement—if the deliverable isn't noted there, it isn't part of the project.

The *Guide to the PMBOK* mentions a WBS dictionary. This contains a description of the work package level and details regarding the activities within the work package. Information such as costs, budgets, resource assignments, and activity descriptions would be found in the WBS dictionary.

Noting Milestones

There's one last thing I should mention regarding the WBS. Some project managers choose to note milestones on their WBS. A milestone is a major accomplishment in a project. The completion of a deliverable could be a milestone, for example. Milestones are like checkpoints along the way in the project to help determine progress. In most cases, the higher levels of the WBS can be flagged as milestones. The higher levels indicate major accomplishments on the project. For example, Asbestos Abatement in the "Lincoln Street Building Renovation" example is a major accomplishment that could be considered a milestone. The project would not be considered successful or complete if this milestone was not met. Sometimes critical activities can be flagged as milestones as well. We'll talk more about milestones in a later chapter.

Scope Statement Updates

Many times, you'll find when you're creating the WBS that deliverables might need further definition or refining. As you work through the decomposition process, you might discover new deliverables that weren't thought of during the Scope Planning process. These changes should be reflected in the scope statement. Scope statement updates are the output of the Scope Definition process that allow you to do just that.

Communicating with Stakeholders

We've talked a good deal about documentation so far, and this topic will continue to come up throughout the remainder of the book. Documentation is only one side of the equation though—communication is the other.

You need to know who gets what information and when. The *Communications Planning* process determines the communication needs of the stakeholders. The *communications management plan*, which is the only output of this process, documents the types of information needs the stakeholders have, when the information should be distributed, and how the information will be delivered.

The type of information you will typically communicate includes status reports, status review meetings, scope statements and scope statement updates, project baseline information, performance measures, project acceptance, and so on. We'll cover all of these topics in the remaining chapters of this book. What's important to know now is that the information needs of the stakeholders should be determined early on in the Planning process so that as you develop more management plans, risk assessments, and so on, you know who gets what information and how it should be delivered.

The information that will be shared with stakeholders and the distribution methods are based on the needs of the stakeholders, the project complexity, and the organizational policies. Some communications may be informal—a chat by the watercooler, for instance—while other communications are written and a copy is filed with the project files.

The communications management plan documents how to collect, store, file, and make corrections or updates to previously published material. It also discusses the timing of the communication. The communications management plan describes how stakeholders can access project information between published dates as well. You might consider setting up an intranet site for your project and posting the appropriate project documentation there for the stakeholders to access anytime they wish.

We will discuss communication methods in more depth in Chapter 8.

Project Case Study: New Kitchen Heaven Retail Store

You're just finishing your phone conversation with Jill and see Dirk headed toward your office. The realtor has found a great location, and you and Jill have set up a time to take a tour later this week.

Dirk walks in, crosses his arms over his chest, and stands next to your desk with an "I'm here for answers" look. "Thought I'd drop by and see if you have signed a lease and gotten Jake started on that build-out yet."

"I just got off the phone with Jill," you reply. "We set up a time to tour a location the end of this week."

"What's been the holdup?" Dirk asks. "I thought we'd be ready to start the build-out about now."

"I've been working on the project plans."

"Project plans," Dirk interrupts. "We already have a plan. That charter thing you drew up last week spelled things out pretty clearly."

"The charter was the project kick-off, and I agree it did include all the deliverables. However, it's not detailed enough to start mapping out the project plans. I wrote a scope statement that further details the project deliverables and other project information. I've already forwarded that to you. I've also drawn up a work breakdown structure with all the deliverables shown in a tree structure that I'd like to go over with you before showing it to the project team."

"We aren't building trees, we're building a new store. I don't understand why you're wasting all this time planning. We all know what the goals are."

"Dirk," you reply. "If we put the right amount of effort and time into the planning stage, the execution stage should go pretty smoothly. Planning is probably one of the most important things we can do on this project. If we don't plan correctly, we might miss something very important that could delay the store opening. That date is pretty firm, I thought."

"Yes the date is firm. But I don't see how we could miss anything. You and I have met several times, and I know you've met with Jill and Jake. They're the other key players on this."

"You're right, I have met with Jill and Jake. And that's a perfect example of why we need to plan. When I met with Jill, she told me how all the store's data is communicated via a satellite network connection on a nightly basis. That means we need to involve the IT group." You glance down at your notes. "Ricardo Ramirez heads up IT. I spoke with him last week about his deliverables, and I've included his group as a subproject on the work breakdown structure."

"Oh," Dirk replies. "I forgot about IT. You're right, that's an important part of the project, and we can't leave them out. Okay, I'm beginning to see why you're taking planning seriously. Let's have a look at this work breakdown structure."

You hand Dirk a copy of the WBS. A partial version is shown here.

Project Case Study Checklist

Interviewed project stakeholders and business process owners for further definition of deliverables

Created project scope statement, which includes:

- Project justification—the business need.

- Project product—the product description.

- Project deliverables—clear and concise deliverables.

- Project objectives—including constraints. Objectives are specific, measurable, and timely.

Decomposed deliverables into a WBS

WBS includes:

- Level one is the project.

- Level two is subprojects or deliverables.

- Level three is deliverables or activities.

- Remaining levels are activities.

- Last level of WBS is the work package level where time and cost estimates can be defined in the next process.

Summary

This chapter started us on the road to project Planning via the Scope Planning process and the Scope Definition process. Scope Planning is where we produced the scope statement, which describes the project goals, deliverables, and requirements. The scope statement forms the baseline we'll use to weigh future project decisions. The scope statement must contain an exhaustive list of project deliverables that will be used in future Planning processes. Measurement criteria agreed upon by the stakeholders and project manager are associated with these deliverables and documented in the scope statement to track project progress.

The deliverables, requirements, and measurement criteria should be spelled out clearly and concisely in the scope statement to avoid any misunderstandings later in the project. Formal acceptance of the scope statement is required by the stakeholders and project manager. Acceptance is usually accompanied by sign-offs on the document indicating that it has been read and the signing party agrees with the deliverables and requirements of the project.

The purpose of the scope management plan is to analyze the reliability and stability of the project scope. The scope management plan documents the process to manage project scope and changes to the scope.

The Scope Definition process is concerned with decomposition and the production of a work breakdown structure. Decomposition is breaking down deliverables into manageable pieces of work, which might be further broken down into activities.

A work breakdown structure (WBS) is a deliverables-oriented group of project essentials. The highest levels of the WBS are described using nouns, and the lowest levels are described with verbs. Each element in the WBS has its own set of objectives and deliverables that must be met in order to fulfill the deliverables of the next highest level, and ultimately the project itself. In this way, the WBS validates the completeness of the work.

The lowest level of the WBS is known as work packages. This breakdown allows the project manager to determine cost estimates, time estimates, resource assignments, and quality controls.

Exam Essentials

Be able to name the Scope Planning outputs. The scope statement, supporting detail, and scope management plan.

Understand the purpose of the scope statement. The scope statement serves as a baseline for future project decisions. The project objectives and deliverables and their quantifiable measurements are documented in the scope statement and are used by the project manager and the stakeholders to determine if the project was completed successfully.

Be able to name the Scope Definition tools and techniques and outputs. The tools and techniques from Scope Definition are decomposition and WBS templates. Decomposition is breaking the deliverables down into workable, manageable units of work. The outputs are the work breakdown structure and scope statement updates.

Be able to describe the purpose of the scope management plan. The scope management plan describes how scope changes will be handled during the project and how to request changes. It details how likely it is that scope changes will occur, their frequency, and their impact.

Be able to define a WBS and its components. The WBS is a deliverables-oriented hierarchy. It uses the deliverables from the scope statement or similar documents and decomposes them into logical, manageable units of work. Level one is the project level, level two is the major deliverable level or subproject level, and so on. The lowest level of any WBS is called a work package.

Be able to describe the purpose of the communications management plan. The communications management plan determines the communication needs of the stakeholders. It documents what information will be distributed, how it will be distributed, to whom, and the timing of the distribution. It also documents how to collect, store, file, and make corrections to previously published material.

Key Terms

Before you take the exam, be certain you are familiar with the following terms:

code of accounts	Scope Planning
communications management plan	scope statement
Communications Planning	supporting detail
decomposition	work breakdown structure (WBS)
Scope Definition	work package
scope management plan	

Review Questions

1. You are a project manager for Laredo Pioneer's Traveling Rodeo Show. You're heading up a project to promote a new line of souvenirs to be sold at the shows. You need to gather the inputs to write the scope statement. You gather which of the following?

    A. Project charter, product description, assumptions, and constraints

    B. Project charter, product analysis, and cost benefit analysis

    C. Product description, product analysis, and project charter

    D. Product description, assumptions, constraints, and product analysis

2. You are a project manager for Laredo Pioneer's Traveling Rodeo Show. You're heading up a project to promote a new line of souvenirs to be sold at the shows. You're ready to write the scope statement, and you know it should contain which of the following?

    A. Project justification, benefit/cost analysis, project deliverables, and product analysis

    B. Product analysis, project product, and project deliverables

    C. Project justification, project product, project deliverables, and project objectives

    D. Product analysis, project deliverables, benefit/cost analysis, and project objectives

3. Which of the following is true regarding the scope statement?

    A. It describes how to make changes to project scope.

    B. It describes project deliverables and serves as a baseline for future project decisions.

    C. It assesses the stability of the project scope and is a baseline for future project decisions.

    D. It assesses the reliability of the project scope and describes the frequency of changes and their impacts.

4. You are a project manager for an agricultural supply company. You have just completed and obtained sign-off on the scope statement for your new Natural Bug Busters project. A key stakeholder has informed you that a deliverable is missing from the scope statement. This deliverable is a critical success factor. You should do which of the following?

   A. Inform the stakeholder that work not stated in the scope statement is excluded from the project.

   B. Modify the scope statement to reflect the new deliverable.

   C. Inform the stakeholder that this deliverable can be included in the next project since sign-off has already been obtained.

   D. Modify the scope statement after an approved change request has been received from the stakeholder.

5. You are a project manager responsible for the construction of a new office complex. You are taking over for a project manager who recently left the company. The prior project manager completed the project charter and the scope statement for this project. In your interviews with some key stakeholders, you conclude that the scope statement was poorly constructed. You know all of the following are true except:

   A. It will be difficult to assess future project decisions from this scope statement.

   B. It will be difficult to decompose the deliverables from this scope statement.

   C. It will be difficult to assess cost and time estimates from this scope statement.

   D. It will be difficult to create an accurate WBS from this scope statement.

6. You are a project manager responsible for the construction of a new office complex. You are taking over for a project manager who recently left the company. The prior project manager completed the scope statement and scope management plan for this project. In your interviews with some key stakeholders, you conclude which of the following?

   A. They understand that the scope statement assesses the stability of the project scope and outlines how to incorporate scope changes into the project.

   B. They understand that the scope management plan assesses the stability of the project scope and outlines how to incorporate scope changes into the project.

   C. They understand that the scope management plan is deliverables oriented and cost estimates can be easily derived from it.

   D. They understand that the scope statement is deliverables oriented and cost estimates can be easily derived from it.

7. All of the following are true about decomposition except:

   A. It's an output of the Scope Definition process.

   B. It's a tool and technique of the Scope Definition process.

   C. It is used to create a WBS.

   D. It subdivides the major deliverables into smaller components.

8. Your company has asked you to be the project manager for the product introduction of their new DeskTop Rock media system. You recently published a document that establishes the scope baseline. Which of the following is true?

   A. This is the scope statement, which is an output of the Scope Planning process.

   B. This is the scope statement, which is an output of the Scope Definition process.

   C. This is the scope statement, which is a tool and technique of the Scope Definition process.

   D. This is the scope management plan, which is an output of the Scope Definition process.

9. What are the outputs of the Scope Planning process?

   A. Product analysis, scope statement, and scope management plan

   B. Scope statement, scope management plan, and WBS

   C. Scope statement, supporting detail, and WBS

   D. Scope statement, supporting detail, and scope management plan

10. Your company has asked you to be the project manager for the product introduction of their new DeskTop Rock media system. You recently published the scope statement and the supporting detail. The supporting detail contains all of the following except:

   A. Constraints

   B. Other project information not noted in the scope statement

   C. Code of accounts

   D. Assumptions

11. You are a project manager for Giraffe Enterprises. You've recently taken over for a project manager who lied about his PMI certification and was subsequently fired. Unfortunately, he did a poor job of Scope Definition. You know if you don't correct this, one of the following could happen:

   A. The stakeholders will require overtime from the project team to keep the project on schedule.

   B. The WBS will adversely affect the deliverable breakdowns, and costs will increase.

   C. The scope management plan will require changes.

   D. The project costs could increase, there might be rework, and schedule delays may result.

12. Scope definition is necessary for all of the following reasons except:

    A. To subdivide project deliverables into smaller components

    B. To assess the stability of the project scope

    C. To facilitate time and cost estimates

    D. To facilitate responsibility and assignment

13. You are working on a project that is similar in scope to a project performed last year by your company. You might consider which of the following?

    A. Using the previous project's alternatives identification as a template

    B. Reusing the previous project's benefit/cost analysis as justification for this project

    C. Using the previous project's WBS as a template

    D. Reusing the previous project's product description when writing the scope statement

14. Your company, Kick That Ball Sports, has appointed you project manager for their new Cricket product line introduction. This is a national effort, and all the retail stores across the country need to have the new products on the shelves before the media advertising blitz begins. The product line involves three new products, some with multiple deliverables. You are ready to create the WBS. Which of the following is true?

    A. The WBS should include the three new products and the advertising campaign as level two deliverables.

    B. The WBS should include the three new products as level two deliverables.

    C. The WBS should include the three new products as level two deliverables and the advertising campaign as a level three deliverable.

    D. The WBS should include the three new products and the advertising campaign as level three deliverables.

15. Your company, Kick That Ball Sports, has appointed you project manager for their new Cricket product line introduction. This is a national effort, and all the retail stores across the country need to have the new products on the shelves before the media advertising blitz begins. The product line involves three new products, some with multiple deliverables. The Scope Definition process is now complete. Which of the following is true?

A. The WBS template, an output of the Scope Definition process, was used from the previous project to create the WBS for this project. The WBS encompasses the major deliverables for the project.

B. The WBS template from the previous project, an output from the Scope Planning process, was used to create the WBS for this project. The WBS encompasses the major deliverables for the project.

C. The WBS, an output of the Scope Planning process, has been created, and it encompasses the full scope of work for the project.

D. The WBS, an output of the Scope Definition process, has been created, and it encompasses the full scope of work for the project.

16. All of the following are true regarding the WBS except:

A. It is a deliverables-oriented grouping of project deliverables and elements.

B. It defines and organizes the work of the project in a hierarchical form.

C. It provides a framework for the work of the project, and work not shown on the WBS is not included in the project.

D. It defines all the deliverables of the project, but the activities level should not be listed on the WBS.

17. You are the project manager for Lucky Stars nightclubs. They specialize in live country and western band performances. Your newest project is in the Planning process. You've published the scope statement and scope management plan. The document that describes who will receive copies of this information as well as future project information, how it should be distributed, and how the information should be stored and filed is which of the following?

    A. Scope management plan

    B. Communications management plan

    C. Information distribution plan

    D. Project charter

18. You are the project manager for Lucky Stars nightclubs. They specialize in live country and western band performances. Your newest project is in the Planning process. You are working on the WBS. The finance manager has given you a numbering system to assign to the WBS. Which of the following is true?

    A. The numbering system is a unique identifier known as the code of accounts, which is used to track the costs of the WBS elements.

    B. The numbering system is a unique identifier known as the WBS dictionary, which is used to track the descriptions of individual work elements.

    C. The numbering system is a unique identifier known as the code of accounts, which is used to track time and resource assignments for individual work elements.

    D. The numbering system is a unique identifier known as the WBS dictionary, which is used to assign quality control codes to the individual work elements.

19. You've constructed the WBS for your recent project. Level two assignments have been made, and you've requested that the subproject managers report back to you in 3 weeks with each of their individual WBSs constructed. All of the following are true except:

A. The work package level facilitates resource assignments.

B. The work package level is the lowest level in the WBS.

C. The work package level defines the agreed-upon deliverables.

D. The work package level facilitates cost and time estimates.

20. The grouping of project elements by deliverables is known as what?

A. The code of accounts

B. The work package

C. The work breakdown structure

D. The work breakdown dictionary

Answers to Review Questions

1. A. The inputs of the Scope Planning process are product description, project charter, constraints, and assumptions.

2. C. The scope statement includes all of the following: project justification, project product, project deliverables, and project objectives according to the *Guide to the PMBOK*.

3. B. The scope statement describes the project deliverables, requirements, and objectives. It serves as a baseline for future project decisions.

4. D. The scope statement will change throughout the project as change requests are received and approved. Project managers must be certain to seek out all deliverables before publishing the scope statement to prevent situations like this.

5. C. Cost estimates, time estimates, and quality controls are derived from the WBS in the Scope Definition process, not from the scope statement, which is an output of the Scope Planning process.

6. B. The scope management plan assesses the stability and reliability of the project scope and addresses how frequently scope changes will occur and what their impacts might be. The scope management plan outlines the method for requesting changes to the project scope and for incorporating those changes into the project.

7. A. Decomposition subdivides the major deliverables into smaller components. It is a tool and technique of Scope Definition, along with WBS templates, and this process is used to create a WBS.

8. A. The scope statement establishes the baseline for the project. The scope statement is an output of the Scope Planning process.

9. D. The outputs of the Scope Planning process are the scope statement, supporting detail, and the scope management plan.

10. C. The code of accounts is assigned to the elements in the WBS.

11. D. Selection A might seem like a correct answer, but selection D is a more correct answer. We don't have enough information to determine if stakeholders will require overtime. We do know that poor Scope Definition leads to cost increases, rework, schedule delays, and poor morale.

12. B. The scope management plan assesses the stability of the project scope.

13. C. WBSs from previous projects can be used as templates on projects that are producing similar products or services. Some companies write WBS templates to be used for projects of similar scope.

14. A. Level one of the WBS is the project itself. There are three new products plus the advertising campaign. Each of these is a subproject under level one.

15. D. The WBS details the entire scope of the project and includes all deliverables. It is an output of the Scope Definition process.

16. D. It is up to the project manager to determine how many levels to detail on the WBS. Small projects can easily show activities on the WBS.

17. B. The communications management plan documents what information will be distributed, how it will be distributed, to whom, and the timing of the distribution. It also documents how to collect, store, file, and make corrections to previously published material.

18. A. Each element in the WBS is assigned a unique identifier. These are collectively known as the code of accounts. Typically, these codes are associated with a corporate chart of accounts and are used to track the costs of the individual work elements in the WBS.

19. C. The work package level is the lowest level in the WBS and facilitates resource assignment and cost and time estimates. The agreed-upon deliverables in selection C would be higher levels in the WBS.

20. C. The WBS is the deliverables-oriented hierarchy of project work.

Chapter

5

Resource Planning and Estimating

PMP EXAM CONTENT FROM THE PROJECT PLANNING PERFORMANCE DOMAIN COVERED IN THIS CHAPTER:

- ✓ 3. Develop Resource Management Plan.
- ✓ 4. Refine Time and Cost Estimates.

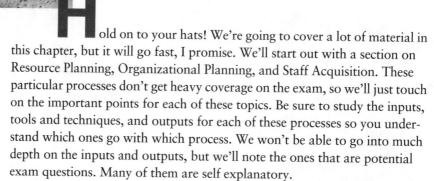

old on to your hats! We're going to cover a lot of material in this chapter, but it will go fast, I promise. We'll start out with a section on Resource Planning, Organizational Planning, and Staff Acquisition. These particular processes don't get heavy coverage on the exam, so we'll just touch on the important points for each of these topics. Be sure to study the inputs, tools and techniques, and outputs for each of these processes so you understand which ones go with which process. We won't be able to go into much depth on the inputs and outputs, but we'll note the ones that are potential exam questions. Many of them are self explanatory.

We'll spend the majority of our time in this chapter looking at the time and cost estimating techniques. You'll find several exam questions on these areas, so spend some time understanding and memorizing the tools and techniques in all of these processes.

Developing a Resource Management Plan

All projects require resources, from the smallest to the largest. *Resources* in this case does not mean just people; it means all the physical resources required to complete the project. This includes people, equipment, supplies, materials, software, hardware—and the list goes on depending on the project you're working on. *Resource Planning* is the process of determining what physical resources are needed, and in what quantity, to perform project activities.

Developing a resource management plan encompasses several processes including Resource Planning, Organizational Planning, Staff Acquisition, Solicitation Planning, and Procurement Planning. The combined outputs from these processes will comprise your resource management plan. We'll cover Solicitation Planning and Procurement Planning in the next chapter.

Resource Inputs

The Resource Planning process has several inputs you are already familiar with, one of which is the WBS. Three inputs are new to this process; they are the resource pool description, organizational policies, and activity duration estimates.

The resource pool description lists the types of resources that might be needed for the project. For example, if you are working on a project that requires the use of specialized equipment during the course of the project, the resource pool description should contain the details concerning this resource, and the specific knowledge or skills needed to use the equipment. The same is true for human resources. Suppose you need an expert in thermodynamics in one or several phases of your project. The resource pool description should list this specific resource requirement. List all the materials, equipment, skills, or special talents you might need during any part of your project in this document.

Organizational policies regarding materials purchases, hiring processes, leases, vendor relationships, and so on should be taken into consideration when performing Resource Planning. Don't confuse this input with the Organizational Planning process, which we'll discuss in the next section. Organizational policies in this case are merely how the company handles obtaining supplies and resources. Are there policies and procedures in place that should be followed? If so, you should take note of the procedures and adhere to them when ordering supplies, hiring staff, and so on.

Activity duration estimates are an estimate of the number of work periods needed to complete the activities listed on the WBS. They are an output of the Activity Duration Estimating process. We'll cover this process in more detail a little later in this chapter.

Documenting Resource Requirements

The resource pool description and organizational policies, along with the other inputs and tools and techniques in this process, will be used to produce the resource requirements output. The resource requirements document is a detailed description of the kinds of resources needed for the project and the quantity needed of each resource. Resource needs and resource quantity should be listed for each element in the WBS.

Staffing requirements are a subset of resource requirements. Remember that the resource requirements document details for all the resources required for the project, not just staffing resources. The staffing requirements list should identify the kinds of skills required and the individuals or groups who might provide these skills to the project. The staffing requirements list should also document the time frames during the project when these skills will be needed. For example, the thermodynamics expert might be needed only during the design phase, so be certain to note where and when on the WBS this expert is needed.

A strange thing happens here. Resource requirements become an input to other Planning processes. But so do staffing requirements, which are a subset of resource requirements. This is the only process where an output is split into two pieces and each piece becomes an input to other processes.

Developing an Organizational Plan

The Organizational Planning process focuses on the human resources aspect of project planning. Its purpose is to document the roles and responsibilities of individuals or groups for various project elements and then document the reporting relationships for each. Communications Planning goes hand in hand with Organizational Planning as the organizational structure will affect the way communications are carried out among project participants and the project interfaces.

Organizational Planning has three inputs: project interfaces, staffing requirements, and constraints. We covered staffing requirements in the last section and don't need to add anything here. Constraints were covered in previous chapters, but there is some new information to introduce after we define project interfaces.

Project Interfaces

The *Guide to the PMBOK* identifies three categories of project interfaces: organizational interfaces, technical interfaces, and interpersonal interfaces. Each of these defines the type of reporting relationships that exist among the different categories.

Organizational interfaces deal with the types of reporting relationships that exist within an organization's structure be it functional, matrix, or projectized. The reporting relationships in the organization might be formal or informal, and as the project manager, you should take these into consideration when outlining the project plan.

The same is true for *technical interfaces*, which deal with the reporting relationships that exist within the technical areas of an organization. You should consider the technical interfaces both within the project itself and between the project process groups during hand-off.

Interpersonal interfaces deal with the relationships that exist among project team members and among other project participants. All projects fall into the interpersonal interfaces and organizational interfaces categories. Whether technical interfaces affect the project depends on the project itself.

The project manager should be aware of these project interfaces and, for purposes of the exam, remember that organizational interfaces are the most difficult project interfaces to deal with.

Constraints

This topic seems to come up a lot, so you probably remember that constraints are things that limit the options available to the project team. These typically involve time, costs, or quality. However, there are a few new constraints regarding project team organizations highlighted in the *Guide to the PMBOK* that you should know.

Organizational Structures

Organizational structures can be a constraint. For example, a strong matrix structure provides the project manager with much more authority and power than the weak matrix structure.

Collective Bargaining Agreements

Collective bargaining agreements with unions and contractual obligations with other organized employee associations or groups may require specialized reporting relationships and are considered constraints.

Team Preferences

Preferences of the project management team might be a constraint. Success with certain organizational structures in the past might lead team members to prefer one type of team or organizational structure over another.

Staffing Assignments

The organization of the project team will likely be influenced by the skills and knowledge of the project team members who will serve on the team. This constraint is called *expected staff assignments*.

The outputs of this process are concerned with identifying resources, documenting their responsibilities, and determining when and how they come on and off the project. You'll need to consider the project interfaces and constraints we talked about when determining project roles and reporting relationships. As an example, collective bargaining agreements might require you to set up your reporting relationships a specific way, and individual assignments will be made based on the skills of the project team members.

Assigning Resources

The tools and techniques of Organizational Planning are used to help produce the following outputs: roles and responsibility assignment, staffing management plan, organization chart, and supporting detail. We'll look at each of these next.

Roles and Responsibility Assignment

Project roles in this context refer to the project manager, project team members, and stakeholders. The roles and responsibilities for this process are tied to the project scope and WBS. Many times a project manager will use a *Responsibility Assignment Matrix (RAM)* to graphically display this information. A RAM is usually depicted as a chart with resource names listed in each row (for example, programmers, testers, trainers, etc.) and WBS elements as the columns with indicators in the intersections where the resources are needed. However, the level of detail is up to you. One RAM might be developed for the level two WBS elements on a complex project with more RAMs subsequently produced for the additional WBS levels. Or a RAM might be constructed with level three elements only. Table 5.1 shows a sample RAM for a software development team.

TABLE 5.1 Sample RAM

	Activity A	Activity B	Activity C
Programmers	X	X	
Testers	X	X	
Trainers		X	X

Staffing Management Plan

This plan documents how and when people resources are introduced to the project and later released. Again, the level and amount of detail contained in this plan are up to you. Note that many staffing management plans make use of a *resource histogram*. This is usually drawn in chart form with project time along the horizontal axis and hours needed along the vertical axis. The example histogram below shows the hours needed for an asphalt crew on a construction project.

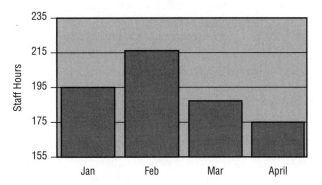

Resource Histogram for Asphalt Crew

Organization Chart

The organization chart is just like the org charts you've seen dozens of times before. It shows the reporting relationships of the project members. An *organizational breakdown structure (OBS)* relates WBS elements, usually the work package level for very large projects, to the organizational unit that's responsible for completing the work.

Supporting Detail

Information that further describes the organization and impacts to the organizational units due to work requests is considered supporting detail. Job descriptions and training needs are other examples of information gathered for this output.

This process ensures roles and responsibilities are clearly outlined and that reporting structures are documented and communicated to all project participants. This process is completed early on in project Planning and should be reviewed regularly throughout the project to assure accuracy and document changes that are needed as project circumstances change.

Acquiring Staff

The *Staff Acquisition* process involves attaining and assigning human resources to the project. Project staff may come from inside the company or outside the company in the form of full-time employees hired specifically for the project, or as contract help. In any case, it's your job as project manager to ensure that resources are available and skilled in the project activities they're assigned to.

The Staff Acquisition process inputs are as follows: the staffing management plan that was produced as an output to Organizational Planning, staffing pool description, and recruitment practices. Recruitment practices are a matter of making certain you consult any organizational procedures or policies currently in place when hiring staff.

Staffing Pool Description

Some project activities may require special skills or knowledge in order to be completed. The staffing pool description involves taking this information into account as well as personal interests, characteristics, and availability of potential team members before making assignments. For example, you will want to consider previous experience of the staff member you're thinking of assigning to a specific activity. Have they performed this function before? Do they have the experience necessary for the level of complexity this project activity calls for?

Personal interests and personal characteristics play a big role as well. If the person you're thinking of just isn't interested in the project, they aren't likely to perform at their best. If you can, think about assigning someone else in a case like this. Unfortunately, some people just don't play well with others. When you're assigning staff, if at all possible, don't put the only two people in the whole company who can't get along together on the same project. If the staff member you need has a skill no one else has or they can perform a function like no one else can, you might not have a choice. In this case, you'll have to employ other techniques to keep the team cohesive and working well together despite the not-so-friendly characteristics of the vital team member.

One final consideration: Check on the availability of key team members. If the team member you must have for the activity scheduled in February is on her honeymoon, you probably aren't going to win the toss.

Negotiating for Team Members

Negotiation, preassignment, and procurement are tools and techniques of the Staff Acquisition process. As the project manager, you will use the negotiation technique quite a lot. You'll have to negotiate with functional managers and other organizational department managers for resources for your project and for the timing of those resources.

Preassignment happens when the project is put out for bid and specific team members are promised as part of the proposal, or when internal project team members are promised and assigned as a condition of the project. This should be spelled out in the project charter in this case. Procurement is the process of hiring individuals or teams of people for certain project activities either as full-time employees or as contract help during the course of the project or project phase.

Assigning Project Staff

After determining the staffing pool description, reviewing recruitment practices, and negotiating for staff, project team members are assigned to project activities, and a project team directory is published listing the names of all project team members and stakeholders. The resulting outputs of the Staff Acquisition process are as follows: assignment of project staff and project team directory.

Now that we know what the project activities are and what resources are needed to perform these activities, we'll need to perform time and cost estimates for these activities. We're working toward the development of the project schedule where we determine actual start and stop dates for activities, but we have several processes to complete before we get there.

 Real World Scenario

The Only Candidate

"Hey, did you hear?" your friend Story asks. "Roger has been assigned to the project team."

"Over my dead body," you reply as you push away from your computer screen. You head straight for the project manager's office and don't wait for a response from Story.

Ann seats the phone into the cradle just as you walk through the door. Fortunately for you, Ann's door is always open and she welcomes drop-ins.

"Seems like something is on your mind," Ann says. "What can I help with?"

"Story just told me that Roger has been assigned to the project team. I can't work with Roger. He's arrogant and doesn't respect anyone's work but his own. He belittles me in front of others, and I don't deserve that. I write good code, and I don't need Roger looking over my shoulder. I want to be on this team, but not if Roger is part of it."

Ann thinks for a minute and replies, "I want you to have the opportunity to work on this project; it's a great opportunity for you. But there isn't anyone else who can work on the analysis phase of this project except Roger. He's the only one left who has a solid understanding of the mainframe legacy code. Unfortunately, those old programs were never documented well, and they've evolved over the years into programs on top of programs. Without Roger's expertise of the existing system, we'd blow the budget and time estimates already established for this project. What would you say to a meeting with you and Roger and me to talk about these issues and see if we can't work this out?"

Time Estimating Techniques

Estimating the duration of project activities involves identifying the activities and sequencing them in the correct order. Then, time estimates are assigned as baseline measurements and used to track project activities to ensure the project is completed on time.

Keep in mind that for purposes of the exam, Activity Definition, Activity Sequencing, Activity Duration Estimating, and Schedule Development are separate processes each with inputs, tools and techniques, and outputs. In practice, especially for small- to medium-sized projects, these processes are condensed into one function or step. We'll take a look at each of the activity-related processes now, and we'll cover Schedule Development in Chapter 7.

Understanding the Activity Definition Process

The *Activity Definition* process is a further breakdown of the work package elements of the WBS. This step is necessary when you are working with large projects where the original WBS goes to only level two or level three elements. At this point, level two or three is then assigned to subproject managers to further break down and identify individual activities. In practice, many times Activity Definition might be accomplished during the construction of the WBS, and the activities themselves are the work package level.

This process produces an output called an *activity list,* which is an extension of the WBS. The activity list should contain all the activities of the project with a description of each activity so that team members understand what the work is and how it is to be completed. Once the activity list is completed, the WBS might need to be updated. This is the second output in this process.

The exam may have a question or two regarding the activity list. All of the other inputs and tools and techniques in Activity Definition have been covered in previous chapters.

Understanding the Activity Sequencing Process

We've identified the activities and now need to sequence them in a logical order and find out if dependencies exist among the activities. Here's a classic example. Let's say you're going to paint your house, but unfortunately, it's fallen into a little disrepair. The old paint is peeling and chipping and will need to be scraped before a coat of primer can be sprayed on the house. After the primer dries, then the painting can commence. In this example, the primer activity depends on the scraping. You can't—okay, *you shouldn't*— prime the house before scraping off the peeling paint. The painting activity depends on the primer activity in the same way. You really shouldn't start painting until the primer has dried.

During *Activity Sequencing*, you will use a host of inputs and tools and techniques to produce the final outputs, a project network diagram, and activity list updates. We're going to look at three of the inputs, and we'll examine all of the tools and techniques needed for this process. The remaining inputs have been discussed previously.

Dependencies

Three of the inputs to Activity Sequencing are as follows: mandatory dependencies, discretionary dependencies, and external dependencies. Dependencies are just like we described in the house-painting example. But as you've probably guessed, the *Guide to the PMBOK* defines dependencies differently depending on their characteristics:

Mandatory Dependencies

Mandatory dependencies, also known as hard logic or hard dependencies, are defined by the type of work being performed. The scraping, primer, painting sequences are examples of mandatory dependencies. The nature of the work itself dictates the order the activities should be performed in.

Discretionary Dependencies

Discretionary dependencies are delineated by the project management team. Discretionary dependencies are also known as *preferred logic*, *soft logic*, or *preferential logic*. These are usually process or procedure driven, or "best practices" techniques based on past experience. For example, past experience on house-painting projects has shown that all trim work should be hand painted while the bulk of the main painting work should be done with a sprayer.

External Dependencies

External dependencies are, well, external to the project. The weather forecast might be an external dependency in the painting example because you wouldn't want to start painting prior to a rain storm.

Once we've identified the dependencies and assembled all the other inputs for the Activity Sequencing process, we'll take this information and produce a diagram, or schematic display, of the project activities. The project network diagram shows the dependencies, or logical relationships, that exist among the activities. We can use one of several tools and techniques to produce this output. We'll examine each in detail below.

Precedence Diagramming Method (PDM)

The *precedence diagramming method (PDM)* is what most project management software programs use today. Precedence diagrams connect activities with arrows that show dependencies between the activities. This method is also called *activity on node (AON)*.

The activity information is written on the nodes with arrows connecting the nodes, or dependent activities. The nodes are shown as rectangles, and you are free to put as much information about the activity on the node as you'd like. The minimum information that should be displayed on the node is the activity name. Sometimes the nodes are displayed with activity name, activity number, start and stop dates, due dates, slack time, and so on. (We'll cover slack time in a later chapter.) For the exam, remember that the PDM uses only one time estimate to determine duration.

The example below shows a PDM, or AON, of the house-painting example.

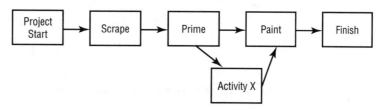

The PDM is further defined by four types of *logical relationships. The Guide to the PMBOK* calls these *dependencies* or *precedence relationships.* You may already be familiar with these if you've used Microsoft Project, or some other similar project management software program. The four dependencies are as follows:

Finish to start (FS)   This is the most frequently used logical relationship. This relationship says that the independent, or *from* activity, must finish before the dependent, or *to* activity, can start.

Start to finish (SF)   The start to finish relationship says that the independent activity must start before the dependent activity can finish. This logical relationship is seldom used.

Finish to finish (FF)   This relationship says that the independent activity must finish before the dependent activity finishes.

Start to start (SS):   I think you're getting the hang of this. This relationship says that the independent activity must start before the dependent activity can start.

Keep these logical relationships in mind when constructing your project network diagram. Remember that finish to start is the most commonly used logical relationship.

Arrow Diagramming Method (ADM)

The *arrow diagramming method (ADM)* is visually the opposite of the PDM. The arrow diagramming method places activities on the arrows, which are connected to dependent activities with nodes. This method is also called *activity on arrow (AOA).* This method is seldom used today. For the record, AOA allows for more than one time estimate to determine duration. The example below shows the AOA method applied to our house-painting example.

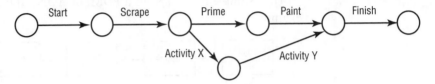

Conditional Diagramming Methods

The only thing you need to know regarding conditional diagramming methods, such as the Graphical Evaluation and Review Technique (GERT) and System Dynamics models, is that they allow for nonsequential activities such as loops and conditional branches. PDM and ADM do not allow loops or conditional branches. We will cover GERT in more depth in a later chapter.

Network Templates

These templates are like the templates we've talked about in other processes. Perhaps the project you're working on is similar to a project that's been completed in the past. You can use a previous project network diagram as a template for the current project.

I recommend you memorize the graphic below to help remember the tools and techniques of the Activity Sequencing process and their characteristics for the exam. This may look a little strange, but I think it will work for you now that you understand what each of these diagramming methods is about. This is information you need to know for the exam. If this graphic isn't useful for you, come up with your own mnemonic or sample that will help you remember which of these is which. Don't say I didn't warn you.

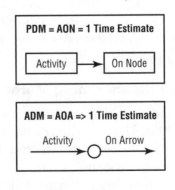

The outputs of Activity Sequencing are the project network diagram and activity list updates. We've just spent a good deal of time describing the different types of project network diagrams you can construct using PDM or ADM techniques. Keep in mind that the construction of these network diagrams might bring activities to light that you missed when defining your activity list, or it might make you break an activity down into two activities in places where you thought one activity might work. If this is the case, you will produce activity list updates based on this new information.

We're sailing right along. One more activity process remains, and then we've completed the time estimating segment of this chapter.

Estimating Activity Durations

The *Activity Duration Estimating* process takes the activities defined in the WBS and activity list and assesses the number of work periods needed to complete these activities. Work periods are usually expressed in hours or days. However, larger projects might express duration in weeks or months.

Keep in mind that when you're estimating activity duration, you are estimating the length of time the activity will take to complete, including any elapsed time needed from the beginning to the ending of the activity. For example, let's look at the house-painting project. We estimate that it will take three days, including drying time, to prime the house. Now, let's say priming is scheduled to begin on Saturday, but our crew doesn't work on Sunday. The activity duration in this case is four days, which includes the three days to prime and dry plus the Sunday the crew doesn't work. Most project management software programs will handle this kind of situation automatically.

Activity Duration Estimating is performed using the following tools and techniques.

Expert Judgment

Activities are most accurately estimated by the staff members who will perform the activities. In this case, expert judgment is used by team members because of their experience with similar activities in the past. You should be careful with these estimates, though, as they are subject to bias and aren't based on any scientific means. It's good practice to combine expert judgment with historical information and use as many experts as you can.

Analogous Estimating

Analogous estimating, also called *top-down estimating*, is a form of expert judgment. With this technique, you will use the actual duration of a similar activity completed on a previous project to determine the duration of the current activity—provided the information was documented and stored with the project information on the previous project. This technique is most useful when the previous activities you're comparing are truly similar to the activity you're estimating and don't just appear to be similar. And you want the folks who are working on the estimate to have experience with these activities.

Top-down estimating techniques are also used to estimate total project duration. The best way to think about top-down techniques is to look at the estimate as a whole. Think about being on a mountaintop where you can see the whole picture as one rather than all the individual items that make up the picture. For instance, let's go back to our house-painting example. You would compare a previous house-painting project to the current house-painting project where the houses are of similar size and the paint you're using is the same quality. The first house-painting project can be used to estimate the project duration for the second house-painting project because of the similarities in the project.

Top-down techniques are useful when you're early on in the project Planning process and are only just beginning to flesh out all the details of the project. Sometimes during the project selection process, the selection committee may want an idea of the project's duration. You can derive a project estimate at this stage by using top-down techniques.

Quantitatively Based Durations

The best way to describe the meaning of quantitatively based durations is with an example. Suppose you are working on a company-wide network upgrade project. This requires you to run new cable to the switches on every floor in the building. Quantitatively based durations can be used to determine activity duration estimates by taking a known element—in this case, the amount of cable needed—and multiplying it by the amount of time it takes to install a unit of cable to come up with an estimate. In other words, suppose we have 10,000 meters of new cable to run. We know from past experience it takes 1 hour to install 100 meters. Using this measurement, we can make a quantitatively based estimate for this activity of 100 hours to run the new cable. Therefore, the cable activity duration estimate is 100 hours.

Reserve Time (Contingency)

Reserve time, also called *buffer* or *contingency time* in the *Guide to the PMBOK*, means adding a portion of time to the activity to account for schedule risk. You might choose to add a percentage of time or a set number of work periods to the activity or the overall schedule. For example, we know it will take 100 hours to run new cable based on the qualitative estimate we came up with earlier. We also know that sometimes we hit problem areas when running the cable. To make sure we don't impact the project schedule, we build in a reserve time of 10 percent of our original estimate to account for the problems we might encounter. This brings our activity duration estimate to 110 hours for this activity.

 Real World Scenario

Desert State University (DSU)

DSU has hired a contract agency to create their new registration website. The website will allow students in good academic standing to register for classes over the Internet. You have been appointed the project manager for the DSU side of this project. You'll be working with Henry Lu from Web Sites International to complete this project.

Henry has given you an activity list and asked for time estimates that he can plug into the project plan.

Your first stop is Jim Mahoney's desk. He's the expert on the mainframe registration system and will be writing the interface programs to accept registration data from the new website. Jim will also create the download that the Internet program will use to verify students' academic standing. Jim has created other programs just like this in the past. His expertise and judgment are very reliable.

The next stop is Gloria Stillwater. She's the new team leader over the testing group. Gloria has been with DSU for only one month. Since she has no experience working with DSU data and staff members, she tells you she'll get back to you within a week with estimates for the testing activities. She plans to read through the project binders of some similar projects and base her estimates against the historical information on similar projects. She'll run the estimates by her lead tester before giving them to you.

Cost Estimating Techniques

We now have an exhaustive breakdown of project activities, and we have some pretty good duration estimates. Now the question that's forever on the mind of the executive management staff: How much is it going to cost? The purpose of the Cost Estimating process is to answer that question.

Every project has a budget, and part of completing a project successfully is completing it within the approved budget. Sometimes project managers are not responsible for the budget portion of the project. This function is assigned instead to a functional manager who is responsible for tracking and reporting all the project costs. I believe project mangers will have more and more responsibility in this area as the project management discipline evolves. Keep in mind that if you, as the project manager, don't have responsibility for the project budget, your performance evaluation for the project should not include budget or cost measurements.

Accuracy in Cost Estimating

As with time estimates, the WBS is the key to determining accurate cost estimates. The *Cost Estimating* process develops a cost estimate for the resources required for each activity outlined in the WBS. This includes weighing alternative options and examining trade-offs. For example, many times software development projects take on a life of their own. The requested project completion dates are unrealistic; however, the project team commits to completing the project on time and on budget anyway. How do they do this? By cutting things like design, analysis, and documentation. In the end, the project might get completed on time and on budget, but was it really? The costs associated with the extended support period due to a lack of design and documentation and the hours needed by the software programmers to fix the reported bugs aren't included in the original cost of the project (but they should have been). Therefore, the costs actually exceed what was budgeted. You should examine trade-offs such as these when determining cost estimates.

When you are determining cost estimates, be certain to include all the costs of the project over its entire life cycle. Include warranty periods and ongoing costs in your estimates. As in the example above, software projects often have warranty periods that guarantee bug fixes or problem resolution within a certain time frame. This is a legitimate cost that should be included in your estimates.

One more note: Don't confuse pricing with Cost Estimating. If you are working for a company that performs IT services on contract, for example, the price you will charge for your services is not the same thing as the costs to perform the project. The costs are centered around the resources needed to produce the product or service of the project. The price your company might charge for the service includes not only these costs, but a profit margin as well.

Cost Estimating Inputs

You are already familiar with most of the Cost Estimating inputs. Two that we haven't seen before are the resource rates and the chart of accounts.

Resource rates are the unit cost of the resources you're considering. If you're hiring contract Java coders, their unit cost might be $135 per hour. To determine the estimate, you multiply the number of hours needed, which was estimated during the Activity Duration Estimating process, by the number of resources needed. If your project requires certain materials or equipment, use the unit cost to calculate the appropriate estimate. When unit costs are not known, you might need to estimate them as well.

Be certain to estimate all the resources you're going to need for the project. This includes staff wages, contractor costs if applicable, materials, supplies, equipment, hardware, software tools, design tools, and so on.

A chart of accounts is the coding system used by the finance department to record transactions in the company's general ledger. The chart of accounts is where the project costs will be tracked. The code of accounts we talked about in association with the WBS comes from the chart of accounts.

Cost Estimating Tools

Cost Estimating has five tools and techniques used to derive estimates: analogous estimating, parametric modeling, bottom-up estimating, computerized tools, and other Cost Estimating methods. We'll look at each of these next.

Analogous Estimating

We talked about this process in the time estimating section earlier in this chapter. The information relayed there applies to Cost Estimating as well. Remember that *analogous estimating* is a top-down estimating technique and is a form of expert judgment. It is a less accurate technique than the others we'll look at.

Parametric Modeling

Parametric modeling is a mathematical model that uses parameters, or project characteristics, to forecast project costs. The idea here is to find a parameter, or multiple parameters, that changes proportionately with project costs and then plug that into the model to come up with a total project cost. In order to use this technique, there must be a pattern that exists in the work so that you can use an estimate from that work element to derive the total project estimate.

For example, we might know from past experience that it costs $275 per square foot to build an office building. The $275 becomes the parameter that we use in the parametric model to come up with an estimate of total project cost. If you're using multiple parameters, each parameter is also assigned a weight that is included in the calculations. This allows for cost estimates to be calculated simultaneously.

Parametric modeling is similar to analogous estimating because it estimates the cost of the entire project (top-down). It is more accurate when historical information is used to help construct the model and when the parameters are easily quantified.

Bottom-up Estimating

The *bottom-up estimating* technique is the opposite of top-down estimating. Here you will estimate every activity or work item individually and then roll up that estimate, or add them all together, to come up with a total project estimate. This is a very accurate means of estimating, provided the estimates at the work package level are accurate. However, it takes a considerable amount of time to perform bottom-up estimating as every work package must be assessed and estimated accurately to be included in the bottom-up calculation.

You wouldn't choose this technique to provide a cost estimate for the project in the Initiation stage if one were requested as you don't have enough information at that stage to use the bottom-up technique. Instead, use the top-down estimation technique when a project cost estimate is needed early on in the project selection stage.

Computerized Tools

Project management software can be a useful tool in Cost Estimating as are spreadsheet programs. Using software can make the job of Cost Estimating easy and fast.

Other Cost Estimating Methods

The first four tools and techniques described in this section are the primary methods you'll use to calculate cost estimates. You may also use other techniques or methods. For example, when your project is performed under contract or you need to procure resources under contract, you might analyze vendor bids to determine cost estimates for these activities. Make certain to document the Cost Estimating method you used in the supporting detail output of this process.

Documenting the Cost Estimates

Obviously, one of the outputs of the Cost Estimating process is the cost estimates. These are quantitative amounts, usually stated in dollars, that reflect the cost of the resources needed to complete the project activities. The tools and techniques we just described help us derive these estimates.

Supporting detail and the cost management plan are the remaining two Cost Estimating outputs. Supporting detail is just as we've seen in other processes. Any information that supports how the estimates were developed, what assumptions were made during the Cost Estimating process, and any other details you think need to be documented go here.

Cost variances will occur, and estimates will be refined, as you get further into your project. As you've probably suspected, there is a plan that defines how these cost variances should be managed. That plan is called the cost management plan and is the last output of the Cost Estimating process. Your cost management plan should define how changes to cost estimates, or changes in resource unit costs, will be reflected in the project budget. Changes or variances with a significant impact should be communicated to the project sponsor and stakeholders. The cost management plan should define how and when this notification process works as well.

Cost Estimating uses several techniques to make an accurate assessment of the project costs. In practice, using a combination of techniques is your best bet to come up with the most reliable cost estimates. The Cost Estimating output will become an input to the Cost Budgeting process, which allows us to establish a baseline for project costs to track against.

Project Case Study: New Kitchen Heaven Retail Store

"Thanks everyone for your timely responses. I'll look over the activity lists and estimates you've assigned and start working on the project plan." The meeting adjourns, and you head back to your office to review the estimates and resource assignments. You'd like to get the project schedule constructed soon and go over it with Dirk. This information is the first cut at the project schedule.

Ricardo Ramirez from the IT department has outlined his activity list and estimates. He reminds you that data is sent from each store over a T1 connection, not over satellite as Jill told you originally. Ricardo's estimates are as follows. He's also taken the trouble to write them in sequential order.

1. Procure the T1 connection. This takes 30 to 45 days and will have ongoing costs of $300 per month. This can be done concurrently with the other activities below. Ricardo will handle this activity.

2. Run Ethernet cable throughout the building. This activity depends on the lease being signed and must finish before the build-out can start. Estimated time to complete is 16 hours using qualitatively based estimates. Ricardo has one person on staff who can complete this specialized activity. His first available date is October 5.

3. Purchase the router, switch, server, and rack for the equipment room and four point-of-service terminals. Estimated costs are $17,000. Delivery time is 2 weeks. Ricardo will do this activity.

4. Install router and test connection. Testing depends on the T1 installation at demarcation. Time estimate to install is 8 hours. Ricardo's staff will do this activity.

5. Install switch. Based on past experience, time estimate to install is 2 hours. Ricardo's staff will do this activity.

6. Install server and test. Testing depends on the T1 connection installation. Based on past experience, time estimate to install is 6 hours. Ricardo's staff will do this activity.

7. Web team to add the new store location and phone number to the lookup function on the Internet site. Time estimate is 8 hours. Ricardo will assign his applications-programming manager to this activity. This activity depends on the lease being signed.

Jake and Jill have each written similar lists with estimates and resource assignments. You begin to align all the activities in sequential order and discover a problem. Jill needs 10 days to stock shelves and train employees, meaning that the build-out must be finished by January 14. Build-out takes approximately 120 days and therefore must start by September 19. The problem is that Ricardo's Ethernet cable expert isn't available until October 5, and he needs two days to complete the cabling. This pushes out the build-out start date by almost 2 weeks, which means the project completion date, or store-opening date, is delayed by 2 weeks.

After gathering more information from Ricardo, you head to Dirk's office.

"So, Dirk," you conclude after filling him in on all the details. "We have two options. Hire a contractor to perform the cable run since Ricardo's person isn't available, or push the store opening out by 2 weeks."

Dirk asks, "How much will the contractor charge to run the cable, and are they available within the time frame you need?"

"Yes, they are available, and I've already requested Ricardo book the week of September 17th to hold this option open for us. They've quoted a price of $10,000."

"Okay, let's bring in the contractor. $10,000 isn't going to break the budget at this point. How is that planning coming anyway? Signed a lease yet?"

"Yes, we've signed the lease. Jake has been meeting with Gomez construction on the build-out. We've used Gomez on three out of the last five new stores and have had good luck with them."

Project Case Study Checklist

Activity Definition

Activity Sequencing

Activity Duration Estimating

- Expert judgment

- Qualitatively based estimates

Cost Estimating

- Other Cost Estimating methods—vendor bids

Summary

The Resource Planning process considers all the resources needed and the quantity of resources needed to perform project activities. This information is tied to the WBS elements and is detailed in the resource requirements document.

Staffing requirements are a subset of the resource requirements output. Staffing requirements are concerned with the human resource aspect of the resource plan and detail special skills or knowledge that might be needed for a project activity.

Organizational planning identifies and assigns roles and responsibilities and reporting relationships. Many times the roles and responsibilities assignments are depicted in a Responsibility Assignment Matrix (RAM). The staffing management plan describes how and when project team members will be brought on and off the project and is an output of the Organizational Planning process.

The Staff Acquisition process details staff assignments and publishes the project team directory.

Duration estimates are produced as a result of the Activity Duration Estimating process. Prior to this process, activities must be identified and sequenced in logical order. Activity Sequencing is performed using PDM, which is an activity on node (AON) method, or ADM, which is an activity on arrow (AOA) method—or with conditional diagramming or network templates. ADM is seldom used today.

Activity duration estimates document the number of work periods needed for each activity including their elapsed time. Analogous estimating, also called top-down estimating, is one way to determine activity duration estimates. Top-down techniques can also be used to estimate project durations and total project costs. Quantitatively based durations multiply a known element—like the quantity of materials needed—by the time it takes to install or complete one unit of materials. The result is a total estimate for the activity. Reserve time takes schedule risk into consideration by adding an additional percentage of time or another work period to the estimate just in case you run into trouble.

The Cost Estimating process determines how much the project resources will cost, which is usually stated in dollars. The cost management plan outlines how costs will be managed throughout the project. Analogous estimating is one technique that can be used to determine cost estimates. Another estimating technique is parametric modeling. This is a mathematical model that forecasts project costs. Bottom-up estimating can be used for project cost estimates. This involves estimating the cost of each work package and then rolling these up to come up with a total cost.

Exam Essentials

Be able to identify the tools and techniques of Activity Sequencing. Precedence diagramming method (PDM), arrow diagramming method (ADM), conditional diagramming method, and network templates.

Be able to discuss the difference between PDM and ADM. PDM uses activity on node (AON) diagrams, and ADM uses activity on arrow (AOA) diagrams.

Be able to name the tools and techniques of Activity Duration Estimating. Expert judgment, analogous estimating, quantitatively based durations, and reserve time.

Be able to identify the tools and techniques of Cost Estimating. Analogous estimating, parametric modeling, bottom-up estimating, computerized tools, and other Cost Estimating methods.

Be able to define the difference between analogous estimating and bottom-up estimating. Analogous estimating is a top-down technique that uses expert judgment and historical information. Bottom-up performs estimates for each work item and rolls them up to a total.

Key Terms

Before you take the exam, be certain you are familiar with the following terms:

Activity Definition	Cost Estimating
Activity Duration Estimating	logical relationship
activity list	organizational breakdown structure (OBS)
activity on arrow (AOA)	Parametric modeling
activity on node (AON)	precedence diagramming method (PDM)
Activity Sequencing	resource histogram
analogous estimating	Resource Planning
arrow diagramming method (ADM)	Responsibility Assignment Matrix (RAM)
bottom-up estimating	Staff Acquisition

Review Questions

1. Which of the following is true regarding the Resource Planning process?

    A. Resource Planning involves the human resource aspect of planning only, and its output is staffing requirements.

    B. Resource Planning involves the human resource aspect of planning only, and its output is resource requirements.

    C. Resource Planning encompasses all the physical resources needed for the project, and its output is staffing requirements.

    D. Resource Planning encompasses all the physical resources needed for the project, and its output is resource requirements.

2. Sally is a project manager working on the Resource Planning process. She should consider all of the following when developing the resource requirements output except:

    A. WBS

    B. Supply purchase policies

    C. Resource rates

    D. Special knowledge and talents

3. Which of the following are constraints that you might find during the Organizational Planning process?

    A. Organizational structure, expected staff assignments, collective bargaining agreements, and project management team preferences

    B. Organizational structure, organizational interfaces, technical interfaces, and interpersonal interfaces

    C. Organizational interfaces, expected staff assignments, collective bargaining agreements, and project management team preferences

    D. Organizational interfaces, technical interfaces, and interpersonal interfaces

4. You are the project manager for a scheduled version release of your company's software tracking product. You have linked the WBS and project scope definition and assigned roles and responsibilities. You might want to display the roles and responsibilities in which of the following?

   A. RDM

   B. PDM

   C. AOA

   D. RAM

5. Which of the following is true regarding the staffing management plan?

   A. It details the resource requirements and the quantity of resources needed for project activities. It is an output of the Resource Planning process.

   B. It details how and when staff resources will be brought on and off the project. It is an output of the Organizational Planning process.

   C. It details how and when staff resources will be brought on and off the project. It is an output of the Resource Planning process.

   D. It details the resource requirements and the quantity of resources needed for project activities. It is an output of the Organizational Planning process.

6. All of the following describe the activity list except:

   A. It's an extension of the WBS.

   B. It includes all activities of the project.

   C. It describes the WBS updates.

   D. It includes a description of project activities.

7. You are the project manager for Design Your Web Site, Inc. Your company is designing the website for a national grocery store chain. You have your activity list in hand and are ready to diagram the activity dependencies using the PDM technique. You know that:

A. PDM uses AON diagramming methods.

B. PDM uses AOA diagramming methods.

C. PDM uses ADM diagramming methods.

D. PDM uses PDM diagramming methods.

8. You are the project manager for Design Your Web Site, Inc. Your company is designing the website for a national grocery store chain. You have your activity list in hand and several time estimates for each activity and are ready to diagram the activity dependencies. You should use which of the following?

A. PDM techniques

B. PDM or ADM techniques

C. AON techniques

D. ADM techniques

9. All of the following are true regarding the tools and techniques of Activity Sequencing except:

A. GERT uses analogous methods.

B. GERT allows for loops.

C. GERT is a conditional diagramming method.

D. GERT allows for conditional branches.

10. You are the project manager for Changing Tides video games. You have produced a project network diagram and have updated the activity list. Which process have you just finished?

    A. The Activity Sequencing process, which identifies all the specific activities of the project

    B. The Activity Sequencing process, which identifies all the activity dependencies

    C. The Activity Duration Estimating process, which diagrams project network time estimates

    D. The Activity Duration Estimating process, which identifies all the dependent activities of the project

11. You are the project manager for Changing Tides video games. You have gathered the inputs for the Activity Duration Estimating process. You will employ which tools and techniques to produce the outputs for this process?

    A. Activity list, analogous estimating, qualitatively based durations, and alternatives identification

    B. Activity list, analogous estimating, expert judgment, and qualitatively based durations

    C. Expert judgment, analogous estimating, quantitatively based durations, and reserve time

    D. Expert judgment, alternatives identification, quantitatively based durations, and reserve time

12. As project manager, you know that all of the following are true concerning analogous estimating techniques except:

    A. It's a qualitatively based estimating technique.

    B. It's a top-down estimating technique.

    C. It's a tool and technique of Activity Duration Estimating and Cost Estimating.

    D. It's a form of expert judgment.

13. You have been hired as a contract project manager for Grapevine Vineyards. Grapevine wants you to design an Internet wine club for their customers. Customers must preregister before being allowed to order wine over the Internet so that legal age can be established. You know that the module to verify preregistration must be written and tested using data from Grapevine's existing database. This new module cannot be tested until the data from the existing system is loaded. This is an example of which of the following?

A. Preferential logic

B. Soft logic

C. Discretionary dependency

D. Hard logic

14. You have been hired as a contract project manger for Grapevine Vineyards. Grapevine wants you to design an Internet wine club for their customers. One of the activities for this project is the installation and testing of several new servers. You know from past experience it takes about 16 hours per server to accomplish this task. Since you're installing 10 new servers, you estimate this activity to take 160 hours. Which of the estimating techniques have you used?

A. Analogous estimating

B. Bottom-up estimating

C. Quantitatively based durations

D. Reserve time

15. Your project sponsor has requested a cost estimate for the project. She would like the cost estimate to be as accurate as possible as this might be her one and only chance to secure the budget for this project due to recent cuts in special projects. You decide:

A. To use analogous estimating techniques

B. To use bottom-up estimating techniques

C. To use top-down estimating techniques

D. To use expert judgment techniques

16. Your project sponsor has requested a cost estimate for the project you're working on. This project is similar in scope to a project you worked on last year. She would like to get the cost estimates as soon as possible. Accuracy is not her primary concern right now. She needs a ball park figure by tomorrow. You decide to use:

    A. Analogous estimating techniques

    B. Bottom-up estimating techniques

    C. Parametric modeling techniques

    D. Computerized modeling techniques

17. All of the following are true regarding parametric modeling except:

    A. It's a form of top-down estimating.

    B. It's a mathematical model.

    C. It's a tool used to estimate project costs.

    D. It's a tool used to estimate project time.

18. Your project's primary constraint is quality. In order to make certain the project team members don't feel too pressed for time and to avoid schedule risk, you decide to use which of the following activity estimating tools?

    A. Expert judgment

    B. Quantitatively based durations

    C. Reserve time

    D. Analogous estimating

19. You are the project manager for BB Tops, a nationwide toy store chain. You are working on estimates for your latest project and have gathered several variables for your model. You've determined the following:

    A. Parametric modeling is a top-down technique that uses variables to produce time estimates.

    B. Parametric modeling is a mathematical formula that uses variables to produce cost estimates.

    C. Contingency estimating is a top-down technique that uses variables to produce cost estimates.

    D. Contingency estimating is a mathematical model that uses variables to produce time estimates.

20. Which logical relationship does the PDM use most often?

    A. Start to finish

    B. Start to start

    C. Finish to finish

    D. Finish to start

Answers to Review Questions

1. D. Resource Planning is the process that determines all the physical resources needed for the project and what quantities of resources are needed. The output is resource requirements.

2. C. Resource rates are an input to Cost Estimating. Supply purchase policies would be found in the organizational policies input, which the project manager should consider when writing the resource requirements.

3. A. Constraints can be anything that limits the option of the project team. Organizational structure, collective bargaining agreements, preferences of the project management team, and expected staff assignments are all constraints that might be encountered during this process.

4. D. The Responsibility Assignment Matrix (RAM) links project roles and responsibilities with project activities.

5. B. The staffing management plan details how and when human resources will be added to and taken off the project. It is an output of Organizational Planning.

6. C. The activity list is produced as an extension of the WBS and includes all the project activities with descriptions of the activities. The activity list and the WBS updates are an output to the Activity Definition process.

7. A. Precedence diagramming methods are also known as activity on node diagramming methods.

8. D. PDM uses one time estimate to determine duration, while ADM can use more than one time estimate.

9. A. GERT is a conditional diagramming method that allows for loops and conditional branches.

10. B. The Activity Sequencing process produces network diagrams and updates to the activity list. The purpose of this process is to identify all activity dependencies.

11. C. The tools and techniques for Activity Duration Estimating are expert judgment, analogous estimating, qualitatively based durations, and reserve time.

12. A. Analogous estimating is not a qualitatively based technique. It is a top-down estimating technique that considers previous similar activities when calculating estimates.

13. D. This is an example of a mandatory dependency, also known as hard logic. Mandatory dependencies are inherent in the nature of the work. Discretionary dependencies, also called preferred logic, preferential logic, and soft logic, are defined by the project management team.

14. C. Quantitatively based durations multiply a known element—like the quantity of materials needed—by the time it takes to install or complete one unit of materials. The result is a total estimate for the activity. In this case, 10 servers multiplied by 16 hours per server gives us a 160-hour total duration estimate.

15. B. Bottom-up techniques are the most time consuming and the most accurate estimates you can use. With bottom-up, each work item is estimated and rolled up to a project total.

16. A. Analogous, or top-down, estimating techniques are a form of expert judgment. Since this project is similar to another recent project, you can use the cost estimates from the previous project to help you quickly determine estimates for the current project.

17. D. Parametric modeling is a Cost Estimating technique.

18. C. Reserve time takes schedule risk into consideration and adds a percentage of time or additional work periods to the estimate to prevent schedule delays.

19. B. Parametric modeling uses variables, or parameters, to produce cost estimates. Contingencies are also known as reserve time and are used in the Activity Duration Estimating process.

20. D. Finish to start is the most commonly used logical relationship in PDM and most project management software packages.

Chapter

6

Establishing Project Planning Controls

PMP EXAM CONTENT FROM THE PROJECT PLANNING PERFORMANCE DOMAIN COVERED IN THIS CHAPTER:

✓ 5. Establish Project Controls.

Each of the project Planning processes we've discussed so far, along with what we'll cover here and in Chapter 7, will culminate in the final output of the project Planning process, which is the project plan. The Execution and Controlling process groups depend on the project plan to measure and track project performance. In order to measure performance, several more plans need to be put into place including a quality plan, a risk response plan, and a procurement plan. We'll cover each of these in the upcoming sections of this chapter.

We have a lot of material to cover in this chapter including several processes on risk management. I recommend you study the inputs, tools and techniques, and outputs of the risk processes from the *Guide to the PMBOK* as we will not be able to cover all of them here. Most of these processes have multiple inputs, many of which were covered previously or are self explanatory. The exam puts the most emphasis on the tools and techniques of these processes, but study the inputs and outputs as well.

This chapter will cover Quality Planning, Risk Management Planning, Risk Identification, Qualitative Risk Analysis, Quantitative Risk Analysis, Risk Response Planning, Solicitation Planning, and Procurement Planning.

Identifying Quality Standards

Quality is one of the triple constraints found in all projects. It's the third leg to the successful completion of a project and more typically defines whether stakeholder expectations were met. Being on time and on budget is one thing—if you deliver the wrong product or an inferior product, on time and on budget suddenly don't mean much. Remember those career-limiting moves we talked about in a previous chapter? This could be one of them if you don't plan and monitor quality properly on your project.

Quality Planning is a process that is concerned with targeting quality standards that are relevant to the project at hand and devising a plan to meet those standards. The quality management plan is an output of this process. It describes how the quality policy will be implemented by the project management team during the course of the project.

The Quality Management knowledge area, which includes Quality Planning, Quality Assurance, and Quality Control, involves the quality management of the project as well as the quality aspects of the product or service the project was undertaken to produce. We'll discuss Quality Assurance and Quality Control in later chapters. Our focus in this chapter is Quality Planning.

Quality Inputs

The Quality Planning process has several inputs: quality policy, scope statement, product description, standards and regulations, and other process outputs. We'll look at two of these inputs now.

Quality Policy

The quality policy is a guideline published by executive management that describes what quality policies should be adopted for projects the company undertakes. It's up to the project manager to understand this policy and incorporate any predetermined company guidelines into the quality plan. If a quality policy does not exist, it's up to the project management team to create one for the project.

Standards and Regulations

As with the quality policy, the project manager should consider any standards or regulations that exist concerning the work of the project when writing the quality plan. A standard is defined by the *Guide to the PMBOK* as something that's approved by a recognized body and that employs rules, guidelines, or characteristics that should be followed. For example, the Americans with Disabilities Act (ADA) has established standards for web page designers that outline alternative viewing options of web pages for people with disabilities. PMI guidelines regarding project management are another example of standards.

Standards aren't mandatory, but it's a good idea to follow them. If your project creates a software product that ignores standard protocols, your customers won't be able to use it.

Standards can be set by the organization, by independent bodies or organizations such as the International Organization for Standardization (ISO), and so on.

A regulation is mandatory. Regulations are almost always imposed by governments or institutions like the American Medical Association. However, organizations may have their own self-imposed regulations that you should be aware of as well. Regulations require strict adherence, particularly in the case of government-imposed regulations, or stiff penalties and fines could result—maybe even jail time if the offense is serious enough. Hmm, might be tough to practice project management from behind bars...not a recommended career move.

If possible, it's a good idea to include information from the quality policy and any standards and regulations that affect the project in the quality management plan. If it's not possible to include this information in the quality management plan, then at least make reference to the information and where it can be found. It's the project manager's responsibility to be certain all stakeholders are aware of and understand the policy issues and standards or regulations that might impact the project.

The remaining inputs to Quality Planning have been covered in previous chapters. One note regarding the "other process outputs" input: Contracts might have certain provisions for quality requirements that you should account for in the quality management plan. This will be discovered during the Procurement Planning process. Therefore, this "other output" from Procurement Planning becomes an input to Quality Planning.

Cost of Quality

The cost of quality must be measured in order to be certain the product or service meets stakeholders' expectations. Three people in particular are responsible for the rise of the quality management movement and the theories behind the cost of quality. They are Philip B. Crosby, Joseph M. Juran, and W. Edwards Deming. Each of these men developed steps or points that led to commonly accepted quality processes that we use today.

Philip B. Crosby

Philip B. Crosby devised the *zero defects* practice, which means, basically, do it right the first time. (Didn't your dad used to tell you this?) Crosby says that costs will increase when quality planning isn't performed up front, which means you'll have to engage in rework, thus affecting productivity. Prevention is the key to Crosby's theory. If you prevent the defect from occurring in the first place, costs are lower, conformance to requirements is easily met, and the cost measurement for quality becomes the cost of nonconformance rather than the cost of rework.

Joseph M. Juran

Joseph M. Juran is noted for his *fitness for use* premise. Simply put, this means stakeholders' and customers' expectations are met or exceeded. This says that conformance to specifications—meaning the product of the project that was produced is what the project set out to produce—is met or exceeded. And, fitness for use specifically reflects the customers' or stakeholders' view of quality. Fitness for use answers the questions, "Did the product or service produced meet the quality expectation," "Did it satisfy a real need," and "Is it reliable and safe?"

Juran also proposed that there could be grades of quality. However, you should not confuse grade with quality. Low quality is usually not an acceptable condition; however, low grade might be. For example, your new Dad's Dollars Credit Card software tracking system might be of high quality, meaning there are no bugs and the product performs as advertised, but of low grade, meaning there are few features. You'll almost always want to strive for high quality, regardless of the acceptable grade level.

W. Edwards Deming

W. Edwards Deming suggested that as much as 85 percent of the cost of quality is a management problem. Once the quality issue has hit the floor, or the worker level, the workers have little control. For example, if you're constructing a new highway and the management team that bid on the project proposed using inferior-grade asphalt, the workers laying the asphalt have little control over its quality. They're at the mercy of the management team that purchased the supplies.

Deming also proposed that workers cannot figure out quality on their own, and thus cannot perform at their best. He believed that workers need to be shown what acceptable quality is, and that they need to be made to understand that quality and continuous improvement are necessary elements of any organization, or project in our case.

Kaizen Approach

The Kaizen approach is a quality technique from Japan. In fact, *Kaizen* means continuous improvement in Japanese. With this technique, all project team members and managers should be constantly watching for quality improvement opportunities. The Kaizen approach states that you should improve the quality of the people first, then the quality of the products or service.

Quality Planning Tools

Quality Planning has five tools and techniques used to help construct the quality management plan. I recommend you understand each of these tools and techniques and its purpose for the exam. Let's take a look at the tools and techniques.

Benefit/Cost Analysis

You've seen this technique before. In the case of quality management, you'll want to consider the trade-offs of the cost of quality. As mentioned earlier, it's cheaper and more efficient to prevent defects in the first place than to have to spend time and money fixing them later. According to the *Guide to the PMBOK*, the benefits of meeting quality requirements are as follows:

- Stakeholder satisfaction is increased.

- Costs are lower.

- Productivity is higher.

- There is less rework.

Benchmarking

Benchmarking is a process of comparing previous similar activities to the current project activities to provide a standard to measure performance against. This comparison will also help you derive ideas for quality improvements on the current project. For example, if your current printer can produce 8 pages per minute and you're considering a new printer that produces 14 pages per minute, the benchmark is 8 pages per minute.

Flowcharting

Flowcharts are diagrams that show the logical steps that must be performed in order to accomplish an objective. They can also show how the individual elements of a system interrelate. In the case of quality management planning, two types of flowcharts are commonly used. They are cause-and-effect diagrams and system or process flowcharts.

Cause-and-effect diagrams show the relationship between the effects of problems and their causes. This diagram depicts every potential cause and subcause of a problem and the effect that each proposed solution will have on the problem. This diagram is also called a fishbone diagram, or Ishikawa diagram after its developer Kaoru Ishikawa. Figure 6.1 shows an example cause-and-effect diagram.

FIGURE 6.1 Cause-and-effect diagram

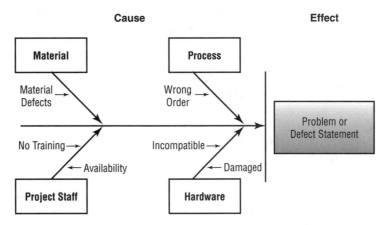

The system or process flowchart shows the logical steps needed to accomplish an objective and the interrelation of individual elements of a system.

Design of Experiments

For exam purposes, you need to know that *design of experiments* is an analytical technique that identifies the elements, or variables, that will have the greatest effect on overall project outcomes. This technique is used most often concerning the product of the project but can also be applied to project management processes. This process designs and sets up experiments to determine the ideal solution for a problem using a limited number of sample cases.

Cost of Quality

The *cost of quality* here refers to the costs to produce the product or service of the project according to the quality standards. These costs include all the work necessary to meet the product requirements whether the work was planned or unplanned.

There are three costs associated with the cost of quality: prevention costs; appraisal costs; and failure costs, which consist of internal and external costs.

Prevention Costs

Prevention means keeping defects out of the hands of customers. *Prevention costs* are the costs associated with satisfying customer requirements by producing a product without defects. These costs are manifested early on in the process and include things like quality planning, training, design review, and contractor and supplier costs.

Appraisal Costs

Appraisal costs are the costs expended to examine the product or process and make certain the requirements are being met. Appraisal costs might include costs associated with things like inspections and testing.

Failure Costs

Failure costs are what it costs when things don't go according to plan. There are two types of failure costs, internal and external.

Internal failure costs result when customer requirements are not satisfied while the product is still in the control of the organization. Internal failure costs may include corrective action, rework, scrapping, and downtime.

External failure costs occur when the product has reached the customer and they determine that their requirements have not been met. Costs associated with external failure costs may include inspections at the customer site, returns, and customer service costs.

Quality Management Plan

Quality Planning uses many techniques to determine the areas of quality improvement that can be implemented, controlled, and measured throughout the rest of the project. The *quality management plan* describes how the project management team will enact the quality policy. It also documents the resources needed to carry out the quality plan, the responsibilities of the project team in implementing quality, and all the processes and procedures the project team and organization use to satisfy quality requirements.

The quality management plan is written by the project manager in cooperation with the project staff. You will assign quality actions to the activities listed on the WBS. Isn't that WBS a handy thing? The quality plan should then document the quality actions associated with the WBS activities. Later in the Quality Control process, measurements will be taken to determine if quality to date is on track with the quality standards outlined in the quality management plan.

Operational Definitions

Operational definitions are an output of the Quality Planning process. They are sometimes called *metrics*, and their purpose is to specifically describe what is being measured and how it will be measured according to the Quality Control plan and process.

Checklists

If you're like me, you start your day at the office with a big to-do list that has so many items on it you won't be able to finish them all. Nevertheless, you faithfully write the list every day and check off the things that you accomplish throughout the day. *Checklists* are like this in that they provide a means to determine if the required steps in a process have been followed. As each step is completed, it's checked off the list. Checklists can be activity specific or industry specific, and might be very complex or easy to follow. Sometimes, organizations may have standard checklists they use for projects. You might also be able to obtain checklists from professional associations.

Checklists are an output of Quality Planning. Remember that checklists are an output of this process but are a tool and technique of the Risk Identification process, and are an input to Quality Control. Many times, outputs of one process become inputs to another, so that isn't unusual. However, I believe this is the only case where an input/output is also a tool and technique in another process.

Inputs to Other Processes

Quality Planning finishes up its outputs with inputs to other processes. In the process of identifying Quality Planning measurements and controls, you might be alerted to other Planning processes that need to be tweaked in order to comply with the new information you've discovered.

Quality is an important planning and measuring tool. We'll revisit quality during the Execution and Controlling processes where we get into quality measurements and controls. But for now, let's move on to defining project risks.

 Real World Scenario

Candy Works

Juliette Walters is a contract project manager for Candy Works. They've introduced a new line of hard candy drops in various exotic flavors: caffe latte, hot buttered popcorn, and jalapeño spice, just to name a few.

Juliette is writing the quality management plan for this project. After interviewing stakeholders and key team members, she's found several quality factors of importance to the organization. Quality will be measured by:

Candy size   Each piece should measure 3 mm.

Appearance   No visible cracks or breaks should appear in the candy.

Flavor   Flavor must be distinguishable when taste tested.

Number produced   9000 pieces per week is the production target. The current machine has been benchmarked at 9200 candies per week.

Intensity of color   There should be no opaqueness in the darker colors.

Wrappers   Properly fitting wrappers cover the candies, folding over twice in back, and twisted on each side. There is a different wrapper for each flavor of candy, which must be matched exactly.

The candy is cooked and then pulled into a long cylinder shape roughly 6 feet long and 2 feet in diameter. This cylinder is fed into the machine that molds and cuts the candy into drops. The cylinders vary a little in size because they're hand stretched by expert candy makers prior to feeding them into the drop maker machine. As a result, the end of one flavor batch, the caffe latte flavor, and the beginning of the next batch, the hot buttered popcorn flavor, merge. This means the drops that fall into the collection bins are intermingled during the last run of the first flavor batch. In other words, the last bin of the caffe latte flavor run has some hot buttered popcorn drops mixed in. And, there isn't a way to separate the drops once they've hit the bin. From here, the drops go on to the candy-wrapping machine where brightly colored wrappers are matched to the candy flavor. According to the quality plan, hot buttered popcorn drops cannot be wrapped as caffe latte drops. Juliette ponders what to do.

As she tosses and turns that night thinking about the problem, it occurs to her to present this problem as an opportunity to the company rather than as a problem. In order to keep production in the 9000 candies per week category, the machines can't be stopped every time a new batch is introduced. So Juliette comes up with the idea to wrap candies from the intermixed bins with wrappers that say "mystery flavor." This way, production keeps pace with the plan, and the wrapper/flavor quality problem is mitigated.

Risk Planning

Every one of us takes risks on a daily basis. Just getting out of bed in the morning is a risk. You might stub your toe in the dark on the way to the light switch or trip over the dog and break a leg. These things don't usually happen, but the possibility exists. The same is true for your project. Risk exists on all projects, and the potential that a particular risk will occur depends on the nature of the risk.

Risk, like much of the information gathered during other Planning processes, will change as the project progresses and should be monitored throughout the project. As you get close to a risk event, that's the time to reassess your original assumptions about the risk and your plans to deal with the risk and to make any adjustments as required.

One consideration to take into account when assessing risk is risk tolerance. Stakeholder risk tolerance is one of the inputs in the Risk Management Planning process. Organizations and stakeholders, as well as individuals, all have different tolerances for risk. One organization might believe that the risk of a potential 17 percent cost overrun is high, while another might think it's low. It's important for the project manager to understand the tolerance level the organization and the stakeholders have for risk before evaluating and ranking risk.

During the risk-planning process, we'll look at Risk Management Planning, Risk Identification, Qualitative Risk Analysis, Quantitative Risk Analysis, and Risk Response Planning. At this stage, we need to identify all potential risks that exist for our project, and we need to understand the probability of risk occurrence. We also want to know what the impact to the project or product outcome will be if the risk does happen. Not all risk is bad, and not all risks have negative impacts, but you need to know about them nevertheless. All risks are caused by something and therefore have consequences. Those consequences will likely impact one or more of the triple constraints.

The idea behind risk planning is that you identify all the risks and then evaluate and quantify the risks to come up with a plan to deal with or avert them.

Risk Management Planning

Risks come about for many reasons. Some are internal to the project, and some are external. The project environment, the planning process, the project management process, inadequate resources, and so on can all contribute to risk. Some risks you'll know about in advance and plan for during this process; others will occur unannounced during the project. The *Risk Management Planning* process determines how you'll plan for risks on your project.

Risks associated with the project generally concern the project objectives, which in turn impact time, costs, or quality, or any combination of the three. The purpose for Risk Management Planning is to create a *risk management plan*, which describes how you will define, monitor, and control risks throughout the project. The risk management plan becomes part of the project plan at the conclusion of the Planning process.

Risk Management Plan

The risk management plan is the only output of this process. The risk management plan details how risk management processes will be implemented, monitored, and controlled throughout the life of the project. It details how you will manage risks but does not attempt to define responses to individual risks. In the risk response plan, individual risk responses are discussed. We'll talk about that a little later in this section.

According to the *Guide to the PMBOK*, the risk management plan might include a description of the methodology you'll use to perform risk management. Roles and responsibilities are included in the document and describe the team of people who are responsible for managing the identified risks and their responses. These teams are usually not the project team. Risk analysis should be unbiased, which may not be possible when project team members are involved.

The budget for risk management is included in the plan as well. Qualitative and quantitative scoring interpretation methods are described in the plan including thresholds for risk. We'll cover these topics later in this section.

The plan also describes the timing of risk management processes and the criteria that establish risk thresholds. And the plan also describes how the risk management information will be maintained and updated, reported to project participants, and documented for future reference.

It's very important to spend time developing this plan as the risk management plan is an input to every other risk-planning process. It is also an input to the Risk Monitoring and Control process, which we'll cover in another chapter.

Identifying Potential Risk

The *Risk Identification* process involves identifying all the risks that might impact the project, documenting them, and documenting their characteristics. Risk Identification should occur over the course of several steps. You can include all project team members, stakeholders, subject matter experts, users, and anyone else whom you think may help in the Risk Identification process. Perhaps in the first round of Risk Identification, you include just the project team and then bring in the stakeholders or risk management team to further flesh out risks during the second round of identification.

Risks may or may not adversely affect the project. However, all risk events and their consequences should be identified. Here's a partial list to get you thinking about where risk may be found:

- Budgets/funding

- Schedules

- Scope or requirements changes

- Technical issues

- Personnel issues

- Hardware

- Contracts

- Political concerns

- Business risk

- Legal risk

- Environmental risk

This is by no means an exhaustive list. Realize that risk is lurking almost anywhere on your project. It's your job to discover all the possible risks using the tools and techniques of this process and document the risks.

Identifying Risk Inputs

The inputs to this process include the risk management plan, project Planning outputs, risk categories, and historical information. Take note of the input titled "project Planning outputs" as they include the project charter, the WBS, your cost and time estimates, assumptions and constraints, and the procurement plan. We'll discuss the procurement plan later in this chapter.

Risk categories involve either industry or application areas. According to the *Guide to the PMBOK*, the risk categories may include technical, quality, or performance risks; project management risks; organizational risks; and external risks.

The historical information input here refers to previous project experiences via the project files and/or published information like commercial databases or academic research that might exist for your application areas. Project team knowledge is another form of historical information.

Tools and Techniques Used to Identify Risk

This process is undertaken using five tools and techniques: documentation reviews, information-gathering techniques, checklists, assumptions analysis, and diagramming techniques.

Documentation reviews involve reviewing project plans, assumptions, and historical information regarding previous projects.

Information gathering includes several techniques like brainstorming, the Delphi technique, interviewing, and strength and weakness analysis. We'll take a brief look at each.

Brainstorming

This is probably the most often used technique of Risk Identification. You've probably used this technique many times for many purposes. *Brainstorming* involves getting subject matter experts, team members, risk management team members, and anyone else who might benefit the process in a room and asking them to start identifying possible risk events. The trick here is that one person's idea might spawn another idea and so on, so that by the end of the session you've identified all the possible risks.

Delphi Technique

The *Delphi technique* is a lot like brainstorming only the people participating in the meeting don't necessarily know each other. In fact, the people participating in this technique don't all have to be located in the same place and can participate anonymously. You can use e-mail to facilitate this technique very easily.

What you do is assemble your experts, both from inside and outside the company, and ask them via a questionnaire to identify potential risks. They in turn send their responses back to you (or the facilitator of this process). All the responses are organized by content and sent back to the Delphi members for further input, additions, or comments. The participants then send their comments back one more time, and a final list of risks is compiled by the facilitator.

The Delphi technique is a great tool that allows consensus to be reached very quickly. It also helps prevent one person from unduly influencing the others in the group and thus prevents bias in the outcome because the participants are usually anonymous and don't necessarily know how others in the group responded.

NOMINAL GROUP TECHNIQUE

Another technique that is similar to the Delphi technique is the *nominal group technique*. It isn't a named tool and technique of this process but is a technique you might find useful.

This technique requires the participants to be together in the same room. Each participant has paper and pencil in front of them, and they are asked to write down what risks they think the project faces. Sticky-backed notes are a good way to do this. Each piece of paper should contain only one risk. The papers are given to the facilitator, who sticks them up to the wall or a white board. The panel is then asked to review all the risks posted on the board; rank them and prioritize them, in writing; and submit the ranking to the facilitator. Once this is done, you should have a complete list of risks.

Interviewing

Interviews are question-and-answer sessions held with others including other project managers, subject matter experts, stakeholders, customers, the management team, project team members, and users. These folks provide you with possible risks based on their past experiences with similar projects.

This technique involves interviewing those folks with previous experience on projects similar to yours, or those with specialized knowledge or industry expertise. Ask them to tell you about any risks that they've experienced or that they think may happen on your project. Show them the WBS and your list of assumptions to help get them started thinking in the right direction.

Checklists

Checklists used during Risk Identification are usually developed based on historical information and previous project team experience. If you typically work on projects that are similar in nature, begin to compile a list of risks. You can then convert this to a checklist that will allow you to identify risks on future projects quickly and easily. However, don't rely solely on checklists for Risk Identification as you might miss important risks.

Assumptions Analysis

This is a matter of identifying and documenting the assumptions you've made regarding the project and then using them as a jumping-off point to further identify risks.

Diagramming Techniques

Cause-and-effect diagrams and flowcharts are usable in the Risk Identification process as well as the Quality Planning process. We discussed these diagramming techniques earlier in this chapter.

A third diagramming technique used during Risk Identification is called *influence diagrams*. These typically show the causes of problems and the order of occurrence over time.

Each of these techniques provides a way for you to help identify project risks. It's important that you identify all the risks early on. The better job you do of identifying the project's risks at the Planning stage, the better your risk response plan will look. Risk Identification is not an area of project Planning that you should skip.

Risk Identification Outputs

The outputs of the Risk Identification process include risks, triggers, and inputs to other processes.

Risks are all the potential events and their subsequent consequences that could occur, as we've discussed in this section. Once you've identified all the potential risks, you might want to log them in a risk database or tracking system to organize them and keep a close eye on their status. This can easily be done in spreadsheet format or whatever means you choose. List the risks and assign each risk a tracking number. This gives you a means to track the risks, their occurrence, and the responses implemented. We'll talk more about risk databases in the Risk Monitoring and Control process in Chapter 10.

Triggers

If you've ever suffered from a hay fever attack, you can't mistake the itchy, runny nose and scratchy throat that can come on suddenly and send you into a sneezing frenzy. Risk symptoms, also known as *triggers*, work the same way. Be on the alert for symptoms that might signal a risk event is about to occur.

If you're planning to host an outdoor gathering and rain clouds start rolling in from the north on the morning of the activity, you probably have a risk event waiting to happen. A key team member hinting about job hunting is a warning sign that they may be thinking of leaving, which in turn can cause schedule delays, increased costs, etc. This is another example of a trigger.

Inputs to other processes may occur as a result of the risks you've identified and can include schedule updates, modifications to the WBS, cost revisions, and other process updates.

Qualitative Risk Analysis

Qualitative Risk Analysis involves determining what impact the identified risks will have on the project and the probability they'll occur. It also puts the risks in priority order according to their effect on the project objectives.

Qualitative Risk Analysis should be performed throughout the project. Using Qualitative Risk Analysis methods allows you to determine the probability a risk will occur and to evaluate its consequences. This technique depends on the project type, data precision, and the scales of probability and impact. We'll take a brief look at these three inputs. The remaining inputs to this process include the risk management plan, identified risks, project status, and assumptions.

Qualitative Inputs

The input project type refers to the complexity of the project and whether you and the team have had experience with projects of this kind. If you're working on a project that is similar in size and scope to others you've worked on, you'll have a much better understanding of the probability of the occurrence of risk events and their consequences. However, if you're working on a new project that's particularly detailed or you're using new technology, you will have little information on the probability of risk events.

Data precision is concerned with the reliability of the data used to identify and describe risks and the level of understanding regarding their consequences.

Scales of probability and impact are used to determine and measure risk probability and the effect of the risk on the project objectives. We'll talk more about these scales in the tools and techniques section (which comes next).

Risk Probability Analysis

The Qualitative Risk Analysis tools and techniques are primarily concerned with discovering the probability of a risk event and determining the impact the risk will have if it does occur. The outputs of this process will prioritize the risks you've scored here using these tools and techniques to determine which ones should receive further Risk Response Planning. All of the information you gather regarding risks and probability needs to be as accurate as possible. It's also important that you gather unbiased information so that you don't unintentionally overlook risks with great potential or consequences.

The purpose of this process is to determine risk event probability and risk impact. You'll use the tools and techniques of this process to establish risk scores. The tools and techniques include risk probability and impact, probability/impact risk rating matrix, project assumptions testing, and data precision ranking.

Risk Probability and Impact

This tool and technique assigns probability to the risk events you've identified and determines their effect on project objectives.

During Qualitative Risk Analysis, you will simply assign a high, medium, or low value, or some similar combination, to the risk. For example, maybe you've identified the departure of a key team member as a potential risk for the project. Depending on how familiar you are with the situation, you may know that this probability is very likely and the consequences would have significant impact. If so, assign a high probability to this risk. If the key team member is happy with the company and wouldn't dream of leaving save for extreme circumstances, assign this risk a low probability.

These assignments include the probability of the risk occurring and the severity of the impact should it occur. The next technique deals with this issue more fully.

Probability/Impact Risk Rating Matrix

A probability matrix might be as simple as listing your risks and assigning a high, medium, or low value to them. This is called an *ordinal scale* as the values are rank ordered from high to low. In practice, ordinal values may also include ranking by position. In other words, the risks are listed in rank order as the first, the second, the third, and so on.

Another matrix format is shown as a combination of the probability of the risk using a probability scale and the severity of the impact using an impact scale.

Probability is the likelihood that an event will occur. The classic example is flipping a coin. There is a .50 probability of getting heads and a .50 probability of getting tails on the flip. One thing to note is that the probability that an event will occur plus the probability that the event will not occur always equals 1.0. In our coin-flipping example, there is a .50 chance that we'll get heads on the flip. There is also, therefore, a .50 chance we will not get heads on the flip. The two responses added together equal 1.0. *Probability scales* are always expressed as a number between 0.0, which means there is no probability of the event occurring, and 1.0, which means there is 100 percent certainty the risk will occur.

The severity of the risk impact, called an *impact scale*, is assigned as a cardinal value. Cardinal scales or values are actual numeric values assigned to the risk.

Assessing the probability and risk impact is typically accomplished using expert judgment and interviewing techniques. Some of the tools and techniques outlined in the Risk Identification process like brainstorming, interviewing, and the Delphi technique can be used during this process to determine probability and impact.

RISK IMPACTS

Another method to determine impact is to develop predefined measurements that describe what value to place on a risk event depending on the project objective or triple constraint it impacts. For example, let's say a risk event impacting project costs has a medium chance of occurring. You've predefined a medium impact to carry a value of 0.4. Further criteria say that a risk event that falls into the medium category for cost must increase cost by 10 percent. An example chart is shown in Table 6.1.

TABLE 6.1 Risk Impacts Rating Matrix

Constraints	Low-Low	Low	Medium	High	High-High
	0.05	0.20	0.40	0.60	0.80
Cost	No significant impact	Less than 6% increase	7–12% increase	13–18% increase	More than 18% increase
Time	No significant impact	Less than 6% increase	7–12% increase	13–18% increase	More than 18% increase
Quality	No significant impact	Few components impacted	Significant impact requiring customer approval to proceed	Unacceptable quality	Product not usable

You can use a chart like this to evaluate and assign risk probability and impact to your list of identified risks. The criteria are determined at the beginning of the project. Later, all the risks are listed and prioritized based on the risk ranking and other factors. We'll get to that when we discuss the outputs of this process.

PROBABILITY/IMPACT MATRIX

A probability/impact (PI) matrix is developed to determine if risks should be classified as high, medium, or low risks. This is accomplished by multiplying the risk probability by the risk impact to determine an overall score. The threshold of risk based on high, medium, and low tolerances is determined by comparing the risk score based on the probability level to the PI matrix.

As an example, we've determined that a cost risk event has a 0.4 probability of occurring and a 0.2 impact on the project cost if it does occur. Therefore, the overall score is as follows: $0.4 \times 0.2 = 0.08$. A score of 0.08 for a probability of 0.4 is in the medium threshold, so this risk is assigned a medium value. Again, the values assigned to the risks will determine how Risk Response Planning is carried out for the risks later during the risk-planning processes.

A further example of this is shown in the "Screen Scrapers, Inc." sidebar later in this section.

Project Assumptions Testing

The important thing to note about this output is that all assumptions are tested against two things according to the *Guide to the PMBOK*. The first is the strength of the assumption or the validity of the assumption. The second is the consequences that may impact the project if the assumption turns out to be false. All assumptions that are false should be evaluated and scored just like the risks you identified and scored earlier in this section.

Data Precision Ranking

This involves determining the usefulness of the data gathered to evaluate risk. According to the *Guide to the PMBOK*, data precision ranking looks at the quality of the data used, the availability of data regarding the risks, how well the risk is understood, and the reliability and integrity of the data.

Screen Scrapers is a software-manufacturing company that produces a software product that looks at your mainframe screens, commonly called *green screens*, and converts them to browser-based screens. The browser-based screens look like any other Windows-compatible screens with buttons, scroll bars, and drop-down lists.

Screen Scrapers devised this product for companies that use mainframe programs to update and store data because many of the entry-level workers beginning their careers today are not familiar with green screens. They're cumbersome and difficult to learn, and no consistency exists from screen to screen or program to program. An F5 key in one program might mean go back one page, while an F5 key in another program might mean clear the screen. New users are easily confused, make a lot of mistakes, and have to write tablets full of notes on how to navigate all the screens.

Your company has purchased the Screen Scraper product and has appointed you the project manager over the installation. There are lots of issues to address on this project, and you've made great headway. You're now at the risk identification and quantification stage. You decide to use the Delphi technique to assist you in identifying risk and assigning probability and impact rankings. There are some experts available in your company who can serve on the Delphi panel, as well as some folks in industry organizations you belong to outside the company.

You assemble the group, and set up a summary of the project and send it out via e-mail requesting responses to your questions about risk. After the first pass, you compile the list of risks as follows (this list is an example and isn't exhaustive as your list will be project specific):

- Vendor viability—will they stay in business?

- Vendor responsiveness with problems after implementation

- Software compatibility risks with existing systems

- Hardware compatibility risk

- Connection to the mainframe risk

- Training IT staff members to maintain the product

You send this list back to the Delphi members and ask them to assign a probability of high-high, high, medium, low, or low-low and an impact level of 0.0–1.0 to each risk. The Delphi members assign probability based on a probability scale designed by the risk management team.

The values of the probability scale are as follows: High-high is 0.8, high is 0.6, medium is 0.4, low is 0.2, and low-low is 0.05.

The PI matrix index shows the probability assignment thresholds listed in Table 6.2 (following this sidebar). The table is populated by multiplying the risk event probability times the impact values of 0.05, 0.2, 0.4, 0.6, and 0.8. The table is read based on the probability of the risk occurring. For example, if the risk event has a 0.8 probability of occurring and the risk score is 0.16, the risk would receive an overall medium rating.

The completed risk list and their rankings that you received from the Delphi members looks like Table 6.3 (following this sidebar).

Based on the PI matrix thresholds, the project risks are assigned the following overall probabilities:

- Vendor viability = high
- Vendor responsiveness = low
- Software compatibility = medium
- Hardware compatibility = medium
- Mainframe connection = high
- Training = low

TABLE 6.2 PI Matrix for Screen Scrapers, Inc.

Probability	Risk Scores (Probability × Impact)*				
.8	.04	.16	*.32*	*.48*	*.64*
.6	.03	.12	.24	*.36*	*.48*
.4	.02	.08	.16	.24	*.32*
.2	.01	.04	.08	.12	.16

*The legend for the PI matrix is as follows: no formatting = low assignment; *italics* = medium assignment; ***bold italics*** = high assignment.

TABLE 6.3   Risk Impacts Rating Matrix for Screen Scrapers, Inc.

Risk	Probability	Impact	Risk Scores
Vendor viability	.4	.8	.32
Vendor responsiveness	.2	.5	.10
Software compatibility	.4	.4	.16
Hardware compatibility	.4	.3	.12
Mainframe connection	.8	.8	.64
Training	.2	.3	.06

Risk Ranking

The outputs of this process include overall risk ranking for the project, list of prioritized risks, list of risks for additional analysis and management, and trends in Qualitative Risk Analysis results.

The goal here is to rank all of the risks, prioritize them, and perform more analysis on the risks with high priority. Let's look at the first three outputs individually.

Overall Risk Ranking for the Project

This output compares the list of risks and their overall rankings to other similar projects. You can use the overall risk scores of the current project as a gauge to determine if it has more or less risk than projects of similar size and scope. Overall risk score comparisons are also used to help determine if further analysis should be performed regarding the project and to make go or no-go decisions about the project or project phase. For example, suppose the project you're considering has an overall risk score that's significantly higher than a previous project of a similar nature. You could consider doing further benefit/cost analysis and revisit some of the project justification techniques to determine if the project is worth pursuing. A relatively high risk score could also indicate that you need to assign more resources to the high-risk areas or perhaps that the project needs to be canceled.

List of Prioritized Risks

As the title implies, the risks you've identified and scored during this process are now listed in priority order. Priority is determined using the risk scores including probability and impact and other criteria, which might include the timing of the risk event, the WBS level impacted, and so on.

List of Risks for Additional Analysis and Management

This output examines the risks and their scores to determine which ones should receive further analysis. Those risks with scores of high-high or high, for example, might need further review and action by the risk management team.

Quantifying Risk

Quantitative Risk Analysis looks at the risks you've identified and assigns numeric probabilities to each risk. Quantitative Risk Analysis, like Qualitative Risk Analysis, examines each risk and its potential impact on the project objectives. You may choose to use both of these processes to assess risk or only one of them depending on the complexity of the project and organizational policy regarding risk planning.

Quantitative Risk Analysis evaluates the impacts of risk and quantifies the risk exposure of the project. It determines any interactions among the risks and assesses the range of potential project outcomes. This includes identifying realistic cost, schedule, and scope issues that need attention. The focus here is to determine which risks you should pay attention to and develop responses for, and which risks you can put on the back burner.

We'll take a look at the tools and techniques of the Quantitative Risk Analysis process, which include interviewing, sensitivity analysis, decision tree analysis, and simulation.

Interviewing

This technique is like the interviewing technique we talked about in Risk Identification. Project team members, stakeholders, and subject matter experts are prime candidates for risk interviews. Ask them about their experiences on past projects and about working with the types of technology or processes you'll use during this project.

Make certain you document the results of the interview and how the interviewees decided upon the risk ranges and criteria they used to place risks in certain categories. This will help you later in developing risk responses as well.

For the exam, you should know that there are several types of probability distributions that are useful in displaying risk information. The type of distribution you use determines the type of information you should gather during the interviewing process. It's beyond the scope of this book to delve into probability distributions and calculations. Remember that continuous probability distributions are commonly used in Quantitative Risk Analysis. According to the *Guide to the PMBOK*, continuous probability distributions include normal and log normal distributions, and triangular, beta, and uniform types. Also remember that triangular distributions use estimates based on pessimistic, most likely, and optimistic values. There is more information on this estimating technique in Chapter 7. Normal and log normal distributions use mean and standard deviations.

Sensitivity Analysis

Sensitivity analysis is a quantitative method of analyzing the potential impact of risk events on the project. Sensitivity analysis can also be used to determine stakeholder risk tolerance levels.

Decision Tree Analysis

Unfortunately, this isn't a tree outside your office door that produces "yes" and "no" leaves that you can pick to help you make a decision. Decision trees are diagrams that show the sequence of interrelated decisions and the expected results of choosing one alternative over the other. Typically, more than one choice or option is available when you're faced with a decision or, in this case, potential outcomes from a risk event. The available choices are depicted in a tree form starting at the left with the risk decision and branching out to the right with possible outcomes. Decision trees are usually used for risk events associated with time or cost.

Figure 6.2 shows a sample decision tree using expected value (EV) as one of its inputs.

FIGURE 6.2 Decision tree

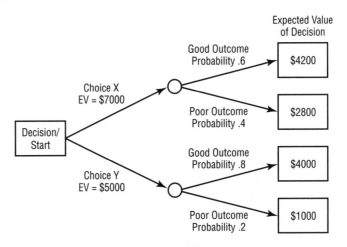

Expected value is the anticipated impact of the decision. This example shows expected value in dollars. The expected value of the decision is a result of the probability of the risk event multiplied by the impact. Impact is shown in dollars in this example. The squares represent decisions to be made, and the circles represent the points where risk events may occur.

The decision with an expected value of $4200 is the correct decision to make as the resulting outcome has the greatest value.

Simulation

Monte Carlo Analysis is a simulation technique that helps you quantify risks associated with the project as a whole. The identified risks and their potential impacts to the project objectives are examined from the perspective of the whole project. Monte Carlo Analysis is used to determine potential outcomes by simulating the project over and over multiple times. Monte Carlo Analysis can also be used during the Schedule Development process.

Simulation techniques are used to predict schedule or cost risks. Schedule simulations are usually performed using the precedence diagramming method schedule, and cost risk simulation typically uses the WBS as its basis.

Listing Quantified Risks

The outputs of the Quantitative Risk Analysis process are prioritized lists of quantified risks, probabilistic analysis of the project, probability of achieving the cost and time objectives, and trends in Quantitative Risk Analysis results.

The prioritized list in this process is similar to the list produced during the Qualitative Risk Analysis process. The list of risks includes those that present the greatest risk to the project and their impacts. It also lists those risks with the greatest opportunities to the project.

Probabilistic analysis of the project is the forecasted results of the project schedule and costs as a result of the outcomes of risk analysis. These results include projected completion dates and costs along with a confidence level associated with each. Confidence levels describe the level of confidence placed on the result. As an example, perhaps the projected schedule completion date is July 12 and the confidence level is .85. This says that we believe the project will finish on or before July 12 and have an 85 percent level of confidence that this date is accurate.

Using the tools and techniques of Quantitative Risk Analysis will also allow you to assign a probability of achieving the cost and time objectives of the project. This output documents those probabilities.

Trends in Quantitative Risk Analysis will likely appear as you repeat the risk analysis processes. This information is useful as you progress, making those risks with the greatest threat to the project more evident, which allows you the opportunity to perform further analysis or go on to develop risk response plans.

Risk Response Planning

Risk Response Planning is a process of deciding what steps to take to reduce threats and take advantage of the opportunities discovered during the risk analysis processes. This process also includes assigning departments or individual staff members the responsibility of carrying out the risk response plans you'll outline in this process.

Generally you'll want to develop risk response plans for those risks with a combination of high probability of occurrence and significant impact to the project. Developing risk response plans for risks of low severity or insignificant impact would not be efficient.

Several strategies are used in this process to reduce or control risk. It's important that you choose the right strategy for each risk so that the risk and its impacts are dealt with effectively. After deciding on which strategy to use, you'll develop an action plan to put this strategy into play should the risk event occur. You may also choose to designate a secondary or backup strategy.

The tools and techniques of this process include the following strategies: avoidance, transference, mitigation, and acceptance.

Avoidance

Risk avoidance involves avoiding the risk altogether or eliminating the cause of the risk event. Let's say you're going to take a car trip from your home to a point 800 miles away. You know, because your friends who just took the same trip told you, that there is a long stretch of construction on one of the highways you're planning on using. To avoid the risk of delay, you plan the trip around the construction work and use another highway for that stretch of driving. In this way, you avoid the risk of getting held up in construction traffic and arrive at your destination on time.

With risk avoidance, you essentially eradicate the risk by eliminating its cause. Here's another example: Suppose your project was kicked off without adequate scope definition and requirements gathering. You run a high probability of experiencing scope creep, or ever-changing requirements, as the project progresses, thus impacting the project schedule. You can avoid this risk by adequately documenting the project scope and requirements during the Planning process and taking steps to monitor and control changes to scope so it doesn't get out of hand.

Risks that occur early in the project might easily be avoided by improving communications, refining requirements, assigning additional resources to project activities, refining the project scope to avoid risk events, and so on.

Transference

The idea behind *risk transference* is to transfer the risk and the consequences of that risk to a third party. The risk hasn't gone away, but the responsibility for the management of that risk now rests with another party. Most companies aren't willing to take on someone else's risk without a little cash thrown in for good measure. This strategy will impact the project budget and should be included in the cost estimate exercises if you know you're going to use it.

Transfer of risk can occur in many forms. Insurance is one form of risk transfer. You are probably familiar with how insurance works. As an example, you purchase car insurance so that if you come upon an obstacle in the road and there is no way of avoiding it, the cost to repair the damage to the car is paid by the insurance company. Okay, minus the deductible and all the calculations for the age of the car, the mileage, the color and make of the car, the weather conditions the day you were driving—but we digress.

Another method of risk transfer is contracting. Contracting transfers specific risks to the vendor depending on the work required by the contract. The vendor accepts the responsibility for the cost of failure. Again, this doesn't come without a price. Contractors charge for their services, and depending on the type of contract you negotiate, the cost might be quite high. For example, in a firm fixed price contract, which we'll talk more about in the Procurement Planning section, the vendor increases the cost of the contract to compensate for the level of risk they're accepting.

However, keep in mind that contracting isn't a cure-all. You might just be swapping one risk for another. For example, say you hire a driver to go with you on your road trip and their job is to do all the driving. If the driver becomes ill or in some way can't fulfill their obligation, you aren't going to get to your destination on time. You've placed the risks associated with the drive on the contract driver; however, you've taken on a risk of delay due to nonperformance, which means you've just swapped one risk for another. You'll have to weigh your options in cases like this and determine which side of the risk coin your organization can more readily accept.

Other forms of transference include warranties, guarantees, and performance bonds.

Mitigation

Risk mitigation attempts to reduce the impact of the risk event by reducing the probability of risk occurrence. This strategy is a lot like defensive driving. You see an obstacle in the road ahead, survey your options, and take the necessary steps to avoid the obstacle and proceed safely on your journey. Seeing the obstacle ahead (identifying risk) allows you to reduce the threat by planning ways around it or planning ways to reduce its impact if the risk does occur.

According to the *Guide to the PMBOK*, the purpose of mitigation is to reduce the probability that a risk will occur and reduce the impact of the risk to a level where you can accept the risk and its outcomes.

Acceptance

Acceptance means that you won't make any plans to try to avoid or mitigate the risk. You're willing to accept the consequences of the risk should it occur. Let's revisit our road trip example. You could plan the trip using the original route and just accept the risk of running into construction. If you get to that point and you're delayed, you'll just accept it. This is called passive acceptance. You could also go ahead and make plans to take an alternate route, but not enact those plans until you actually reach the construction and know for certain that it is going to impede your progress. This is called active acceptance.

Contingency Planning

Contingency planning is a lot like mitigation in that you plan alternatives to deal with the risks should they occur. For example, perhaps you have identified the departure of a key team member as one of your project risks. A contingency plan might be to train one or two other team members in the area of expertise needed so that if the key team member leaves, you have someone else to put in their place.

Contingency comes into play when the risk event occurs. This implies you need to plan for your contingencies well in advance of the threat. After the risks have been identified and quantified, contingency plans should be developed and kept at the ready.

Contingency allowances or reserves are project funds that are held in reserve to offset any unavoidable threats that might occur to project scope, schedule, cost overruns, or quality.

In practice, you'll find that identifying risks, quantifying risks, and developing responses for potential threats may happen simultaneously. In any case, you don't want to be taken by surprise, and that's the point of the risk processes. If you know about potential risks early on, you can very often mitigate or avoid them altogether.

Risk Response Planning Outputs

Risk Response Planning has several outputs including risk response plan, residual risks, secondary risks, contractual agreements, contingency reserve amounts needed, inputs to other processes, and inputs to a revised project plan. The last four of these outputs are self explanatory. Remember that you might need to revisit other Planning processes after performing Risk Response Planning to modify project plans as a result of risk responses.

Now we'll examine the first three outputs of this process.

Risk Response Plan

The *risk response plan* describes the actions you'll take should the identified risks occur. It should include all the identified risks, descriptions of the risks, and the area of the project in which the impact will occur. The risk detail should also describe the causes of risk and how they'll impact the project objectives.

The department or staff members responsible for risk management are documented here. All of the results of the qualitative and quantitative processes and the details regarding risk strategies (acceptance, avoidance, and so on) are documented here as well.

The meat of this plan contains the responses to risks whether this includes one of the risk strategies or a detailed action plan. All of the responses should document the time and cost needed to implement the response.

The contingency plans and reserves are part of the risk response plan as well.

Residual Risks

A *residual risk* is a leftover risk so to speak. After you've implemented a risk response strategy—say mitigation, for example—some minor risk may still remain. The contingency reserve is set up to handle situations like this.

Secondary Risks

Secondary risks are risks that come about as a result of implementing a risk response. The example given previously where you transferred risk by hiring a driver to take you to your destination but they became ill along the way is an example of a secondary risk. Their illness delayed your arrival time, which is risk directly caused by hiring the driver, or implementing a risk response. When planning for risk, identify and plan responses for secondary risks that could occur as well.

Risks exist on all projects. And risk planning is an important part of the project Planning process. Just the act of identifying risks and planning responses can decrease their impact if they occur. Don't take the "what I don't know won't hurt me" approach to risk planning. This is definitely a case where not knowing something can be devastating. Risks that are easily identified and have planned responses aren't likely to kill projects or your career. Risks that you should have known about but ignored could end up costing the organization thousands or millions of dollars, causing schedule delays, or ultimately killing the project. There could be a personal cost as well as cost and schedule overruns due to poor planning on your part are not easily explained on your resume.

Understanding Procurement Planning

*P*rocurement *Planning* is a process of identifying what goods or services you're going to purchase from outside of the organization. Part of what you'll accomplish in this process is determining whether you should purchase the goods or services, and if so, how much and when. Keep in mind that we're discussing the Procurement Planning process from the buyer's perspective as this is the approach the *Guide to the PMBOK* takes.

Sometimes, your entire project will be procured from a vendor. In cases like these, the vendor will have a project manager assigned to the project. Your organization may choose to have an internal project manager assigned as well to act as the conduit between your company and the vendor and to provide information and monitor your organization's deliverables. When this happens, the vendor or contracting company is responsible for fulfilling all of the project management processes as part of the contract. In the case of an outsourced project, the seller—also known as the vendor, supplier, or contractor—manages the project, and the buyer becomes the stakeholder.

Procurement Planning has many inputs. We've covered some of them before, and the ones we haven't looked at are self explanatory. I recommend you study the inputs to this process on your own. The exam focuses primarily on the tools and techniques and outputs of this process. We'll look at two of the tools and techniques now. Expert judgment is also a tool and technique in this process, but we've already covered that ground.

Make or Buy Analysis

The main decision you're trying to get to in make or buy analysis is whether it's more cost effective to buy the products and services or more cost effective for the organization to produce the goods and services needed for the project.

One of the things you should consider in make or buy analysis is cost. Costs should include both direct costs—in other words, the actual cost to purchase the product or service—and indirect costs such as the salary of the manager overseeing the purchase process or ongoing maintenance costs.

Other considerations might include things like capacity issues, skills, availability, and trade secrets. Strict control might be needed for a certain process and thus the process cannot be outsourced. Perhaps your organization has the skills in-house to complete the project, but their current project list is so back-logged that they can't get to the new project for months so you need to bring in a vendor.

Make or buy analysis concludes with the decision to do one or the other.

Contract Type Selection

A *contract* is a compulsory agreement between two or more parties and is constructed such that one party gives something up (money) in exchange for something (goods or services) provided by the other party. There are different types of contracts for different purposes. The *Guide to the PMBOK* divides contracts up into three categories. Within each category are different types of contracts. We'll look at each. There is an exam question or two regarding contract types, so spend some time getting familiar with them.

Fixed Price or Lump Sum Contracts

These contracts set a specific, firm price for the goods or services rendered. The buyer and seller agree on a well-defined deliverable for a set price. In this kind of contract, the biggest risk is borne by the seller. The seller, or contractor, must take great strides to assure they've covered their costs and will make a comfortable profit on the transaction. The seller assumes the risks of increasing costs, nonperformance, or other problems. However, to counter these unforeseen risks, the seller builds in the cost of the risk to the contract price.

Fixed price contracts are usually used for projects that will take a long time to complete and have a high value to the company.

Fixed Price plus Incentive Contracts

Fixed price plus incentive contracts are another type of fixed price contract, but the difference here is that the buyer includes an incentive, or bonus, for early completion or for some other agreed-upon performance criteria that's exceeded according to contract specifications. The criteria for early completion, or other performance enhancements, must be spelled out in the contract so both parties understand the terms and conditions.

Another thing to note with this type of contract is that some of the risk is borne by the buyer as opposed to the firm fixed price contract where all of the risk is borne by the seller. The buyer takes some risk, albeit minimal, by offering the incentive to get the work done earlier, etc. For example, the buyer really would like the product delivered 30 days prior to when the seller thinks they can deliver, so the buyer assumes the risk for the early delivery via the incentive.

Unit Price Contracts

This type of contract is used quite often. The seller specifies a set amount for the goods or services rendered by some measurement. For example, a contracting agency might charge you $135 per hour for a Java programmer, or a leasing company may charge you $2000 per month for the hardware you're renting during the testing phase of your project. These rates are preset and agreed upon by the buyer and seller ahead of time.

Cost Reimbursable Contracts

These types of contracts are as the name implies. The costs associated with producing the goods or services are charged to the buyer. All the costs the seller takes on during the project are charged back to the buyer, thus the seller is reimbursed.

Cost reimbursable contracts carry the highest risk to the buyer as the total costs are uncertain. As problems arise, the buyer will have to shell out even more money to correct the problems. Cost reimbursable contracts are risky for the buyer and have a lot of uncertainty associated with them. Be certain to audit your statements when using a contract like this so that charges from some other project the vendor is working on don't accidentally end up on your bill.

Cost reimbursable contracts are used when there is a lot of uncertainty regarding the project, when a large investment must be made in the project well before completion of the project, and when there is a high amount of risk.

Cost plus Fixed Fee

The first type of cost reimbursable contract is *cost plus fixed fee (CPFF)*. Cost plus contracts charge back all project costs to the seller and include a fixed fee upon completion of the contract. This is how the seller makes money on the deal as the fixed fee portion is the seller's profit. The fee is always firm in this kind of contract, but the costs are variable. The seller doesn't necessarily have a lot of motivation to control costs with this type of contract as you can imagine. And the only motivation to complete the project is driven by the fixed fee portion of the contract.

Cost plus Incentive Fee

The next category of cost reimbursable contract is *cost plus incentive fee*, also known as *cost plus percentage of cost*. This type of contract is just like the CPFF contract, only an incentive has been added for exceeding the performance criteria laid out in the contract. The qualification for exceeded performance must be written in the contract and agreed to by both parties. The incentive is calculated as a percentage of cost or by some method that compares estimated project costs to actual project costs.

This type of contract is the riskiest of all contracts for the buyer. There is no guarantee what the final costs will be, and since the profit to the seller is some percentage of the total cost, anything goes.

Time and Materials (T&M) Contracts

Time and materials contracts are a cross between the fixed price and cost reimbursable contract. The full amount of the material costs is not known at the time the contract is awarded. This resembles a cost reimbursable contract as the costs will continue to grow during the contract's life.

Unit rates may be used in a time and materials contract to preset the rate of a technician or the use of equipment, for example. This is like the fixed price contract arrangement where unit prices are preset ahead of time.

For the exam, I recommend understanding the difference between a fixed price contract and a cost reimbursable contract, when you should use each type of contract, and that risk to the buyer is highest on a cost reimbursable contract.

Procurement Outputs

There are only two outputs in this process. The first is the *procurement management plan*. We've seen a lot of other outputs with the wording, "___ management plan," so you're probably already ahead of me on this one. But hold the phone—let's make sure we touch on the important points. The second output is the statement of work.

Procurement Management Plan

This plan details how the procurement process will be managed. It defines the type of contract to use, what authority the project team has, if more than one contractor will be used, and how the procurement process will be integrated with other project processes. This document, like all the other management plans, becomes a part of the project plan document that we'll talk about in Chapter 7.

Statement of Work

A *statement of work (SOW)* contains the details of the procurement item in clear, concise terms. It includes the project objectives, a description of the work of the project, concise specifications of the product or services required, and a project schedule.

The SOW may be prepared by either the buyer or the seller. Buyers might prepare the SOW and give it to the sellers who, in turn, rewrite it so that they can price the work out properly. If the buyer does not know how to prepare a SOW, the seller may prepare it for them and then give it to the buyer to review.

The seller uses the SOW to determine whether they are able to produce the goods or services as specified in the SOW. It wouldn't hurt to include a copy of the WBS with the SOW as well. Any information the seller can use to properly price the goods or services helps both sides understand what's needed and how it will be provided.

Projects may require some or all of the work of the project to be provided by a vendor. The Procurement Planning process determines if goods or services should be procured from outside of the organization—and if so, describes what will be outsourced and what kind of contract to use, and documents the information in the SOW and procurement management plan.

Solicitation Planning

Solicitation Planning is the last process we'll cover in this chapter. (I hear you cheering out there!) We'll look at one tool and technique and two of the outputs.

In *Solicitation Planning*, you prepare the documents you'll use in the Solicitation process. Standard forms are a tool used to facilitate the procurement process. These are forms that are standardized for your organization and for the types of goods or services typically procured by the organization. Your organization may or may not have standard forms. They are usually found in organizations that write a lot of contracts and procure a significant number of goods and services.

Procurement Documents

Procurement documents are an output of this process. These documents are used to solicit vendors to bid on your procurement needs. You're probably familiar with some of the titles of procurement documents. They might be called request for proposal (RFP), request for information (RFI), invitation for bid (IFB), request for quotation (RFQ), and so on. Procurement documents should clearly state the description of the work requested, they could include the SOW, and they should explain how vendors should respond. Any special provisions or contractual needs should be spelled out as well. For example, many organizations have data concerning personal information like social security numbers and account information on their systems. The vendor will have access to this private information, and in order to ensure they maintain confidentiality, you should require they sign a nondisclosure agreement.

Evaluation Criteria

Evaluation criteria is the last output we'll discuss in this process. This refers to the method your organization will use to choose a vendor from among the proposals you receive. Scoring models might be used as well as rating models, or purely subjective methods of selection might be utilized. An example weighted scoring method was shown in Chapter 3 under the "Describing Project Selection Methods" section. This method could easily be used to score vendor proposals. Sometimes, the evaluation criteria is made public in the procurement process so that vendors know exactly what you're looking for. There are pros and cons to this approach.

Project Case Study: New Kitchen Heaven Retail Store

Ricardo knocks on your office door and asks if you have a few minutes to talk. "Of course," you reply, and he takes a seat on one of the comfy chairs at the conference table. You have a feeling this might take a while.

"I think you should know that I'm concerned about the availability of the T1 line. I've already put in the call to get us on the list because, as I said last week, there's a 30- to 45-day lead time on these orders."

"We're only midway through the Planning process. Do you need to order the T1 so soon? We don't even know the store location yet," you say.

"Even though they say lead time is 30 to 45 days, I've waited as much as 5 or 6 months to get a T1 installed in the past. I know we're really pushing for the early February store opening, so I thought I'd get the ball rolling now. What I need from you is the location address, and I'll need that pretty quick."

"We're narrowing down the choices between a couple of properties, so I should have that for you within the next couple of weeks. Is that soon enough?"

"The sooner the better," Ricardo replies.

"Great. I'm glad you stopped by, Ricardo. I wanted to talk with you about risk anyway, and you led us right into the discussion. Let me ask you, what probability would you assign to the T1 line installation happening 6 months from now?"

"I'd say the probability for 6 months is low. It's more likely that if there is a delay, it would be within a 3- to 4-month time frame."

"If they didn't get to it for 6 months, would it be a showstopper? In other words, is there some other way we could transfer Jill's data until the T1 did get installed?"

"Sure, there are other methods we could use. Jill won't want to do that for very long, but there are workarounds available."

"Good. Now, what about the risk for contractor availability and hardware availability and delivery schedules?" you ask.

You and Ricardo go on to discuss the risks associated with the IT tasks. Later, you ask Jill and Jake the same kinds of questions and compile a list of risks. In addition, you review the project information for the Atlanta store opening, as it's very similar in size and scope to this store, and add those risks to your list as well. You divide some of the risks into the following categories: IT, Facilities, and Retail. A sample portion of your list appears below with overall assignments made based on Qualitative Risk Analysis and the PI matrix.

Category/Risk: IT

- T1 line availability and installation. Risk score: Low

- Contractor availability for Ethernet install. Risk score: Medium

- POS and server hardware availability. Risk score: Medium

Category/Risk: Facilities

- Desirable location in the right price range. Risk score: High

- Contractor availability for build-out. Risk score: Low

- Availability of fixtures and shelving. Risk score: Low

Category/Risk: Retail

- Product availability. Risk score: Medium

- Shipment dates for product. Risk score: Medium

After examining the risks, you decide that response plans should be developed for the last two items listed under the IT source, the first item under Facilities, and both of the risks listed under Retail.

Ricardo has already mitigated the T1 connection and installation risk by signing up several months ahead of when the install is needed. The contractor availability can be handled with a contingency plan that specifies a backup contractor should the first choice not be available. For the POS terminals and hardware, you decide to use the transfer strategy. As part of the contract, you'll require these vendors to deliver on time, and if they cannot, they'll be required to provide and pay for rental equipment until they can get your gear delivered.

The Facilities risk and Retail risks will be handled with a combination of acceptance, contingency plans, and mitigation.

You've calculated the expected value for several potential risk events. Two of them are detailed here.

Desirable location has an expected value of $780,000. The probability of choosing an incorrect or less than desirable location is 60 percent. The potential loss in sales is the difference between a high-producing store that generates $2.5 million in sales per year versus an average store that generates $1.2 million in sales per year.

The expected value of the product availability event is $50,000. The probability of the event occurring is 40 percent. The potential loss in sales is $125,000 for not opening the store in conjunction with the Garden and Home Show.

Kitchen Heaven has a file drawer full of standard forms as they've opened several retail stores each year for the last 3 years. You'll use these standard forms to secure the contracts with the vendors and order the retail items.

Project Case Study Checklist

Risk Management Planning

Risk Identification

- Documentation reviews
- Information-gathering techniques

Qualitative Risk Analysis

- Risk probability and impact
- Probability/impact risk rating
- List of prioritized risks

Quantitative Risk Analysis

- Interviewing
- Expected value

Risk Response Planning

- Avoidance, transference, mitigation, and acceptance strategies
- Risk response plan

Procurement Planning

- Standard forms

Solicitation Planning

- Procurement documents

Summary

Congratulations! You've completed another fun-filled, action-packed chapter. We covered a lot of material in this chapter starting with Quality

Planning and risk-related planning, and ending up with Procurement and Solicitation Planning.

Quality Planning targets the quality standards that are relevant to your project. You need to consider the cost of quality when considering stakeholder needs. Three men led to the rise of the cost of quality theories. Crosby is known for his zero defects theory, Juran for the fitness for use theory, and Deming for contributing 85 percent of cost of quality to the management team. The Kaizen approach says that people should be improved first, then the quality of the products or services.

Flowcharting is a tool and technique in Quality Planning that diagrams the logical steps that must be performed to accomplish your objective. Cause-and-effect diagrams show the relationship between the effects of quality problems and their causes. Design of experiments is an analytical technique that determines what variables have the greatest effect on the project outcomes.

The quality management plan outlines how the project team will enact the quality policy.

Risk is inherent in all projects. The Risk Management Planning process determines how you will plan for risks on your project. Its only output is the risk management plan, which details how you will manage risks.

The Risk Identification process seeks to identify and document the project risks using brainstorming, the Delphi technique, interviewing, and checklists.

Qualitative Risk Analysis and Quantitative Risk Analysis involve evaluating risks and assigning probability and impact factors to the risks. Many tools and techniques are used during these processes including risk probability and impact, probability/impact risk rating matrix, interviewing, sensitivity analysis, decision tree analysis, and simulation.

A probability/impact risk matrix uses the combination of the probability score multiplied by the impact value to determine the risk score and assignment. The threshold of risk based on high, medium, and low tolerances is determined by comparing the risk score based on the probability level to the PI matrix.

Monte Carlo simulation is a technique used to quantify schedule or cost risks. Decision trees graphically display decisions and their various choices and outcomes.

The Risk Response Planning process is the last risk-planning process and culminates with the risk response plan. The risk response plan details the strategies you'll use to respond to risk and assigns individuals to manage each risk response. Risk response strategies include avoidance, mitigation, acceptance, and transfer. Insurance and contracting are examples of transferring risk.

Contingency planning involves planning alternatives to deal with risk events should they occur. Part of the risk management plan should detail the contingency plans for high-probability, high-impact risk events.

Procurement Planning involves performing analysis to determine if the goods and services needed to perform the project should be procured from a vendor or produced internally. Several types of contracts are considered during procurement. The risk impact with fixed price contracts typically rests on the seller, while the risk impact with cost reimbursable contracts rests on the buyer.

The procurement management plan details how the procurement process will be managed during the course of the project. Solicitation Planning is a matter of preparing the documents you'll use in the Solicitation process during the Executing process of the project.

Exam Essentials

Be able to identify what produces increased stakeholder satisfaction, lower costs, higher productivity, and less rework. These are the benefits of meeting quality requirements and are discovered during benefit/cost analysis in Quality Planning.

Be able to name the purpose of Risk Identification. To identify all risks that may impact the project, document them, and identify their characteristics.

Be able to define the purpose of Qualitative Risk Analysis. Qualitative Risk Analysis determines the impact the identified risks will have on the project and the probability they'll occur, and puts the risks in priority order according to their effect on the project objectives.

Be able to define the purpose of the risk response plan. It describes the actions to take should the identified risks occur. It should include all the identified risks, a description of the risks, how they'll impact the project objectives, and the people assigned to manage the risk responses.

Be able to name the purpose for the Procurement Planning process. To identify which project needs should be obtained from outside the organization.

Be able to identify the contract types and their usage. Use fixed price contracts for long-term projects with a high value to the company, and use cost reimbursable contracts for projects with uncertainty and large investments early in the project life. Time and materials contracts are a cross between fixed and cost reimbursable.

Key Terms

Before you take the exam, be certain you are familiar with the following terms:

benchmarking	quality management plan
cause-and-effect diagram	Quality Planning
checklist	Quantitative Risk Analysis
Delphi Technique	Risk Identification
flowchart	risk management plan
impact scale	Risk Management Planning
probability scale	Risk Response Planning
procurement management plan	Solicitation Planning
Procurement Planning	statement of work (SOW)
Qualitative Risk Analysis	

Review Questions

1. What are the Quality Planning process outputs?

   A. Quality management plan, benchmarking, checklists, evaluation criteria

   B. Quality management plan, benchmarking, operational definitions

   C. Quality management plan, checklists, inputs to other processes

   D. Quality management plan, operational definitions, checklists, inputs to other processes

2. Three people are responsible for establishing cost of quality theories. Crosby and Juran are two them, and their theories respectively are:

   A. Grades of quality, fitness for use

   B. Fitness for use, zero defects

   C. Zero defects, fitness for use

   D. Cost of quality, zero defects

3. The theory that 85 percent of the cost of quality is a management problem is attributed to:

   A. Deming

   B. Kaizen

   C. Juran

   D. Crosby

4. All of the following are benefits of meeting quality requirements except:

   A. An increase in stakeholder satisfaction

   B. Less rework

   C. Low turnover

   D. Higher productivity

5. You are a project manager for Fountain of Youth Spring Water bottlers. You are installing a new accounting system and have identified several problems and their causes. You decide to use which of the following flowcharts to diagram the problems' causes and effects?

   A. Decision tree diagram

   B. Fishbone diagram

   C. Benchmark diagram

   D. Simulation tree diagram

6. You are a project manager for Fountain of Youth Spring Water bottlers. You are installing a new accounting system and have identified several problems and their causes. You decide to use which of the following to identify the variables that will have the greatest effect on project outcomes?

   A. Design of experiments

   B. Benchmarking

   C. Benefit/cost analysis

   D. Flowcharting

7. Each of the following is true regarding the risk management plan except:

   A. The risk management plan is an output of the Risk Management Planning process.

   B. The risk management plan includes a description of the responses to risks and triggers.

   C. The risk management plan includes thresholds, scoring and interpretation methods, responsible parties, and budgets.

   D. The risk management plan is an input to all the remaining risk-planning processes.

8. Information-gathering techniques used in the Risk Identification process include all of the following except:

    A. Brainstorming

    B. Delphi technique

    C. Interviewing

    D. Kaizen technique

9. Which of the following processes assess the likelihood of risk occurrences and their consequences using numeric probability assignments?

    A. Qualitative Risk Analysis

    B. Risk Identification

    C. Quantitative Risk Analysis

    D. Risk Response Planning

10. You are the project manager for a new website for the local zoo. You need to perform Qualitative Risk Analysis. When you've completed this process, you'll produce all of the following outputs except:

    A. Overall risk ranking for the project

    B. List of prioritized risks

    C. Inputs to other processes

    D. List of risks for additional analysis and management

11. You are the project manager for a new website for the local zoo. You need to perform Quantitative Risk Analysis. You'll use all of the following tools and techniques to accomplish this except:

    A. Data precision ranking

    B. Sensitivity analysis

    C. Decision tree analysis

    D. Interviewing

12. Which of the following tools and techniques shows the impacts of one decision over another as well as the probability and cost of each risk along a logical path?

    A. Simulation

    B. Decision tree

    C. Probability/impact risk matrix

    D. Sensitivity analysis

13. Which of the following describes the cost of quality associated with scrapping, rework, and downtime?

    A. Internal failure costs

    B. External failure costs

    C. Prevention costs

    D. Appraisal costs

14. Your hardware vendor left you voicemail saying that a potential snowstorm in the Midwest might prevent your equipment from arriving on time. She wanted to give you a heads-up and asked that you return the call. Which of the following is true?

    A. This is a secondary risk, which is an output of Risk Response Planning.

    B. This is a contingency plan, which is an output of Risk Response Planning.

    C. This is a risk, which is an output of Risk Identification.

    D. This is a trigger, which is an output of Risk Identification.

15. You are constructing a probability/impact risk rating matrix for your project. Which of the following is true?

A. The PI matrix multiplies the risk's probability by the cost of the impact to determine an expected value of the risk event.

B. The PI matrix multiplies the risk's probability scales, which fall between 0.0 and 1.0, and the risk's impact scales to determine a risk score.

C. The PI matrix multiplies the risk's probability by the expected value of the risk event to determine the risk impact and assign a risk score based on a predetermined threshold.

D. The PI matrix multiplies the risk's probability scales and the risk's impact scales, which fall between 0.0 and 1.0, to determine a risk score.

16. All of the following strategies are tools and techniques of Risk Response Planning used to reduce or control risk except?

A. Mitigation

B. Simulation

C. Avoidance

D. Acceptance

17. Your hardware vendor left you voicemail saying that a snowstorm in the Midwest will prevent your equipment from arriving on time. You identified a risk response for this risk and have arranged for a local company to lease you the needed equipment until yours arrives. This is an example of which risk response strategy?

A. Transference

B. Acceptance

C. Mitigation

D. Avoidance

18. You are the project manager for an upcoming outdoor concert event. You're working on the procurement plan for the computer software program that will control the lighting and screen projections during the concert. You're comparing the cost of purchasing a software product to the cost of your company programmers writing a custom software program. You are engaged in which of the following?

    A. Procurement planning

    B. Sensitivity analysis

    C. Transference of risk

    D. Make or buy analysis

19. You are the project manager for an outdoor concert event scheduled for 1 year from today. You're working on the procurement plan for the computer software program that will control the lighting and screen projections during the concert. You've decided to contract with a professional services company that specializes in writing custom software programs. You want to minimize the risk to the organization, so you'll opt for which contract type?

    A. Fixed price plus incentive

    B. Cost plus fixed fee

    C. Fixed price

    D. Cost plus incentive

20. You are the project manager for Heart of Texas casual clothing company. They're introducing a new line of clothing called Black Sheep Ranch Wear. You will outsource the production of this clothing line to a vendor. The vendor has requested a SOW. All of the following are true except:

    A. The SOW contains a description of the new clothing line.

    B. As the purchaser, you are required to write the SOW.

    C. The SOW contains the objectives of the project.

    D. The vendor requires a SOW to determine if they can produce the clothing line given the very detailed specifications of this project.

Answers to Review Questions

1. D. Quality Planning has four outputs: quality management plan, operational definitions, checklists, and inputs to other processes. Benchmarking is a tool and technique of this process.

2. C. Philip Crosby devised the zero defects theory, meaning do it right the first time. Proper Quality Planning leads to less rework and higher productivity. Joseph Juran's fitness for use says that stakeholders' and customers' expectations are met or exceeded.

3. A. W. Edwards Deming conjectured that the cost of quality is a management problem 85 percent of the time and that once the problem trickles down to the workers, it is outside their control.

4. C. The benefits of meeting quality requirements are increased stakeholder satisfaction, lower costs, higher productivity, and less rework.

5. B. The cause-and-effect flowcharts, also called fishbone diagrams or Ishikawa diagrams, show the relationship between the causes and effects of quality problems.

6. A. Design of experiments is an analytical technique that identifies the elements or variables that will have the greatest effect on overall project outcomes.

7. B. The risk management plan details how risk management processes will be implemented, monitored, and controlled throughout the life of the project. The risk management plan does not include responses to risks or triggers. Responses to risks are detailed in the Risk Response Planning process.

8. D. The Kaizen approach is a quality technique that says project team members and managers should always be on the lookout for quality improvement opportunities.

9. C. Quantitative Risk Analysis analyzes the probability of risks and their consequences using numeric probability assignments. Qualitative Risk Analysis may use numeric probability analysis, but the *Guide to the PMBOK* distinguishes between these two processes by stating that Quantitative Risk Analysis analyzes probability numerically. The Quantitative Risk Analysis process evaluates risk impacts and assesses the range of possible project results.

10. C. Inputs to other processes are an output of Risk Identification and Risk Response Planning. The other output of Qualitative Risk Analysis not listed here is trends in Qualitative Risk Analysis results.

11. A. Data precision ranking is a tool and technique of the Qualitative Risk Analysis process. The remaining tool and technique of Quantitative Risk Analysis is simulation.

12. B. Decision trees allow you to show the sequence of choices and their outcomes in a tree form starting with the decision or risk event at the left and each option branching out from there to the right. This is a tool and technique of the Quantitative Risk Analysis process.

13. A. Internal failure costs are costs associated with not meeting the customer's expectations while you still had control over the product. This results in rework, scrapping, and downtime.

14. D. The best answer is D. Triggers are also called risk symptoms, which are an output of Risk Identification. Triggers are warning signs of an impending risk.

15. B. The PI matrix multiplies the probability—determined with the risk's probability scales, which fall between 0.0 and 1.0—and impact, which is determined with impact scales, to determine a risk score and assign a high, medium, or low designation to the risk based on a predetermined threshold.

16. B. The tools and techniques of Risk Response Planning are avoidance, transference, mitigation, and acceptance.

17. C. Mitigation tries to reduce the impact of a risk event should it occur. Making plans to arrange for the leased equipment reduces the consequences of the risk.

18. D. Make or buy analysis is determining whether it's more cost effective to purchase the goods or services needed for the project or more cost effective for the organization to produce them internally.

19. C. Fixed price contracts have the highest risk to the seller and the least amount of risk to the buyer. However, the price the vendor charges for the product or service will compensate for the amount of risk they're taking on.

20. B. The SOW can be written by either the buyer or the seller. Sometimes the buyer will write the SOW, and the seller may modify it and send it back to the buyer for verification and approval.

Chapter

7

Creating the Project Plan

PMP EXAM CONTENT FROM THE PROJECT PLANNING PERFORMANCE DOMAIN COVERED IN THIS CHAPTER:

✓ 6. Develop Project Plan.

✓ 7. Obtain Plan Approval.

The Planning process group has more processes than any other *Guide to the PMBOK* process group. As a result, a lot of time and effort goes into the Planning process of any project. You'll find on some projects you spend as much time planning the project as you do executing and controlling the project. This isn't a bad thing. The better planning you do up front, the more likely you'll have a successful project. The Planning, Executing, and Controlling process groups together account for almost 70 percent of the PMP exam questions, so you'll want to spend about the same percentage of your study time on these areas.

We'll spend this chapter wrapping up the remaining Planning processes and conclude with a discussion of the Project Plan Development process. This process takes the outputs of other Planning processes and creates a project plan that's used throughout project Executing and project Controlling processes to track project performance. All other processes in the Planning process group have to be completed before working on the Project Plan Development process. We'll cover Schedule Development and Cost Budgeting in this chapter as well and begin the Executing process group in the next chapter.

Developing the Project Schedule

The *Schedule Development* process is the heart of the Planning process group. This is where you will lay out the schedule for your project tasks, determine their start and finish dates, and finalize activity sequences and durations. This process, along with Activity Duration Estimating and Cost

Estimating, is repeated several times before you actually come up with the project schedule. We'll learn later in this section that project management software comes in very handy during this process. In fact, it is one of the tools and techniques of this process.

Although there are no exam questions regarding the order that processes are performed in, it might help to understand that Schedule Development cannot be performed until all of the following core processes of project Planning are completed: Scope Planning, Scope Definition, Resource Planning, Activity Definition, Activity Sequencing, Activity Duration Estimating, Risk Management Planning, and Cost Estimating. Schedule Development must be completed prior to the Cost Budgeting process, which we'll cover later in this chapter. Both of these processes then feed the final Planning process, Project Plan Development.

Scheduling Inputs

Schedule Development has 10 inputs, 7 of which are outputs from previous Planning processes. As we've discussed, you can see how important it is to perform all of the Planning processes accurately, as the information you derive from almost every process is used somewhere else in Planning or in the later process groups. Your project schedule will reflect the information you know at this point in time. If you have incorrectly estimated activity durations or didn't identify the right dependencies, for example, your project schedule will not be correct. It's definitely worth the time investment to correctly plan your project and come up with accurate outputs for each of the Planning processes.

Three of the inputs to this process are new: calendars, leads and lags, and activity attributes. A short description of each is given next.

Calendars

Calendars are divided into two types: project calendars and resource calendars. *Project calendars* concern all the resources involved in the project, while *resource calendars* look at particular resources or groups of resources and their availability.

Leads and Lags

Leads and lags are related to Activity Sequencing. Remember that Activity Sequencing puts tasks in logical order and determines if there are dependencies that exist among the activities. We then take these tasks and develop a network diagram from them. (We discussed this in Chapter 5 if you need a quick review.) Leads and lags come in when there are delays between dependent and independent activities. *Lags* require the dependent activity to have time added either to the start date or to the finish date of the activity. *Leads*, conversely, require time to be subtracted from the start date or the finish date of the dependent activity. Lead time is not used as often as lag time.

Let's go back to the classic house-painting example to put all this in perspective. In order to paint, we first need to scrape the peeling paint and then prime. However, we can't begin painting until the primer has dried. So we shouldn't schedule priming for Monday and painting for Tuesday if we need the primer to dry on Tuesday. Therefore, the priming activity requires lag time, so we need to add time to the end of this activity to allow for the drying time needed before we can start painting.

Lead time works just the opposite. Suppose, for this example, we could start priming before the scraping is finished. Maybe there are areas on the house that don't require scraping, so we don't really need to wait until the scraping activity finishes to begin the priming activity. Priming in this example has lead time subtracted from the beginning of the activity so that this activity begins prior to the finish of the previous activity.

Activity Attributes

Activity attributes are the characteristics of the activity. These might include a description of where the activity will take place, who will perform the activity, and whether the activity is a summary-level activity—level two or three on the WBS perhaps—or a detailed activity with particular specifications.

Understanding the Tools and Techniques of Schedule Development

The two primary outputs of Schedule Development are the project schedule and the schedule management plan. You can employ several tools and techniques in order to produce these outputs. The tools and techniques you choose will depend on the complexity of the project. For the exam, however, you'll need to know them all.

There are six tools and techniques used in Schedule Development. A lot of information is packed into some of these tools and techniques, and you will want to dedicate study time to each of them for the exam. The first tool and technique, called mathematical analysis, includes several techniques, each of which are thoroughly covered on the exam. So, let's get to it!

Mathematical Analysis

Mathematical analysis includes three commonly known techniques: Critical Path Method (CPM), Graphical Evaluation and Review Technique (GERT), and Program Evaluation and Review Technique (PERT). CPM and PERT are very similar network-planning methods, and in some organizations, CPM and PERT are used synonymously. We'll examine each of these techniques momentarily. Keep in mind that CPM and PERT are methods to determine schedule durations without regard to resource availability.

Critical Path Method

Critical Path Method (CPM) calculates the earliest start date, earliest finish date, latest start date, and latest finish date for each activity. The *critical path (CP)* on any project is the longest full path. Any project activity with a float time that equals zero is considered a critical path task. We will walk through an example to explain how all these dates and float times are calculated after a short description of float time.

Float time is also called *slack time*, and you'll see these terms used interchangeably. There are two types of slack: total slack and free slack. *Total slack* is the amount of time you can delay the start of a task without delaying the ending of the project. *Free slack* is the amount of time you can delay the start of a task without delaying the start of a successor task.

We'll calculate the CP for a sample project and illustrate how all the dates, the CP, and the float times are derived.

You are the project manager for a new software project. The company you are working for is venturing into the movie rental business over the Web. You need to devise a software system that tracks all the information related to rentals and also supplies the management team with reports that will help them make good business decisions. For purposes of illustration, I'm showing only a limited portion of the tasks that you would have on a project like this.

We'll start our example by plugging information into Table 7.1 (see below) from the processes that we've already completed. The list of activities comes from the work package level of the WBS and the activity list compiled during the Activity Definition process. The durations for each activity are listed in the column by that title and were derived during the Activity Duration Estimating process. The duration times are listed in days. The Dependency column lists the activities that require a previous activity to finish before the current activity can start. We're using only finish-start relationships. For example, you'll see that activity number 2 and activity number 4 each depend on activity 1 to finish before they can begin. The dependency information came from the Activity Sequencing process. Now, we'll proceed to calculating the dates.

Project Deliverables is the first activity and, obviously, where the project starts. This activity begins on April 1. Project Deliverables has a 12-day duration. So now take April 1 and add 12 days to this to come up with an early finish date of April 12. Watch out, because you need to count day one, or April 1, as a full work day. The simplest way to do this calculation is to take the early start date, add the duration, and subtract one. Therefore, the early finish date for the first activity is April 12. By the way, we are ignoring weekends and holidays for this example. Activity 2 depends on activity 1, so it cannot start until activity 1 has finished. Its earliest start date is April 13. Add the duration to this date minus one to come up with the finish date.

You'll notice that activity 4 depends on activity 1 finishing, so its earliest start date is also April 13. Continue to calculate the remaining early start and early finish dates in the same manner. This calculation is called a *forward pass*.

To calculate the late start and late finish dates, you begin with the last activity. The late finish for activity 9 is July 10. Since the duration is only 1 day, July 10 is also the late start date. You know that activity 8 must finish before activity 9 can begin, so activity 8's late finish date, July 9, is 1 day prior to activity 9's late start date, July 10. Subtract the duration of activity 8 (3 days) from July 9 and add one to get the late start date of July 7. We're performing the opposite calculation that we did for the forward pass. This calculation is called a *backward pass*, as you might have guessed. Continue calculating the late start and late finish through activity 4.

Activity 3 adds a new twist. Here's how it works. Activity 7 cannot begin until activity 3 and activity 6 are completed. No other activity depends on the completion of activity 3. If activity 7's late start date is June 29, activity 3's late finish date must be June 28. June 28 less 8 days plus one gives us a late start date of June 21. Activity 3 depends on activity 2, so activity 2 must be completed prior to beginning activity 3. Calculate these dates just like you did for activities 9 through 4.

Activity 1 still remains. Activity 4 cannot start until activity 1 is completed. If activity 4's late start date is April 13, the late finish date for activity 1 must be April 12. Subtract the duration of activity 1 and add one to come up with a late start date of April 1.

Alternatively, the forward pass and backward pass can be calculated by saying the first task starts on day zero and then adding the duration to this. As an example, activity number 1's early start date is April 1, which is day zero. Add 12 days to day zero and you come up with an early finish date of April 12.

The calculation for float/slack time is determined by subtracting the early start date from the late start date. If the float time equals zero, the activity is on the critical path.

To determine the CP duration of the project, add up the duration of every activity with zero float. You should come up with 101 days, as we're adding the duration for all activities except for activity 2 and activity 3. A critical path task is any task that cannot be changed without impacting the project end date. By definition, these are all tasks with zero float.

TABLE 7.1 CPM Calculation

Activity Number	Activity Description	Dependency	Duration	Early Start	Early Finish	Late Start	Late Finish	Float/ Slack
1	Project Deliverables	—	12	4/1	4/12	4/1	4/12	0
2	Procure Hardware	1	2	4/13	4/14	6/19	6/20	68
3	Test Hardware	2	8	4/15	4/22	6/21	6/28	68
4	Procure Software Tools	1	10	4/13	4/22	4/13	4/22	0
5	Write Programs	4	45	4/23	6/6	4/23	6/6	0
6	Test and Debug	5	22	6/7	6/28	6/7	6/28	0
7	Install	3, 6	8	6/29	7/6	6/29	7/6	0
8	Training	7	3	7/7	7/9	7/7	7/9	0
9	Acceptance	8	1	7/10	7/10	7/10	7/10	0

Another way to determine the critical path is by looking at the network diagram. If the duration is included with the information on the node, or if start and end dates are given, you simply calculate the duration and then add up the duration of the longest path in the diagram to determine CP. However, this method is not as accurate as what's described in Table 7.1. Shown in Figure 7.1 is the same project in diagram form. Duration is printed in the top-right corner of each node. Add up the duration of each path to determine which one is the critical path.

FIGURE 7.1 Critical path diagram

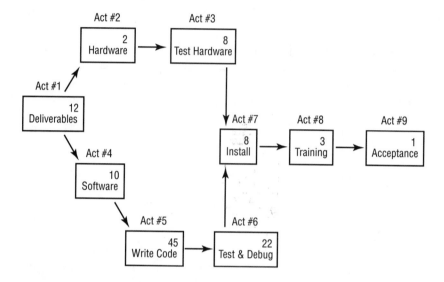

Remember that CP is always the path with the longest duration. In the figure, path 1-2-3-7-8-9 equals 34 days. Path 1-4-5-6-7-8-9 equals 101 days; therefore this path is the critical path.

Graphical Evaluation and Review Technique

The only thing you need to understand about the Graphical Evaluation and Review Technique (GERT) for the exam is that GERT allows for conditional branching and looping, and probabilistic treatment. In practice, GERT is similar to PERT except that GERT allows you to loop back through a process or perform branching to show alternatives. For example, our software project in the CPM example might require unit testing of individual modules before the entire program can be tested, and each module must pass its unit test. If the unit test fails, GERT allows you to depict a looping condition so that you can come back through unit testing and then progress to the next activity once the unit test is passed.

Program Evaluation and Review Technique

The *Program Evaluation and Review Technique (PERT)* was developed in the 1950s by the United States Navy. They were working on one of the most complex engineering projects in history at the time, the Polaris Missile Program, and needed a way to manage the project and forecast the project schedule with a high degree of reliability. PERT was developed to do just that.

PERT and CPM are similar techniques. The difference is CPM uses the most likely duration to determine project duration, while PERT uses what's called expected value (or the weighted average) to determine project duration. *Expected value* is calculated using three time estimates for activity duration instead of one and then finding the weighted average of the three time estimates. If we take this one step further and determine the standard deviation of each activity, we can assign a confidence factor to our project estimates. Without getting too heavily involved in the mathematics of probability, understand that for data that fits a bell curve, which is what we're about to calculate with the PERT technique, the following is true:

- Work will finish within plus or minus three standard deviations 99.73 percent of the time.

- Work will finish within plus or minus two standard deviations 95.44 percent of the time.

- Work will finish within plus or minus one standard deviation 68.26 percent of the time.

The three time estimates used to calculate expected value are the optimistic estimate, the pessimistic estimate, and the most likely estimate. Going back to our software example, let's find out what these three time estimates might look like for the activity called Write Programs. You get these estimates by asking the lead programmer, or key team member, to estimate the optimistic, pessimistic, and most likely duration for the activity based on their past experience. Other historical information could be used to determine these estimates as well. We'll say in this case that we're given 38 days for the optimistic time, 57 days for the pessimistic, and 45 days for the most likely. (Remember that 45 days is what we used to calculate CPM and was derived from the Activity Duration Estimating process.)

The formula to calculate expected value is as follows:

$$[\text{optimistic} + \text{pessimistic} + (4 \times \text{most likely})] \div 6$$

The expected value for the Write Programs activity is as follows:

$$[38 + 57 + (4 \times 45)] \div 6 = 45.83$$

The formula for standard deviation, which helps us determine confidence level, is as follows:

(pessimistic − optimistic) ÷ 6

The standard deviation for our activity is as follows:

(57 − 38) ÷ 6 = 3.17

We could say the following given the information we now have:

- There is a 68.26 percent chance that the Write Programs activity will be completed between 42.66 days and 49 days.

- There is a 95.44 percent chance that the Write Programs activity will be completed between 39.49 days and 52.17 days.

We calculated the range of dates for the 68.26 percent chance by adding and subtracting one standard deviation, 3.17, from the expected value, 45.83. The 95.44 percent chance was calculated by multiplying the standard deviation times two, which equals 6.34, and adding and subtracting that result from the expected value to come up with the least number of days and the most number of days it will take to finish the activity. Generally speaking, two standard deviations, or 95.44 percent, is a close enough estimate for most purposes.

The higher the standard deviation is for an activity, the higher the risk. Since standard deviation measures the difference between the pessimistic and the optimistic times, a greater spread between the two, which results in a higher number, indicates a greater risk. Conversely, a low standard deviation means less risk.

Let's bring our table of activities back and plug in the expected values and the standard deviation for each (please see Table 7.2).

TABLE 7.2   PERT Calculation

Activity Number	Activity Description	Optimistic	Pessimistic	Most Likely	Expected Value	Standard Deviation	SD Squared
1	Project Deliverables	10	14	12	12.00	0.67	0.45
2	Procure Hardware	—	—	—	—	—	—

TABLE 7.2 PERT Calculation *(continued)*

Activity Number	Activity Description	Optimistic	Pessimistic	Most Likely	Expected Value	Standard Deviation	SD Squared
3	Test Hardware	—	—	—	—	—	—
4	Procure Software Tools	8	14	10	10.33	1.00	1.0
5	Write Programs	38	57	45	45.83	3.17	10.05
6	Test and Debug	20	30	22	23.00	1.67	2.79
7	Install	5	10	8	7.83	0.83	0.69
8	Training	3	3	3	3.00	0	0
9	Acceptance	1	1	1	1.00	0	0
Totals for CP tasks					102.99		14.98

Now we'll look at the total project duration using PERT and the standard deviation to determine a range of dates for project duration. You should add only the tasks that are on the critical path. You'll remember from the CPM example that tasks 2 and 3 are not on the critical path, so their expected value and standard deviation calculations have been left blank in this table. When we add all the remaining tasks, the total expected value duration is 102.99 days, or 103 days rounded to the nearest day.

Your next logical conclusion might be to add the Standard Deviation column to get the standard deviation for the project. Unfortunately, you cannot add up the standard deviations because you will come out with a number that is much too high. Totaling the standard deviations assumes that all of the tasks will run over schedule, and that's not likely. It is likely that a few tasks will run over, but not every one of them. So, now you're probably wondering how to calculate the magic number.

You might have noticed an extra column at the right called SD Squared. This is the standard deviation squared—or for those of you with math phobias out there, the standard deviation multiplied by itself.

Once you have calculated standard deviation squared for each activity, add up the squares for a total of 14.98. There's one more step and we're done. Take the square root of 14.98 (you'll need a calculator) to come up with 3.87. This is the standard deviation you will use to determine your range of projected completion dates. Here's a recap of these last few calculations:

Total expected value = 103.00

Sum of SD Squared = 14.98

Square root of SD Squared = 3.87

We can now make the following predictions regarding our project:

- There is a 68.26 percent chance that the project will be completed between 99.13 days and 106.87 days.

- There is a 95.44 percent chance that the project will be completed between 95.26 days and 110.74 days.

PERT is used for very large, highly complex projects. PERT is also a useful technique to determine project duration when your activity durations are uncertain. For the exam, it's recommended that you know one standard deviation gives you a 68 percent (rounded) probability and two standard deviations gives you a 95 percent (rounded) probability. Also know how to calculate the range of project duration dates based on the expected value and standard deviation calculation. You probably don't need to memorize how to calculate the standard deviation as I believe most of the questions give you this information. You should, however, memorize the PERT formula and know how it works. It wouldn't hurt to go ahead and memorize the standard deviation formula as well—you never know what might show up on the exam.

Duration Compression

Duration compression takes on two forms according to the *Guide to the PMBOK*, crashing and fast tracking. Compression is simply shortening the project schedule to accomplish all the activities sooner than estimated.

Schedule compression might happen when the project end date has been predetermined and after performing the CPM or PERT techniques, you discover that the project is going to take longer than the original promised date. In our CPM example, we calculated the end date to be July 10. What if the project was undertaken and a July 2 date was promised? That's when you'll need to employ crashing or fast tracking.

Crashing is a compression technique that looks at cost and schedule trade-offs. One of the things you might do to crash the schedule is add resources, from either inside or outside the organization, to the critical path tasks. It wouldn't help you to add resources to noncritical path tasks as these tasks don't impact the schedule end date anyway because they have float time. You might also limit or reduce the project requirements. Ask stakeholders if the features or functions are "nice to have" or necessary. You might also try changing the sequence of tasks. This sometimes shortens the schedule, but isn't always possible.

Be certain to check the critical path when you've used the crashing technique as crashing might have changed the critical path. Crashing doesn't always come up with a reasonable result. It will often increase the costs of the project as well. The idea with crashing is to try to gain the greatest amount of schedule compression with the least amount of cost.

We talked about fast tracking in Chapter 1. *Fast tracking* is starting two tasks at the same time that were previously scheduled to start sequentially. Fast tracking can increase project risk and might cause the project team to have to rework tasks. As an example, fast tracking is often performed in object-oriented programming. The programmers might begin writing code on several modules at once, out of sequential order, and prior to the completion of the design phase.

Simulation

Monte Carlo Analysis is a simulation technique that produces a range of values for each activity with multiple duration possibilities. Probability durations are then chosen for each activity, and the simulation starts. Monte Carlo will run the possible activity durations and schedule projections many, many times to come up with the schedule projections and their probability, critical path duration estimates, and float time. For the exam, remember that Monte Carlo is a simulation technique that shows the probability of all the possible project completion dates.

Resource Leveling Heuristics

Earlier I said that CPM and PERT do not consider resource availability. Now that you have a schedule of activities, it's time to plug in resources for those activities and adjust the schedule according to any resource constraints you discover.

Remember that you identified resources and acquired staff during the Resource Planning and Staff Acquisition processes, which we discussed in Chapter 5. Skill sets, previous experience, availability, and personal interests were documented during these processes, and staff was assigned to the project. Staff members were not assigned directly to tasks at that point, just to the project itself. Organizational development described roles and responsibilities as they related to scope definition and produced the staffing management plan, which describes how to bring resources on and off the project.

Now during Schedule Development, resources are assigned to specific activities. Usually, you'll find that your initial schedule has periods of time with more activities than you have resources to work on them. You will also find that it isn't always possible to assign 100 percent of your team members' time to tasks. Sometimes your schedule will show a team member who is over allocated, meaning they're assigned to more work than they can physically perform in the given time period. Other times, they might not be assigned enough work to keep them busy during the time period. This problem is easy to fix. You can assign under-allocated resources to multiple tasks to keep them busy.

Having over-allocated resources is a little more difficult problem to resolve. *Resource leveling* attempts to smooth out the resource assignments to get tasks completed without overloading the individual while trying to keep the project on schedule. There are several ways the project manager can do this. You might delay the start of a task to match the availability of a key team member. Or you might adjust the resource assignments so that more tasks are given to team members who are under allocated. Perhaps you can split some tasks so that the team member with the pertinent knowledge or skill performs the critical part of the task and the noncritical part of the task is given to a less skilled team member. All of these methods are forms of resource leveling.

Generally speaking, resource leveling of over-allocated team members will extend the project end date. If you're under a date constraint, you'll have to go back and rework the schedule after assigning resources to keep the project on track with the committed completion date. This might include moving key resources off of noncritical tasks and assigning them to critical path tasks or adjusting assignments as previously mentioned. Reallocating those team members with slack time to critical path tasks to keep them on schedule is another option.

 Real World Scenario

Sunny Surgeons, Inc.

Kate Newman is a project manager for Sunny Surgeons, Inc. Sunny Surgeons is a software company that produces software for handheld display devices for the medical profession. The software allows surgeons to keep notes regarding patients, upcoming surgeries, and ideas about new medicines and techniques to research. Kate's latest project is to write an enhanced version of the patient-tracking program with system integration capabilities to a well-known desktop software product used by the medical industry.

There has been some recent turnover in the programming department. Fortunately, Stephen, the senior programmer who led the development effort on the original version of the patient tracker, still works for Sunny. His expertise with handheld technologies as well as his knowledge of the desktop software product make him an invaluable resource for this project.

Kate discovered a problem during the development of the project schedule. Stephen is over allocated for three key activities. Kate decides to see what his take is on the situation before deciding what to do.

Stephen, the eternal optimist programmer who loves his job and does all but sleep in his office at night, says he can easily complete all the activities and that Kate shouldn't give it a second thought. He also suggests to Kate that Karen Wong, a junior programmer on his team, worked on the last project with him and might be able to handle the noncritical path task on her own with a little direction from Stephen.

Kate thinks better of the idea of over allocating her key project resource even if he does think he can do the entire thing single-handed. She decides to try some resource leveling to see what that turns up.

Kate discovers that rearranging the order of activities along with assigning Karen to handle the noncritical path activity might be a possible solution. However, this scenario lengthens the project by a total of 8 days. Since Kate knows the primary constraint on this project is quality, she's fairly sure she can get buy-off from the project sponsor and stakeholders on the increased schedule date. She can also sell the resource-leveled schedule as a low-risk option as opposed to assigning Stephen to all the activities and keeping the project end date the same. Over allocating resources can cause burnout and stress-related illnesses, which will ultimately have a negative impact on the project schedule.

Project Management Software

Given the examples we've gone through on Schedule Development and resource leveling, you probably already have concluded how much project management software might help you with these processes. Project management software will automate the mathematical calculations and perform resource leveling functions for you. Obviously, you can then print the schedule that's been produced for final approval and ongoing updates. It's common practice to e-mail updated schedules with project notes so that stakeholders know what activities are completed and which ones remain to be done.

It's beyond the scope of this book to go into all the various software programs available to project managers. Suffice it to say that project management software ranges from the very simple to the very complex. The level of sophistication and the types of project management techniques that you're involved with will determine which software product you should choose. Many project managers that I know have had great success with Microsoft Project software and use it exclusively. It contains a robust set of features and reporting tools that will serve most projects well.

Don't forget that you are the project manager and your good judgment should never be usurped by the recommendation of a software product. Your finally tuned skills and experience will tell you if relationship issues between team members might cause bigger problems than what the resource leveling function indicates. Constraints and stakeholder expectations are difficult for a software package to factor in. Rely on your expertise when in doubt. If you don't have the experience yet to make knowledge-based decisions, seek out another project manager or a senior stakeholder, manager, or team member and ask them to confirm if you're on the right track. Project management software is a wonderful tool, but it is not a substitute for sound project management practices or experience.

Producing the Schedule Development Outputs

The Schedule Development process has four outputs: project schedule, supporting detail, schedule management plan, and resource requirements updates. The two primary outputs from this process that will carry forward throughout the rest of the project are the project schedule and the schedule management plan.

Project Schedule

The purpose of the Schedule Development process is to determine the start and finish dates for your project activities. One of the primary outputs of this process is the *project schedule*, which details this information as well as the resource assignments.

The project schedule should be approved and signed off by stakeholders and functional managers. This assures you that they have read the schedule, understand the dates and resource commitments, and will likely cooperate. You'll also need to obtain confirmation that resources will be available as outlined in the schedule when you're working in a functional organization. The schedule cannot be finalized until you receive approval and commitment for the resource assignments outlined in the schedule. Approval and finalization of the schedule should be completed prior to the end of the Project Plan Development process.

Once the schedule is approved, it will become your baseline for the remainder of the project. Project progress and task completion will be monitored and tracked against this original plan to determine if the project is on course as planned.

The schedule can be displayed in a variety of ways, some of which are variations on what we've already seen. Network diagrams, like the ones we talked about in Chapter 5, will work as schedule diagrams when you add the start and finish dates to each activity. These diagrams usually show the activity dependencies and critical path. Figure 7.2 shows a sample portion of a network diagram highlighting our programming activities.

FIGURE 7.2   Network diagram with activity dates

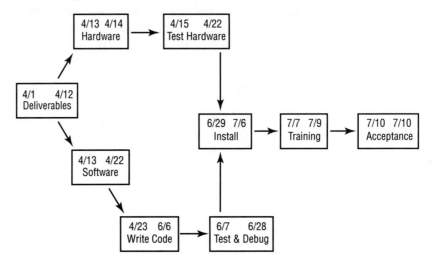

Gantt charts are easy to read and commonly used to display schedule activities. Depending on the software you're using to produce the Gantt chart, it might also show activity sequences, activity start and end dates, resource assignments, activity dependencies, and the critical path. Figure 7.3 is a simple example that plots various activities against time. These activities do not relate to the activities in the tables or other figures shown so far.

FIGURE 7.3   Gantt chart

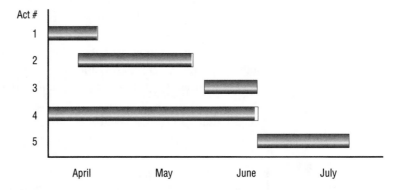

Milestone charts are another way to depict schedule information. *Milestones* mark the completion of major deliverables or some other key event in the project. For example, approval and sign-off on project deliverables might be considered a milestone. Other examples might be completion of a prototype, system testing, contract approval, and so on.

Milestone charts might show the key events and their start or completion dates in a bar chart form similar to a Gantt chart. Or they can be written in a simple table format with milestones listed in the rows and expected schedule dates in one column and actual completion dates in another. As the milestones are met, the actual date column is filled in. This information can be included with the project status reports.

Milestone	Scheduled Date	Actual Date
Sign off on deliverables	4/12	4/12
Sign off on hardware test	4/22	4/25
Programming completed	6/06	
Testing completed	6/28	
Acceptance and sign-off	7/10	
Project closeout	7/10	

Time-scaled network diagrams are rarely used. They combine the network diagrams with the bar chart format to display schedule information.

Supporting Detail

The minimum amount of information in the supporting detail output is the project constraints and assumptions. Other information that should be documented but doesn't necessarily fit into the other categories would get documented here. Always err on the side of too much documentation, rather than not enough.

You will have to be the judge of what other information to include here as it will depend on the nature of the project. The *Guide to the PMBOK* suggests that you might include resource histograms. There is an example resource histogram in Chapter 5 if you need to review. Resource histograms typically display hours needed on one axis and period of time (months, weeks, days, years) on the other. You might also include alternative schedules or schedule reserves in this section.

Schedule Management Plan

The schedule management plan should be published and distributed along with your other project Planning documents. Like other management plan outputs, the schedule management plan describes how schedule changes will be managed and is an important part of your overall project plan.

Resource Requirements Updates

Resource requirements are an output of the Resource Planning process. As a result of scheduling activities and leveling resources, you may have to make adjustments to the resource requirements document. As I've noted during some of the other Planning processes, project planning and project management are an iterative process. Rarely is anything cast in cement. You will continue to revisit processes throughout the project to refine and adjust. Eventually, processes do get put to bed. You wouldn't want to come back to the Planning process at the conclusion of the project, for example, but keep in mind that the Planning, Executing, and Controlling process groups are iterative, and it's not unusual to have to revise processes within these phases as you progress on the project.

In practice, Activity Definition, Activity Sequencing, Activity Duration Estimating, and Schedule Development are easily completed at the same time with the aid of good project management software. Gantt charts, critical path, PERT charts, resource allocation, activity dependencies, what-if analysis, and various reports are easily produced after plugging in your scheduling information to most project management software tools. Regardless of your methods, be certain to obtain sign-off of the project schedule and provide your stakeholders and project sponsor with regular updates. And keep your schedule handy—there will likely be changes and modifications as you go.

Establishing the Cost Budget Baseline

Our next step is to determine the cost budget baseline. The budget will be used as a plan for allocating costs and resources to project activities. The Schedule Development and Cost Estimating processes must be completed prior to working on Cost Budgeting as their outputs become the inputs to this process. The inputs for Cost Budgeting are cost estimates, WBS, risk management plan, and project schedule.

The same tools and techniques we discussed for the Cost Estimating process in Chapter 5 are used in the Cost Budgeting process. A quick reminder here of those tools and techniques wouldn't hurt:

Analogous estimating   This a top-down technique that uses historical information to determine estimates and is a form of expert judgment.

Parametric modeling   This is a mathematical model used to estimate project costs.

Bottom-up estimating   This involves estimating the individual costs of each activity and then rolling them up to come up with a total project cost.

Computerized tools   These are used to perform the above estimating techniques automatically.

The *Cost Budgeting* process assigns cost estimates to activities and is used to measure the variance and performance of the project throughout the remaining process groups. Thus, it serves as a baseline for cost measurements as the *cost baseline* is now the expected cost for the project. Remember that costs are tied to the financial system through the chart of accounts, or code of accounts, and are assigned to project activities at the work package level of the WBS.

The cost baseline can be displayed graphically with time increments on one axis against dollars expended on the other as shown in Figure 7.4. The costs shown on this graph are cumulative costs, meaning that what we spent this period is added to what was spent last period and then charted. Many variations of this graph exist showing dollars budgeted against dollars expended to date and so on. Cost budgets can be displayed using this type of graph as well by plotting the sum of the estimated costs excepted per period.

FIGURE 7.4   Cost baseline

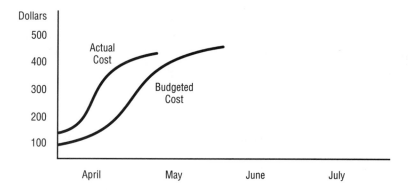

For the exam, remember that cost baselines are displayed as an S-curve. The reason for this is that project spending starts out slowly and gradually increases over the project's life until it reaches a peak, then tapers off again as the project wraps up. Large projects are difficult to graph in this manner, as the timescale isn't wide enough to accurately show fluctuations in spending. There are other methods that more accurately graph costs, which we'll look at in the Cost Control process.

The budget should contain all the costs for all of the expected work on the project. You would have identified most of these costs in the Cost Estimating process. Schedule Development might have uncovered additional activities that need to be added to the budget as well.

The budget should also contain appropriations for risk response. We covered several categories and tools of Risk Response Planning in Chapter 6 including avoidance, mitigation, insurance, and contingency plans. Some of the budget should be allocated to each of these techniques that you identified in your risk management plan. Additionally, you'll want to set aside money for reserves. This is for the unforeseen, unplanned risks that may occur. Even with all of the time and effort we spend on planning, unexpected things do crop up. Better to have the money set aside and not need it than to need it and not have it.

The cost baseline is the only output of the Cost Budgeting process. We'll revisit the cost baseline when we talk about the Cost Control process and examine different ways to measure costs.

Developing the Project Plan

We've finally made it to Project Plan Development. All the work we've done up to this point culminates in this final Planning process.

Project Plan Development takes the outputs from all the other Planning processes and brings them together in a concise, logical format. This might end up being one main document with reference to other pertinent documents, or several documents organized in a logical fashion. The project plan, which is an output of this process, is used throughout the Executing and Controlling processes for decision making and guidance based on the original plan.

Project Plan Development has five inputs that we've seen before. They are other planning outputs, historical information, organizational policies, constraints, and assumptions. The *Guide to the PMBOK* points out that organizational policies should be consulted when developing your project plan. Some policies might include things like quality management, personnel administration, and financial controls according to the *Guide to the PMBOK*.

Tools and Techniques

The tools and techniques of this process are all new. They are project planning methodology, stakeholder skills and knowledge, project management information system (PMIS), and earned value management (EVM). We'll describe each below.

Project Planning Methodology

We've been explaining and employing project planning methodology since the beginning of the first chapter. This is simply a formal, structured technique that the project manager uses to help develop the project plan. It might involve using what the *Guide to the PMBOK* calls *hard* tools like Microsoft Project software, or *soft* tools like paper templates or project meetings. Some organizations have project management offices with standardized forms and templates that project managers can use to facilitate the Planning process.

Keep in mind that Monte Carlo Analysis can be used during this process as well. Since Planning is such an iterative process, Monte Carlo comes in handy when you're looking at schedule risks, project durations, and the like.

Stakeholder Skills and Knowledge

Yes, stakeholders have skills and knowledge that might be helpful to the project manager during project Planning. Believe it or not, and I'm positive you are not one of these types, there are project managers who think stakeholders have no business helping with any aspect of the project Planning, Executing, or Controlling process groups. I'm not certain how you would end up with a successful project (as defined by meeting or exceeding stakeholder expectations) when stakeholders have not been included in the project process groups. Don't let this happen to you. As the project manager, one of your most important jobs is to create an open, communicative atmosphere so that stakeholders are able to contribute to the process.

It's important that stakeholders participate in the project Planning processes and sign off on the final project plan. This assures you that stakeholders agree to, or at least know, the details regarding project activities, duration, activity costs, risks, and budgets, and how each of these things impacts the project scope and their own departments and resources. Stakeholders usually have less of a say in how the project is executed and controlled as the objectives and scope are firmly defined by then. This makes their cooperation and participation in the Planning processes even more important. Do everything you can to ensure stakeholders take the project seriously and actively solicit their input during Project Plan Development.

Project Management Information System (PMIS)

This is an information system that stores all the information related to your project. It allows you to gather information, incorporate it with other project information, and produce reports for distribution to stakeholders and team members. The information system is used from the beginning of the project through closeout. Keep in mind that the information system could be a software product or a combination of software and a manual system.

As the project manager, you need to be certain that you're managing the project, and not just managing the project management information system. It's easy to get caught up in the software features and in the processes and planning logic and not pay attention to the project itself. Be certain that the project is where your attention is and not just the software or information system you're using to manage the software.

Earned Value Management (EVM)

Earned value management (EVM) is concerned with measuring and reporting on the progress of the project. It incorporates the project schedule, scope, and resources as a whole to determine if variances exist in the project. Earned value analysis is a technique used to calculate performance measures that we'll explore in more detail in Chapter 9.

Project Plan Development Outputs

This brings us to the outputs of the Project Plan Development process, which are the project plan and supporting detail. Let's talk a little bit more about each of these.

Project Plan

The *project plan* will be used as the guideline throughout the project Executing and project Controlling process groups. You'll use the project plan to track and measure project performance and to make future project decisions.

The project plan encompasses everything we've talked about up to now and is represented in a formal document, or collection of documents. This document will contain the project scope statement, deliverables, assumptions, risks, WBS, milestones, activity schedule, resources, and more. It becomes the baseline you'll use to measure and track progress against. It's also used to control the components that tend to stray from the original plan and get them back in line.

The project plan will be used as a communication and information tool for stakeholders, team members, and the management team. They will use the project plan to review and gauge progress as well.

The *Guide to the PMBOK* makes a point of the difference between the project performance measurement baselines and the project plan. The project plan is the document, or assortment of documents, that constitutes what the project is, what the project will deliver, and how all the processes will be managed. There will be changes to the project plan throughout the remaining process groups, and the document, or documents, will need to be updated to reflect those changes.

The performance measurement baselines are the management controls in place that should change only infrequently. Examples of the performance measurement baselines we've looked at so far are Cost Budgeting baselines and schedule baselines. The project plan itself also becomes a baseline. If changes in scope or schedule do occur after Planning is complete, there's a formalized process that you should go through to implement the changes, which we'll cover in a later chapter.

Supporting Detail

We've seen this output before. The supporting detail for the Project Plan Development process will include any information not previously included in the other project Planning processes. Technical information such as design specifications might be included here as well. Back in Chapter 6, we talked about standards and policies. If they're applicable to the project, you could include the standards here or reference where they might be found. Again we're back to our project management mantra, "Document, document, document." If you cannot find any other logical place to put information that you know should be included with the project, put it in supporting detail. Last but not least, don't forget to include assumptions and constraints that were discovered during this phase of the Planning process.

Don't forget that sign-off is an important part of this process. Your last step in the Planning process group will be to obtain sign-off of the project plan from stakeholders, the sponsor, and the management team.

Project Case Study: New Kitchen Heaven Retail Store

You've spent a couple of days working on the project schedule in Microsoft Project 2000, clarifying tasks and activities with Jake, Ricardo, and Jill. You decide that a Gantt chart will work excellently for reporting status for this project. A portion of your first draft of the Gantt chart shows the following at the end of the project:

The detail behind the Gantt chart snapshot is shown below. This is a limited amount of detail for example purposes.

You stare intensely at the problem you see on the screen. The Grand Opening task (number 18) is scheduled to occur 2 weeks later than when you need it! Grand opening must happen February 1 and 2, not February 15 and 16 as the schedule shows. You trace the problem back and see that Grand Opening depends on Train Store Personnel, which itself depends on several other tasks including Hire Store Personnel, Install and Test Hardware, and Build-out. Digging deeper, build-out can't begin until the Ethernet cable is run throughout the building. Ricardo already set up the time with the contractor to run the cable September 17. This date cannot move, which means build-out cannot start any sooner than September 19.

You pick up the phone and dial Jake's number. "Jake," you say into the receiver. "I'm working on the project schedule, and I have some issues with the Gomez activity."

"Shoot," Jake says.

"Gomez Construction can't start work until the Ethernet cable is run. I've already confirmed with Ricardo that there is no negotiation on this. Ricardo is hiring a contractor for this activity, and the earliest they can start is September 17. It takes them 2 days to run the cable, which puts the start date for build-out at September 19."

"Right," Jake replies. "That's just about when we thought. What's the problem?"

"Jill wants to have the build-out finished prior to hiring the store personnel. During the last store opening, those activities overlapped, and she said it was unmanageable. She wants to hire folks and have them stock the shelves in preparation for store opening but doesn't want contractors in there while they're doing it. A September 19 start date for Gomez puts us at a finish date of February 12, which is too late regardless of the problem with Jill. Hence, my question, is 120 days to finish a build-out a firm estimate?"

"Always—I've got this down to a science. Gomez has worked with me on enough of these build-outs that we can come within just a couple of days of this estimate either way," Jake says.

You pick up your schedule detail and continue. "I've scheduled Gomez's resource calendar as you told me originally. Gomez doesn't work Sundays and neither do we. Their holidays are Labor Day, a couple of days at Thanksgiving, Christmas and New Year's, but this puts us too far out on the schedule. I know Dirk won't go for a later date; he's firm on the February 1 opening."

"I can't change the 120 days. Sounds like you have a problem."

"I need to crash the schedule," you say. "What would the chances be of Gomez agreeing to split the build-out tasks? We could hire a second contractor to come in and work alongside Gomez's crew to speed up this task. That would shorten the duration to 100 days, which means we could meet the February 1 date."

"Won't happen. I know Gomez. They're a big outfit and have all their own crews. We typically work with them exclusively. If I brought another contractor into the picture, I might have a hard time negotiating any kind of favors with them later if we get into a bind."

"Alright," you say. "How about this? I'm making some changes to the resource calendar while we're talking. What if we authorize Gomez's crew to work six 10-hour days, which still leaves them with Sundays off, and we ask them to work Labor Day and take only one day at each of the other holidays instead of two?"

The detail showing these changes is shown below.

"I think Gomez would go for that. You realize it's going to cost you?"

"Project management is all about trade-offs. We can't move the start date, so chances are the budget might take a hit to accommodate schedule changes or risk. Fortunately, I'm just now wrapping up the final cost budget baseline, so if you can get me the increased cost from Gomez soon, I'd appreciate it. This change will keep us on track and resolve Jill's issues too."

"I don't think Gomez's crew will mind the overtime during the holiday season. Everyone can use a little extra cash at that time of year, it seems. I'll have the figures for you in a day or two."

Project Case Study Checklist

Developing project schedule

- Calendars

- Lead and lag time

- Critical path

Duration compression

- Crashing

Utilizing project management software

Producing project schedule

- Milestones

- Gantt chart

- Resource leveling

Cost baseline

Finalized project plan

Summary

Great job, you've made it through the entire Planning process. We covered three processes in this chapter: Schedule Development, Cost Budgeting, and Project Plan Development.

Schedule Development is the process in which you assign beginning and ending dates to tasks and determine their duration. You can use several methods to do this including CPM, GERT, and PERT. The CPM calculates early start, early finish, late start, and late finish dates. It also determines float time. All tasks with zero float are critical path tasks. The critical path is the longest path in the project.

GERT allows for conditional branching and looping; CPM and PERT do not.

PERT calculates a weighted average estimate for each activity by using the optimistic, pessimistic, and most likely times and then determines variances, or standard deviations, to come up with a total project duration within a given confidence range. 68.26 percent of the time, work will finish within plus or minus one standard deviation. 95.44 percent of the time, work will finish within plus or minus two standard deviations.

Schedules sometimes need to be compressed to meet promised dates or to shorten the schedule times. Crashing looks at cost and schedule trade-offs. Adding resources to critical path tasks and limiting or reducing the project requirements or scope are ways to crash the schedule. Fast tracking involves beginning two tasks that were originally scheduled to start one after the other at the same time. Fast tracking increases project risk.

Monte Carlo Analysis can be used in the Schedule Development process to determine project duration.

Resource leveling attempts to smooth out the schedule and properly allocate resources to critical path tasks. This may require updates to the resource management plan.

The project schedule details the activities in graphical form through the use of network diagrams with dates, Gantt charts, milestone charts, or timescaled network diagrams.

The schedule management plan details how the project schedule will be managed and how changes will be incorporated into the project schedule.

The Cost Budgeting baseline will be used throughout the project to measure project expenditures, variance, and project performance. The cost baseline is graphically displayed as an S-curve.

Project Plan Development is the last process in the Planning process group. The project plan is used as a guideline throughout the project Executing and Controlling processes to help make future project decisions. It's also used to measure and track project performance. The project plan might be one document or several documents stored together in an organized, logical format.

Exam Essentials

Be able to calculate the critical path.   The critical path is the activities whose durations add up to the longest full path utilizing the forward pass, backward pass, and float calculations.

Be able to define a critical path task.   A critical path task is a project activity with zero float.

Be able to describe and calculate PERT duration estimates.   This is a weighted average technique that uses three estimates: optimistic, pessimistic, and most likely. The formula is as follows: [optimistic + pessimistic + (4 × most likely)] ÷ 6.

Be able to name the duration compression techniques.   They are crashing and fast tracking.

Be able to describe the cost baseline.   This is the expected cost of the project and is used to measure performance. It's displayed as an S-curve.

Key Terms

Before you take the exam, be certain you are familiar with the following terms:

cost baseline	project plan
Cost Budgeting	Project Plan Development
critical path (CP)	project schedule
Critical Path Method (CPM)	resource leveling
float time	Schedule Development
milestones	slack time
Program Evaluation and Review Technique (PERT)	

Review Questions

1. The project schedule is used to determine all of the following except:

   A. Cost estimates

   B. Activity start dates

   C. Float times

   D. Activity end dates

2. You are a project manager for Picture Shades, Inc. They manufacture window shades for hotel chains that have replicas of Renaissance-era paintings on the inside of the shades. Picture Shades is taking their product to the home market, and you're managing the new project. They will offer their products at retail stores as well as on their website. You're developing the project schedule for this undertaking and have determined the critical path. Which of the following is true?

   A. You calculated the most likely start date and most likely finish dates, float time, and weighted average estimates.

   B. You calculated the activity dependency, and the optimistic and pessimistic activity duration estimates.

   C. You calculated the early and late start dates, early and late finish dates, and float times for all activities.

   D. You calculated the optimistic, pessimistic, and most likely duration times and the float times for all activities.

3. You are a project manager for Picture Shades, Inc. They manufacture window shades for hotel chains that have replicas of Renaissance-era paintings on the inside of the shades. Picture Shades is taking their product to the home market, and you're managing the new project. They will offer their products at retail stores as well as on their website. You're developing the project schedule for this undertaking. Looking at the graph below, which path is the critical path?

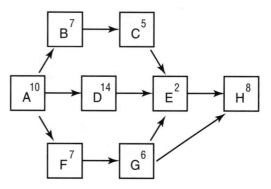

A. A-B-C-E-H

B. A-D-E-H

C. A-F-G-H

D. A-F-G-E-H

4. Use the example graphic shown below to answer this question. If the duration of activity B was changed to 10 days and the duration of activity G was changed to 9 days, which of the following is the critical path?

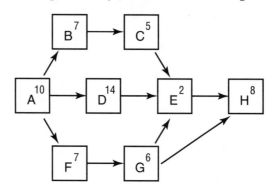

A. A-B-C-E-H

B. A-D-E-H

C. A-F-G-H

D. A-F-G-E-H

5. Which of the following is true regarding the critical path?

   A. It should never be compressed.

   B. It allows for looping and branching.

   C. The critical path technique is the same as PERT.

   D. It's the duration of all tasks with zero float.

6. All of the following are tools and techniques of the Schedule Development process except?

   A. CPM

   B. RAM

   C. GERT

   D. PERT

7. You are a project manager for a new software development project. You have a few activities that require specialized testing. The testing might need to be repeated more than once. Which of the following do you choose?

   A. The Graphical Evaluation and Review Technique because it allows for conditional branching and looping for the testing activity

   B. The Critical Path Method because it allows for float time to be calculated for the testing activity

   C. The Program Evaluation and Review Technique because it allows for conditional branching and looping for the testing activity

   D. The Program Evaluation and Review Technique because it allows for a weighted average distribution, which will even out the time needed for the testing activity

8. You are a project manager for Move It Now trucking company. Your company specializes in moving household goods across the city or across the country. Your project involves upgrading the nationwide computer network for the company. Your lead engineer has given you the following estimates for a critical path activity: 60 days most likely, 72 days pessimistic, 48 days optimistic. What is the expected value, or weighted average?

A. 54

B. 66

C. 60

D. 30

9. You are a project manager for Move It Now trucking company. Your company specializes in moving household goods across the city or across the country. Your project involves upgrading the nation-wide computer network for the company. Your lead engineer has given you the following estimates for a critical path activity: 60 days most likely, 72 days pessimistic, 48 days optimistic. What is the standard deviation?

A. 22

B. 20

C. 2

D. 4

10. If you know expected value is 500 and the standard deviation is 12, you can say with approximately a 95 percent confidence rating which of the following?

A. The activity will take between 488 and 512 days.

B. The activity will take between 464 and 536 days.

C. The activity will take between 494 and 506 days.

D. The activity will take between 476 and 524 days.

11. If your expected value is 110 and the standard deviation is 12, which of the following is true?

   A. There is approximately a 99 percent chance of completing this activity between 86 and 134 days.

   B. There is approximately a 68 percent chance of completing this activity between 98 and 122 days.

   C. There is approximately a 95 percent chance of completing this activity between 98 and 122 days.

   D. There is approximately a 75 percent chance of completing this activity between 86 and 134 days.

12. You are the project manager working on a research project for a new drug treatment. Your preliminary project schedule runs past the due date for a federal grant application. The manager of the R&D department has agreed to release two resources to work on your project in order to meet the federal grant application date. This is an example of:

   A. Crashing

   B. Fast tracking

   C. Resource leveling

   D. Adjusting the resource calendar

13. You are the project manager working on a research project for a new drug treatment. Your preliminary project schedule runs past the due date for a federal grant application. You adjust the schedule and find that two activities previously scheduled to start sequentially can be started at the same time. This is an example of:

   A. Crashing

   B. Fast tracking

   C. Resource leveling

   D. Adjusting the resource calendar

14. You are the project manager for Rivera Gourmet Adventure Vacations. Rivera combines the wonderful tastes of great gourmet food with outdoor adventure activities. Your project involves installing a new human resources software system. Jason, the database analyst working on this project, is over allocated. Which of the following is true?

    A. You should use resource requirements updates to determine availability and smooth out resource over allocation.

    B. You should use crashing to resource level the critical path tasks.

    C. You should use resource leveling heuristics to smooth out resource assignments.

    D. You should use fast tracking to resource level the critical path tasks.

15. What is one of the problems with project management software?

    A. The project manager manages the software instead of the project.

    B. Project duration calculations are sometimes approximate.

    C. You cannot override the project management software decisions regarding schedules.

    D. It's expensive and difficult to use.

16. Obtaining formal project plan approval and sign-off is important for all of the following reasons except:

    A. Stakeholders are able to recommend a project Planning methodology to follow throughout the remaining process groups.

    B. Stakeholders are aware of the project details, which makes them more likely to participate in future project decisions.

    C. Stakeholders will be more likely to cooperate.

    D. Stakeholders are aware of the specific details regarding project schedules, budgets, and risks.

17. Which of the following are the tools and techniques of the Cost Budgeting process?

    A. Project management information system, analogous estimating, bottom-up estimating, mathematical analysis

    B. Analogous estimating, bottom-up estimating, mathematical analysis, computerized tools

    C. Project management software, analogous estimating, bottom-up estimating, parametric modeling

    D. Analogous estimating, bottom-up estimating, parametric modeling, computerized tools

18. You are the project manager for a custom home-building construction company. You are working on the model home project for the upcoming Show Homes Tour. The model home includes Internet connections in every room and talking appliances. You are working on the cost budget for this project. All of the following are true except:

    A. This process assigns cost estimates to project activities including risks and contingency plans.

    B. The cost baseline will be used to measure variances and future project performance.

    C. This process assigns cost estimates for expected future period operating costs.

    D. The cost baseline is the expected cost for the project.

19. Which of the following is displayed as an S-curve?

    A. Gantt

    B. Cost baseline

    C. Critical path

    D. PERT

20. All of the following are true regarding the project plan except:

   A. Some of its inputs are outputs from other Planning processes.

   B. It's used to guide the project Executing and Controlling processes and is the baseline used to measure project performance.

   C. It consists of one document that should be formally approved and signed by stakeholders.

   D. It contains things like the WBS, project schedule, and resource assignments.

Answers to Review Questions

1. A. The project schedule determines start and ending dates of activities, determines float times, generally shows resource assignments, and details the activity sequences and durations.

2. C. The CPM calculates a single early and late start date and a single early and late finish date for each activity. Once these dates are known, float time is calculated for each activity to determine the critical path. The other answers contain elements of PERT calculations.

3. B. The only information you have for this example is activity duration, therefore the critical path is the path with the longest duration. Path A-D-E-H with a duration of 34 days is the critical path.

4. D. The only information you have for this example is activity duration, so you must calculate the critical path based on the durations given. The duration of A-B-C-E-H increased by 3 days for a total of 35 days. The duration of A-F-G-H and A-F-G-E-H each increased by 3 days. A-F-G-E-H totals 36 days and becomes the new critical path.

5. D. The critical path is calculated by adding together the durations of all the tasks with zero float. The critical path can be compressed using crashing techniques.

6. B. A RAM is a Responsibility Assignment Matrix used in the Organizational Planning process.

7. A. GERT is the only Schedule Development tool that allows for conditional branching and looping.

8. C. The calculation for PERT is the sum of optimistic time plus pessimistic time plus four times the most likely time divided by 6. The calculation for this example is as follows: $[48 + 72 + (4 \times 60)] \div 6 = 60$.

9. D. The standard deviation is calculated by subtracting the optimistic time from the pessimistic time and dividing the result by 6. The calculation for this example looks as follows: $(72 - 48) \div 6 = 4$

10. D. There is a 95 percent probability that the work will finish within plus or minus two standard deviations. The expected value is 500, and the standard deviation times 2 is 24, so the activity will take between 476 and 524 days.

11. B. A 68 percent probability is calculated using plus or minus one standard deviation, a 95 percent probability uses plus or minus two standard deviations, and a 99 percent probability uses plus or minus three standard deviations.

12. A. Crashing the schedule includes things like adding resources to the critical path tasks or limiting project requirements.

13. B. Fast tracking is starting two tasks at the same time that were previously scheduled to start one after the other.

14. C. Resource leveling heuristics attempt to smooth out resource assignments by splitting tasks, assigning under-allocated team members to more tasks, or delaying the start of tasks to match team members' availability.

15. A. Project management software is a very useful tool for the project manager, and it automates project scheduling allowing for what-if analysis and easy changes. But if you focus too much on the tool and ignore the project, the tool becomes a hindrance.

16. A. Stakeholders ordinarily will not have much say in the project Planning methodology used by the project manager. The methodology employed is usually determined by either the organization, the project office, or the project manager.

17. D. Cost Budgeting's tools and techniques are the same tools and techniques of the Cost Estimating process: analogous estimating, parametric modeling, bottom-up estimating, and computerized tools.

18. C. Future period operating costs are considered ongoing costs and are not part of project costs.

19. B. The cost baseline is displayed as an S-curve because of the way project spending occurs. Spending begins slowly, picks up speed until the spending peak is reached, and then tapers off as the project winds down.

20. C. The project plan might be one document or a collection of documents organized in a logical format.

Chapter

8

Developing the Project Team

✓ 1. Commit Resources.

✓ 2. Implement Resources.

✓ 3. Manage Progress.

✓ 4. Communicate Progress.

This chapter begins the project Executing process group. We'll cover three processes in the project Executing group including Project Plan Execution, Team Development, and Information Distribution. You'll get a reprieve in this chapter as there is only one math equation you need to memorize.

Project Plan Execution is the action process so to speak. This is where you'll put the plans into action and begin working on the project activities. Execution also involves keeping the project in line with the original project plan and bringing wayward activities back into alignment.

Several things happen during the Executing processes. The majority of the project budget will be spent during this process, and often the majority of the project time is expended here as well. The greatest conflicts you'll see during the project Executing process are schedule conflicts. And, the product description will be finalized here and contain more detail than it did in the Planning process.

Project Plan Execution is the only core process in the Executing process group. All the other processes we'll discuss are facilitating processes to Project Plan Execution. In other words, the facilitating processes assist you with executing the project plan.

We'll start out this chapter with the Project Plan Execution process and then discuss Team Development and communication processes. There are several exam questions on every process within the Executing process group. You'll find the majority of questions regard the Project Plan Execution process, the Team Development process, and the Contract Administration process, which we'll talk about in the next chapter. Don't skip studying the other processes, however, as roughly a quarter of the exam questions concern the entire Executing process. Are you ready to dive into Executing? Let's go.

Executing the Project Plan

The purpose of the *Project Plan Execution* process is to carry out the project plan. This is where your project comes to life and the work of the project happens. Activities are clarified, and the work is authorized to begin. Resources are committed and assigned to activities, and the product or service of the project is created. One of the most difficult aspects of this process is coordinating and integrating all the elements of the project. The largest portion of the project budget will be spent in Project Plan Execution.

Executing Inputs

Project Plan Execution has five inputs: project plan, supporting detail, organizational policies, preventive action, and corrective action. We covered supporting detail earlier in this book, which included constraints and assumptions. There are a few new things to add to organizational policies, so we'll look at that one again along with the others.

Project Plan

The project plan is the output of the Planning process group, specifically the Project Plan Development process. The important thing to note here is that all the management plans we discussed during the Planning process—such as the scope management plan, the schedule management plan, the resource management plan, and so on, plus the cost budgeting baseline and the schedule baseline—are used throughout the Executing process to manage the project and keep the performance of the project on track with the project objectives. If you don't have a project plan, you'll have no way of managing the process. You'll find that even with a plan, project scope has a way of changing. Stakeholders and others tend to sneak in a few of the "oh, I didn't understand that before" statements and hope that they slide right by you. With that signed, approved plan in your files, you are allowed to gently remind them that they read and agreed to the project plan and you're sticking to it. They can request a formal change, but that's another topic, which we'll get to shortly.

Organizational Policies

It's important for the project manager to understand organizational policies as they may impact Project Plan Execution. For example, the organization may have purchasing approval processes that must be followed. Perhaps orders for goods or services that exceed certain dollar amounts need different levels of approval. As the project manager, you need to be aware of policies like this so you're certain you can execute the project smoothly. It's very frustrating to find out after the fact that you should have followed a certain process or policy, and now because you didn't, you've got schedule delays or worse. You could consider using the "sin now, ask forgiveness later" technique in extreme emergencies, but you didn't hear that from me. By the way, that's not an authorized PMI technique.

The project manager and the project team will be responsible for coordinating all the organizational interfaces for the project including technical, human resource, purchasing, finance, and so on. It will serve you well to understand the policies and politics involved in each of these areas in your organization.

Preventive Action

Preventive action involves anything that will reduce the potential impacts of risk events should they occur. Contingency plans and risk responses are examples of preventive action. These and other risk responses were described in the Risk Response Planning process in Chapter 6.

Corrective Action

In my organization, a corrective action means an employee has big trouble coming. Fortunately, this isn't what's meant here. Corrective actions are taken to get the anticipated future project outcomes to align with the project plan. Maybe you've discovered one of your programmers is adding an unplanned feature to the software project because he's friends with the user. You'll have to redirect him to the activities assigned him originally to avoid schedule delays.

Corrective actions are outputs of processes in the Controlling process group but serve as inputs to the Project Plan Execution process. For the exam, remember that the Executing and Controlling process results are inputs to each other.

We'll cover corrective action again in the chapters that discuss the Controlling process.

Meetings and More

As with the Project Plan Development process, almost everything we've done to date is utilized by the Project Plan Execution process. The primary output here is work results, meaning actually producing the product or service we set out to produce. Without having completed the prior processes, we wouldn't know what the work of the project should look like. Several tools and techniques are used to facilitate the work results. We'll look at all of them, with the exception of project management information system, which we've covered previously.

General Management Skills

We covered some general management skills in an earlier chapter. What's important to note here is that leadership, negotiation, and communications skills are especially useful during Project Plan Execution. You might recall that leadership is about imparting vision and rallying people around that vision. Leaders motivate and inspire and are concerned with strategic vision. Leaders understand the difference between power and politics. Power is the ability to get people to do what they wouldn't do ordinarily, or the ability to influence behavior. Politics impart pressure to conform regardless of whether the person agrees with the decision.

One other thing to consider in this category is that you're going to monitor other departments that have assignments on the project and manage their progress. Again this implies that you'll need general knowledge management skills to understand what the assignments entail and strong leadership skills to influence the departments to stay on schedule.

Product Skills and Knowledge

The Resource Planning process defined the skills that are required of project team members, and the Staff Acquisition process provided the resources for the project. Product skills and knowledge are also needed by the project team members to understand the product or service of the project. If your project is constructing a mass spectrometer and no one on your team knows what a mass spectrometer looks like, you've got a problem. Key team members should have knowledge, skills, and experience with the products of the project.

Work Authorization System

Work authorization systems clarify and initiate the work of each work package. This is a formal procedure that authorizes work to begin in the correct sequence and at the right time. Work authorization systems are usually written procedures defined by the organization. They might include e-mail–based or paper-based systems or even verbal instructions, which work well with smaller projects. Usually, work is authorized using a form that describes the task, the responsible party, anticipated start and end dates, special instructions, and whatever else is particular to the activity or project. Depending on the organizational structure, the work is assigned and authorized by either the project manager or the functional manager.

Status Review Meetings

Status review meetings are important functions of Project Plan Execution. Status meetings are a way to formally exchange project information. They can occur between the project team and project manager, the project manager and stakeholders, the project manager and users or customers, the project manager and the management team, and so on.

The purpose of the status meeting is to provide updated information regarding the progress of the project. These are not show-and-tell meetings. If you have a prototype to demo, set up a different time to do that. Status meetings are meant to exchange information and provide project updates.

Regular, timely status meetings prevent surprises down the road. They alert the project manager to potential risk events and provide the opportunity to discover and manage problems before they get to the uncontrollable stage.

The project manager is usually the expediter of the status meeting. As such, it's your job to use status meetings wisely. Don't waste your team's time or stakeholders' time either. Notify attendees in writing of the meeting time and place. Publish an agenda prior to the meeting and stick to the agenda during the meeting. Every so often, summarize what's been discussed during the meeting. Don't let side discussions lead you down rabbit trails, and keep irrelevant conversations to a minimum. It's also good to publish status meeting notes at the conclusion of the meeting, especially if any action items resulted from the meeting. This will give you a document trail and serves as a reminder to the meeting participants of what actions need to be resolved and who is responsible for the action item.

It's important that project team members are honest with the project manager and that the project manager is in turn honest about what they report. A few years ago, a department in my agency took on a project of gargantuan proportions and unfortunately didn't employ good project management techniques. One of the biggest problems with this project was that the project manager did not listen to the highly skilled project team members. The team members warned of problems and setbacks, but the project manager didn't want to hear of it. The project manager took their reports to be of the "Chicken Little" ilk and refused to believe the sky was falling. Unfortunately, the sky *was* falling! The project manager, because they didn't believe it, refused to report the true status of the project to the stakeholders and oversight committees. Millions of dollars were wasted on a project that was doomed for failure, while the project manager continued to report that the project was on time and activities were completed when in fact they were not.

There are hundreds of project stories like this, and I'll bet you've got one or two from your experience as well. Don't let your project become the next bad example. Above all, be honest in your reporting. No one likes bad news, but bad news delivered too late along with millions of dollars wasted is a guaranteed career showstopper.

Organizational Procedures

This is very similar to organizational policies, except organizational policies are an input, and organizational procedures are a tool and technique of this process.

The project manager should take organizational procedures into consideration when doing the work of the project. Maybe your finance department requires special requisitions for certain purchases, or your human resources department might require formal procedures for full-time as well as contract personnel. Be aware of policies like this ahead of time so that they don't interfere with the project Executing process.

Resulting Outputs

We've already touched on the outputs of this process. Obviously, the product or service of the project is our end result. The *Guide to the PMBOK* calls this work results. The second output we'll look at is change requests.

Work Results

During Project Plan Execution, you'll gather and record information regarding the activity completion dates, milestone completions, the status of the deliverables, the quality of the deliverables, costs, schedule progress and updates, and so on. All of this information gets used during the Performance Reporting process, which we'll discuss during the Controlling process.

Project Executing and Controlling are two processes that work hand in hand. As you gather the information from work results, you'll measure the outputs and take corrective actions where necessary. This means you'll loop back through the Executing process to put the corrections into place. The *Guide to the PMBOK* breaks these processes up for ease of explanation, but in practice, you'll work through several of the Executing and Controlling processes together.

Change Requests

As a result of working through activities and producing your product or service, you will inevitably come upon things that need to be changed. This might encompass schedule changes, scope changes, or requirements or resource changes. The list really could go on. Your job as project manager, if you choose to accept it (wasn't that a movie theme?), is to collect the change requests and make determinations on their impact to the project. We'll discuss change requests in the coming chapters. Change requests are an output of this process and an output of the Performance Reporting process in the Controlling process group. Remember that Executing and Controlling outputs feed each other as inputs.

Project Plan Execution is the primary process, and the only core process, in the Executing process group. The work of the project is performed here, and the project plan is put into action and carried out. This process is where the project manager is like an orchestra conductor signaling the instruments to begin their activities, monitoring what should be winding down, and keeping that smile going to remind everyone that they should be enjoying themselves. I recommend that you know the tools and techniques and the outputs of this process for the exam.

Developing the Project Team

Projects exist to create a unique product or service within a limited time frame. Projects are performed by people, and most projects require more than one person to perform all of the activities. If you've got more than one person working on your project, you've got a team. And if you've got a team, you've got a wide assortment of personalities, skills, needs, and issues in the mix. Couple this with part-time team members, teams based in functional organizations whose loyalty lies with the functional manager, or teams based in matrix organizations that report to two different managers and you could have some real challenges on your hands. Good luck. Okay, I won't leave you hanging like that.

Team Development according to the *Guide to the PMBOK*, is about creating an open, encouraging environment for stakeholders to contribute as well as developing your team into an effective, functioning, coordinated group. Projects are performed by individuals, and the better they work together, the smoother and the more efficient the execution of the project will be.

Team Development inputs include project staff, project plan, staffing management plan, performance reports, and external feedback. All of the inputs have been discussed elsewhere with the exception of external feedback. External feedback, as it implies, is information relayed to the project team from those outside of the project team regarding performance expectations. This feedback might come from stakeholders, the management team, users, customers, etc.

The tools and techniques of Team Development include team-building activities, general management skills, reward and recognition systems, collocation, and training. We'll cover these topics next. As I said earlier, there are a lot of exam questions regarding team building, so dig out all your favorite memorization techniques and put them to use.

Implementing Team Building

Many times, project teams are made up of folks who don't know each other. They aren't necessarily aware of the project objectives and may not even want to be a part of the team. The project manager may not have worked with the people assigned to the project team before either. Sound like a recipe for disaster? It's not. Thousands of projects are started with team members and project managers who don't know each other and come to a successful completion. How is that done? It's a result of the project manager's team-building and communication skills.

The project manager's job is to bring the team together, get them all headed in the right direction, and provide motivation, reward, and recognition to keep the team in tip-top shape. This is done using a variety of team-building techniques and exercises. Team building is simply getting a diverse group of people to work together in the most efficient and effective manner possible. There are entire volumes on this subject, and it's beyond the scope of this book to go into all the team-building possibilities. The exam tends to focus more on the theories behind team building, so that's what we'll spend our time looking at.

All newly formed teams go through four stages of development: forming, storming, norming, and performing. You've probably seen this elsewhere, but since these stages are on the exam, you'll want to memorize them. Let's take a brief look at each of them.

Forming

This one's easy. It's the beginning stage of team formation when all the members are brought together, introduced, and told the objectives of the project. This is where team members learn why they're working together. During this stage, team members tend to be formal and reserved and take on an "all business" approach.

Storming

This stage is where the action begins. Team members become confrontational with each other as they're vying for position and control during this stage. They're working through who is going to be the top dog and jockeying for status.

Norming

Now things begin to calm down. Team members know each other fairly well by now; they're comfortable with their position in the team and begin to deal with project problems instead of people problems. In this stage, they confront the project concerns and problems instead of each other. Decisions are made jointly at this stage, and team members exhibit affection and familiarity with one another.

Performing

Ahh, perfection. Well, almost, anyway. This is where great teams end up. This stage is where the team is productive and effective. The level of trust among team members is high, and great things are achieved. This is the mature development stage.

Different teams progress through these stages at different rates. When you have to bring new team members on board for whatever reason, the team-forming stages start all over again. It doesn't matter where the team is in the forming process—a new member will start the cycle over again.

🌐 **Real World Scenario**

Micro-Robotics Research and Development

Micro-Robotics is working on a prototype microscopic robot that's inserted into inoperable brain tumors. The robot is controlled using a remote control joystick device that allows a trained brain surgeon to excise the brain tumor. You are the project manager for this project and have recently assembled your team.

You've got a diverse group of highly skilled team members including medical doctors, medical researchers, computer programmers, and bio-mechanical engineers.

You've held a few project meetings and have called the next one to order. The agenda has been read, and you're discussing the progress of one of the computer programs that controls the robot.

"I did hear what you said, Amiel," Noelle the brain surgeon says. "And it won't work like that."

Amiel is the lead computer programmer on the project. "But when we met last week, you said…"

Noelle interrupts, "How many brain surgeries have you performed? Fix it or I'm off this team."

You tell everyone to take five. It occurs to you that this really isn't unusual behavior. Highly skilled experts are sometimes difficult to manage, but all teams go through certain stages prior to hitting the peak performance stage. You realize this team is in the storming stage and will benefit from some team-building exercises. A few off-site team-building activities is just what the doctor ordered.

Team Focus

Did you ever watch any of those old pirate movies on late-night TV? Remember the scenes where the captain went down into the bowels of the ship to check on the teams of rowers? Imagine your project team members are like those rowing teams. If the members on the left are rowing one way and the members on the right are rowing another, you're creating a lot of energy and looking very busy, but in the end you aren't making any progress. All the team members need to understand the direction you're headed and work toward that end.

It's paramount that the team members know and understand the objectives of the project. After all, that's the reason they've been brought together in the first place. Keep in mind that people see and hear things from their own perspective. A room full of people attending a speech will all come away with something a little different because what was said speaks to their particular situation in life at the time. In other words, their own perceptions filter what they hear. It's your job as project manager to make certain the team members understand the objectives and their assignments correctly. Ask them to tell you in their own words what they believe the project objectives to be. This is a great way to know if you've got everyone on board.

Effective Team Characteristics

Effective teams are typically very energetic teams. Their enthusiasm is contagious, and it feeds on itself. They generate a lot of creativity and become good problem solvers. Teams like this are every project manager's dream. Investing yourself in team building as well as relationship building, especially when you don't think you have the time to do so, will bring many benefits. Here's a sample of the benefits:

- Better conflict resolution

- Commitment to the project

- Commitment to the project team members and project manager

- High job satisfaction

- Enhanced communication

- A sense of belonging and purpose

Dysfunctional teams will typically produce the opposite results of the benefits we just listed. Dysfunctional teams don't just happen by themselves any more than great teams do. Sure, sometimes you're lucky enough to get the right combination of folks together right off the bat. But usually, team building takes work and dedication on the part of the project manager. Even in the situations where you do get that dynamite combination of people, they will benefit from team-building exercises and feedback.

Unfortunately, sour attitudes are just as contagious as enthusiasm. Watch for these symptoms among your team members and take action to correct the situation before the entire team is affected:

- Lack of motivation or "don't care" attitudes

- Project work that isn't satisfying

- Status meetings that turn into whining sessions

- Poor communication

- Lack of respect and lack of trust for the project manager

Keep in mind that no amount of team building will make up for poor project planning or ineffective project management techniques. Neglecting these things and thinking that your project team is good enough to make up for the poor planning or poor techniques could spell doom for your project. And besides that, it's not fair to your project team to put them in that position.

Collocation

Team members are often located in the same physical location—for example, the same office building or office complex. This is called *collocation*. Collocation enables teams to function more effectively than if they're spread out among different localities. Many times on large projects, the project manager will make provisions in the project budget to bring the team together at the same site. It's difficult, but not impossible, to manage project team members who are not physically located together. One way to achieve collocation might be to set aside a common meeting room, sometimes called a war room, for team members who are located in different buildings or across town to meet and exchange information.

Training

Training is a matter of assessing your team's skills and abilities, plus the project needs, and providing the training necessary for the team members to carry out their assigned activities. Training can sometimes be a reward as well. In the software industry, programmers seek out positions that offer training on the latest and greatest technologies, and they consider it a benefit or bonus to attend training on the company dollar and time.

Motivating the Team

Team building starts with project planning and doesn't stop until the project is completed. It involves employing techniques to improve your team's performance and keeping team members motivated. Motivation helps people work more efficiently and produce better results. If clear expectations, clear procedures, and the right motivational tools are used, project teams will excel.

Motivation can be extrinsic or intrinsic. Extrinsic motivators are material things and might include bonuses, the use of a company car, stock options, gift certificates, training opportunities, and so on.

Intrinsic motivators are specific to the individual. Some people are just naturally driven to achieve—it's part of their nature. Cultural and religious influences are forms of intrinsic motivators as well. Reward and recognition, which we'll look at next, are examples of extrinsic motivators.

Reward and Recognition

Reward and recognition systems are an important part of team interaction. These are formal ways of recognizing and promoting desirable behavior. Reward and recognition should occur in proportion to the achievement. In other words, appropriately link the reward to the performance. Team members should be rewarded for going above and beyond the call of duty. Perhaps they put in a significant amount of overtime to meet a project goal or spent nights round-the-clock babysitting ill-performing equipment. These types of behaviors should get rewarded and formally recognized by the project manager and the management team. On the other hand, if the ill-performing equipment was a direct result of mistakes made or if it happened because of poor planning, rewards would not be appropriate in this case, obviously.

Rewards should be linked to performance. A project manager who has responsibility for the project budget and the procurement process and keeps the costs in line with the budget should get rewarded for this achievement. If these functions are assigned to a functional manager in the organization, it wouldn't be appropriate to reward the project manager as they were not the one responsible for keeping the costs in line.

Consider individual preferences and cultural differences as well when using rewards and recognitions. Some people don't like to be recognized in front of a group; others thrive on it. Some people appreciate an honest thank-you with minimal fanfare, and others just won't accept individual rewards as their culture doesn't allow it. Keep this in mind when devising your reward system.

🌐 Real World Scenario

Bakers Gift Baskets

You're a contract project manager for Bakers Gift Baskets. This company assembles gift baskets of all styles and shapes with every edible treat imaginable. The company has recently experienced explosive growth, and you've been brought on board to manage their new project. They want to offer "pick your own" baskets that allow customers to pick the individual items they want included in the basket. And, they're introducing a new line of containers to choose from, including things like miniature golf bags, flowerpots, serving bowls, and the like. This means changes to the catalog and the website to accommodate the new offerings.

The deadline for this project is the driving constraint. The web changes won't cause any problems with the deadline. However, the catalog must go to press quickly to meet holiday mailing deadlines, which in turn are driving the project deadline.

Your team put their heads together and came up with an ingenious plan to meet the catalog deadline. It required lots of overtime and some weekend work on their part to pull it off, but they met the date.

You decide this is a perfect opportunity to recognize and reward the team for their outstanding efforts. You've arranged a slot on the agenda at the next all-company meeting to bring your team up front and praise them for their cooperation and efforts to get the catalog to the printers on time. You'll also present each of them with 2 days of paid time off and a gift certificate for a dinner with their family at an exclusive restaurant in the city.

Motivational Theories

There are many theories on motivation. You will encounter questions on these theories on the exam, so know their names and their primary points.

Motivational theories came about during the modern age. Prior to today's information and service type jobs and yesterday's factory work, the majority of people worked the land and barely kept enough food on the table to feed their family. No one was concerned about motivation at work. You worked because you would starve to death if you didn't. Fortunately, that isn't the case today.

Today we have a new set of problems in the workplace. Workers in the U.S. today aren't concerned with starvation—that need has been replaced with other needs like job satisfaction, a sense of belonging and commitment to the project, good working conditions, and so on. Motivational theories present ideas on why people act the way they do, and how we can influence them to act in certain ways to get the results we want. Again, there are libraries full of books on this topic. We'll cover four of them here.

Maslow's Hierarchy of Needs

You have probably seen this classic example of motivational theory. Abraham Maslow hypothesized that humans have five basic needs arranged in hierarchical order. The first of those needs are physical needs like the need for food, clothing, and shelter. The idea is these needs must be met before the person can move to the next level in the hierarchy, which is safety and security needs. Here the concern is for the person's physical welfare and the security of their belongings. Once that need is met, they progress to the next level, and so on. The theory suggests that once a lower level need has been met, it no longer serves as a motivator and the next higher level becomes the driving motivator in a person's life. Maslow conjectures that humans are always in one state of need or another. Here is a recap of each of the needs starting with the highest level and working down.

Self-actualization   Performing at your peak potential

Self-esteem needs   Accomplishment, respect for self, capability

Social needs   A sense of belonging, love, acceptance, friendship

Safety and security needs   Your physical welfare and your belongings

Basic physical needs   Food, clothing, shelter

The highest level of motivation in this theory is the state of self-actualization. The United States Army had a slogan a few years ago that I think encapsulates self-actualization very well; it went something like this: "Be all you can be." When all the physical, safety, social, and self-esteem needs have been met, a person reaches a state of independence where they're able to express themselves and perform at their peak. They'll do good work just for the sake of doing good work. Recognition and self-esteem have already been fulfilled at lower levels; now the need for being the best they can be is reached.

Hygiene Theory

Fredrick Herzberg came up with the Hygiene theory, also known as the Motivation-Hygiene theory. He postulates that there are two factors that contribute to motivation: hygiene factors and motivators. Hygiene factors deal with work environment issues. The thing to remember about hygiene factors is that they prevent dissatisfaction. Examples of hygiene factors are pay, benefits, the conditions of the work environment, and relationships with peers and managers. Pay is considered a hygiene factor as Herzberg believed that over the long term, pay is not a motivator. In other words, being paid for the work done prevents dissatisfaction but doesn't necessarily bring satisfaction in and of itself. He believed this to be true as long as the pay system is equitable. If two workers performing the same functions have large disparities in pay, then pay can become a motivator.

Motivators deal with the substance of the work itself and the satisfaction one derives from performing the functions of the job. Motivators lead to satisfaction. The ability to advance, the opportunity to learn new things, and the challenges involved in the work are all motivators according to Herzberg.

For the exam, remember that Herzberg was the inventor of the Hygiene theory and that this theory claims that hygiene factors prevent dissatisfaction while motivators lead to satisfaction.

Expectancy Theory

The Expectancy theory says that the expectation of a positive outcome drives motivation. People will behave in certain ways if they think there will be good rewards for doing so. Also note that this theory says the strength of the expectancy drives the behavior. In other words, the expectation or likelihood of the reward is linked to the behavior. For example, if you tell your 2-year-old to put the toys back in the toy box and you'll give her a cookie, chances are she'll put the toys away. This is a reasonable reward for a reasonable action. However, if you promise your project team members vacations in Hawaii if they get the project done early and they know there is no way you can deliver that reward, there is little motivation to work toward that reward.

This theory also says that people become what you expect of them. If you openly praise your project team members and treat them like valuable contributors, you'll likely have a high-performing team on your hands. Conversely, when you publicly criticize people or let them know that you have low expectations regarding their performance, they'll likely live up (or down as the case may be) to that expectation as well.

Achievement Theory

Achievement theory says that people are motivated by the need for three things: achievement, power, and affiliation. The achievement motivation is obviously the need to achieve or succeed. The power motivation involves a desire for influencing the behavior of others. And the need for affiliation is relationship oriented. Workers want to have friendships with their co-workers and a sense of camaraderie with their fellow team members. The strength of your team members' desire for each of these will drive their performance on various activities.

We'll cover two more theories in the leadership section, which is next. These deal specifically with how leaders deal with their project team members.

Getting to Leadership vs. Management

Leaders have a knack for getting others to do what needs done and rallying them around a vision. Good leaders have committed team members who believe in the vision of the leader. Leaders set direction and time frames, and have the ability to attract good talent to work for them.

We talked about leaders versus managers back in Chapter 1. Leaders inspire a vision and get things done through others by garnering loyalty, respect, and cooperation from team members. They set the course and lead the way. Leaders are usually concerned about the big picture, so to speak. Good leaders are directive in their approach, but allow for plenty of feedback and input. Good leaders commonly have strong interpersonal skills and are well respected.

Managers are generally task oriented, concerned with things like plans, controls, budgets, policies, and procedures. They're generalists with a broad base of planning and organizational skills, and their primary goal is satisfying stakeholder needs. They also posses motivational skills and the ability to recognize and reward behavior.

Project managers need to use the traits of both leaders and managers at different times during the project. On very large projects, a project manager will act more like a leader inspiring the subproject managers to get on board with the objectives. On small projects, project managers will act more like managers as they're responsible for all the planning and coordinating functions.

There are two theories that we'll discuss regarding leadership. They are McGregor's Theory of X and Y and the Contingency theory. Then we'll end this section with a discussion of the types of power leaders use and the outputs of Team Development.

Theory X and Theory Y

Theory X and Theory Y attempt to explain how different managers deal with their team members. Theory X managers believe most people do not like work and will try to steer clear of it; they have little to no ambition, need constant supervision, and won't actually perform the duties of their job unless threatened.

As a result, Theory X managers are like dictators and impose very rigid controls over their people. They believe people are motivated only by punishment, money, or position. Unfortunately for them, Theory X managers unknowingly also subscribe to the Expectancy theory. If they expect people to be lazy and unproductive and treat them as such, their team members probably will be lazy and unproductive.

Theory Y managers believe people are interested in performing their best given the right motivation and proper expectations. These managers provide support to their teams, are concerned about their team members, and are good listeners. Theory Y managers believe people are creative and committed to the project goals, that they like responsibility and seek it out, and that they are able to perform the functions of their positions with limited supervision.

Contingency Theory

This theory builds on a combination of Theory Y and the Hygiene theory. The Contingency theory, in a nutshell, says that people are motivated to achieve levels of competency and will continue to be motivated by this need even after competency is reached.

The Power of Leaders

Power is the ability to influence others to do what you want them to do. This can be used in a positive manner or a negative one. But that old saying of your grandmother about attracting more flies with honey than vinegar still holds true today.

Leaders, managers, and project managers use power to convince others to do things a specific way. The kind of power they use to accomplish this depends on their personality, their personal values, and the company culture.

Types of Power

There are several forms of power that a project manager might use. We've already talked about reward power, which is the ability to grant bonuses or incentive awards for a job well done. Let's look at a few more.

Punishment Power

Punishment, also known as coercive or penalty power, is just the opposite of reward power. The employee is threatened with consequences if expectations are not met.

Expert Power

Expert power occurs when the person being influenced believes the manager, or the person doing the influencing, is knowledgeable on the subject or has special abilities that make them an expert. The person goes along just because they think the influencer knows what they're doing and it's the best thing for the situation.

Legitimate Power

Legitimate, or formal, power comes about as a result of the influencer's position. Because that person is the project manager, or executive vice president, or CEO, they have the power to call the shots and make decisions.

Referent Power

Referent power is inferred to the influencer by their subordinates. Project team members who have a great deal of respect and high regard for their project managers willingly go along with decisions made by the project manager because of referent power.

Punishment power should be used as a last resort. There are times when you'll have to use this method, but hopefully much less often than the other three forms of power. Sometimes, you'll have team members who won't live up to expectations and their performance suffers as a result. This is a case where punishment power is enacted to get the employee to correct their behavior.

Defining Team Development Outputs

We're now ready to close out the Team Development process outputs. There are several questions regarding team-building and motivational techniques on the exam, so it's good you've just spent the time learning all about them.

The outputs to Team Development are performance improvements and input to performance appraisals. These are pretty straightforward. As a result of positive team-building experiences, you'll see individuals improving their skills, team behaviors and relationships improving, conflict resolutions going smoothly, and team members recommending ways to improve the work of the project.

Performance appraisals are typically annual affairs where managers let their employees know what they think of their performance for the past year and rate them accordingly. Project managers should contribute to the performance appraisals of all project team members. In functional organizations, the functional manager is responsible for the performance appraisal. If project managers do not have an equal say, or at least some say in the employee's performance, it will cause the team member to be loyal to the functional manager and show little loyalty to the project or project manager.

Project managers need to wear a lot of hats. This is one of the things that makes this job so interesting. You need organization and planning skills to plan the project. You need motivation and sometimes disciplinary skills to execute the project plans. You need to exercise leadership and power where appropriate. And all the while, you have a host of relationships to manage, including team members, stakeholders, managers, and customers. It's a great job and brings terrific satisfaction.

Developing Great Communication Skills

Every aspect of your job as a project manager will involve communications. It's been estimated that project managers spend as much as 90 percent of their time communicating in one form or another. Therefore, communication skills are arguably the most important skills a project manager can have. They are even more important than technical skills. Good communication skills foster an open, trusting environment. The ability to communicate well is a project manager's best asset.

We talked about how important good communication skills are in Chapter 1. In this section, we'll discuss the act of communication, listening behaviors, and conflict resolution. You'll employ each of these techniques with your project team, stakeholders, customers, and management team.

Information Exchange

Communication is the process of exchanging information. There are three elements to all communication: the sender, the message, and the receiver.

The sender is the person responsible for putting the information together in a clear and concise manner. The information should be complete and presented in a way that the receiver will be able to correctly understand it. Make your messages relevant to the receiver. Junk mail is annoying, and information that doesn't pertain in any way whatsoever to the receiver is nothing more than that.

The message is the information being sent and received. It might be written, verbal, non-verbal, formal, informal, internal, external, horizontal, or vertical. Horizontal communications are messages sent and received to peers. Vertical communications are messages sent and received down to subordinates and up to executive management.

Make your messages as simple as you can to get your point across. Don't complicate the message with unnecessary detail and technical jargon that others may not understand. A simple trick that helps clarify your messages, especially verbal messages, is to repeat the key information periodically. Public speakers are taught that the best way to organize your speech is to first tell the audience what you're going to tell them; second, tell them; and third, tell them what you just told them.

The receiver is the person the message is intended for. They are responsible for understanding the information correctly and making sure they've received all of the information.

Keep in mind that receivers filter the information they receive through their knowledge of the subject, culture influences, language, emotions, attitudes, and geographic locations. The sender should take these filters into consideration when sending messages so that the receiver will clearly understand the message that was sent.

Methods of Information Exchange

Senders, receivers, and messages are the elements of communication. The way the sender packages or encodes the information and transmits it, and the way the receiver unpacks or decodes the message are the methods of communication exchange.

Senders encode messages. Encoding is a method of putting the information into a format the receiver will understand. Language, pictures, and symbols are ways to encode messages. Encoding formats the message for transmitting.

Transmitting is the way the information gets from the sender to the receiver. Spoken words, written documentation, memos, e-mail, voice mail, and so on are all transmitting methods.

Decoding is what the receiver does with the information when they get it. They convert it into an understandable format. Usually, this means they read the memo, listen to the speaker, etc.

Forms of Communication

Communication occurs primarily in written or verbal form. Granted, we can point to something or indicate what you need with motions, but usually we use the spoken or written word to get our message across.

Verbal communication is easier and less complicated than written communication, and it's usually a fast method of communication. Written communication, on the other hand, is an excellent way to get across complex, detailed messages. Detailed instructions are better provided in written form as it provides the reader the ability to go back over information they're not quite sure about.

Both verbal and written communications might take a formal or an informal approach. Speeches or lectures are an example of formal verbal communications. Most project status meetings take more of a formal approach as do most written project status reports. Generally speaking, the project manager should take an informal approach when communicating with stakeholders and project team members outside of the status meetings. This makes you appear more open and friendly and easier to approach with questions and issues.

Lines of Communication

Project communication will always involve more than one person, even on the tiniest of projects. As such, communication network models have been devised to try to explain the relationships between people and the number or type of interactions needed between project participants. What you need to remember for the exam is that network models consist of nodes with lines connecting the nodes that indicate the number of lines of communication. See Figure 8.1 for an example of a network communication circle with six participants.

FIGURE 8.1 Circular communication network

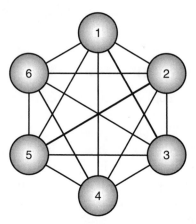

Nodes = participants
Lines = lines of communication between participants

The nodes are the participants, and the lines show the connection between them all. You'll need to know how to calculate the lines of communication when you take the exam. You could draw them out like this example and count up the lines, but there's an easier way. The formula for calculating the lines of communication is as follows: [number of participants × (number of participants less one)] divided by two. Here's the calculation in math terms:

$$[n \times (n - 1)] \div 2$$

Figure 8.1 shows six participants, so let's plug that into our formula to determine the lines of communication:

$$[6 \times (6 - 1)] \div 2 = 15$$

I recommend you memorize this formula before taking the exam.

Effective Listening Skills

What did you say? Often we think we're listening when we really aren't. In all fairness, we can take in only so much information at one time. But it's important to perform active listening when someone else is speaking. As a project manager, you will spend the majority of your time communicating with team members, stakeholders, customers, vendors, and others. This means you should be as good a listener as you are a communicator.

Listening Techniques

One of the things you can do to listen more actively is to appear interested. This will make the speaker feel at ease and will benefit you as well. By acting interested, you become interested and thereby retain more of the information being presented.

Making eye contact with the speaker is another effective listening tool. This lets the speaker know you are paying attention to what they're saying and are interested.

Put your speaker at ease by letting them know beforehand that you're interested in what they're going to talk about and that you're looking forward to hearing what they have to say. While they're speaking, nod your head, smile, or make comments when and if appropriate to let the speaker know you understand the message. If you don't understand something and are in the proper setting, ask clarifying questions.

Another great trick that works well in lots of situations is to recap what the speaker said in your own words and tell it back to them. Start with something like this, "Let me make sure I understand you correctly, you're saying…" and ask the speaker to confirm that you did understand them correctly.

Just like your mother always said, it's impolite to interrupt. Interrupting is a way of telling the speaker that you aren't really listening and you're more interested in telling them what you have to say than listening to them. Interrupting gets the other person off track, they might forget their point, and it may even make them angry.

Not to disagree with mom, but there probably are some occasions where interrupting is appropriate. As an example, if you're in a project status meeting and someone wants to take the meeting off course, sometimes the only way to get the meeting back on track is to interrupt them. You can still do this politely. Start first by saying their name to get their attention. Then let them know that you'd be happy to talk with them about their topic outside of the meeting or add it to the agenda for the next status meeting if it's something everyone needs to hear. Sorry, mom.

Resolving Conflicts

I said earlier in this chapter that if you have more than one person working on your project, you have a team. Here's another fact: If you have more than one person working on your project, you'll have conflict. I put conflict resolution in the communication section because conflict resolution involves communication, as we'll see in a moment.

Everyone has desires, needs, and goals. Conflict comes into the picture when the desires, needs, or goals of one party are incompatible with the desires, needs, or goals of another party (or parties). Conflict, simply, is the incompatibility of goals and one party resisting or blocking the attainment of those goals by the other party. This doesn't sound like a party!

There are five ways of resolving conflict that may show up on the exam: forcing, smoothing, compromise, confrontation, and withdrawal. Each technique will not necessarily have long-term benefits. The smoothing and withdrawal techniques have temporary results and aren't always good techniques to use to resolve problems. Forcing, compromise, and confrontation techniques, however, tend to have lasting effects.

Forcing

Forcing is just like it sounds. One person forces a solution on the other parties. This is where the boss puts on the "because I'm the boss and I said so" hat. While this is a permanent solution, it isn't necessarily the best solution. People will go along with it because, well, they're forced to go along with it. It doesn't mean they agree with the solution. This isn't the best technique to use when you're trying to build a team. This is an example of a win-lose conflict resolution technique. The forcing party wins, and the losers are those who are forced to go along with the decision.

Smoothing

Smoothing does not lead to a permanent solution. It's a temporary way to resolve conflict where someone attempts to make the conflict appear less important than it is. Everyone looks at each other and scratches their head and wonders why they thought the conflict was such a big deal anyway. As a result, a compromise is reached and everyone feels good about the solution until they get back to their desk and start thinking about the issue again. When they realize that the conflict was smoothed over and really is more important than what they were led to believe, they'll be back at it and the conflict will resurface. This is an example of a lose-lose conflict resolution technique as neither side wins.

Compromise

Compromise is achieved when each of the parties involved in the conflict gives up something to reach a solution. Everyone involved decides what they will give on and what they won't give on, and eventually through all the give and take a solution is reached. Neither side wins or loses in this situation. As a result, neither side is really gung ho on the decision that was reached. They will drag their feet and reluctantly trudge along. If, however, firm commitments are made by both parties to the resolution, then the solution becomes a permanent one.

Confrontation

This technique is also called problem solving and is the best way to resolve conflict. A fact-finding mission results in this scenario. The thinking here is that one right solution to a problem exists and the facts will bear out the solution. Once the facts are uncovered, they're presented to the parties and the decision will be clear. Thus the solution becomes a permanent one and the conflict expires. This is the conflict resolution approach project mangers use most often and is an example of a win-win conflict resolution technique.

Withdrawal

Withdrawal never results in resolution. This occurs when one of the parties gets up and leaves and refuses to discuss the conflict. It is probably the worst of all the techniques as nothing gets resolved. This is an example of a lose-lose conflict resolution technique.

Keep in mind that group size makes a difference when you're trying to resolve conflict or make decisions. Groups of 5 to 11 people have been shown to make the most accurate decisions.

Use communication, listening, and conflict resolution skills wisely. As a project manager, you'll find that your day-to-day activities encompass these three areas the majority of the time. Project managers with excellent communication skills can work wonders. Communication won't take the place of proper planning and management techniques, but a project manager who communicates well with their team and the stakeholders can make up for a lack of technical skills any day, hands down. If your team and your stakeholders trust you, and you can communicate the vision and the project goals and report on project status accurately and honestly, the world is your oyster.

Distributing Project Information

Information Distribution is concerned with getting stakeholders information regarding the project in a timely manner. This can come about in several ways: status reports, project meetings, review meetings, etc. In the Information Distribution process, the communications management plan that was defined during the Communications Planning process is put into action. Communication and Information Distribution work together to report the progress of the project team.

The Information Distribution process inputs are work results, communications management plan, and project plan. These have all been discussed previously. The tools and techniques for this process are communication skills, information retrieval systems, and information distribution methods. We covered communication skills in the last section, so we'll skip ahead to the information systems.

Information Retrieval Systems

Retrieval systems are ways that information is stored and shared among project team members. They include things like project management software, manual filing systems, and electronic databases. Don't confuse retrieval systems with distribution methods. Remember that retrieval systems are ways for the project team to get at project information.

Information Distribution Methods

Distribution methods are ways of getting the project information to the project team or stakeholders. As the name implies, these are ways to distribute the information and might include e-mail, hard copy, voice mail, video-conferencing, etc.

Outputs of Information Distribution

The first output of the Information Distribution process is *project records*. These include, as you might guess, memos, correspondence, and other documents concerning the project. The best place to keep information like this is in a project binder or a set of project binders, depending on the size of the project. The project binders are ordinary three-ring binders where project information gets filed. They are maintained by the project manager or project office, and contain all information regarding the project. These records serve as historical information once the project is closed.

Project reports, the second output of this process, include the project status reports and minutes from project meetings. If you're keeping an issues log, they would be included with this as well.

The final output of this process is project presentations. These involve presenting project information to the stakeholders and other appropriate parties when necessary. The presentations might be formal or informal and depend on the audience and the information being communicated.

Project Case Study: New Kitchen Heaven Retail Store

Dirk Perrier logs on and finds the following e-mail addressed to all the stakeholders and project team members from you.

Project Progress Report

Project Name   Kitchen Heaven Retail Store

Project Number   081501-1910

Prepared by   Project Manager

Date   September 20, 2001

Section 1: Action Items

- Action Item 1: Call Cable Vendor—Responsible Party: Ricardo; Resolution Date: 9/12

- Action Item 2: T1 Connection Status—Responsible Party: Ricardo; Resolution Date: Pending

- Action Item 3: Build-out Begins—Responsible Party: Jake; Resolution Date: Pending

Section 2: Scheduled and Actual Completion Dates

- Sign Lease—Scheduled: 8/20/01; Completed: 8/20/01

- Gomez Contract Signed—Scheduled: 9/11/01; Completed: 9/11/01

- Ethernet Cable Run—Scheduled: 9/18/01; Completed: 9/18/01

- Build-out Started—Scheduled: 9/19/01; Completed: Open

Section 3: Activity That Occurred in the Project This Week

The Ethernet cable run was completed without a problem.

Gomez construction started the build-out process. This task was fast tracked with the Ethernet cable run as planned.

Jill made initial calls regarding retail products order.

Section 4: Progress Expected This Reporting Period Not Completed

None. Project is on track to date.

Section 5: Progress Expected Next Reporting Period

Build-out will continue. Jake reports that Gomez expects to have electrical lines run and drywall started prior to the end of the next reporting period.

Ricardo should have a T1 update. There's a slim possibility that the T1 connection will have occurred by next reporting period.

Section 6: Issues

We had to start the build-out on the last day of the cable run (this is called fast tracking) to keep the project on schedule. Jake and Ricardo reported only minor problems with this arrangement in that the contractors got into each other's way a time or two. This did not impact the completion of the cable run as most of day two this team was in the back room and Gomez's crew was in the storefront area.

A key member of the Gomez construction crew was out last week due to a family emergency. Gomez assures us that it will not impact the build-out schedule. They replaced the team member with someone from another project so it appears so far that build-out is on schedule.

Ricardo is somewhat concerned about the T1 connection as the phone company won't return his calls inquiring about status. We're still ahead of the curve on this one as hardware isn't scheduled to begin testing until January 23. Hardware testing depends on the T1 connection. This is a heads-up at this point, and we'll carry this as an issue in the status report going forward until it's resolved.

One of the gourmet food item suppliers Jill uses regularly went out of business. She is in the process of tracking down a new supplier to pick up the slack for the existing stores and supply the gourmet food products for the new store.

"Good job on the status," Dirk says as you pick up the phone. "I was beginning to wonder when we'd see some action on the project, but it looks like things are under way."

"A lot has happened in just the past 2 weeks as you can see. I'll publish these project status updates twice a month in conjunction with the regular project status meetings. Starting in January, I'll publish them once a week until project completion."

"Keep me posted on that T1 line. That isn't going to be a showstopper, is it?"

"We have a contingency plan in place," you reply. "We talked about that last week."

"Okay. I'll see you at the project meeting Friday."

"See you then," you say.

Project Case Study Checklist

Communication

- Sender makes it clear and concise.

- There's no unnecessary technical jargon.

- Formal written communication is provided.

- It's the receiver's responsibility to understand information.

- Status report is a vertical and horizontal communication method.

Project Plan Execution

- Status review meetings

- Work results

Team Development

Information Distribution

- Project information is delivered to stakeholders in a timely manner.

- Information distribution method is status reports via e-mail and project meetings.

- Status report is part of the project reports filed in the project binder or file for future reference as historical information.

Summary

This chapter detailed three processes from the Executing process group: Project Plan Execution, Team Development, and Information Distribution.

Project Plan Execution is where the project plans come to life. Activities are authorized to begin using a work authorization system, the product or service of the project is actually produced, and status review meetings are held to inform stakeholders of project progress and updates.

Team building involves creating an open, inviting atmosphere where stakeholders and project team members will become efficient and cooperative teams increasing productivity during the course of the project. It's the project manager's job to bring the team together into a functioning, productive group.

There are four stages of Team Development: forming, storming, norming, and performing. All groups proceed through these stages, and the introduction of a new team member will always start the process over again.

Collocation is physically placing team members together in the same location. This might also include a common meeting room or gathering area where team members can meet and collaborate on the project.

Several motivational theories exist including reward and recognition, Maslow's Hierarchy of Needs, Hygiene theory, Expectancy theory, and Achievement theory. These theories conjecture that motivation is driven by needs, anticipation of expected outcomes, or needs for achievement, power, or affiliation. The Hygiene theory proposes that hygiene factors prevent dissatisfaction.

Leaders inspire vision and rally people around common goals. Theory X leaders think most people are motivated only through punishment, money, or position. Theory Y leaders think most people want to perform the best job they can. The Contingency theory says that people naturally want to achieve levels of competency and will continue to be motivated by competency needs even after competency is reached.

Leaders exhibit five types of power: reward, punishment, expert, legitimate, and referent power.

Communication skills are the most important skills a project manager exercises. People who send messages are responsible for making sure the message is clear, concise, and complete. Receivers are responsible for understanding the message correctly and making sure they've received all of the information.

Listening skills put speakers at ease. Several techniques tell your speaker you're listening attentively including making eye contact, nodding, asking clarifying questions, and limiting interruptions.

Information Distribution is a matter of getting project information out to the stakeholders. Information retrieval systems generally store project information and include project management software, filing cabinets, and electronic databases. Information distribution methods are ways to get the information to the stakeholders and include e-mail, paper, voice mail, or videoconferencing.

Exam Essentials

Be able to identify distinguishing characteristics of Project Plan Execution. It's the only core process in the Executing group, and the majority of the project budget is spent during this process.

Be able to name the four stages of group formation. Forming, storming, norming, and performing.

Be able to define Maslow's highest level of motivation. Self-actualization occurs when a person performs at their peak and all lower level needs have been met.

Be able to name the five levels of power. Reward, punishment, expert, legitimate, and referent.

Be able to differentiate between senders and receivers of information. Senders are responsible for clear, concise, complete messages, while receivers are responsible for understanding the message correctly.

Be able to identify the five styles of conflict resolution. Forcing, smoothing, compromise, confrontation, and withdrawal.

Key Terms

Before you take the exam, be certain you are familiar with the following terms:

collocation	project record
Information Distribution	Team Development
Project Plan Execution	

Review Questions

1. You are a project manager for an international marketing firm. You are ready to assign resources to your new project using a work authorization system. All of the following are true except:

   A. Work authorization systems clarify and initiate the work for each work package.

   B. Work authorization systems are written procedures defined by the organization.

   C. Work authorization systems are tools and techniques of the Project Plan Execution process.

   D. Work authorization systems are an output of the Project Plan Execution process.

2. Your project is progressing as planned. The project team has come up with a demo that the sales team will use when making presentations to perspective clients. You will do which of the following at your next stakeholder project status meeting?

   A. Report on the progress of the demo and note that it's a completed task

   B. Preview the demo for stakeholders and obtain their approval and sign-off

   C. Review the technical documentation of the demo and obtain approval and sign-off

   D. Report that the demo has been noted as a completed task in the information retrieval system

3. All of the following are tools and techniques of the Project Plan Execution process except:

   A. Project management information system

   B. Work authorization system

   C. Organizational policies

   D. General management skills

4. You are a project manager for a growing dairy farm. They offer their organic dairy products regionally and are expanding their operations to the West Coast. They're in the process of purchasing and leasing dairy farms to get operations under way. You are in charge of the network operations part of this project. An important deadline is approaching that depends on the successful completion of the testing phase. You've detected some problems with your hardware in the testing phase and discover that the hardware is not compatible with other network equipment. You take corrective action and exchange the hardware for more compatible equipment. Which of the following is true?

   A. This is not a corrective action as corrective action involves human resources, not project resources.

   B. Corrective action is taken here to make sure the future project outcomes are aligned with the project plan.

   C. Corrective action is not necessary in this case as the future project outcomes aren't affected.

   D. Corrective action serves as the change request to authorize exchanging the equipment.

5. You are a project manager for a growing dairy farm. They offer their organic dairy products regionally and are expanding their operations to the West Coast. They're in the process of purchasing and leasing dairy farms to get operations under way. The subproject manager in charge of network operations has reported some hardware problems to you. You're also having some other problems coordinating and integrating other elements of the project. Which of the following is true?

   A. You are in the Project Plan Execution process.

   B. Your project team doesn't appear to have the right skills and knowledge needed to perform this project.

   C. You are in the Information Distribution process.

   D. Your project team could benefit from some team-building exercises.

6. Which of the following processes serve as inputs to each other?

   A. Executing and Controlling

   B. Planning and Executing

   C. Planning and Controlling

   D. Executing and Initiation

7. You are the project manager for a cable service provider. Your team members are amiable with each other and are careful to make project decisions jointly. Which of the following is true?

   A. They are in the smoothing stage of Team Development.

   B. They are in the norming stage of Team Development.

   C. They are in the forming stage of Team Development.

   D. They are in the forcing stage of Team Development.

8. You are the project manager for a cable service provider. Your project team is researching a new service offering. They have been working together for quite sometime and are in the performing stage of Team Development. A new member has been introduced to the team. Which of the following is true?

   A. The Team Development process will start all over again with the storming stage.

   B. The team will continue in the performing stage.

   C. The Team Development process will start all over again with the forming stage.

   D. The team will start all over again at the storming stage but quickly progress to the performing stage.

9. You are the project manager for a cable service provider. Your project team is researching a new service offering. They have been working together for quite some time and are in the performing stage of Team Development. This stage of Team Development is similar to which of the following?

    A. Smoothing

    B. Achievement theory

    C. Hygiene theory

    D. Self-actualization

10. Receivers in the communication model filter their information through all of the following except:

    A. Culture

    B. Knowledge of subject

    C. Conflict

    D. Language

11. You've promised your team two days of paid time off plus a week's training in the latest technology of their choice if they complete their project ahead of schedule. This is an example of which of the following?

    A. Achievement theory

    B. Expectancy theory

    C. Maslow's theory

    D. Contingency theory

12. What are the outputs of the Team Development process?

    A. Performance improvements, input to performance appraisals

    B. Input to performance appraisals, reward and recognition systems

    C. Performance improvements, input to performance appraisals, performance reports

    D. Work results, input to performance appraisals, performance reports

13. Your team is split between two buildings on either side of town. As a result, the team isn't very cohesive because the members don't know each other very well. The team is still in the storming stage because of the separation issues. Which of the following should you consider?

    A. Corrective action

    B. Collocation

    C. Training

    D. Conflict resolution

14. Your project team is a close group all busily working on project activities. They're close to approaching the performing stage of Team Development. All six members must communicate frequently with each other. How many lines of communication are there?

    A. 12

    B. 15

    C. 18

    D. 14

15. Project managers use this conflict resolution technique most often:

    A. Smoothing

    B. Confronting

    C. Norming

    D. Forcing

16. You are the project manager for a web development project. You hold regular project status meetings and publish status reports on a timely basis. You know that communication is one of your most important functions. As such, all of the following are true except:

    A. Senders are responsible for sending clear, concise, complete messages.

    B. Receivers are responsible for understanding the message.

    C. Communication can be vertical or horizontal or both.

    D. Effective communication techniques include making eye contact, nodding, and asking clarifying questions.

17. You are a fabulous project manager, and your team thinks highly of you. You are well respected by the stakeholders, management team, and project team. When you make decisions, others follow your lead as a result of which of the following?

    A. Referent power

    B. Expert power

    C. Legitimate power

    D. Punishment power

18. Theory Y managers believe which of the following?

    A. That people are motivated only by money, power, or position

    B. That people will perform their best if they're given proper motivation and expectations

    C. That people are motivated to achieve a high level of competency

    D. That people are motivated by expectation of good outcomes

19. You have accumulated project information throughout the project and need to distribute some important information you just received. All of the following are part of information distribution methods except:

    A. Electronic mail

    B. Videoconferencing

    C. Electronic databases

    D. Voice mail

20. You know that the next status meeting will require some discussion and a decision for a problem that has surfaced on the project. In order to make the most accurate decision, you know that the number of participants in the meeting should be limited to:

    A. 1 to 5

    B. 5 to 11

    C. 7 to 16

    D. 10 to 18

Answers to Review Questions

1. C. Work authorization systems are a tool and technique of the Project Plan Execution process. They formally initiate the work of each work package and clarify the assignments.

2. A. Status meetings are to report on the progress of the project. They are not for demos or show-and-tell. Answer C is not correct as stakeholders are not concerned about the content of the technical documentation. They need to know that the technical documentation has been reviewed by a qualified technician and that the documentation task is accurate and complete.

3. C. Organizational policies are an input to this process. Organizational procedures are a tool and technique.

4. B. Corrective action brings anticipated future project outcomes back into alignment with the project plan. Since there is an important deadline looming that depends on a positive outcome of this test, the equipment is exchanged so that the project plan and project schedule are not impacted.

5. A. The most difficult aspect of the Project Plan Execution process is coordinating and integrating all the project elements. The clue to this question was the next-to-last sentence, which contained this wording.

6. A. The Executing process group and Controlling process group serve as inputs to each other.

7. B. Teams in the norming stage of Team Development exhibit affection and familiarity with one another and make joint decisions. Smoothing and forcing are conflict resolution techniques, not Team Development stages.

8. C. The introduction of a new team member will start the Team Development process all over again with the forming stage, which is the first stage of Team Development.

9. D. The performing stage is similar to Maslow's self-actualization. They are both at the peak of performance, concerned with doing good and being the best.

10. C. Receivers filter information through cultural considerations, knowledge of the subject matter, language abilities, geographic location, emotions, and attitudes.

11. B. The Expectancy theory says that people are motivated by the expectation of good outcomes. The outcome must be reasonable and attainable.

12. A. Performance improvements and input to performance appraisals are the Team Development outputs.

13. B. Collocation would bring your team members together in the same location and allow them to function more efficiently as a team. At a minimum, team members meeting in a common room, such as a war room, for all team meetings would bring the team closer together.

14. B. The formula to calculate lines of communication for this question is as follows: $[6 \times (6 - 1)] \div 2 = 15$.

15. B. Confronting is a problem-solving technique that seeks to determine the facts and find solutions based on the facts, and that results in a win-win resolution for all parties.

16. D. Making eye contact, nodding, and asking clarifying questions are good listening skills, which are related to communication skills.

17. A. Referent power is power that is inferred on a leader by their subordinates as a result of the high level of respect for the leader.

18. B. Theory Y managers believe that people will perform their best if they're provided with the proper motivation and the right expectations.

19. C. Electronic databases are a type of information retrieval system, not a distribution method.

20. B. Group sizes of 5 to 11 participants make the most accurate decisions.

Chapter

9

Measuring and Controlling Project Performance

FROM THE PROJECT EXECUTION PERFORMANCE DOMAIN:

✓ 3. Manage Progress.

✓ 5. Implement Quality Assurance Procedures.

FROM THE PROJECT CONTROL PERFORMANCE DOMAIN:

✓ 1. Measure Performance.

✓ 2. Refine Control Limits.

✓ 3. Take Corrective Action.

✓ 4. Evaluate Effectiveness of Corrective Action.

✓ 5. Ensure Plan Compliance.

This chapter will wrap up the Executing process group and introduce the Controlling process group. The Executing processes we'll cover in this chapter are Solicitation, Source Selection, Contract Administration, and Quality Assurance. There are several questions on the exam that involve the Solicitation, Source Selection, and Contract Administration processes. These processes are usually performed in the order given here.

The Solicitation process obtains vendor proposals in the form of responses to requests for proposals (RFPs), requests for information (RFIs), and other documents. Source Selection marks the receipt of bids and proposals and selects a vendor from among the bidders. The Contract Administration process monitors the contract to ensure the vendor meets all the requirements of the contract.

The Controlling process group involves taking measurements and performing inspections to find out if there are variances in the plan. If variances are discovered, corrective action is taken to get the project back on track, and the affected project Planning processes are repeated to make adjustments to the plan as a result of the variances. We will examine two Controlling processes in this chapter: Scope Verification and Performance Reporting.

During Performance Reporting, we'll talk about performance measurements and look at the various techniques used to get to these measurements. We'll discuss the remaining Controlling processes in Chapter 10.

Contracting Foundations

Contracts exist because two or more parties want to exchange goods or services for consideration (usually money) and want a dependable means to assure fulfillment of both sides of the agreement. Contracts are a way to assure the goods are delivered and the money is paid and are enforceable by a court of law if necessary.

Many times project managers must purchase goods or services to complete the project. Sometimes the entire project is completed on contract. That means project managers should have an understanding of the contracting process.

Depending on the size of the organization, administering the contract might fall to someone in the procurement department. This doesn't mean that you're off the hook as the project manager. It's still your responsibility to oversee the process and make sure the project objectives are being met regardless of whether a vendor is performing the activities or your project team members are performing the activities.

You'll be the one monitoring the performance of the vendor and informing them when and if performance is lacking. If administering the contract is your responsibility, you may have to terminate the contract when the vendor violates the terms or doesn't meet agreed-upon deliverables. If the procurement department has this responsibility, you'll have to document the situation and provide this to the procurement department so that they can enforce or terminate the contract.

Contracting Life Cycles

Contracts, like projects, have a life cycle of their own. The four contract life cycles are requirement, requisition, solicitation, and award. These life cycles are intertwined with the following processes from the *Guide to the PMBOK:* Procurement Planning, Solicitation Planning, Solicitation, Source Selection, and Contract Administration. A description of each of these life cycles follows.

Requirement—Procurement Planning Process

The requirement cycle is the equivalent of the *Guide to the PMBOK*'s Procurement Planning process, which was discussed in Chapter 6. The project and contract needs are established in this cycle, and the requirements of the project are defined. The statement of work (SOW) is used to define the work of the project, the objectives, and a high-level overview of the deliverables. A work breakdown structure (WBS) is developed, a make or buy analysis takes place, and cost estimates are determined.

The SOW is provided by the buyer when the project is performed under contract to describe the requirements of the project. The product description can serve as the SOW.

Requisition—Solicitation Planning Process

This cycle combines the *Guide to the PMBOK*'s Solicitation Planning process, discussed in Chapter 6, and the inputs from the *Solicitation* process, which occurs during the Executing process group. Here the project objectives are refined and confirmed. A review of the potential qualified vendors takes place including checking references and reviewing other projects the vendor has worked on that are similar to your proposed project. Solicitation materials such as the request for proposals (RFP), request for information (RFI), and request for quotations (RFQ) are prepared during the Solicitation Planning process, but the solicitation materials are actually presented to the vendors in the next cycle. Generally, the project manager is the one responsible for preparing the RFP, RFI, and so on, and the vendors respond to the RFP during the Solicitation process.

The inputs to the Solicitation process are the procurement documents and a qualified seller list. Some organizations require vendors to register and maintain information regarding their experience and offerings on a qualified seller list. Vendors must go through the procurement department to get placed on the list. Project managers then must choose their vendors from among the list of prequalified vendors assembled by the procurement department. If a list isn't available, you'll have to work with the project team to come up with your own requirements for selecting vendors.

Solicitation—Solicitation Process

Soliciting bids involves requesting vendors to compete for the contract. This is where vendors will respond to the RFP. You will use the tools and techniques of the *Guide to the PMBOK*'s Solicitation process during this contract cycle. The resulting output is the vendor proposals.

The vendors bear the majority of work in the Solicitation process by preparing responses to the RFPs. Depending on the RFP and the effort needed to respond, costs to the vendor can become quite substantial.

There are two techniques of the Solicitation process, bidder conferences and advertising. Bidder conferences allow all prospective vendors to attend a prearranged meeting with the buyers to ask questions and clarify issues they have regarding the project and the RFP. The meeting is held once, and all vendors attend at the same time. The bidder conference is held before the vendor prepares their responses so that they are sure their RFP response will address the project requirements.

Advertising is letting potential vendors know that an RFP is available. The company's Internet site, professional journals, or newspapers are examples of where advertising might appear.

Obtaining bids and proposals is the official output of the Solicitation process. The *Guide to the PMBOK* makes a distinction between Solicitation and Source Selection that you should know: Solicitation obtains bids and proposals; Source Selection is the receipt of bids and proposals. We'll look at Source Selection next.

Award—Source Selection Process

Vendors are chosen and contracts are awarded and signed during the award cycle. The *Guide to the PMBOK* equivalent to the award cycle is the *Source Selection* process.

The project manager, or the selection committee depending on the organizational policy, receives the bids and proposals during the Source Selection process and applies evaluation criteria to each. We've discussed each of the Source Selection inputs previously, but let's do a quick recap:

Proposals   These are the response to the RFPs, RFIs, etc.

Evaluation criteria   These might include things like purchase price, technical qualifications of the vendor, PMP certification of the project manager, etc.

Organizational policies   Selection committees might evaluate RFP responses instead of the project manager depending on the size of the contract and the organizational policy.

The Source Selection process uses several tools and techniques to select the final vendor. This is usually a complicated process, except for the cases where price is the only determining factor. Let's examine each of the tools and techniques of this process.

Contract Negotiation

In *contract negotiation*, both parties come to an agreement regarding the contract terms. Negotiation skills are put into practice here as the details of the contract are ironed out between the parties. At a minimum, contract language should include price, responsibilities, regulations or laws that apply, and the overall approach to the project.

You might see a term called *fait accompli* show up on the exam. This happens during contract negotiation when one party tries to convince the other party discussing a particular contract term that it is no longer an issue. It's a distraction technique, as the party practicing fait accompli is purposely trying to keep from negotiation an issue and claims the issue cannot be changed. For example, during negotiations the vendor tells you that the key resource they're assigning to your project must start immediately or you'll lose that resource and they'll get assigned work elsewhere. However, you don't know, because the vendor didn't tell you, that they can reserve this resource for your project and hold them until the start date. They used fait accompli to push you into starting the project, or hiring this resource, sooner than you would have otherwise.

Weighting Systems

Weighting systems assign numerical weights to evaluation criteria, then multiply this by the weight of each criteria factor to come up with total scores for each vendor. Weighting systems are useful when you have multiple vendors to choose from, as they allow you to rank order the proposals to determine the sequence of negotiations.

There is an example of a weighted scoring system in Chapter 3. These systems are commonly used to evaluate vendor proposals.

Screening Systems

Screening systems use predetermined performance criteria to screen out vendors. Perhaps your project requires board-certified engineers. One of the screening criteria would be that vendors propose project team members who are board-certified engineers. If they don't, they're eliminated from the selection process.

Weighting systems and screening systems are often used in combination to come up with a selection.

Independent Estimates

Your procurement department might conduct an *independent estimate* of the costs of the proposal and use this to compare to the vendor prices. If there are large differences between the independent estimate and the proposed vendor cost, one of two things is happening: The SOW, or the terms of the contract, was not detailed enough to allow the vendor to come up with an accurate cost, or the vendor simply failed to respond to all the requirements laid out in the contract or in the SOW.

After all the RFPs are examined and scored, a vendor is selected and the contract is awarded. The only output of the Source Selection process is the contract. We've spent a great deal of time discussing contracts previously. Remember to memorize the types of contracts—fixed price, cost plus, etc.—discussed in Chapter 6.

Once you have a contract, someone has to administer it. In large organizations, this responsibility will fall to the procurement department. But as we mentioned previously, the project manager should still have a solid understanding of administering contracts as they'll work with the procurement department to determine satisfactory fulfillment of the contract. This brings us to our last contract topic for this chapter, Contract Administration.

 Real World Scenario

Vendor Selection for Fitness Counts HR System

Amanda Jacobson is the project manager for Fitness Counts, a nationwide chain of gyms containing all the latest and greatest fitness equipment, aerobics classes, swimming pools, and such.

Fitness Counts is converting their human resources system. They have several requirements that were specifically addressed in the RFP including the following: the new system must run on a platform that's compatible with the company's current operating system; hardware must be compatible with company standards; data conversion of existing HR data must be included in the price of the bid; Fitness Counts wants to have the ability to add their own custom modules using internal programmers; and training of Fitness Counts programmers must be included in the bid.

They are in the Source Selection process and have received bids based on the RFP published earlier this month. Fitness Counts is using a combination of selection criteria and weighted scoring model to choose a vendor.

One of the selection criteria said that the vendor must have prior experience with a project like this. Four vendors met that criteria and proceeded to the weighted scoring selection process.

Amanda is one of the members of the selection committee. She and four other members on the committee rated the four vendors who met the initial selection criteria. The results are shown in Table 9.1 (following this sidebar).

Vendor C is the clear winner of this bid. Based on the weighted scoring model, their responses to the RFP came out ahead of the other bidders. Amanda calls them with the good news and also calls the other vendors to thank them for participating in the bid. Vendor C is awarded the contract, and Amanda moves on to the Contract Administration process.

TABLE 9.1 Example Weighted Scoring Model

Criteria	Weight*	Vendor A	Vendor B	Vendor C	Vendor D
Platform	5	15	10	20	15
Hardware	4	12	12	16	12
Data Conversion	5	15	20	20	10
Custom Modules/ Training	4	16	12	12	16
Totals	—	58	54	68	53

*1–5; 5 highest

Administering the Contract

The *Contract Administration* process entails monitoring the vendor's performance and ensuring all the requirements of the contract are met. It's imperative that the project manager and project team are aware of any contract agreements that may impact the project so the team does not inadvertently take action that violates the terms of the contract.

Administering the contract is closely linked with project processes. You'll coordinate the contract with the project processes and monitor progress, execute plans, track costs, measure outputs, approve changes, take corrective action, and report on status just like you do for the project itself.

Contracting Inputs

The inputs to Contract Administration are contract, work results, change requests, and seller invoices. We've already discussed contracts, so let's move on to work results.

Work Results

Monitoring work results involves an examination of the deliverables to determine which ones are complete and which ones have not been completed to date. It also looks at the quality of the deliverables and the cost of the deliverables. You will monitor work results against the project plan and make certain activities are performed correctly and in sequence.

Change Requests

Sometimes as you get into the project, you'll discover changes need to be made. This could entail changes to the contract as well. Change requests might include things like modifications to deliverables, changes in contract terms, or termination for poor performance. Changes that cannot be agreed upon are called *contested changes*. Contested changes usually result in disputes, claims, or appeals. These can be settled directly between the parties themselves, through the court system, or by a process called arbitration. *Arbitration* involves bringing all parties to the table with a third, disinterested party who is not a participant in the contract to try and reach an agreement. The purpose of arbitration is to reach an agreement without having to go to court.

Seller Invoices

Your vendors will submit invoices for payment for the goods or services delivered in the form of seller invoices. Remember that this is an input of Contract Administration and not an output of Solicitation. Also, don't confuse this with the payment system, which is a tool and technique of this process.

Administering Contracts with Tools and Techniques

Administering the contract requires several tools and techniques according to the *Guide to the PMBOK:* contract change control system, performance reporting, and payment system. Here's a review of each.

Contract Change Control System

Much like the management plans found in the Planning processes, the contract change control system describes the processes needed to make contract changes. The change control system is a formal process that requires authorization to make changes. The authorization levels are defined by the organizational policies of your organization.

This system tracks disputes and their resolution and all the paperwork for submitting changes, and contains a tracking system to number the change requests and record their status. The change control system, along with all the management plan outputs, becomes part of the Integrated Change Control process that we'll discuss in a later chapter.

Performance Reporting

Reporting is a large part of project management. This entails providing your managers and stakeholders with information regarding the contract and the vendor's progress regarding project objectives. We'll discuss performance reporting in depth later in this chapter.

Payment Systems

Vendors submit seller invoices as an input to this process, and the payment system is the tool and technique used to issue payment. The organization may have a dedicated department, such as accounts payable, that handles vendor payments, or it might fall to the project manager. In either case, follow the policies and procedures the organization established to track vendor payments.

There is an output to this process called *payment requests*, which is where the actual check is cut and mailed to the vendor. Don't confuse payment systems with payment requests. Payment systems include reviews and authorization to issue the check. The payment request output is where the check gets sent to the vendor.

Before authorizing the payment, you'll want to verify that the terms of the contract to date have been satisfied. Many times, contracts are written such that payment is made based on a predetermined performance schedule. As an example, perhaps the first payment is made after 25 percent of the product or service is completed. As the project manager, you will verify that the delivery meets the expectations to date before the payment is authorized.

Managing Contract Outputs

The outputs to this process include correspondence, contract changes, and payment requests. These are really extensions of the tools and techniques we've already discussed. There are a few more points to examine, so let's get to it.

Correspondence

Correspondence is information that needs to be communicated in writing to either the seller or the buyer. An example might be changes to the contract or notification of performance issues. You would also use correspondence to notify a vendor that you're terminating the contract because performance is below expectations and is not satisfying the requirements of the contract.

Contract Changes

Contract changes are coordinated with the Project Plan Execution process so that any changes impacting the project itself are communicated to the project team and appropriate actions are put into place to realign the objectives. However, contract changes will not always impact the project plan. For example, late delivery of key equipment probably would impact the project plan, but changes in the vendor payment schedule probably would not. It's important that you are kept abreast of any changes to the contract so that you can evaluate whether the project plan needs adjusting.

Payment Requests

This is where the payment is physically delivered to the vendor. Again, don't confuse payment requests with payment systems. Authorization occurs through the payment system tool and technique and then actual payment is made here. I recommend remembering the inputs, tools and techniques, and outputs of the contracting processes including Solicitation, Source Selection, and Contract Administration, as there are several exam questions regarding these processes.

Laying Out Quality Assurance Procedures

The Quality Planning process laid out the quality standards for the project and determined how those standards are satisfied. The *Quality Assurance* process involves performing quality audits to determine how the project is proceeding. Quality Assurance is concerned with making certain the project will meet and satisfy the quality standards of the project defined during the Quality Planning process. The Quality Assurance process should be carried out through the rest of the project. This is how you will know and guarantee the project specifications will be met. Quality Assurance will also improve the quality of future projects because the information gained from one project in the form of lessons learned can be applied to the quality process during the next project.

The Quality Assurance process integrates project scope, project costs, and project time. All three of these elements are brought together and measured during this process.

Project team members, the project manager, and the stakeholders are responsible for the Quality Assurance of the project. The project manager will have the greatest impact on the quality of the project during this process.

Cost of Quality

In Chapter 6, we discussed Quality Planning and some of the ideas behind cost of quality. Quality Assurance further defines the cost of quality by examining the project quality management processes and measuring and evaluating them for effectiveness. This process is concerned with the correctness of work. We already discussed some of the cost of quality practices including zero defects, fitness for use, doing it right the first time, and Deming's suggestion that 85 percent of the cost of quality is a management problem. Most of these theories came about in the 1950s and 1960s and progressed into full-fledged practices. Today, quality assurance has moved more into the strategic realm and is concerned with integrating quality into the strategic-planning process so that quality becomes a companywide theme. Today quality also means allowing your customers, whether internal or external, to define quality and using the quality edge to smash your competition.

Inputs to Quality Assurance

The inputs to Quality Assurance are what we use to measure the organizational project quality management processes against. The quality management processes were defined during Quality Planning. The inputs to the Quality Assurance process are quality management plan, results of quality control measurements, and operational definitions.

Quality Management Plan

The quality management plan we talked about during project Planning defined the quality management processes that we'll use here. The quality management processes ensure that the project will satisfy the quality standards laid out in the plan. The project plan outlined quality improvements, quality control, and quality assurance.

Results of Quality Control Measurements

According to the *Guide to the PMBOK*, these are quality control testing records and quality control measurements that are used to compare and analyze quality standards. Some of the tools you'll use to take quality measurements include inspecting, sampling, statistical sampling, and other monitoring techniques. We'll talk more about the tools and techniques of Quality Control in Chapter 10.

Operational Definitions

Operational definitions are an output of the Quality Planning process and become an input to the Quality Assurance process. You'll remember from Chapter 6 that operational definitions describe in detail what it is that's being measured and how to perform the measurements according to the Quality Control process.

We've recapped the inputs to Quality Assurance here because they're important elements of this process and you may encounter an exam question regarding these inputs. However, the most important thing to remember about Quality Assurance is that quality management processes are what we use to make certain the project satisfies the quality standards laid out in the project plan.

Now let's take a look at the tools and techniques of this process, which will lead us to the final output, quality improvements.

Quality Tools and Quality Audits

There are only two tools and techniques of the Quality Assurance process: Quality Planning tools and techniques and quality audits.

We discussed Quality Planning tools and techniques during the Quality Planning process. You'll recall that the tools and techniques are benefit/cost analysis, benchmarking, flowcharting, design of experiments, and cost of quality. These tools can be used during this process as well to measure project performance.

Quality audits serve a threefold purpose. First, they periodically review quality management activities and assure that they're examining the right quality elements. Second, quality audits measure how the project is progressing and identify corrective actions when variances are detected in the measurements. You'll use the tools and techniques of this process to take performance measurements. And third, quality audits identify lessons learned for the benefit of future projects. Lessons learned allow project managers to learn from prior projects what things worked and what things didn't work so as not to repeat the same mistakes.

Quality audits are performed on a regular schedule or at random depending on the organizational policies. Quality audits performed correctly will provide the following benefits:

- The product of the project is fit for use and meets safety standards.

- Applicable laws and standards are adhered to.

- Corrective action is implemented where necessary.

- The quality plan for the project is adhered to.

- Quality improvements are identified.

Quality audits are generally performed by experienced specialists. The specialist's job is to produce an independent evaluation of the quality process. Some organizations are large enough to have their own quality assurance departments or quality assurance teams; others may have to hire contract personnel to perform this function. Internal quality assurance teams report results to the project team and management team of the organization. External quality assurance teams report results to the customer.

Quality Improvements

Quality improvements are the only output of this process. Quality improvements come about as a result of the quality audits. During the course of the audit, you may discover ways of improving the efficiency or effectiveness of the project thereby increasing the value of the project and more than likely exceeding stakeholder expectations.

Quality improvements are implemented by submitting change requests or taking corrective action. Quality improvements interface with the Controlling processes because of the need to file change requests. We'll look at change requests and change request procedures in Chapter 10.

We've completed the Executing process group with the Quality Assurance section. Remember that the Executing and Controlling processes serve as inputs to each other and that Executing and Controlling are both iterative process groups. As your project progresses and it becomes evident controls need to be exercised to get the project back on track, you'll come back through the Executing process group to reexamine Project Plan Execution, Quality Assurance, and others and then proceed back through the Controlling processes again. Let's move on to the Controlling process group now and find out what it's all about.

Managing Project Progress

Managing and reporting on project progress is the primary focus of the Controlling processes. Many of the tools we talked about in the Project Plan Execution and the Information Distribution processes are used to manage and report project status. Another process that helps manage and control project progress is the *Scope Verification* process.

The most important thing you should know about Scope Verification for the exam is that Scope Verification formalizes the acceptance of the project scope and is primarily concerned with the acceptance of work results. Don't confuse this process with Quality Assurance, which we covered earlier in this chapter. Remember it this way:

- Verification = *accepting* work results.

- Quality Assurance = checking for *correct* work results.

Scope Verification involves evaluating the inputs of this process including work results, product documentation, WBS, scope statement, and project plan to determine if the work is complete and if it satisfies the project objectives. Evaluation is performed using inspection, which is the only tool and technique of this process. You should perform Scope Verification even if the project is canceled to document the degree to which the project was completed. This serves as historical information, and if the project is ever started up again, you've got documentation that tells you what was completed and how far the project progressed.

The output of Scope Verification is formal acceptance. Stakeholders are the people who will accept the work results. Remember that stakeholders include customers, the project sponsor, the management team, etc. Document their acceptance with formal sign-off and file it in your project notebook.

Establishing Performance Measurements

Performance Reporting is part of the Communications Management knowledge area. Thus, it involves collecting and reporting information regarding project progress and project accomplishments to the stakeholders, project team members, management team, and other interested parties. It also involves forecasting future project progress. Reporting might include information concerning project quality, costs, scope, project schedules, procurement, and risk. There are several tools and techniques we can use to do that. The inputs to this process—project plan, work results, and other project records—have been discussed previously.

Performance Reporting Tools and Techniques

There are five tools and techniques in this process: performance reviews, variance analysis, trend analysis, earned value analysis, and information distribution tools and techniques. You'll need to fully understand the variance analysis, trend analysis, and earned value analysis techniques. We'll spend most of our time on the earned value analysis techniques in this section, which involve several formulas. I strongly recommend you memorize every formula I present. I'll pass on a memorization tip I used to commit these formulas to memory when we get to the earned value section. On to the first tool and technique.

Performance Reviews

Performance reviews are project status meetings held with the project team and stakeholders to collect status and report on project progress. We covered the purpose and proper etiquette of status meetings in Chapter 8.

Variance Analysis

Variance analysis compares the expected project plan results with the actual results as the project progresses to determine if variances exist. Typically, the project schedule and project costs are the two areas most often measured. However, quality, performance specifications, risk, and project scope are measurable as well. For the exam, remember that this tool and technique uses project plan results and compares them to actual results to determine variances.

Trend Analysis

According to the *Guide to the PMBOK*, *trend analysis* determines if project performance is improving or worsening over time by periodically analyzing project results. These results are measured with mathematical formulas that attempt to forecast project outcomes based on historical information and results. There are several formulas you can use to predict project trends, but it's outside the scope of this book to go into them. The exam expects you to understand the concept behind trend analysis, not the formulas used to calculate it. You'll want to remember that the results you've analyzed using trend analysis formulas are used to predict future project behavior, or trends.

Earned Value Analysis

Earned value analysis is the most often used performance measurement method. Simply stated, it compares what you got to what you spent. Earned value looks at schedule, cost, and scope project measurements together. To perform the earned value calculations, we need to first determine three measurements: the planned value (PV), actual cost (AC), and earned value (EV).

Each of these measurements has recently been renamed in the *Guide to the PMBOK*. You may see their original names in other publications. Here is a quick reference in case you come across the original names of these measurements:

- PV = budgeted cost of work scheduled (BCWS).
- AC = actual cost of work performed (ACWP).
- EV = budgeted cost of work performed (BCWP).

Let's look at a definition of each of these before we dive into the actual calculations. I recommend you memorize each of these acronyms and make certain you understand the meaning of each before progressing. If you confuse PV for AC or EV, which is easy to do, you'll miss several exam questions.

Planned Value

The *planned value (PV)* is the cost of work that's been budgeted for an activity during a certain time period. These estimates and budgets were established during the Planning process. Remember that PV is the planned costs for activities scheduled during a given time period.

Actual Cost

Actual cost (AC) is the cost of the work to date, including direct and indirect costs. Remember that AC is money that's actually been expended to date. Later we'll see how to compare this to PV to come up with variance calculations results.

Earned Value

Earned value (EV) is a measurement of the project's progress to date, or the value of the work completed to date.

EV is the sum of the cumulative budgeted costs for completed work for all activities that have been accomplished as of the measurement date. If your total budget is $1000 and 50 percent of the work has been completed as of the measurement date, your EV would equal $500. The exam will usually always provide the EV figure—you don't have to calculate it.

These three measurements can be plotted graphically to show the variances between them. If there are no variances in the measurements, all the lines on the graph remain the same, which means the project is progressing as planned. Figure 9.1 shows an example that plots these three measurements.

FIGURE 9.1 Earned value

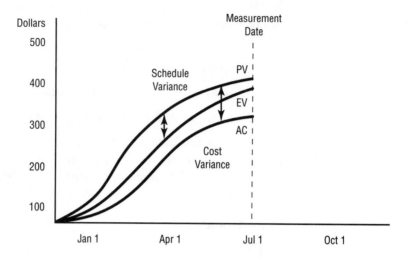

All of these measurements include a cost component. Costs are displayed in an S-curve because spending is minimal in the beginning of the project, picks up steam toward the middle, and then tapers off at the end of the project. This means our earned value measurements will also take on the S-curve shape.

Now we can calculate whether the project is progressing as planned using a variety of formulas. We'll use Figure 9.1 as our example for the formulas below. Figure 9.1 totals are as follows: PV = 400; EV = 375; AC = 325.

Cost Variance

This variance tells us if costs are higher than budgeted (with a resulting negative number) or lower than budgeted (with a resulting positive number).

The cost variance (CV) is calculated as follows:

$$CV = EV - AC$$

Let's calculate the CV using our numbers:

$$375 - 325 = 50$$

The CV is positive, which means we're spending less than what we planned as of July 1.

If we come up with a negative number as the answer to this formula, it would mean that costs are higher than what we'd planned as of July 1.

Schedule Variance

This variance tells us if the schedule is ahead or behind what was planned for this period in time.

The schedule variance (SV) is calculated as follows:

$$SV = EV - PV$$

Let's plug in our numbers:

$$375 - 400 = -25$$

The resulting schedule variance is negative, which means we are behind schedule, or behind where we planned to be as of July 1.

Performance Indexes

Cost and schedule performance indexes are primarily used to calculate performance efficiencies. They're often used in trend analysis to predict future performance. You'll need to know the calculations and what the results mean. If your result in either formula is greater than one, you've got better than expected performance. If the result is less than one, you've got poor performance. If it equals one, you're right on target.

The cost performance index (CPI) is calculated this way:

$$CPI = EV \div AC$$

Let's plug in our numbers and see where we stand.

$$375 \div 325 = 1.15$$

This means cost performance is better than expected. We get an A+ on this assignment.

The schedule performance index (SPI) is calculated this way:

$$SPI = EV \div PV$$

Again, let's see where we stand with our example:

$$375 \div 400 = .94$$

Uh oh, not so good. Schedule performance is not what we expected. We won't grade this one.

Estimate at Completion

There are only a few calculations remaining that will help us finish up our analysis of project progress. EAC is the estimate at completion. This estimates the total cost of the project at completion based on what we know today, or performance to date. It's the best estimate available to determine total costs at completion of the project.

This measurement is used during the Cost Control process, which we'll talk about in Chapter 10. However, I believe it's easier for you to review all these formulas in one place since they all use similar measurements. This should also help you when memorizing the formulas, which I recommend you do.

There are several ways to calculate EAC. The *Guide to the PMBOK* identifies three methods, which we'll cover here. The first one looks like this:

EAC = AC + ETC

The estimate to completion (ETC) formula is discussed in a later section. Essentially, it's the mathematical opposite of the EAC formula.

The EAC formula calculates the actual cost of the project to date plus the cost of the remaining work. Use this calculation when past estimating assumptions are no longer valid or you discover that they were incorrect.

The calculation for EAC using this formula looks like this when ETC = 50:

325 + 50 = 375

You will use this next EAC formula when you believe the current variances are not typical. In other words, you do not expect the variances that have occurred to date to continue to occur. The formula looks like this:

EAC = (AC + BAC) − EV

Budget at completion (BAC) is the remaining budget less the work that's been done to date. The exam will give you the BAC figure. Let's plug in our numbers and see what we get. Assume that BAC = 390.

(325 + 390) − 375 = 340

Only one more EAC formula to go. Use this version of EAC when you expect project performance to continue with the same type of variances occurring in the future as you've experienced to date.

EAC = AC + ((BAC − EV) ÷ CPI)

Putting our numbers into the formula, using BAC = 390, gives us the following:

325 + ((390 − 375) ÷ 1.15)) = 338

We'll look at two more formulas—variance at completion and estimate to completion—and then we'll recap them in an easy-to-memorize form.

Variance at Completion

Variance at completion (VAC) calculates the difference between the budget at completion and the estimate at completion. It looks like this:

VAC = BAC – EAC

We'll use the most optimistic EAC number:

390 – 375 = 15

Again, the positive number means we're doing better with costs than we anticipated.

Estimate to Completion

Estimate to completion (ETC) tells us how much more budget is required to finish the project if everything continues at the current levels of performance. This is our last formula, and you need to memorize it as well:

ETC = EAC – AC

One more time, let's put in our numbers using 375 as EAC:

375 – 325 = 50

This formula tells us from July 1 through project completion on October 1, we'll need $50 more to complete the project if the project continues at the current level of performance.

Recap of Formulas

There are a lot of formulas to memorize. Keep in mind that you'll be given a calculator when you take the exam, so you don't have to do the math manually. Here are the formulas we've covered in this chapter:

CV = EV – AC

SV = EV – PV

CPI = EV ÷ AC

SPI = EV ÷ PV

EAC = AC + ETC (use when past assumptions are incorrect)

EAC = (AC + BAC) – EV (use when variances are not typical)

$EAC = AC + ((BAC - EV) \div CPI)$ (use when variances are expected to remain the same)

$ETC = EAC - AC$

$VAC = BAC - EAC$

Remember that there are nine formulas. You might want to devise an acronym for the first letters of each formula to help you memorize their order: C-S-C-S-E-E-E-E-V.

You'll be given some scratch paper when you go into the exam. I recommend that you write these calculations down on a piece of your scratch paper before you start answering questions and keep it handy. That way, the calculations are off your mind and you've got them in front of you to reference when you get to the portion of the exam where these questions appear.

One tool and technique remains, and then we'll get into the outputs of the Performance Reporting process.

Information Distribution Tools and Techniques

Once you've collected and calculated the variances for your project, you'll need to report on them. Information distribution tools and techniques include communication skills, information retrieval systems, and information distribution methods. We discussed each of these during the Information Distribution process in Chapter 8.

Performance Reporting Outputs

This process has two outputs: performance reports and change requests. We've already discussed change requests and will talk more extensively about them in Chapter 10.

Performance reports contain the information you've gathered from this process. You'll summarize the performance of the project and present it to the stakeholders, management team, and customers if appropriate via the information distribution system.

As a result of performance measures and corrective actions, changes are often needed. This requires that change control processes exist to deal with the changes as they happen. The next chapter will look at all of the change control processes.

Project Case Study: New Kitchen Heaven Retail Store

Your regularly scheduled status meeting is coming up. Stakeholders have asked for an updated status on the project schedule as well as a remaining cost projection. You decide to provide several performance figures for the project on the status report. You'll update these figures for every status report from now through the rest of the project. Let's see how the status meeting is progressing.

"Build-out is behind schedule. They were scheduled to be completed by the 11th of January but aren't going to finish up until the 23rd."

"What's that do to my schedule?" Jill asks. "I'm starting interviews for the store positions on the 14th. I hope to have that wrapped up by the 19th even though the schedule gives me more time. As long as I have the majority of the staff hired by the 19th, we can have them stocking shelves starting the 21st."

You tell Jill, "Let's finish up the status of the other items and I'll come back to that.

"Gomez construction has submitted a seller invoice for the work completed through December 31st. Shelly in our contract management office manages the payment system and handles all payment requests. She'll get a check cut and out to Gomez by the end of this month. Thanks to Jake for overseeing the quality control of the build-out process.

"The contract management office used a fixed price contract on the hardware and IT supplies order. Ricardo's group will manage the quality control and testing once it's all arrived.

"Jill has ordered all the retail products, the cookware line, and has lined up the chef demos. The costs for the new gourmet supplier are higher than our original vendor. This impacts ongoing operations, but the hit to the project budget is minimal.

"I've calculated some performance measurements, including earned value measures, as follows (all figures are in millions of dollars):

BAC = 2; PV = 1.86; EV = 1.75; AC = 1.70

CPI = 1.75 ÷ 1.70 = 1.03

SPI = 1.75 ÷ 1.86 = .94

EAC = 1.70 + ((2 − 1.75) ÷ 1.03)) = 1.89

ETC = 1.94 − 1.70 = .24

"What is all this telling us?" Dirk asks.

"The cost performance index tells us we're getting a good return for the money spent on the project so far. In other words, we've experienced a $1.03 value for every dollar spent to date.

"The schedule performance index isn't as cheery, but it's not dreadful news either. This performance indicator says that work is progressing at 94 percent of what we anticipated by this point.

"The estimate at completion tells us that based on what we know today, the total project will cost $1.89 million. That's coming in under the original $2 million we had budgeted for completion, so we're on track with the project budget.

"The last figure is the estimated cost of the remaining work."

"It looks like we're a little behind schedule based on what you have figured here," Dirk says.

"Yes, that's correct," you reply. "That brings us back to Jill's question. I have two alternatives to propose. One, we overlap the schedule and allow Gomez's crew to complete their work while Jill's staff starts stocking shelves."

Jill says, "I don't like this option. We'll be tripping over each other, and I don't want merchandise damaged by workers who are still dragging equipment around inside the store. What's your other option?"

"We could ask Gomez to increase the crew size so that they complete on time according to the contract. We have a provision in the contract that stipulates they add crew members if they miss the scheduled completion date. I will instruct the contract management department to inform Gomez that we're requiring additional crew members."

"That will do the trick," Jill says. "We need the storefront to ourselves when stocking and preparing for opening. I'm glad you had that stipulation in the contract."

> "Any other questions or concerns?" you ask. With that, the meeting is adjourned.
>
> **Project Case Study Checklist**
>
> Contract Administration
>
> - Work results
>
> - Seller invoices
>
> - Payment systems
>
> - Payment requests
>
> Quality Assurance, quality audits
>
> - Correctness of work results
>
> Scope Verification
>
> - Acceptance of work results
>
> Performance Reporting
>
> - Performance reviews (status meetings)
>
> - Earned value analysis

Summary

We finished up the Executing process group with this chapter and looked at the first process in the Controlling process group. We discussed Solicitation, Source Selection, Contract Administration, and Quality Assurance from the Executing process group and Scope Verification and Performance Reporting from the Controlling process group.

Solicitation, Source Selection, and Contract Administration are generally performed in that order. Solicitation is the process of requesting vendors to compete for the contract through RFPs, RFQs, and so on. The Solicitation process concerns obtaining vendor bids.

Source Selection involves choosing a vendor among the potential qualified vendors that bid on the project. Source Selection uses evaluation criteria, weighting systems, screening systems, and independent estimates to determine who will win the contract.

Contracts have cycles of their own, much like projects. Contracting life cycles include requirement, requisition, solicitation, and award. Contract Administration is concerned with monitoring the vendor's performance and making certain it adheres to the contract requirements. Changes to the contract are managed with change requests.

Changes that cannot be agreed upon are called contested changes. These take the form of disputes, claims, or appeals. They might be settled among the parties directly, through a court of law, or through arbitration.

Seller invoices are submitted as an input to the Contract Administration process. Payment systems process and track vendor invoices, while payment requests are the output of the Contract Administration process and result in the actual payment to the vendor.

During the Quality Assurance process, quality audits are performed to assure the project will meet and satisfy the project's quality standards set out in the quality plan.

Scope Verification formalizes the acceptance of the work results. It determines if the work is complete and if it satisfies the project objectives. Performance Reporting is one of the core processes in the Controlling process group. This process collects and reports on project accomplishments. Stakeholders, team members, the management team, and the customer may all have interest in the performance progress reports. Performance reviews are status meetings where the performance measures are reported.

Performance reviews, variance analysis, trend analysis, earned value analysis, and information distribution tools and techniques are the tools and techniques of Performance Reporting. Variance analysis compares the expected results with the actual results. Trend analysis shows if the project is improving or worsening.

Earned value analysis is the most often used performance measurement method. It includes several calculations that show the status of the project based on three primary values: planned value, actual cost, and earned value.

Exam Essentials

Be able to describe the difference between the Solicitation process and Source Selection. Solicitation obtains bids and proposals from vendors. Source Selection is the receipt of bids and proposals and the selection of a vendor.

Be able to name the tools and techniques of Source Selection. Contract negotiation, weighting systems, screening systems, and independent estimates.

Be able to describe the purpose of Quality Assurance. It's a quality management process concerned with making certain the project meets and satisfies the quality standards of the project. It's concerned with the correctness of the work.

Be able to distinguish between seller invoices, payment systems, and payment requests. They are an input, a tool and technique, and an output of the Contract Administration process respectively.

Be able to name the purpose of Scope Verification. Scope Verification formalizes acceptance of project scope and acceptance of work results.

Be able to define the purpose of Performance Reporting. This process collects and reports information regarding project progress and project accomplishments. The technique used often to report on project performance is earned value analysis.

Key Terms

Before you take the exam, be certain you are familiar with the following terms:

Contract Administration	planned value (PV)
actual cost (AC)	Quality Assurance
earned value (EV)	Scope Verification
earned value analysis	Solicitation
Performance Reporting	Source Selection

Review Questions

1. You are a project manager for Dakota Software Consulting Services. You're working with a major retailer that offers their products through mail-order catalogs. They're interested in knowing customer characteristics, the amounts of first-time orders, and similar information. As a potential bidder for this project, you worked on the RFP response and submitted the proposal. When the selection committee received the RFP responses from all the vendors bidding on this project, they used a weighted system to make a selection. Which process did this occur in?

   A. Source Selection

   B. Solicitation

   C. Requisition

   D. Contract Administration

2. You have been asked to submit a proposal for a project that has been put out for bid. First, you attend the bidders conference to ask questions of the buyers and to hear the questions some of the other bidders will ask. Which of the following is true?

   A. Bidders conferences are a tool and technique of the Source Selection process.

   B. Bidders conferences are an output of the Source Selection process.

   C. Bidders conferences are an output of the Solicitation process.

   D. Bidders conferences are a tool and technique of the Solicitation process.

3. You have been asked to submit a proposal for a project that has been put out for bid. Prior to submitting the proposal, your company must register so that their firm is on the qualified seller list. Which of the following is true?

    A. The qualified seller list provides information about the sellers and is a tool and technique of the Solicitation process.

    B. The qualified seller list provides information about the project and the company that wrote the RFP and is an input to the Solicitation process.

    C. The qualified seller list provides information about the project and the company that wrote the RFP and is a tool and technique of the Source Selection process.

    D. The qualified seller list provides information about the sellers and is an input to the Solicitation process.

4. The tools and techniques of the Source Selection process include all of the following except:

    A. Contract negotiation

    B. Correspondence

    C. Independent estimates

    D. Screening system

5. Which of the following processes negotiates the sequence of award by rank ordering the proposals?

    A. Source Selection

    B. Solicitation

    C. Contract Administration

    D. Procurement

6. During the opening rounds of contract negotiation, the other party uses a fait accompli tactic. Which of the following is true?

A. One party agrees to accept the offer of the other party but secretly knows they will bring the issue back up at a later time.

B. One party claims the issue under discussion was documented and accepted as part of Scope Verification.

C. One party claims the issue under discussion has already been decided and can't be changed.

D. One party claims to accept the offer of the other party provided a contract change request is submitted describing the offer in detail.

7. Your procurement department has obtained independent estimates. The vendor's proposal is substantially different than the independent estimates. All of the following are true except:

A. The SOW was not detailed enough.

B. The vendor failed to respond according to the terms of the proposal.

C. The vendor failed to respond to all items in the SOW.

D. The vendor failed to respond to all items in the contract.

8. What are the tools and techniques of the Contract Administration process?

A. Contract change control system, payment system, payment requests

B. Contract change control system, contract negotiations, payment system

C. Contract change control system, contract negotiations, contract changes

D. Contract change control system, performance reporting, payment system

9. You are a project manager for an engineering company. Your company won the bid to add ramp-metering lights to several on-ramps along a stretch of highway at the south end of the city. You subcontracted a portion of the project to another company. The subcontractor's work involves digging the holes and setting the lamp poles in concrete. The subcontractor's performance is not meeting the contract requirements. All of the following are valid options except:

A. You document the poor performance in written form and send the correspondence to the subcontractor.

B. You terminate the contract for poor performance and submit a change request through Contract Administration.

C. You submit a change request through Contract Administration to ask the subcontractor to comply with the terms of the contract.

D. You agree to meet with the subcontractor to see if a satisfactory solution can be reached.

10. You are a project manager for an engineering company. Your company won the bid to add ramp-metering lights to several on-ramps along a stretch of highway at the south end of the city. You subcontracted a portion of the project to another company. The subcontractor's work involves digging the holes and setting the lamp poles in concrete. You've discovered the subcontractor's work is not correct because the poles are not buried to the correct depth. Which of the following is true?

A. You are in the Quality Assurance process and have performed a quality audit to assure correctness of work.

B. You are in the Scope Verification process and have performed a quality audit to assure correctness of work.

C. You are in the Contract Administration process and have completed a contract audit to assure the subcontractor's performance meets the contract requirements.

D. You are in the Performance Reporting process and have completed a performance review of the contractor's work.

11. The purpose of a quality audit includes all of the following except:

    A. Examines the work of the project and formally accepts the work results

    B. Determines how the project is progressing and makes corrections

    C. Identifies lessons learned

    D. Reviews quality management activities to ensure the right quality elements are being examined

12. You are a project manager for Dakota Software Consulting Services. You're working with a major retailer that offers their products through mail-order catalogs. They're interested in knowing customer characteristics, the amounts of first-time orders, and similar information. The stakeholders have accepted the project scope. Work has begun on the project, and you're confirming some of the initial work results with the stakeholders. You've asked for acceptance of the work results. Which process are you in?

    A. Quality Assurance

    B. Quality Control

    C. Scope Verification

    D. Performance Reporting

13. All of the following are tools and techniques of the Performance Reporting process except:

    A. Variance analysis

    B. Performance reporting

    C. Information distribution

    D. Performance reviews

14. This measurement is the value of the work that's been completed to date:

    A. PV

    B. AC

    C. EV

    D. EAC

15. You are a contract project manager for a wholesale flower distribution company. Your project is to develop a website for the company that allows retailers to place their flower orders online. You will also provide a separate link for individual purchases that are ordered, packaged, and mailed to the consumer directly from the grower's site. This project involves coordinating the parent company, growers, and distributors. You are preparing a performance review and have the following measurements at hand: PV = 300; AC = 200; and EV = 250. What do you know about this project?

    A. The EAC is a positive number, which means the project will finish under budget.

    B. You do not have enough information to calculate CPI.

    C. The CV is a negative number in this case, which means you've spent less than what you planned as of the measurement date.

    D. The CV is a positive number in this case, which means you're under budget as of the measurement date.

16. A negative result from an SV calculation means which of the following?

    A. PV is higher than EV.

    B. PV equals one.

    C. EV is higher than PV.

    D. EV is higher than AC.

17. You are a contract project manager for a wholesale flower distribution company. Your project is to develop a website for the company that allows retailers to place their flower orders online. You will also provide a separate link for individual purchases that are ordered, packaged, and mailed to the consumer directly from the grower's site. This project involves coordinating the parent company, growers, and distributors. You are preparing a performance review and have the following measurements at hand: PV = 300; AC = 200; and EV = 250. What is the CPI of this project?

    A. 0.80

    B. 1.25

    C. 1.5

    D. 0.83

18. You do not expect the types of variances that have occurred on the project to date to continue. If BAC = 300, ETC = 275, PV = 300, AC = 200, EV = 250, and CPI = 1.25, what is the EAC?

A. 240

B. 250

C. 475

D. 150

19. You know that BAC = 375, PV = 300, AC = 200, and EV = 250. Variances that have occurred on the project to date are not expected to continue. What is the ETC?

A. 75

B. 50

C. 125

D. 150

20. What are the outputs of the Performance Reporting process?

A. Performance reports and change requests

B. Performance reports and other project records

C. Change requests and performance reporting

D. Change requests and performance measurements

Answers to Review Questions

1. A. Source Selection involves the receipt of bids and proposals. Weighted systems are one of the tools and techniques of this process used to evaluate vendors based on selection criteria defined by the organization.

2. D. Bidders conferences are a tool and technique of the Solicitation process. Solicitation is where proposals are submitted by vendors, and obtained by the organization.

3. D. Qualified seller lists are an input to the Solicitation process. Their purpose is to provide information about the sellers.

4. B. Correspondence is an output of the Contract Administration process. One additional tool and technique of Source Selection not shown in the question is weighting systems.

5. A. Source Selection uses varying tools and techniques to rank order proposals in sequence, starting with the top scoring proposal.

6. C. Fait accompli is a tactic used during contract negotiations where one party convinces the other that the particular issue is no longer relevant or cannot be changed. Answer B is not correct because Scope Verification does not generally occur during contract negotiations since the work of the project has not yet been performed.

7. B. Estimates that differ from bids are the result of incomplete details in the SOW or the vendor failing to respond to the items in the SOW or the items in the contract.

8. D. The tools and techniques of the Contract Administration process are contract change control system, performance reporting, and payment system.

9. C. The contract change control describes the processes you'll use to make changes to the contract. This might include contract term changes, date changes, and termination of a contract.

10. A. You have just performed a quality audit to verify the correctness of the work. Contract audits are not part of the Contract Administration process, so answer C is not correct. Answer D is not correct as performance reviews are status meetings, or similar meetings, that report on the performance of the project to stakeholders and other interested parties.

11. A. The acceptance of work results happens during the Scope Verification process, not during Quality Assurance.

12. C. The Scope Verification process is concerned with the acceptance of work results. It also formalizes the acceptance of the project scope.

13. B. Performance reporting is a tool and technique of the Contract Administration process. The other tools and techniques of Performance Reporting not listed in this question are trend analysis and earned value analysis.

14. C. Earned value is referred to as the value of the work that's been completed to date.

15. D. The CV is a positive number and is calculated by subtracting AC from EV as follows: $250 - 200 = 50$. A positive CV means the project is coming in under budget, meaning you've spent less than what you planned as of the measurement date.

16. A. The SV calculation is $EV - PV$. If PV is a higher number than EV, you'll get a negative number as a result.

17. B. CPI is calculated as follows: $EV \div AC$. In this case, $250 \div 200 = 1.25$.

18. B. When variances are not expected to continue, or are atypical in nature, EAC is calculated as follows: $(AC + BAC) - EV$. Therefore, the calculation for this question looks like this: $(200 + 300) - 250 = 250$.

19. C. To answer this question, you'll first have to calculate EAC because you need that result to plug into the ETC formula. The correct formula for EAC for this question is as follows: $(AC + BAC) - EV$. Therefore, EAC for this question is as follows: $(200 + 375) - 250 = 325$. ETC is calculated this way: $EAC - AC$. Therefore, ETC is as follows: $325 - 200 = 125$.

20. A. Performance Reporting outputs include performance reports and change requests.

Chapter 10

Controlling Change

his chapter will close out the Controlling process group. We started examining the Controlling processes with Performance Reporting and Scope Verification in Chapter 9. Performance reports, which are an output of the Performance Reporting process, serve as an input to every other Controlling process except for Risk Monitoring and Control and Quality Control.

Performance reports are used during the Controlling processes along with the tools and techniques of the Controlling processes to measure project performance. These measurements and control tools allow the project manager to take corrective action during the Controlling processes to remedy wayward project results and realign future project results with the project plan.

We'll cover several processes in this chapter including Integrated Change Control, Scope Change Control, Schedule Control, Cost Control, Quality Control, and Risk Monitoring and Control.

Integrated Change Control lays the foundation for all of the change control processes. We'll spend time during this process to explain how change control works. The Scope Change Control, Schedule Control, and Cost Control processes are very similar to Integrated Change Control. There's no need to repeat the information from Integrated Change Control in the other processes. When we get to the Scope Change Control, Schedule Control, and Cost Control sections, we'll highlight any potential exam questions. Just remember when you're reading these sections that the information from the Integrated Change Control process applies to these areas as well.

Quality Control involves several new tools and techniques, which show up on the exam. Take some time here to understand them and to differentiate between Quality Planning tools and Quality Control tools. Some of the tools and techniques are used in both processes, but the others pertain to the particular process where they're listed.

This chapter concludes the Controlling process group. From here, we move on to the Closing processes and wrap up the project. You've learned a lot about project management by this point and have just a few more things to add to your study list. Keep up the good work. You're getting closer to exam day.

Managing Integrated Change Control

Changes come about on projects for many reasons. It's the project manager's responsibility to manage these changes and see to it that organizational policies regarding changes are implemented. Changes don't necessarily mean negative consequences. Changes can produce positive results as well. It's important that you manage this process carefully, because too many changes—even one significant change—will impact cost, schedule, scope, and/or quality.

Once a change request has been submitted, you've got some decisions to make. Ask yourself questions such as, "Should the change be implemented? If so, what's the cost to the project in terms of the triple constraints: cost, time, and quality? Will the benefits gained by making the change increase or decrease the chances of project completion?"

Just because a change is requested doesn't mean you have to implement it. You'll always want to discover the reasons for the change and determine if they're justifiable, and you'll want to know the cost of the change. Remember that cost can take the form of increased time. Let's say the change you're considering increases the schedule completion date. That means you'll need human resources longer than expected. If you've leased equipment or project resources for the team members to use during the course of the project, a later completion date means your team needs the leased equipment for a longer period of time. All this translates to increased costs. Time equals money as the saying goes, so manage time changes wisely and dig deep to find the impacts that time changes might make on the budget.

How Change Occurs

As the project progresses, the stakeholders or customers may request a change directly. We'll talk about how they submit those change requests in the next major section.

Team members might recommend changes as the project progresses. Once the project is under way, they may discover more efficient ways of performing tasks or producing the product of the project and will recommend changes to accommodate the new efficiencies.

Changes to the project may occur indirectly as a result of contingency plans, other changes, or team members performing favors for the stakeholders by making that one little change without telling anyone about it. Many times, the project manager is the last to know about changes like this one. There's a fine line here as you don't want to discourage good working relationships between team members and stakeholders, yet at the same time you'll want to ensure that all changes come through the change control process. A dozen little changes slipped through like this and your project scope suddenly exits stage left.

Change Control Concerns

Integrated Change Control, according to the *Guide to the PMBOK*, is concerned with three things: influencing the things that cause change, determining that change is needed or has happened, and managing change.

Influencing those things that bring about change includes factors such as the triple constraints, stakeholder requests, team member recommendations, and others. You'll want to understand these factors and the impact they have on the project if implemented. Obviously, you'll want to implement those changes that are most beneficial to the project. Performance measures and corrective actions may dictate that a project change is needed as well. Modifications to the project are submitted in the form of change requests and managed through the change control process. We'll talk more about change requests later in the chapter.

Managing the changes may involve changes to the project plan, project schedule, or cost baseline, also known as the *performance measurement baselines*. It's your responsibility to maintain the reliability of the performance measurement baselines. If changes are not appropriately reflected in the baselines, they become meaningless. Changes that impact a previous process will require updates to those processes, which might mean additional planning is needed. The management plans created during those processes should reflect the changes as well. I would caution you to not change baselines at the drop of a hat. Examine the changes, their justification, and their impacts thoroughly before making changes to the baselines.

Change Control Techniques

The Integrated Change Control process uses five tools and techniques to implement and manage change: change control system, configuration management, performance measurement, additional planning, and project management information system. We'll look at the change control system and configuration management tools. The other tools and techniques have been covered elsewhere or are self explanatory.

Change Control System

If you were to allow changes to occur to the project whenever requested, you would probably never complete the project. Stakeholders, the customer, and end users would continually change the project requirements if given the opportunity to do so. That's why careful planning and scope definition are important in the beginning of the project. It's your job as project manager to drive out all the compelling needs and requirements of the project during the Planning process so that important requirements aren't suddenly "remembered" halfway through the project. However, we're all human, and sometimes things are not known or weren't thought about until a certain point during the project. Stakeholders start thinking in a direction they weren't considering during the Planning process, and new requirements come to light. This is where the *change control system* comes into play.

Purpose of the Change Control System

Change control systems are documented procedures that describe how to submit change requests, how to manage change requests, and the management impacts of the changes as they pertain to project performance. They can include preprinted change request forms that provide a place to record general project information such as the name and project number, the date, and the details regarding the change request.

The change control system also tracks the status of change requests including their approval status. Not all change requests will receive approval to implement. Those changes that are not approved are also tracked and filed in the project notebook for future reference.

The change control system defines the level of authority needed to approve changes. Some change requests could receive approval based on the project manager's decision; others may need more formal approval or more levels of approval such as the project sponsor, executive management, and so on.

Many organizations have formal change control or change request systems in place. If that's the case, you can easily adopt those procedures and use the existing system to manage project change. If no procedures exist, you'll have to define them.

Requirements for Change

There are two things you should require at the beginning of all projects regarding change. First, I recommend that you require all change requests be submitted in writing. This is to clarify the change and make sure no confusion exists regarding what's requested. It also allows the project team to accurately estimate the time it will take to incorporate the change. Keep in mind that you will get verbal change requests as well. According to *Guide to the PMBOK*, change requests come in verbal or written forms, but it's good practice to require them in writing.

Second, all change requests must come through the formal change control system. Make sure no one is allowed to go directly to team members and request changes without the project manager knowing about it. Also make certain your stakeholders understand that this can cause schedule delays, cost overruns, and sacrifices to quality and isn't good change management practice. Encourage them from the beginning of the project to use the formal procedures laid out in the change control system to request changes.

Configuration Control Board

In some organizations, a *configuration control board (CCB)* is established to review all change requests. They are given the authority to approve or deny change requests as defined by the organization. It's important that their authority is clearly defined and that separate procedures exist for emergency changes. The CCB may meet only once a week, once every other week, or even once a month depending on the project. When emergencies arise, the pre-established procedures allow the project manager to implement the change on the spot. This will always require a follow-up with the CCB and the completion of a formal change request even though it's after the fact.

CCB members may include stakeholders, managers, project team members, and others who may not have any connection to the project at hand. Some organizations have permanent CCBs that are staffed by full-time employees dedicated to managing change for the entire organization, not just project change. You may want to consider establishing a CCB for your project if the organization does not have one.

Some organizations use other types of review boards that have the same responsibilities as the CCB. Some other names you might see are technical assessment board (TAB), technical review board (TRB), and engineering review board (ERB).

Configuration Management

Configuration management in most organizations is a subset of the change control process. Sometimes the configuration management system is the change control system. The exam will expect you to know that configuration management involves identifying the physical characteristics of the product of the project (or of the individual components of the product) and documenting their functionality as well.

Configuration management describes the characteristics of the product of the project and makes sure the description is accurate and complete. Configuration management controls changes to the characteristics of an item, and tracks the changes made or requested and their status. Audits are performed as part of configuration management to determine if the requirements have been met.

Integrated Change Control Results

Changes to the project will require updates to the project plan or the supporting detail of the project plan. These changes are noted as such in the project plan, and stakeholders are informed at the status meetings of the changes that have occurred, their impacts, and where the description of the changes can be found. Project plan updates are an output of the Integrated Change Control process.

Two other outputs occur in this process. They are corrective action and lessons learned. We've talked about each of these before. *Corrective action* is any action taken to ensure the product of the project, or future project performance, adheres to the requirements described in the scope document and to the project plan. Remember that corrective action is an output of all of the change control processes except for Quality Control. And, corrective action is an output of the Controlling processes and an input to the Executing processes.

Lessons learned document the causes of the variances that occur in the project. The corrective action taken and the justification for choosing that particular corrective action are noted as part of lessons learned as well. At the conclusion of the project, lessons learned become part of the historical information that is used as inputs to some of the Planning processes. When you take on a new project, it's a good idea to review the lessons learned of similar projects so that you can plan appropriately and avoid the variances that occurred in the first project.

 Real World Scenario

Mustang Enterprises' New Accounting System

You are a stakeholder of the New Accounting System project for Mustang Enterprises. The existing accounting system lives on a mainframe, and some of the programs used to process data on this system are over 15 years old. Your company decided to hire a contract software services firm to write a thin-client, browser-based version of the accounting system so that the mainframe programs could be retired.

The project is in the Controlling process, and the contract project manager keeps reporting everything is okay and on schedule. When you asked him detailed questions and requested performance data, the project manager patted you on the back and said, "Don't worry, I've got everything under control."

You are a little worried, because some of the key project team members have come to you confidentially to inform you of the progress of the project.

After further investigation, you discover that the project manager changed the database midway through the project and didn't tell anyone except the project team. The project scope stated specifically that project development required database product A. The change in database products changed the project scope and product scope without letting the stakeholders know.

This change has caused schedule delays, because the project team members have told you they need training in the new database development tools before they can proceed. Additionally, many of the programs already written were to interface with database A, not database B, and will have to be modified in order to work with database B. To add insult to injury, the database switch will impact the project budget in two ways. First, database B involves substantially more money than database A and requires the purchase of new development tools for the programming team. Second, several members of the programming staff will have to attend multiple training sessions on the new database product to fully integrate the programs and system. Training is currently running $2200 per session per person.

> Since you're a key stakeholder, you decide to bring the information you've discovered out into the open at the next project status meeting. Additionally, you plan to meet with the project sponsor and the procurement department to determine what alternatives you have to request the contracting firm replace the current project manager with a new project manager. This may cause further setback to the project, but the project plan and project schedule will require updates anyway as a result of the existing project manager's decisions. You also determine to document all that's happened as a lesson learned and to set up a change control process to prevent this from happening in the future.

Controlling Scope Changes

The Scope Management knowledge area involves Initiation, Scope Planning, Scope Definition, Scope Verification, and Scope Change Control. You'll recall that project scope describes the work required to produce the product or service of the project. This includes the requirements of the product, which describe the features and functionality of the product or service. Product scope, on the other hand, is the description of the product features. The product description is the document that defines the characteristics of the product or service of the project.

You can conclude from this that the *Scope Change Control* process involves changes to the project scope. Any modification to the agreed-upon WBS is considered a scope change. Changes in product scope will require changes to the project scope as well. Let's say one of your project deliverables is the design of a piece of specialized equipment that's integrated into your final product. Now let's say that due to engineering setbacks and some miscalculations, the specialized equipment requires design modifications. The redesign of this equipment impacts the end product, or product scope. Since changes to the product scope impact the project requirements, which are detailed in the scope document, changes to project scope are also required.

Change Requests

Change requests, according to the *Guide to the PMBOK*, come in written or verbal forms. As stated earlier, I recommend that you require all change requests in written form. They are easier to track this way and provide a paper trail of the action taken. The *Guide to the PMBOK* also says change requests are direct or indirect, might come from inside or outside the organization, and may result from optional requests or from legal requirements. Change requests are an input to the Scope Change Control process.

Another input we've seen before is performance reports. Performance reports tell us which deliverables have been completed and if the project is proceeding as planned. When it's not proceeding as planned, change requests will result.

The WBS and the scope management plan are the remaining inputs to this process. These have been covered previously. You'll recall the scope management plan details how scope changes get integrated into the project and how scope changes are managed as well.

Scope Tracking Systems

There are three tools and techniques of the Scope Change Control process: scope change control, performance measurements, and additional planning. *Scope change control* is a system that tracks changes and, along with all the other change control systems we'll detail in this chapter, is integrated with the integrated change control system. Depending on the size and complexity of the project, the integrated change control system may suffice for all changes to the project.

Scope change control is a lot like the integrated change control system. It tracks and records change requests, describes the procedures to follow to implement scope change, and details the authorization levels needed to approve the changes. When your project is performed under contract, scope changes will require conformance to the provisions of the contract and the contract change system as well.

Scope Changes

The outputs of the Scope Change Control process are scope changes, corrective action, lessons learned, and adjusted baseline. Let's take a brief look at scope changes.

Scope changes will likely require you to run back through the project Planning processes and make any needed adjustments. Scope changes include any changes to the WBS that were previously agreed to as well.

Schedule revisions are needed as a result of scope changes. But not all scope changes will necessarily cause increases to the project budget or project schedule. Some scope changes may reduce the number of hours needed to complete the project and or reduce the project budget.

When scope changes are requested, all areas of the project should be investigated to determine what the changes will impact. The project team should perform estimates of the impact and of the amount of time needed to make the change. Sometimes, however, the change request is so extensive that even the time to perform an estimate should be evaluated before proceeding. In other words, if the project team is busy working on estimates, they aren't working on the project. That means extensive change requests could impact the existing schedule because of the time and effort needed just to evaluate the change. Cases like these require you to make a determination, or ask the CCB to decide, if the change is important enough to allow the project team time to work on the estimates.

Changes in scope may require updates to the schedule or cost baselines or other baselines established during the Planning process. *Adjusted baseline* is the output where revisions to baselines are made.

Always remember to update your stakeholders regarding the changes you're implementing and their impacts. They'll want to know how the changes impact the performance baselines including the project costs, project schedule, project scope, and quality.

Controlling Schedule Changes

According to the *Guide to the PMBOK*, scope changes will impact the project schedule and require schedule changes and revisions as a result. *Schedule Control* is the process that manages changes to the schedule.

Schedule Control inputs include project schedule, performance reports, change requests, and schedule management plan. We've looked at all these inputs before. Remember that the schedule management plan details the process to implement schedule changes.

This process is very similar to the Integrated Change Control and Scope Change Control processes covered earlier. The schedule change control system is a tool and technique of Schedule Control and works just like scope change control, except that it defines how changes to the schedule are made and managed. The remaining tools and techniques of this process are performance measurements, additional planning, project management software, and variance analysis. We'll look at variance analysis next.

Schedule Variances

Variance analysis is a tool and technique of this process that helps determine variances in schedule start and end dates. Comparing the estimated dates to the actual or forecasted dates will show you where variances have occurred, or will occur, and will allow you to implement corrective actions. You'll want to be certain to examine the float variance of the critical path activities and subcritical activities. Remember that *float* is the amount of time you can delay starting an activity without increasing the amount of time it takes to complete the project. Because the activities with the least amount of float have the potential to cause the biggest schedule delay, examine float variance in ascending order of critical activities.

However, not all schedule variances will impact the schedule. For example, a delay to a non–critical path task will not delay the integrated schedule and may not need corrective action. But delays to critical path tasks will always cause delays to the project completion date and do require corrective action.

The outputs of this process include schedule updates, corrective action, and lessons learned. Updates to the schedule sometimes require what the *Guide to the PMBOK* terms *revisions*. In a revision, changes are made to the scheduled start dates and scheduled completion dates of project activities. These generally occur only as a result of a scope change. When revisions are necessary, you may have to establish a new schedule baseline that reflects the changed project activity dates.

Managing Cost Changes

The *Cost Control* process manages changes to project costs as outlined in the cost management plan. The inputs to Cost Control are similar to the inputs we've seen for the other control processes and include cost baseline, performance reports, change requests, and cost management plan. These inputs are examined using the tools and techniques of this process to determine if revised cost estimates or budget updates are required.

Cost variances are calculated using the performance measurement and earned value management tools and techniques. You'll recall from Chapter 9 that earned value management (EVM) continuously monitors the planned value (formerly BCWS), earned value (formerly BCWP), and actual costs (formerly ACWP) expended to produce the work of the project. When variances that result in cost changes are discovered, those changes are managed using the cost change control system. Like the other processes we've examined so far, the cost change control system is closely linked with the integrated change control system.

You may have to do some additional planning if your cost changes are significant. Remember that many times cost, scope, and schedule changes are closely linked. Cost changes may drive schedule changes due to budget cuts, poor-quality products, and so on. The Planning, Executing, and Controlling processes are iterative, and changes to one may require changes or modification to another. Additional planning and computerized tools are the remaining tools and techniques of this process.

It's important to take the right corrective actions as a result of cost variances, because other problems can result from not dealing with cost issues. Impacts to the budget, quality, or schedule or increased risk may result from incorrect responses to cost variances.

Cost Control problems come about for many reasons including incorrect estimating techniques, predetermined or fixed budgets with no flexibility, schedule overruns, inadequate WBS development, and so on. Good project management planning techniques during the Planning processes may prevent cost problems later in the project. At a minimum, proper planning will reduce the impact of these problems if they do occur.

Revising Costs

Cost Control has several outputs that involve revising your original cost estimates and calculating new estimates at completion. We talked about estimate at completion (EAC) calculations in Chapter 9, so be certain to review them before taking the exam. And remember that the EAC calculations determine the estimated total cost of the project at completion and are an output of the Cost Control process.

Cost Control outputs include revised cost estimates, budget updates, corrective action, estimate at completion, project closeout, and lessons learned. We'll look at three of these outputs next. Corrective action, EAC, and lessons learned were covered previously.

Revised Cost Estimates

Revised cost estimates include updating original cost estimates and other areas of the project plan that these estimates may impact. As an example, perhaps the cost estimate for new hardware required for your project was recently revised. Suppose the cost estimate was needed because the equipment originally planned for in the project is no longer available and new equipment is ordered in its place. This may require revisions to other project activities, which will require you to revisit the project Planning processes.

Always inform appropriate stakeholders of revised cost estimates and any changes of significant impact on the project. Keep them updated on changes, status, and risk conditions during regularly scheduled project meetings.

Budget Updates

The Cost Control process tracks project performance to detect variances. Approved changes as a result of those variances are considered budget updates, which are a type of revised cost estimate. The cost baseline is changed as a result of the budget updates to reflect the new cost estimates. Significant updates to the budget as a result of corrective action or variances may require rebaselining of the project costs.

Project Closeout

Make certain that you're familiar with the regulations and standards that are required for project closures and cancellations for your industry. Some industries require the costs of failed or cancelled projects be written off in a specific manner. Familiarize yourself with these standards. You may contact the American Institute of Certified Public Accountants for more information regarding accounting and finance standards for your particular industry.

Cost Control, like many of the other Controlling processes, is concerned with monitoring project performance for variances. As the project manager, you'll want to keep a close eye on the factors that cause variance to keep their impacts to a minimum. An important thing to remember is that Cost Control makes certain all appropriate parties agree to any changes to the cost baseline. This process is ongoing and continues to manage cost changes throughout the project.

Utilizing Quality Control Techniques

Quality Planning, Quality Assurance, and Quality Control are part of the project Quality Management knowledge area. These processes work together to define and monitor the work of the project and to make certain the results meet the quality requirements laid out in the plan.

Quality Control is specifically concerned with monitoring work results to see if they comply with the standards set out in the quality management plan. Quality Control should be practiced and performed throughout the project to identify and remove the causes of unacceptable results. Remember that Quality Control is concerned with project results both from a management perspective, such as schedule and cost performance, and from a product perspective. In other words, the end product should conform to the requirements and product description defined during the Planning processes.

Quality Control inputs include work results, a quality management plan, operational definitions, and checklists. We've discussed each of these inputs previously, so we'll move on to tools and techniques. There are several new tools and techniques in this process including inspection, control charts, Pareto diagrams, statistical sampling, flowcharting, and trend analysis. The primary purpose of each of these tools is to examine the product and/or the project processes for conformity to standards. Spend time understanding them and their individual uses, because there are exam questions on each of them.

Inspection

Inspection involves physically looking at, measuring, or testing results to determine if they conform to the requirements or quality standards. It's a tool used to gather information and improve results. Inspections might occur after the final product is produced or at intervals during the development of the product to examine individual components.

Don't confuse inspection with prevention, as they're two different things. Inspection keeps errors in the product from reaching the customer. Prevention keeps errors from occurring in the process. It always costs less to prevent problems in the first place than it does to fix problems built into the product after the fact. Rework, labor costs, material costs, and potential loss of customers are all factors to consider when weighing prevention costs versus the cost of rework. Philip Crosby developed the theory of zero defects, which deals with prevention costs. Loosely translated, zero defects means doing it right the first time.

Inspection may take actual measurements of components to determine if they meet requirements. Maybe a component part for your product must be exactly 5 mm in length. In order to pass inspection, the parts are measured and must meet the 5 mm length requirement. If they measure 5 mm, they pass; if they do not, they fail.

Measurements can vary even if the variances are not noticeable. Machines wear down, people make mistakes, the environment may cause variances, and so on. Measurements that fall within a specified range are called *tolerable results*. So, instead of 5 mm exactly, maybe a range between 4.98 mm and 5.02 mm is an acceptable or a tolerable measurement for our component. If the samples that are measured fall within the tolerable range, they pass; otherwise they fail inspection.

One inspection technique uses measurements called *attributes*. The measurements determine whether the attributes meet one of two options, conforming or nonconforming. In other words, the measurements conform or meet the requirement, or they do not conform. This can also be considered a pass/fail or go/no-go decision.

Attribute conformity and inspections are not necessarily performed on every component part or every end product that's produced. That's time consuming and inefficient when you're producing numerous components. Inspection in cases like this is usually performed on a sampling of parts or products. In other words, every X number of parts are tested for conformity or measurement specifics. This measurement technique is called *statistical sampling*. Statistical sampling is another tool and technique of the Quality Control process that we'll get to shortly.

Inspection will tell you where problems exist and give you the opportunity to correct them, thus leading to quality improvements. The other tools and techniques we'll talk about in this section also lead to quality improvements in the product or process, or both. Quality improvements are an output of the Quality Control process.

Control Charts

Control charts measure the results of processes over time and display the results in graph form. Control charts are a way to measure variances to determine if process variances are in control or out of control.

Common causes of variances are a result of random variances, known or predictable variances, or variances that are always present in the process.

🌐 Real World Scenario

The Never-Ending Bridge Project

One of the main thoroughfares into your city requires a bridge replacement. You were appointed the project manager for the city and have managed this project since its initiation 15 months ago.

The project entailed hiring a contractor to build and construct the new bridge and then managing the contract and the work of the contracting agency to bring the project to a successful completion.

Approximately 28,000 vehicles travel across this bridge on a daily basis carrying commuters and college students back and forth to the downtown area. One of the requirements was the closure of no more than three of the six lanes of traffic at one time during construction. Another requirement stated that two coats of paint were to be applied to the steel before bringing it on-site, and a third coat of paint was to be applied at the site after construction. The paint is guaranteed to last 25 to 30 years.

You assisted the quality control department with a recent inspection. The inspection revealed that some of the paint was peeling. After further investigation, you discovered that the contractor did not allow the first coat of paint to cure properly, so when the second coat was applied, it didn't stick correctly and peeled and flaked in places.

You've instructed the contractor that according to the terms of the contract and the RFP specifications, they're required to apply three coats of paint to the bridge as part of the work of the project. Corrective action is needed to get this project back on track. As a result, the contract company decides to subcontract out the paint work to another company while they finish up their remaining tasks on the project.

Unfortunately, the subcontractor that was hired found they were in way over their heads and were not able to complete the paint job. Several months have passed, and the original project completion date was missed long ago. This obviously required revisions to the project schedule when it became clear that the subcontractor wasn't going to make the date. Now another revision to the project schedule is necessary due to the subcontractor's failure to complete the painting task.

The original contractor did some searching and found another subcontractor capable of completing the painting job. It's now the middle of winter. Because the temperatures are cold, the painting crew must hang insulated tarps between the bays on the bridge and use heaters to warm up small areas of steel to the proper temperature to apply the paint. This process has extended the completion date of this activity by over three times its original estimate and ultimately delayed the completion of the project by two years.

Corrective action was taken as a result of the inspection and eventually the project was completed, but not without schedule delays, schedule changes, scope changes, and rework—not to mention the increased cost to the original contractor. Since the contract was a fixed price contract, the contractor's profit was eaten away paying for the painting job. The cost to correct the quality issue did not impact the city, but it did impact the contractor. This is a case where an ounce of prevention would have been worth a pound of cure as the old saying goes.

The process itself will have inherent variability that is perhaps caused by human mistakes, machine variations or malfunctions, the environment, and so on. Common cause variances that do not fall within the acceptable range are difficult to correct and usually require a reorganization of the process. This has the potential for significant impact, and decisions to change the process always require management approval.

Special cause variances are easily controlled at the operational level. Perhaps a machine needs to be calibrated or procedures for the process need to be refined. Perhaps your process is very detailed with specific procedures that are carried out to produce the output. Not following these detailed procedures could result in variances known as *special cause variances*.

According to the *Guide to the PMBOK*, processes in control can be changed to bring about improvements, but if processes are in control, you should not adjust the process.

Monitoring Processes

Control charts are used mostly to monitor repetitive activities like you'd find in the manufacturing industry. For example, the process that produces widgets by the case lot must meet certain specifications and fall within certain variances to be considered in control. However, you can use control charts to monitor project variances such as scope and schedule variances as well.

A control chart is based on sample variance measurements. From the samples chosen and measured, the mean and standard deviation are determined. Quality Control is usually maintained, or said to be in control, within plus or minus three standard deviations. In other words, Quality Control says that if the process is in control, we know that 99.73 percent of the parts going through the process will fall within an acceptable range of the mean. If you discover a part outside of this range, you should investigate and determine if corrective action is needed.

An example control chart is shown in Figure 10.1.

FIGURE 10.1 Control chart

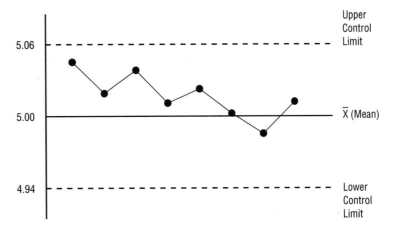

We've determined from our samples measurements that 5 mm is the mean in our example control chart. One standard deviation equals 0.02. Three standard deviations on either side of the mean becomes our upper and lower control points on this chart. Therefore, if all control points fall within plus or minus three standard deviations on either side of the mean, the process is in control. If points fall outside of the acceptable limits, the process is not in control and corrective action is needed.

Pareto Diagrams

You have probably heard of the 80/20 rule. Vilfredo Pareto is the person credited with discovering this rule. He observed that 80 percent of the wealth and land ownership in Italy was held by 20 percent of the population. Over the years, others have observed that the 80/20 rule applies across many disciplines and areas. As an example, generally speaking, 80 percent of the deposits of any given financial institution are held by 20 percent of its customer base. Let's hope that rule doesn't apply to project managers, though, with 20 percent of the project managers out there doing 80 percent of the work!

According to Pareto, the 80/20 rule as it applies to quality says that a small number of causes create the majority of the problems. Have you ever noticed that with your project staff or department staff? It always seems just a few people cause the biggest headaches, but we're off track.

Pareto diagrams are displayed as histograms that rank order the most important factors such as delays, costs, defects, or other factors by their frequency over time. His theory was you'd get the most benefit if you spent the majority of your time fixing the most important problems. The information shown in Table 10.1 is plotted on an example Pareto diagram shown in Figure 10.2.

TABLE 10.1 Frequency of Failures

Item	Defect Frequency	Percent of Defects	Cumulative Percent
A	800	.27	.27
B	700	.23	.50
C	400	.19	.69
D	300	.17	.86
E	200	.14	1.0

FIGURE 10.2 Pareto diagram

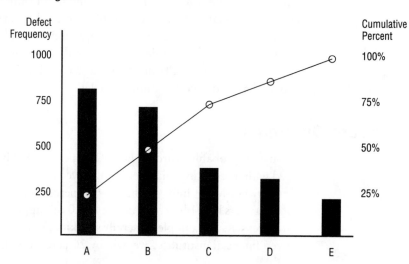

The problems are rank ordered according to their frequency and percentage of defects. The defect frequencies in this figure are shown as black bars, and the cumulative percentages of defects are plotted as circles. You can see in Figure 10.2 that problem A should receive priority attention, because the most benefit will come from fixing this problem.

Scatter Diagrams

You're probably checking that *Guide to the PMBOK* tool and technique list now and have discovered that scatter diagrams are not on the list. You are correct. The *Guide to the PMBOK* does not list scatter diagrams as a tool and technique of Quality Control; however, you might encounter a question on the exam regarding them.

Scatter diagrams use two variables, one called an independent variable, which is an input, and one called a dependent variable, which is an output. Scatter diagrams display the relationship between these two elements as points on a graph. As an example, maybe your scatter diagram plots the ability of your employees to perform a certain task. Their experience performing this task in months is plotted as the independent variable on the X axis, and their score, the dependent variable, is plotted on the Y axis.

The important thing to remember about scatter diagrams is that they plot the dependent and independent variables. A sample scatter diagram is shown in Figure 10.3.

FIGURE 10.3   Scatter diagram

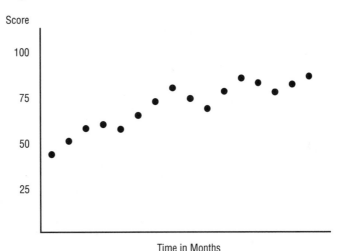

Statistical Sampling

Statistical sampling involves taking a sample number of parts from the whole population and examining them to determine if they fall within the variances outlined by the quality control plan. Perhaps you determine to statistically sample 25 parts out of a lot or run. The quality plan outlines that the lot will pass if four parts or less fall outside the allowable variance.

Statistical sampling may also involve determining the standard deviation for a process as discussed in the control chart tool and technique. The quality plan determines if plus or minus two standard deviations, which is 95.44 percent of the population, is adequate, or if plus or minus three standard deviations, which is 99.73 percent, is adequate.

Flowcharting

Flowcharting is also a tool and technique of the Quality Planning process. We discussed the different methods of flowcharting in Chapter 6 including cause-and-effect diagrams and system or process flowcharts. These show how various elements of a system relate. Flowcharts are used in the Quality Control process to examine how problems happen.

Trend Analysis

Trend analysis, according to the *Guide to the PMBOK*, is a mathematical technique that uses historical results to predict outcomes. Trend analysis often tracks variances in cost and schedule performance by monitoring the number of activities completed with significant variances within a certain time period. This information can then be used to forecast future performance. Trend analysis also tracks technical performance by determining the number of defects observed and the number of defects not corrected.

Quality Control Outputs

Quality Control has several outputs including quality improvement, acceptance decisions, rework, completed checklists, and process adjustments. You should remember two things about Quality Control outputs.

First, rework will cause a project to take longer than originally planned or estimated to complete. You should try to keep rework to a minimum so as not to impact the project schedule. Rework has the potential to cause morale issues as well, especially if the team members thought they were doing a good job all along. Monitor quality periodically so that rework is kept to a minimum.

Second, process adjustments are taken when corrective action or preventive measures are needed as a result of Quality Control variances. Remember, though, that processes in control can be changed to bring about improvements, but processes in control should not be adjusted. Processes out of control may require adjusting, but this should occur only as a result of a management decision and as part of the Integrated Change Control process.

Organizing Risk Response

*R*isk Monitoring and Control involves responding to risks as they occur. The risk management plan and the risk response plan are two of the inputs to this process. You'll recall that the risk management plan details how risk is managed and the risk response plan describes how you will implement plans and strategies in the event of an actual risk event. Keep in mind that some risk events identified in risk planning will happen and some will not. You will have to stay alert for risk event occurrences and be prepared to respond to them when they do occur.

Performance measurements taken during the Performance Reporting process and scope changes may identify new risks. Additional risk identification and analysis is an input to the Risk Monitoring and Control process, and the newly identified risks get documented here. Additional risk response planning may be needed to deal with the new risks or with expected risks whose impact was greater than expected. This may require repeating the Risk Response Planning process to create new contingency plans or alternative plans to deal with the risk, or it may require modification to existing plans. The remaining inputs to this process are project communication and scope changes.

Risk Monitoring and Control Tools and Techniques

The tools and techniques of Risk Monitoring and Control are used to monitor risks throughout the life of the project. Periodic reviews, audits, and new earned value analysis should be performed to check the pulse of risk activity and to make certain risk management is enacted effectively.

The tools and techniques are project risk response audits, periodic project risk reviews, earned value analysis, technical performance measurements, and additional risk response planning. Let's look at a few of these tools now.

Project Risk Response Audits

Risk audits are carried out during the entire life of the project by risk auditors. Risk auditors are not typically project team members and are expertly trained in audit techniques and risk assessment. These audits are specifically interested in looking at the implementation and the effective use of the transference, avoidance, and mitigation risk strategies.

Periodic Project Risk Reviews

Periodic, scheduled reviews of identified risks, risk responses, and risk priorities should occur during the project. The idea here is to monitor risks and their status and determine if their consequences still have the same impact on the project objectives as when they were originally planned. You may have to revisit the Qualitative and Quantitative Risk Analysis processes when new risk consequences are discovered or risk impacts are found to be greater than what was originally planned.

Technical Performance Measurements

This tool and technique compares the technical accomplishments of project milestones during the Executing process to the technical milestones defined in the project Planning process. Variances may indicate a project risk is looming, which you'll want to analyze and prepare a response to if appropriate.

Risk Monitoring and Control Outputs

The outputs of this process include workarounds, corrective action, project change requests, updates to the risk response plan, risk database, and updates to the risk identification checklist. Risk Monitoring and Control should occur throughout the life of the project. Identified risks are monitored and plans are reexamined to determine if they will adequately resolve the risk as it approaches. Additional responses are documented when new risks are identified or when known risk events impact the project more significantly than anticipated.

If no risk response plan exists for a risk, or an unplanned risk occurs, workarounds are implemented to deal with the risk. A *workaround* is an unplanned response to a risk event because the risk was unknown until it happened. The workaround attempts to deal with the risk in a productive, efficient manner as the risk occurs. Workarounds are put into place as a result of a negative risk event and are an output of the Risk Response Planning process.

Project Case Study: New Kitchen Heaven Retail Store

Ricardo submitted a change request regarding the hardware installation at the new store site. A new, much anticipated operating system was just released, and Ricardo has plans to upgrade the entire company to the new operating system. Since he must purchase new equipment for this store anyway, he contends that it makes sense to go ahead and purchase the hardware with the newest operating system already loaded. His staff won't have to upgrade this store as part of the upgrade project, because the store will already have the new operating system.

Ricardo's change request was submitted in writing through the change control system. A CCB was set up during the Planning stages of this project to handle change requests. At the CCB meeting, the following questions come up regarding Ricardo's request.

Has the new operating system been tested with the existing system? Are there compatibility problems? If so, what are the severity and risk potential of getting the problems resolved and the equipment installed by opening day? Is the vendor ready to ship with the new operating system?

The CCB defers their decision for this request until Ricardo gives them answers to these questions.

During the next CCB meeting, the board reviews a change request from Jill Overstreet. The gourmet food supplier she used went out of business a month or so ago, and Jill contracted with a new vendor. She received a sample shipment from the new vendor and was very unhappy with the results. Upon inspecting the products, she found broken containers and damaged packaging. Meanwhile, Jill found another vendor, who has sent her a sample shipment. She is very pleased with the new vendor's products and service. However, this vendor's prices are even higher than the first replacement vendor she contracted with. Jill submitted a cost change request to the CCB because of the increased cost of the gourmet food product shipment. The change in cost does not have a significant impact on the budget, because the new EAC with this change is $1.90 million. The original project budget estimate was $2 million, so the project is still coming in under budget.

You hold a seat on the CCB and are aware of the change requests and their impacts to the project. Ricardo satisfactorily answered all the questions the CCB had, so his request and Jill's request are both approved during the meeting.

Project Case Study Checklist

Integrated change management

Change control systems

Formal change request procedures

Configuration control board

Cost change

Quality control

- Inspection

- Corrective action

Summary

We closed out the Controlling process group with this chapter by covering all the change control processes with the exception of Performance Reporting. Change control is an important part of the project process. It's your responsibility as project manager to manage change and implement corrective action where needed to keep the project on track with the plan.

Integrated Change Control concerns influencing the things that cause change and managing the change once it has occurred. One or more of the triple constraints are generally affected when change occurs. Managing change may involve changes to the project plan, the project schedule, or the budget. Changes that impact processes you've already completed require updates to those processes. Corrective action is often a result of change and assures the future performance of the project lines up with the project plan.

Change control systems document the procedures to manage change and how change requests are implemented. Change requests may come in written or verbal forms, but it's recommended that you ask for all your change requests in writing. Change requests are processed through a formal change control system, and configuration control boards have the authority to approve or deny change requests.

Lessons learned are important for future projects and become part of the historical information used as inputs to the Planning processes on future projects. They also are used to document the causes of the variances that occur on the project.

Quality Control monitors work results to see if they fulfill the quality standards outlined in the quality management plan. Quality Control should occur throughout the life of the project. Quality Control uses many tools and techniques. Inspection measures results to determine if the results conform to the quality standards. Attributes are measurements that either conform or do not conform. Control charts measure the results of processes over time, and Pareto diagrams are histograms that rank order the most important quality factors by their frequency over time. You should not adjust processes that are in control; however, you can change these processes to realize improvements.

Risk Monitoring and Control responds to risks as they occur and implements workarounds for unplanned risk events. Some risks planned for during the Risk Response Planning process will occur, and some will not. Perhaps risks that were previously identified do occur and their impacts are much greater than anticipated during the Risk Response Planning process. These will require updates to the risk management plan or workarounds.

Exam Essentials

Be able to name the control processes that are integrated whenever a scope change occurs.   Schedule Control, Cost Control, and Quality Control.

Be able to define the purpose of a change control system.   They are documented procedures that describe how to submit change requests and how changes are tracked and approved, and they document the level of authority needed for approval.

Be able to describe a CCB.   The configuration control board has the authority to approve or deny change requests. Their authority is defined and outlined by the organization.

Be able to define configuration management.   It's a subset of change control that describes the characteristics of the product of the project and assures accuracy and completeness of the description.

Be able to name the tools and techniques of Quality Control.   Inspection, control charts, Pareto diagrams, statistical sampling, flowcharting, and trend analysis.

Key Terms

Before you take the exam, be certain you are familiar with the following terms:

change control system	Quality Control
configuration control board (CCB)	Risk Monitoring and Control
configuration management	Schedule Control
Cost Control	Scope Change Control
Integrated Change Control	

Review Questions

1. You are a project manager for Bluebird Technologies. Bluebird writes custom billing applications for several industries. A scope change has been requested. You know change is concerned with all of the following except:

   A. Managing change

   B. Verifying change

   C. Influencing causes of change

   D. Determining that a change occurred

2. You are a project manager for Bluebird Technologies. Bluebird writes custom billing applications for several industries. One of your users verbally requests changes to one of the screen displays. You explain to her that the change needs to go through the change control system. You explain that a change control system does all of the following except:

   A. Document procedures for change requests

   B. Track the status of change requests

   C. Describe the management impacts of change

   D. Determine if changes are approved or denied

3. Change control system, configuration management, performance measurement, additional planning, and project management information system are tools and techniques of which process?

   A. Integrated Change Control

   B. Scope Change Control

   C. Schedule change control

   D. Cost change control

4. You are a project manager for Star Light Strings. Star Light manufactures strings of lights for outdoor display. Their products range from simple light strings to elaborate lights with animal designs, bug designs, memorabilia, and so on. Your newest project requires a scope change. You have documented the characteristics of the product and its functionality using which of the following tools and techniques?

   A. Change control system

   B. Corrective action

   C. Configuration management

   D. Updates to the scope management plan

5. You are a project manager for Star Light Strings. Star Light manufactures strings of lights for outdoor display. Their products range from simple light strings to elaborate lights with animal designs, bug designs, memorabilia, and so on. Your newest project requires a change. One of the business unit managers submitted a change through the change control system, which utilizes a CCB. Which of the following is true regarding the CCB?

   A. Describes how change requests are managed

   B. Requires all change requests in writing

   C. Approves or denies change requests

   D. Requires updates to the appropriate management plan

6. You are working on a project that was proceeding well until a manufacturing glitch occurred that requires corrective action. It turns out the glitch was an unintentional enhancement to the product, and the marketing people are absolutely crazy about its potential. The corrective action is canceled, and you continue to produce the product with the newly discovered enhancement. As the project manager, you know that a change has occurred to the product scope as the glitch changed the characteristics of the product. Which of the following is true?

A. Changes to product scope are reflected in the project scope.

B. Changes to product scope are reflected in the integrated change control plan.

C. Changes to product scope are a result of changes to the product description.

D. Changes to product scope are a result of corrective action.

7. You are working on a project that was proceeding well until a manufacturing glitch occurred that requires corrective action. It turns out the glitch was an unintentional enhancement to the product, and the marketing people are absolutely crazy about its potential. The corrective action is canceled, and you continue to produce the product with the newly discovered enhancement. As the project manager, you know that a change has occurred to the project scope. Which of the following is true?

A. Project scope changes do not require CCB approval.

B. Performance measurement baselines are affected by scope changes.

C. Project scope change uses inspection to determine if change has occurred.

D. Project scope change uses workarounds to correct unexpected problems with scope change.

8. Your project has recently experienced change. Some of the agreed-upon WBS elements have been changed as a result. What kind of change has occurred?

A. Schedule change

B. Risk response change

C. Quality change

D. Scope change

9. Your project has experienced some changes to the agreed-upon WBS elements. The changes were approved through the proper change control process. The WBS changes may in turn require which of the following?

    A. Scope changes

    B. Cost changes

    C. Schedule revisions

    D. Risk response changes

10. Which of the following is true regarding schedule variances?

    A. They impact scope, which impacts the schedule.

    B. They sometimes impact the schedule.

    C. They always impact the schedule.

    D. They never impact the schedule.

11. You are a project manager for Laurel's theater productions. Your new project is coming in over budget and requires a cost change through the cost change control system. The cost variance was projected using which of the following tools and techniques?

    A. Performance measurements

    B. Cost baseline measurements

    C. Computerized tools

    D. Performance reports

12. You are a project manager for Laurel's theater productions. Your new project is coming in over budget and requires a cost change through the cost change control system. You know all of the following are true regarding Cost Control except:

    A. Performance is monitored to detect variances.

    B. Changes are reflected in the cost baseline.

    C. Changes are monitored and reflected in the project scope.

    D. Changes are monitored so that inappropriate changes do not get into the cost baseline.

13. Which of the following might require rebaselining of the cost baseline?

A. Corrective action

B. Revised cost estimates

C. Updates to the cost management plan

D. Budget updates

14. You are working on a project to develop a new website for your company. You are monitoring results of the project to determine if they comply with standards set out during the Planning processes. You are also taking steps to eliminate unsatisfactory results. This might mean rework in some cases. Which process are you in?

A. Risk Monitoring and Control

B. Quality Control

C. Integrated Change Control

D. Scope Change Control

15. This tool and technique of Quality Control keeps errors from reaching the customer:

A. Inspection

B. Prevention

C. Corrective action

D. Performance measurements

16. Common causes of variances are a result of all of the following except:

A. Random variances

B. Predictable variances

C. Special variances

D. Variances that are always present in the process

17. You are a project manager in the manufacturing industry. You are using sample variance measurements to monitor the results of the process over time. Which tool and technique of Quality Control are you using?

    A. Statistical sampling

    B. Scatter diagrams

    C. Control charts

    D. Pareto diagrams

18. All of the following are true regarding Pareto diagrams and Pareto theory except:

    A. Pareto diagrams are histograms.

    B. Pareto diagrams rank order factors.

    C. A small number of causes create the majority of problems.

    D. Pareto diagrams use two variables.

19. You are preparing a diagram that plots two variables, the dependent variable and the independent variable, to see the relationship between the two elements. What kind of diagram are you using?

    A. Cause-and-effect diagram

    B. Control chart

    C. Flowchart

    D. Scatter diagram

20. Your project progressed as planned up until yesterday. Suddenly, an unexpected risk event occurred. You quickly devised a response to deal with this negative risk event using which of the following outputs of Risk Monitoring and Control?

    A. Risk management plan updates

    B. Workarounds

    C. Corrective action

    D. Additional risk identification

Answers to Review Questions

1. B. Integrated Change Control, Scope Change Control, Schedule Control, and Cost Control are all concerned with three things: influencing the things that cause change, determining that change is needed or has happened, and managing the change.

2. D . Change control systems are documented procedures that describe how to submit change requests. They track the status of the change requests, document the management impacts of change, track the change approval status, and define the level of authority needed to approve changes. Change control systems do not approve or deny the changes—that's the responsibility of the configuration control board.

3. A. The tools and techniques of Integrated Change Control are change control system, configuration management, performance measurement, additional planning, and project management information system.

4. C. The key to this question was that the characteristics of the product were documented with this tool. Configuration management documents the physical characteristics and the functionality of the product of the project.

5. C. Configuration control boards (CCBs) review change requests and have the authority to approve or deny them. Their authority is defined by the organization.

6. A. Changes to product scope should be reflected in project scope.

7. B. Project scope change affects the performance measurement baselines, which may include schedule baselines and cost baselines.

8. D. Scope changes include changes to the agreed-upon WBS.

9. C. WBS element changes are scope changes. Schedule revisions are often required as a result of scope changes.

10. B. Schedule variances will sometimes, but not always, impact the schedule. Changes to non–critical path tasks will not likely impact the schedule, but changes to critical path tasks will always impact the schedule.

11. A. Performance measurements are a tool and technique of the Cost Control process and determine variances in cost using formulas discussed in the Performance Reporting process.

12. C. Cost Control tracks project performance to detect variances and reflect them in the cost baseline. It's also used to prevent inappropriate changes from getting into the cost baseline.

13. D. Budget updates may require cost rebaselining.

14. B. Quality Control is concerned with monitoring work results to see if they fulfill the quality standards set out in the quality management plan. Rework is an output of the Quality Control process.

15. A. Inspection is a tool and technique of the Quality Control process that keeps errors from reaching the customer. Prevention keeps errors from occurring in the process, but it is not a tool and technique of Quality Control.

16. C. Common causes of variances are a result of random variances, known or predictable variances, or variances that are always present in the process.

17. C. Control charts monitor repetitive activities like those in the manufacturing industry. They are based on sample variance measurements and monitor the results of the process over time.

18. D. Pareto diagrams are displayed as histograms. They rank order the most important factors by their frequency over time. Pareto is known for the 80/20 rule and also said that a small number of causes create the majority of problems.

19. D. Scatter diagrams use an independent and a dependent variable and display the relationship between these two elements as points on a graph.

20. B. Workarounds are unplanned responses. Workarounds deal with negative risk events as they occur. As the name implies, workarounds were not previously known to the project team. The risk event was unplanned, so no contingency plan existed to deal with the risk event and thus it required a workaround.

Chapter

11

Closing Out the Project

PMP EXAM CONTENT FROM THE PROJECT CLOSING PERFORMANCE DOMAIN COVERED IN THIS CHAPTER:

✓ 1. Obtain Acceptance of Deliverables.

✓ 2. Document Lessons Learned.

✓ 3. Facilitate Closure.

✓ 4. Preserve Product Records and Tools.

✓ 5. Release Resources.

You've made it to the homestretch. This chapter covers the last group of project processes. Most of the hard part is over, but we aren't quite done yet. Seven percent of the questions on the exam concern the Closing process group, so you'll want to study the main points of project closure.

The Closing process group has two processes, which we'll cover in this chapter: Contract Closeout and Administrative Closure. The Contract Closeout process is performed and completed before the Administrative Closure process begins. You might see an exam question regarding this order, so keep it in mind. Contract Closeout and Administrative Closure are both concerned with verifying that the work of the project was completed correctly and to the stakeholders' satisfaction.

Project closeout is the most often neglected process of all the project processes. Once the project is over, it's easy to pack things up, throw some files in a drawer, and start moving right into planning the next project. However, don't be so quick to chuck your project just yet. There are a few things to take care of during this process that might make life easier for you on the next project.

One of the most important functions of this process is obtaining formal acceptance of the product of the project from stakeholders and customers. You'll want to get an official sign-off from the stakeholders acknowledging acceptance of the product and then file this with the project documents.

Formulating Project Closeout

All good projects must come to an end, as the saying goes. Hopefully, you've practiced all the things we've talked about that have led up to this point and you've delivered a successful project to the stakeholders and customers. You've also put some of the vital tools of project management into play including planning, executing, controlling, and communicating to help you reach that goal. But how do you know when a project has ended successfully? Delivering the product or service of the project doesn't mean it's been completed satisfactorily. You'll remember that back in the opening chapters, I said a project is completed successfully when it meets or exceeds stakeholders' expectations. During the Closing process, you'll document acceptance of the product of the project with a formal sign-off and file it with the project records for future reference. This is how the stakeholders will indicate that the project has met or exceeded their expectations and the project ends.

Characteristics of Closing

There are a few characteristics common to all projects during the Closing process. One is that the probability of completing the project is highest during this process and risk is lowest. You've already completed the majority of the work of the project, if not all of the work, therefore the probability of not finishing the project is very low.

Stakeholders have the least amount of influence during the Closing processes, while project managers have the greatest amount of influence. Costs are significantly lower during this process as the majority of the project work and spending has already occurred. Remember those cost S-curves we talked about in Chapter 7? This is where they taper off as project spending comes to an end.

One last characteristic is that weak matrix organizations tend to experience the least amount of stress during the Closing process.

All projects do eventually come to an end. Let's examine a few of the reasons for project endings before getting into the Contract Closeout and Administrative Closure processes.

Project Endings

Projects come to an end for several reasons: They're completed successfully, they're canceled or killed prior to completion, or they evolve into ongoing operations and no longer exist as projects. There are four formal types of project endings you might need to know for the exam: addition, starvation, integration, and extinction. Let's look at the definition of each of these ending types.

Addition

Projects that evolve into ongoing operations are considered projects that end due to addition; in other words, they become their own ongoing business unit. An example of this is the installation of an enterprise resource planning system. These systems are business management systems that integrate all areas of a business including marketing, planning, manufacturing, sales, financials, and human resources. After the installation of the software, these systems can develop into their own business unit because ongoing operations, maintenance, and monitoring of the software require full-time staff. These systems usually evolve into an arm of the business reporting system that no one can live without once it's installed.

A project is considered a project when it meets these criteria: It is unique, has a definite beginning and ending date, and is temporary in nature. When a project becomes an ongoing operation, it is no longer a project.

Starvation

When resources are cut off from the project or are no longer provided to the project, it's starved prior to completing all the requirements, and you're left with an unfinished project on your hands. Starvation can happen for any number of reasons: Other projects come about and take precedence over the current project thereby cutting the funding or resources for your project, the customer curtails an order, the project budget is reduced, a key resource quits, and so on. Resource starving can include cutting back or withholding human resources, equipment and supplies, or money. In any case, if you're not getting the people, equipment, or money you need to complete the project, it's going to starve and probably end abruptly.

This is one of those cases where documentation becomes your best friend. Organizations tend to have short memories. As you move on to bigger and better projects, your memory regarding the specifics of the project will fade. That's why project documentation is such an important function. Six months from now when someone important wonders why that project was never completed and begins the finger-pointing routine, the project documents will clearly outline the reasons the project ended early. We'll talk more about documenting project details shortly.

Integration

Integration occurs when the resources of the project including people, equipment, property, and supplies are distributed to other areas in the organization or are assigned to other projects. Perhaps your organization begins to focus on other areas or other projects, and the next thing you know functional managers come calling to retrieve their resources for other, more important things. Again, your project will come to an end due to lack of resources because they have been reassigned to other areas of the business or have been pulled from your project and assigned to another project. The difference between starvation and integration is that starvation results in funding or resource cuts, while integration results in reassignment or redeployment of the resources.

Again, good documentation describing the circumstances that brought about the ending of a project due to integration should be archived with the project records for future reference.

Extinction

This is the best kind of project end because extinction means the project has been completed and accepted by the stakeholders. As such, it no longer exists as it had a definite ending date, the goals of the project were achieved, and the project was closed out.

 Real World Scenario

Pied Piper

Jerome Reeds is the project manager for Pied Piper's newest software project. His team is working on a program that will integrate the organization's human resource information including payroll records, leave time accruals, contact information, and so on. His top two programmers, Lance and Kathy, are heading up the coding team and are in charge of the programming and testing activities.

Pied Piper recently hired a new CIO who started working with the company just a few weeks ago. Jerome is concerned about his human resources project. It was the former CIO's pet project, but he's not sure where it falls on the new CIO's radar screen.

Jerome is in the computer room checking out the new hardware that just arrived for his project. Liz Horowitz, the director of network operations, approaches Jerome.

"That's a nice piece of hardware," Liz comments.

"It sure is. This baby is loaded. It's going to process and serve up data to the users so fast they'll be asking us to upgrade all the servers."

Liz replies, "You're right about that. I've asked Richard to burn it in and load the software."

"What software?" Jerome asks.

"You know, the new customer relationship management software. The CIO hired some vendor she's worked with before to come in and install their CRM system here. She said it was our top priority. I knew this new server was already on order, and it happens to be sized correctly for the new CRM system."

"I purchased this server for the human resources project. What am I supposed to use for that?"

Liz answers, "I've got a server over there on the bottom of the third rack that might work, or maybe you can order another one. But you should take this up with the CIO. All I know is she authorized me to use this server. She understood I was taking it from your project, so maybe she's thinking about going another direction with the human resources project.

You probably should know I also asked to have Lance and Kathy assigned to the CRM project. Even though it's a vendor project, it still requires some of our coders. The CIO wanted the best, and they're the best we've got. It shouldn't take them long to make the changes I need, and then you can have them back for your project. In the meantime, they can give directions to your other programmers so they can keep working."

"I'm going to go see if the CIO is in," Jerome replies.

This is a case where Jerome's project ends by integration due to the reassignment of resources. The new CIO came on board and changed the direction and focus of the project priorities making her new project a higher priority than the previous project. As a result, Jerome's hardware and his top two resources were reassigned to the new project. Had the CIO cut the resources and equipment on the original project altogether, it would have ended due to starvation.

Contract Closeout

Contracts have life cycles of their own just like projects. We talked about the contract life cycles in Chapter 9. As such, contracts come to a close just like projects come to a close. As you might guess, the *Guide to the PMBOK* has a process that deals with contract closings: Contract Closeout.

The *Contract Closeout* process is concerned with completing and settling the terms of the contract. It also determines if the work described in the contract was completed accurately and satisfactorily. This process is called product verification. For the exam, remember that product verification performed during the Closing process determines if all of the work of the project was completed correctly and satisfactorily according to stakeholder expectations. And remember that product documentation is verified and accepted during the Scope Verification process. One more note: When projects end prematurely, the Scope Verification process is where the level of detail concerning the amount of work completed gets documented.

Contract Closeout also updates records and archives the information for future reference. These records detail the final results of the work of the project. We'll look at the specifics of this when we examine the Contract Closeout outputs.

Contracts may have specific terms or conditions for completion and closeout. You should be aware of these terms or conditions so that project closure isn't held up because you missed an important detail. If you are not administering the contract yourself, be certain to ask your procurement department if there are any special conditions that you should know about so that your project team doesn't inadvertently delay contract or project closure.

Contract Closeout Inputs and Tools

Contract Closeout has one input and one tool and technique. The input to this process is contract documentation. This includes the contract itself and all the supporting documents that go along with the contract. These might include things such as the WBS, the project schedule, change control documents, technical documents, financial and payment records, quality control inspection results, and so on. This information along with all the other information gathered during the project is filed once the project is closed out so that anyone considering a future project of similar scope can reference what was already done.

Procurement Audits

The only tool and technique of this process is procurement audits. Audits are reviews of processes to determine if they are meeting the right needs and are being performed correctly or according to standards. The *Guide to the PMBOK* says procurement audits are concerned with reviewing the procurement process starting with the Procurement Planning stage all the way through Contract Administration. In practice, procurement audits should occur all the way through the Contract Closeout process. Closeout is where the project is formally accepted and the contract file is prepared for the Administrative Closure process and archiving. If you miss these steps, the procurement audit will discover that Contract Closeout was not completed and will allow you to correct it.

The primary purpose of the procurement audit is to identify lessons learned during the procurement process. It examines the process to determine areas of improvement and allows you to correct any flawed processes or procedures discovered during the audit.

Procurement audits may be used by either the buyer or the vendor, or by both, as an opportunity for improvement. Documenting the lessons learned, including the successes and failures that occurred, allows you to improve other procurement processes currently under way on this project or other projects. It also gives you the opportunity to improve the process for future projects.

Contract Acceptance

One of the purposes of the Contract Closeout process is to provide formal notice to the seller, usually in written form, that the contract is complete. It's your responsibility as project manager to document the formal acceptance of the contract. Many times the provisions for formalizing acceptance of the product and closing the contract are spelled out in the contract itself.

If you have a procurement department that handles contract administration, they will expect you to inform them when the contract is completed and will in turn follow the formal procedures to let the seller know the contract is complete. However, you'll still note the contract completion in your copy of the project records.

This process is your organization's way of formally accepting the product of the project from the vendor and closing out the contract. If the product or service does not meet expectations, the vendor will need to correct the problems before you issue a formal acceptance notice. Hopefully, quality audits have been performed during the course of the project and the vendor was given the opportunity to make corrections earlier in the process than the Closing stage. It's not a good idea to wait until the very end of the project and then spring all the problems and issues on the vendor at once. It's much more efficient to discuss problems with your vendor as the project progresses as it provides the opportunity for correction when the problems occur.

Formal acceptance and closure is one of the outputs of the Contract Closeout process. The other output is called contract file. This is simply all the contract records and supporting documents. These records are indexed for easy reference and included as inputs to the Administrative Closure process. Then, at the conclusion of Administrative Closure, project archives, which include the contract records, are filed for future reference.

Administrative Closure

The key activity of the *Administrative Closure* process is concerned with gathering and disseminating information to formalize project closure. Every project requires closure, and according to the *Guide to the PMBOK*, the completion of each project phase requires Administrative Closure as well. The exam will likely have a question that expects you to know that Administrative Closure occurs at the end of each phase of the project in order to properly document project information and keep it safe for future reference. Administrative Closure shouldn't wait until project completion but rather should be performed at the end of every phase.

Administrative Closure verifies and documents the project outcomes just like the Contract Closeout process. Keep in mind that not all projects are performed under contract but all projects require Administrative Closure. Since verification and documentation of the project outcomes occur in both processes, projects that are performed under contract need to have project results verified only one time.

Once the project outcomes are documented, formal acceptance is requested of the stakeholders. We'll look at formal acceptance in more detail in a later section.

Administrative Closure Inputs

The Administrative Closure process gathers all the project records and verifies that they are up to date and accurate. The project records must correctly identify the final specifications of the product or service the project set out to produce. Administrative Closure is the place to assure this information accurately reflects the true results of the project.

The three inputs to this process are performance measurement documents, product documentation, and other project records. We talked quite extensively about performance measurements in Chapter 9, so we'll do a recap here.

Performance Measurement Documents

All of the performance measurements that were used to analyze project progress during the Controlling processes are included as part of the documentation for the Administrative Closure process. Any document that helped establish the basis for the performance measurements, including the project plan, the cost budget, cost estimates, the project schedule, and so on, are also collected here. These documents are then reviewed to make certain the goals and objectives of the project were met.

You should make each of these documents available for review during the Administrative Closure process. Stakeholders, the executive management team, or the customer may request to see this information prior to formally accepting the project. You'll want to have these documents available in case they ask.

Product Documentation

The second input of Administrative Closure is product documentation. This documentation includes anything that details the product or service of the project. The *Guide to the PMBOK* includes things like the requirements documents, specifications, plans, technical documents, electronic files, drawings, and so on. This input includes any information that details or lists product specifications or requirements. As with the performance documents, you should make these documents available for review.

Other Project Records

This last input is a catchall input for the remaining documents not gathered in the first two inputs. It includes things like project reports, memos or correspondence generated during the project, and any other records that describe the work of the project.

Administrative Closure Tools and Techniques

We've seen all of the tools and techniques of Administrative Closure in other processes. They include performance reporting tools and techniques, project reports, and project presentations. Here's a pop quiz. Without looking, can you name the nine performance measurements and their formulas?

$CV = EV - AC$

$SV = EV - PV$

$CPI = EV \div AC$

$SPI = EV \div PV$

$EAC = AC + ETC$ (use when past assumptions are incorrect)

$EAC = (AC + BAC) - EV$ (use when variances are not typical)

$EAC = [AC + (BAC - EV) \div CPI]$ (use when variances are expected to remain the same)

$ETC = EAC - AC$

$VAC = BAC - EAC$

So you've been studying. That's very good because you need to know these formulas for the exam. These same performance measurements that were examined throughout the Controlling process can be used during Administrative Closure to verify and document project outcomes. They are included with the project documents gathered and archived during this process. We'll look at project archives next.

Administrative Closure Outputs

Sometimes you'll work on projects where everything just clicks. Your project team functions at the performing stage, the customers and stakeholders are happy, and things just fall into place according to plan. I often find it difficult to close projects that have progressed particularly well just because I don't want them to end. Believe it or not, the majority of your projects can fall into this category if you practice good project management techniques and exercise those great communication skills.

These are the last outputs of the last process of your project: project archives, project closure, and lessons learned.

Project Archives

When all the work of the project is completed, the vendor is paid, the contract is closed, and the records are gathered, you'll create project archives. These include any project documents completed during the project. All of the inputs to this process I mentioned are included here as well as the contract documents. Keep in mind that when projects are performed under contract, the archiving of financial records is especially important. These records may need to be accessed if there are payment disputes. And this information is especially useful when estimating future projects. Projects with large financial expenditures also require particular attention to the archiving of financial records for the same reasons.

All of these documents are indexed for reference and filed in a safe place. Don't forget to include electronic databases and electronic documents as part of your project archives as well. These records can be stored on a network drive or copied onto a CD that's kept with the project binder. Organizational policies will dictate how you should file your project records. If no policies exist, you'll have to create them. I recommend archiving all the information you have regarding your project.

Project Closure and Formal Acceptance

The project closure output concerns verifying that the product of the project meets all the requirements and obtains formal sign-off of the acceptance of the product. Formal acceptance also includes distributing notice of the acceptance of the product or service of the project by the stakeholders, customer, or project sponsor to stakeholders and customers. You should require formal sign-off on a sign-off document indicating that the person or persons signing accept the product of the project. Documenting formal acceptance is important because it signals the official closure of the project and it is your proof that the project was completed satisfactorily.

Another function of sign-off is that it kicks off the beginning of the warranty period. Sometimes project managers or vendors will warranty their work for a certain time period after completing the project. Projects that produce software programs are often warranted from bugs for a 60- or 90-day time frame from the date of implementation or acceptance. Typically in the case of software projects, bugs are fixed for free during the warranty period. Watch out because users will try to squeeze new requirements into the "bug" category mold. If you offer a warranty, it's critical that the warranty spells out exactly what is covered and what is not.

Lessons Learned

Lessons learned are the final output of this process. The purpose of lessons learned is the same as we've seen before. They're used to document the successes and failures of the project. As an example, lessons learned document the reasons why specific corrective actions were taken, their outcomes, the causes of performance variances, unplanned risks that occurred, mistakes that were made and could have been avoided, and so on.

Unfortunately sometimes projects do fail. There are things that can be learned from failed projects as well as successful projects, and this information should be documented for future reference. Most project managers, however, do not document lessons learned. The reason for this is that employees don't want to admit to making mistakes or learning from mistakes made during the project. And they do not want their name associated with failed projects or even mishaps on successful projects.

You and your management team will have to work to create an atmosphere of trust and assurance that lessons learned are not reasons for dismissing employees but are learning opportunities that benefit all those associated with the project. Lessons learned allow you to carry knowledge gained on this project to other projects you'll work on going forward. They'll also prevent repeat mistakes in the future if you take the time to review the project documents and lessons learned prior to undertaking your new project.

Post-implementation audits aren't an official output, but they are a good idea. These go hand in hand with lessons learned as they examine the project from beginning to end and look at what went right and what went wrong. They evaluate the project goals and determine if the product or service of the project satisfies the objectives. Post-implementation audits also examine the activities and project processes to determine if improvements are possible on future projects.

Organizations that do not document lessons learned probably do conduct post-implementation audits. Documenting and gathering information during this procedure can serve the same function as lessons learned if you're honest and include all the good, the bad, and the ugly. Let's hope there's very little ugly.

Real World Scenario

Cimarron Research Group

The Cimarron Research Group researches and develops organic pesticides for use on food crops. They are a medium-sized company and have established a project management office to manage all aspects of project work. The PMO consists of project managers and administrative staff who assist with information handling, filing, and disbursement.

Terri Roberts is the project manager for a project that has just closed. Terri diligently filed all the pertinent project documents as the project progressed and has requested the research files and engineering notes from the director of engineering to include them with the project archives as well. All information regarding the research on this project is included with the project archives. The engineering department chooses to keep their own set of research records as well, but it's important to keep a copy of these notes with the project archives so that all the information about the project is located in one place.

Terri's assistant has indexed all the project documents and recently sent notice of formal acceptance of this project to the stakeholders, project sponsor, and management team. This notice officially closes the project. The next step is to archive the files onto CDs and store them.

Releasing Project Team Members

Releasing project team members is not an official process. However, it should be noted that at the conclusion of the project, you will release your project team members and they will go back to their functional managers or get assigned to a new project in a matrix type organization.

You will want to keep the functional managers or other project managers informed as you get closer to project completion so that they have time to adequately plan for the return of their employees. Start letting them know a few months ahead of time what the schedule looks like and how soon they can plan on using their employees on new projects. This gives the other managers the ability to start planning activities and scheduling activity dates.

Celebrate!

I think it's a good idea to hold some kind of celebration at the conclusion of your project. The project team should celebrate their accomplishment, and you should officially recognize their efforts and thank them for their participation. Any number of ideas come to mind here including a party, a trip to a ball game, pizza and sodas at lunch time, and so on. This shouldn't be the only time you've recognized your team, as we discussed during the Team Development process, but now is the time to officially close the project and thank your team members.

A celebration helps team members formally recognize the project end and brings closure to the work they've done. It also encourages them to remember what they've learned and to start thinking about how their experiences will benefit them and the organization during the next project.

Project Case Study: New Kitchen Heaven Retail Store

Dirk strolls into your office maintaining his formal and dignified manners as always then sits down in the chair beside your desk.

"I just want to congratulate you on a job well done," he says. "The grand opening was a success, and the store had a better than expected week the first week. I'm impressed you were able to pull this off and get the store opened prior to the Garden and Home Show. That was the key to the great opening week."

"Thank you, Dirk. Lots of people put in a lot of hard work and extra hours to get this job done. I'm glad you're happy with the results."

"I thought the banner with our logo, 'Great Gadgets for People Interested in Great Food,' was a wonderful touch."

"That was Jill's idea. She had some great ideas that made the festivities successful. As you know, though," you continue, "we did have some problems on this project. Fortunately they weren't insurmountable, but I think we learned a thing or two during this project that we can carry forward to other projects."

"Like what?" Dirk asks.

"We should have contracted with Gomez construction sooner so that we didn't have to pay overtime. We had a very generous budget, so the overtime expense didn't impact this project, but it might impact the next one.

"And we came fairly close to having a hardware disaster on our hands. Next time, we should order the equipment sooner and test it here at headquarters first, then ship it out to the site after we know everything is working correctly."

"Good ideas. But that's old news. Now that this project is over, I'd like to get you started on the next project. We're going to introduce cooking classes in all of our retail stores. The focus is the home chef, and we might just call the classes the Home Chef Pro series. We'll offer basic classes all the way to professional series classes if the project's a hit. We'll bring in guest chefs from the local areas to give demos and teach some of the classes as well."

"I'm very interested in taking on this project and can't wait to get started. I'm thrilled that you want me to head this up. But I do have a few things here to wrap up before I start work on the new project," you reply.

Dirk says, "The project's over. The grand opening was a success. It's time to move on. Let Jill take over now as retail stores are her responsibility."

"Jill has taken over the day-to-day operations. However, I've got to finish collecting the project information, close out the contract with Gomez, and make final payment. Jake verified that all the work was completed correctly and to his satisfaction. Then I need to publish the formal acceptance notice to all of the stakeholders via e-mail. I will also create a document that outlines those things I told you earlier about that we should remember and reference during the next project; that document is called lessons learned. Then after all those things are completed, all of the project records need to be indexed and archived. I can have all that done by the end of the week and will be free starting Monday to work on requirements gathering and the charter document for the new project."

"This is just like the planning process discussion we got into with the tree, breakdown structure thing and all the planning I suspect. I do have to admit all the planning paid off. I'll give you until the end of the week to close out this project. Come see me Monday to get started on Home Chef Pro."

Project Case Study Checklist

Contract Closeout

- Product verification (work was correct and satisfactory)

> - Formal acceptance and closure
>
> Administrative Closure
>
> - Product verification (work was correct and satisfactory)
>
> - Collecting project documents
>
> - Disseminating final acceptance notice
>
> - Documenting lessons learned
>
> - Archiving project records

Summary

Project closure is the most often neglected process of all the project management processes. The four most important aspects of closure are checking the work for completeness and accuracy, documenting formal acceptance, disseminating project closure information, and archiving records and lessons learned.

Closure involves checking that the work of the project was completed correctly and to the satisfaction of the stakeholders. Documenting formal acceptance of the product of the project is an important aspect of project closure as well. This assures that the stakeholder or customer is satisfied with the work and that it meets their needs.

Projects come to an end in one of four ways: addition, starvation, integration, or extinction. Addition is when projects evolve into their own business unit. Starvation happens because the project is starved of its resources. Integration occurs when resources are taken from the existing project and dispersed back into the organization or assigned to other projects. And extinction is the best end as the project was completed, accepted, and closed.

The two processes in the Closing group are Contract Closeout and Administrative Closure. Contract Closeout is performed before Administrative Closure and is concerned with settling the contract and completing the contract according to its terms. Its two outputs are contract file and formal acceptance and closure.

Administrative Closure is performed at the end of each phase of the project as well as at the end of the project. Administrative Closure involves documenting formal acceptance and disseminating notice of acceptance to the stakeholders, customer, and others. All documentation gathered during the project and collected during this process is archived and saved for reference purposes on future projects.

Lessons learned document the successes and failures of the project. Many times lessons learned are not documented because staff members do not want to assign their names to project errors or failures. You and your management team need to work together to assure employees that lessons learned are not exercises used for disciplinary purposes but benefit both the employee and the organization. Documenting what you've learned from past experiences lets you carry this forward to new projects so that the same errors are not repeated. It also allows you to incorporate new methods of performing activities that you learned on past projects.

Exam Essentials

Be able to name the purpose of the Closing process.   To verify the work was satisfactorily completed, to disseminate information, and to document formal acceptance.

Be able to describe product verification.   Confirms that all the work of the project was completed accurately and to the satisfaction of the stakeholder.

Be able to name the primary activity of the Closing process.   To distribute information that formalizes project completion.

Be able to describe when Administrative Closure is performed.   At the close of each project phase and at the close of the project.

Be able to define the purpose for lessons learned.   To describe the project successes and failures and to use the information learned on future projects.

Key Terms

Before you take the exam, be certain you are familiar with the following terms:

Administrative Closure   Contract Closeout

Review Questions

1. You are the project manager for a top secret software project for an agency of the United States Government. Your mission, should you choose to accept it, is to complete the project using internal resources. The reason is because getting top secret clearances for contractors takes quite a bit of time and waiting for clearances would jeopardize the implementation date. Your programmers are 80 percent of the way through the programming and testing work when your agency appoints a new executive director. Slowly but surely your programmers are taken off this project and reassigned to the executive director's hot new project. Which of the following type of project ending is this?

   A. Starvation

   B. Extinction

   C. Addition

   D. Integration

2. You are the project manager for a top secret software project for an agency of the United States Government. Your mission, should you choose to accept it, is to complete the project using internal resources. The reason is because getting top secret clearances for contractors takes quite a bit of time and waiting for clearances would jeopardize the implementation date. Your programmers are 80 percent of the way through the programming and testing work when your agency appoints a new executive director. Your programmers are siphoned off this project to work on the executive director's hot new project. Which of the following addresses the purpose of Scope Verification in this case?

   A. It determines the correctness and completion of all the work.

   B. It documents the level and degree of completion.

   C. It determines if the project results comply with quality standards.

   D. It documents the correctness of the work according to stakeholders' expectations.

3. You are a project manager for Cinema Snicker Productions. Your company specializes in producing comedy films for the big screen. Your latest project has just been canceled due to budget cuts. Which of the following is true?

   A. This project ended due to starvation because the funding was cut off.

   B. This project ended due to integration because the resources were distributed elsewhere.

   C. This project ended due to starvation because the resources were distributed elsewhere.

   D. This project ended due to integration because the funding was cut off.

4. All of the following are types of project closures or endings except:

   A. Addition

   B. Integration

   C. Verification

   D. Extinction

5. You are a project manager for Cinema Snicker Productions. Your company specializes in producing comedy films for the big screen. Your latest project has just been completed and accepted. You've been given your next project, which starts right away. Which of the following is true?

   A. This project ended due to extinction because it was completed and accepted.

   B. This project ended due to integration because it was completed and accepted and the project manager moved on to a new project.

   C. This project ended due to addition because it was completed and accepted and archived into the company's catalog of available films.

   D. This project ended due to integration because it was completed and accepted.

6. Which of the following processes are performed in the Closing process group and in what order?

   A. Administrative Closure then Contract Closeout

   B. Scope Verification then Administrative Closure

   C. Contract Closeout then Scope Verification

   D. Contract Closeout then Administrative Closure

7. You are a project manager for Dutch Harbor Consulting. Your latest project involved the upgrade of an organization's operating system on 236 servers. You performed this project under contract. You are in the Contract Closeout process and know that you should document:

   A. Lessons learned

   B. Performance measurements

   C. Formal acceptance

   D. Product verification

8. Which of the following are the outputs of the Contract Closeout process?

   A. Project archives, formal acceptance and closure, contract file

   B. Contract file, formal acceptance and closure

   C. Project archives, contract file

   D. Contract file, formal acceptance and closure, lessons learned

9. You are a project manager for Dutch Harbor Consulting. Your latest project involved the upgrade of an organization's operating system on 236 servers. You performed this project under contract. You are in the Closing process and know that product verification is for what purpose?

   A. To verify the goals of the project and assure the product of the project is complete

   B. To evaluate all the work of the project and compare results to project scope

   C. To verify all the work was completed correctly and satisfactorily

   D. To evaluate project goals and assure the product of the project meets the requirements

10. You are a project manager for Dutch Harbor Consulting. Your latest project involved the upgrade of an organization's operating system on 236 servers. You performed this project under contract. You are in the Contract Closeout process and have reviewed the contracting process to identify lessons learned. What is the name of the tool and technique of Contract Closeout you used to perform this function?

    A. Procurement audits

    B. Performance reviews

    C. Performance audits

    D. Procurement reviews

11. All of the following are inputs to the Administrative Closure process except:

    A. Performance measurement documents

    B. Documentation of the product of the project

    C. Other documents

    D. Contract documents

12. You are a project manager for Penguin Software. Your company creates custom software programs for hospitals and large dental offices. You have just completed a project and are gathering the documentation of the product of the project. This might include all of the following except:

    A. Technical specifications

    B. Electronic files

    C. Programming plans

    D. Performance measurements

13. The outputs of the Administrative Closure process include all of the following except:

    A. Project archives

    B. Project closure

    C. Lessons learned

    D. Formal acceptance

14. You are a project manager for Penguin Software. Your company creates custom software programs for hospitals and large dental offices. You have just completed a project and are performing earned value analysis, trend analysis, and performance reviews. Which of the following is true?

    A. This is performance measurement documentation, which is an input to the Contract Closeout process.

    B. This is performance measurement documentation, which is an input to the Administrative Closure process.

    C. These are performance reporting tools and techniques of the Administrative Closure process.

    D. These are performance reporting tools and techniques of the Contract Closeout process.

15. You have collected the performance measurement documentation for your project to be included in the project archives. What is the purpose of the performance measurement documentation?

    A. It's used as part of the formal acceptance process to verify contract expenditures.

    B. It's reviewed to make certain the project goals and objectives were met.

    C. It's included in the project archive documentation after confirming the accuracy of the measurements.

    D. It's used as historical information for future projects that are similar in scope to this project.

16. Your project was just completed. Due to some unfortunate circumstances, the project was delayed causing cost overruns at the end of the project. Which of the following is true?

    A. You document the circumstances as lessons learned.

    B. You pay particular attention to archiving the financial records for this project.

    C. Your project ended due to starvation because of the cost overruns.

    D. You document the circumstances surrounding the project completion during the Scope Verification process.

17. Your project was just completed. Due to some unfortunate circumstances, the project was delayed causing cost overruns at the end of the project. This information might be useful on future projects in all of the following activities except:

    A. Cost estimating

    B. Allocating resources

    C. Product verification

    D. Activity estimating

18. Your project was just completed, accepted, and closed. As is customary for your organization, you conduct a post-implementation audit. The purpose of this audit includes all of the following except:

    A. Evaluating project goals and comparing them to project product

    B. Reviewing successes and failures

    C. Documenting the acceptance of the work results

    D. Documenting possible improvements for future projects

19. Contract documentation is an input to the Contract Closeout process. Contract documentation might include all of the following except:

    A. Supporting documents

    B. Contract changes

    C. Financial documents

    D. Procurement audit documents

20. Procurement audits review what?

    A. The procurement process from Procurement Planning through Contract Administration

    B. The contract administration process from Solicitation Planning through Contract Administration

    C. The procurement process from Procurement Planning through Contract Closeout

    D. The contract administration process from Solicitation Planning through Contract Closeout

Answers to Review Questions

1. D. Integration occurs when resources, equipment, or property are reassigned or redeployed back to the organization or to another project.

2. B. Scope Verification should document the level and degree of completion of the project. If you come back at a later date and restart this project, Scope Verification will describe how far the project progressed and give you an idea of where to start.

3. A. Starvation occurs because the project no longer receives the resources needed to continue. Resources could include people, equipment, money, and the like.

4. C. Verification is not a type of project ending.

5. A. Extinction is the best type of project end because it means the project was completed successfully and accepted by the sponsor or customer.

6. D. Contract Closeout and Administrative Closure are the processes in the Closing process group and are performed in that order.

7. C. The project manager is responsible for documenting the formal acceptance. This should be done during Contract Closeout when projects are performed under contract or during Administrative Closure if no work was performed under contract. In cases where part of the work was performed under contract and part with in-house staff, formal acceptance should occur in both of these processes. Lessons learned are an output of the Administrative Closure process, not the Contract Closeout process.

8. B. The contract file and formal acceptance and closure are the only outputs of the Contract Closeout process.

9. C. Product verification examines all the work of the project and verifies the work was completed correctly and satisfactorily.

10. A. Procurement audits are the only tool and technique of the Contract Closeout process. They're used to review the procurement process and identify and document any lessons learned during the procurement process for future reference.

11. D. Contract documents are an input to the Contract Closeout process but are part of the project archives, which are an output of the Administrative Closure process.

12. D. Performance measurement documentation is an input to the Administrative Closure process and wouldn't be included in the documentation of the product of the project.

13. D. Formal acceptance is included in the project closure process and isn't a separate output.

14. C. Earned value analysis, trend analysis, and performance reviews are tools and techniques included in the performance reporting tools and technique of the Administrative Closure process.

15. B. The performance measurement documentation is reviewed to make certain the project goals and objectives were met. This is an input to the Administrative Closure process.

16. A. Lessons learned document the experiences, successes, and failures that occurred during this project for future reference. There isn't enough information in the question to determine if answer B or answer D are correct. Answer C is not correct as the project was completed.

17. C. Product verification involves examining the work of the project for completeness and correctness. This process occurs on the existing project and isn't of much benefit to future projects as you'll perform product verification on future project work at the close of the project. By definition, a project is unique and creates a unique product or service.

18. C. Post-implementation audits are similar to lessons learned in that they review and document the project successes and failures, look for possible improvements for future projects, and evaluate the project goals and compare these to the end product.

19. D. Procurement audits are a tool and technique of Contract Closeout and not an input. Contract documentation might include all of the other answers shown as well as the contract itself, technical documentation, quality inspection reports related to the contract, and so on.

20. A. According to the *Guide to the PMBOK*, the procurement audit examines the procurement process from the Procurement Planning process through the Contract Administration process.

Chapter 12

Professional Responsibility

PMP EXAM CONTENT FROM THE PROFESSIONAL RESPONSIBILITY PERFORMANCE DOMAIN COVERED IN THIS CHAPTER:

- ✓ 1. Ensure Integrity.
- ✓ 2. Contribute to Knowledge Base.
- ✓ 3. Apply Professional Knowledge.
- ✓ 4. Balance Stakeholder Interests.
- ✓ 5. Respect Differences.

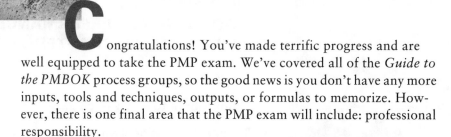

Congratulations! You've made terrific progress and are well equipped to take the PMP exam. We've covered all of the *Guide to the PMBOK* process groups, so the good news is you don't have any more inputs, tools and techniques, outputs, or formulas to memorize. However, there is one final area that the PMP exam will include: professional responsibility.

Once you've obtained the Project Management Professional (PMP) designation, you have an obligation to maintain integrity, apply your subject matter knowledge and project management knowledge, and maintain the code of conduct published by PMI. You'll also be required to balance the interests and needs of stakeholders versus the organization's needs. The exam will include questions on each of these topics.

As a project manager, you'll find yourself in many unique situations, different organizations, and possibly even different countries. Even if you never get involved in international project management, you will still come in contact with others from different cultures and backgrounds than yours. If you work as a contract project manager, you'll be exposed to many different organizations that each have their own cultures and ways of doing things. You should always strive to act in a professional, nonoffensive manner in these situations.

We'll talk about each of these things in this chapter. You'll find most of the questions in this area are based on common sense or are self-evident.

Ensuring Integrity

As a project manager, one of your professional responsibilities is to ensure integrity of the project management process, the product, and your own personal conduct. We've spent the majority of this book discussing how to achieve project management integrity by following the project management processes. Accurately applying your knowledge of these processes to your next project will ensure integrity of the process.

A product that has integrity is one that is complete and sound, or fit for use. Again, the correct application of the project management processes you've learned will ensure integrity of the product. You will accurately describe the product and the requirements of the product in the scope document. The project Planning, Executing, and Controlling processes, which include quality inspections and so on, will also ensure that a quality product is produced by following the requirements, monitoring the process, and taking corrective action where needed. And as you learned in the last chapter, you will seek acceptance of the product from the stakeholders and customer during the Closing process.

Personal Integrity

Personal integrity means sticking to an ethical code. As a certified Project Management Professional, you are required to adhere to PMI's *Project Management Professional Code of Professional Conduct*. You can find a copy of this code at the following PMI website address:

`www.pmi.org/certification/certprog/conductcode.htm`

You should read and understand this code as you will be agreeing to adhere to its terms as part of the certification process. One of the aspects of personal integrity includes your truthfulness about your PMP application and certification, your qualifications, and the continued reporting you provide to PMI to maintain your certification.

Personal Gain

Truthfulness and integrity involve not only information regarding your own background and experience, but regarding the project circumstances as well. For example, let's say you're a project manager working on contract. Part of your compensation consists of a bonus based on total project billing. Now let's suppose your project is finishing sooner than anticipated and this means your personal profit will decrease by $1500. Should you stretch the work to meet the original contracted amount so that your personal bonus comes in at the full amount even though your project team is finished up? I think you know the answer is of course not.

Your personal gain should never be a consideration when billing a customer or completing a project. Personal gain should never be a factor in any project decision. If the project finishes sooner than planned, you should bill the customer for the work completed, not for the full contracted amount. Compromising the project for the sake of your personal gain shows a lack of integrity, which could ultimately cost you your PMP status and even your job.

Conflict of Interest

Another area the *Project Management Professional Code of Professional Conduct* discusses is your responsibility to report to the stakeholders, customers, or others any actions or circumstances that could be construed as a *conflict of interest*.

A conflict of interest is when your personal interests are put above the interests of the project or when you use your influence to cause others to make decisions in your favor without regard for the project outcome. In other words, your personal interests take precedence over your professional obligation, and you make decisions that allow you to personally benefit regardless of the outcome of the project. Let's take a look at a few examples.

Associations and Affiliations

Conflicts of interest may include your associations or affiliations. As an example, perhaps your brother-in-law owns his own construction company and you are the project manager for a construction project that's just published an RFP. Your brother-in-law bids on the project and ends up winning the bid.

If you sat on the decision committee and didn't tell anyone about your association with the winning bidder, that is clearly a conflict of interest. If you influenced the bid decision so that it would go to your brother-in-law, he benefited from your position. Therefore, you put your personal interests or the interests of your associations, in this case, above the project outcome. Even if you did not influence the decision in any way, when others on the project discover the winning bidder is your brother-in-law, they will assume a conflict of interest occurred. This could jeopardize the awarding of the bid and your own position as well.

The correct thing to do in this case would be, first, inform the project sponsor and the decision committee that your brother-in-law intends to bid on the project. Second, you should refrain from participating on the award decision committee so as not to unduly influence others in favor of your brother-in-law. And last, if you've done all these things and your brother-in-law still wins the bid, appoint someone else in your organization to administer the contract and make the payments for the work performed by him. Also make certain you document the decisions you make regarding the activities performed by him and keep them with the project files. The more documentation you have, the less likely someone can make a conflict of interest accusation stick.

Vendor Gifts

Many professionals work in situations where they are not allowed to accept gifts in excess of certain dollar amounts. This might be driven by company policy, the department manager's policy, and so on. In my organization, it's considered a conflict of interest to accept any gift or meal in excess of $25 in value.

Vendors and suppliers often provide their customers and potential customers with lunches, gifts, ball-game tickets, and the like. It's your responsibility to know if a policy exists that forbids you from accepting these gifts. It's also your responsibility to inform the vendor if they've gone over the limit and you are unable to accept the gift.

The same situation can occur here that occurred with the brother-in-law example earlier. If you accept an expensive gift from a vendor and later award that vendor a contract or a piece of the project work, it looks like and probably is a conflict of interest. This violates PMI guidelines and doesn't look good for you personally either.

Don't accept gifts that might be construed as a conflict of interest. If your organization does not have a policy regarding vendor gifts, set limits for yourself depending on the situation, the history of gift acceptance by the organization in the past, and the complexity of the project. It's always better to decline a gift you're unsure about than to accept it and later lose your credibility, your reputation, or your PMP status because of bad judgment.

Stakeholder Influence

Another potential area for conflict of interest comes from stakeholders. Stakeholders are usually folks with a good deal of authority and an important position in the company. Make certain you are not putting your own personal interests above the interests of the project when you're dealing with powerful stakeholders. They may have the ability to promote you or reward you in other ways. That's not a bad thing, but if you let that get in the way of the project or let a stakeholder twist your arm with promises like this, you're getting mighty close to a conflict of interest. Always weigh your decisions with the objectives of the project and the organization in mind, not your own personal gain.

Keep in mind that you may not always be on the receiving end of the spectrum. You should not offer inappropriate gifts or services or use confidential information you have at your disposal to assist others as this also could be considered a conflict of interest.

Acting Professionally

Acting in a professional manner is required of most everyone who works in the business world. While you are not responsible for the actions of others, you are responsible for your own actions and reactions. Part of acting professionally involves controlling yourself and your reactions in questionable situations. For example, a stakeholder or customer may lash out at you but have no basis for their outburst. You can't control what they said or did, but you can control how you respond. As a professional, your concern for the project and the organization should take precedence over your concern for your own feelings. Therefore, lashing out in return would be unprofessional. I don't have room here to go into all the different situations that surround an example like this, but I think you get the idea. Maintain your professional demeanor and don't succumb to shouting matches or ego competitions with others.

Team Members

As project manager, you have a good deal of influence over your project team members. When you see project team members acting out of turn or with less than desirable customer service attitudes, you should coach and influence those team members to conform to the standard of conduct expected by you and your organization. Your team members represent you and the project. As such, they should act professionally. It's your job as the project leader to ensure they do.

You probably remember another saying your mother always told you that goes something like this: Actions speak louder than words. Always remember that you lead by example. Your team members are watching. If you are driven by high personal ethics and a strong desire to produce excellent customer service, those who work for you will likely follow your lead.

 Real World Scenario

The Golf Trip

Amanda Lewis is a project manager for a network upgrade project for her organization. This project will be outsourced to a vendor. Amanda will manage the vendor's work. She also wrote the RFP and is a member of the selection committee.

The project consists of converting the organization's network from 100MB Ethernet to Gigabit Ethernet. This requires replacing all of the routers and switches. Some of the cabling in the buildings will need to be replaced as well. The RFP requires the vendor that wins the bid to install all the new equipment and replace the network interface cards in each of the servers with Gigabit Ethernet cards. The grand total for this project is estimated at $1.2 million.

Don James is a vendor whom Amanda has worked with in the past. Don is very interested in winning this bid. He drops in on Amanda one day shortly after the RFP was posted.

"Amanda, it's good to see you," Don says. "I was in the neighborhood and thought I'd stop in to see how things are going."

"Just great Don," Amanda replies. "I'll bet you're here to talk to me about that RFP. You know I can't say anything until the whole process closes."

"You bet we bid on the project. I know you can't talk about the RFP, so I won't bring it up. I wanted to chat with you about something else. My company is sending 15 lucky contestants and one of their friends to Scottsdale, Arizona, for a 'conference.' The conference includes the use of the Scottsdale golf club, green fees paid of course, and all hotel and meal expenses are on us for the length of the trip. I know Scottsdale is one of your favorite places to golf, so I thought of you. What do you say?"

Amanda sits forward in her chair and looks at Don for a minute. "That sounds fabulous, and I do love Scottsdale. But you and I both know this isn't a conference. I wouldn't feel right about accepting it."

> "Come on, Amanda. Don't look a gift horse in the mouth. It is a conference. I'll be there and so will the top brass from the company. We have some presentations and demonstrations we'd like to show you while you're there, no obligation of course, and then you're free to spend the rest of the time however you'd like."
>
> "I appreciate the offer. Thanks for thinking of me, but no thanks. I'm on the selection committee for the RFP, and it would be a conflict of interest if I attended this conference. Besides, the value of the conference is over the $100 limit our company sets for vendor gifts and meals," Amanda says.
>
> "Okay. We'll miss you. Maybe next time."

Applying Professional Knowledge

Professional knowledge involves knowledge of project management practices as well as specific industry or technical knowledge required to complete an assignment.

As a PMP, you should apply project management knowledge to all your projects. You can take the opportunity to educate others regarding project management practices by keeping others up to date on project management practices, training your team members to use the correct techniques, and informing stakeholders of the correct processes and then sticking to those processes throughout the course of the project. This isn't always easy, especially when the organization doesn't have any formal processes in place. But once the stakeholders see the benefits of good project management practices, they'll never go back to the "old" way of performing their projects.

Project Management Knowledge

Project management is a growing field. Part of your responsibility as a PMP is to stay abreast of project management practices, theories, and techniques. There are many ways to do this, one of which includes joining a local PMI chapter. There are hundreds of local chapters in every state and in other countries as well. You can check the PMI website (`www.pmi.org`) to find a chapter near you.

Chapter meetings give you the opportunity to meet other project managers, find out what techniques they're using, and seek advice regarding your project. Usually guest speakers appear at each chapter meeting and share their experiences and tips. Their stories are always interesting, and they give you the opportunity to learn from someone else's experiences and avoid making wrong turns on your next project. You may have a few stories of your own worth sharing with your local chapter. Volunteer to be a speaker at an upcoming meeting and let others learn from your experiences.

One of the things you'll get when you join the PMI organization and pay your yearly dues is their monthly magazine. This details real-life projects and the techniques and issues project managers have to deal with on those projects. Reading the magazine is a great way to learn new project management techniques or reinforce the things you already know. You might discover how to apply some of the knowledge you've already learned in more efficient ways as well.

PMI offers educational courses through their local chapters and at the national level as well. These are yet another way for you to learn about project management and meet others in your field.

Honesty Is the Best Policy

We talked about honesty earlier in this chapter, but it's worth repeating: Don't mislead others regarding your experience in the project management field. The *Project Management Professional Code of Professional Conduct* requires that you honestly report your qualifications, your experience, and your past performance of services to potential employers, customers, PMI, and others.

Be honest about what you do know and what you don't know. For example, the Quality Control processes as described in the *Guide to the PMBOK* are used extensively in the manufacturing industry. However, the information technology field looks at quality issues in different ways. If you're a project manager in the information technology field, you've probably never used control charts and cause-and-effect diagramming techniques. Don't lead others to believe that you have used techniques you haven't used or that you have experience you don't have.

Emphasize the knowledge you do have and how you've used it in your specific industry and don't try to fudge it with processes and techniques you've never used. Potential clients and employers would much rather work with you and provide training where you might need it than think they've got someone fully experienced with the project or industry techniques needed for this project when they don't.

Industry Knowledge

Contributing and applying professional knowledge goes beyond project management experience. You likely have specific industry or technical experience as well. Part of applying your professional knowledge includes gaining knowledge of your particular industry and keeping others informed of advances in these areas.

Information technology has grown exponentially over the last few years. It used to be that if you specialized in network operations, for example, it was possible to learn and become proficient with all the knowledge out there related to this area. Today that is no longer the case. Each specialized area within information technology has grown to become a knowledge area in and of itself. Many other fields have either always had individual specialties or just recently experienced this phenomenon including the medical field, bioengineering, manufacturing, pharmaceuticals, and so on. You will want to stay up to date regarding your industry so that you can apply that knowledge effectively. Today's fast-paced advances can leave you behind fairly quickly if you don't stay on top of things.

I mentioned in the beginning of the book that as a project manager you are not required to be a technical expert, and that still holds true. But it doesn't hurt to stay abreast of industry trends and knowledge in your field and have a general understanding of the specifics of your business. Again, you can join industry associations, take educational classes, and so on to stay on top of breaking trends and technology in your industry.

Truthful Reporting

As a project manager, you are responsible for truthfully reporting all information in your possession to stakeholders, customers, the project sponsor, and the public. Always be up front regarding the project's progress. Nothing good will come of telling stakeholders or customers that the project is on track and everything looks great when in fact the project's behind schedule or several unplanned risks have occurred that have thrown the project team a curveball. I've personally witnessed the demise of the careers of project managers who chose this route.

Tell the truth regarding project status even when things don't look good. Stakeholders will likely go to great lengths to help you solve problems or brainstorm solutions. Sometimes, though, the call needs to be made to kill the project. This decision is usually made by the stakeholders based on your recommendation and predictions of future project activities. Don't skew the reporting to prevent stakeholders from making this decision when it is the best solution based on the circumstances.

Truthful reporting is required when working with the public as well. When working in situations where the public is at risk, truthfully report the facts of the situation and what steps you're taking to counteract or reduce the threats. I recommend you get approval from the organization regarding public announcements prior to reporting the facts. Many organizations have public relations departments that will handle this situation for you.

Complying with Laws and Regulations

This may seem obvious, but since it's part of the *Project Management Professional Code of Professional Conduct*, we'll mention it here. As a professional, you're required to follow all applicable laws and rules and regulations that apply to your industry, organization, or project. You should also follow any ethical standards and principles that may govern your industry or the state or country you're working in. Remember that rules or regulations you're used to in the United States may or may not apply to other countries and vice versa.

Respecting Confidential Information

Many project managers work for consulting firms where their services are contracted out to organizations that need their expertise for particular projects. If you work in a situation like this, you will likely come across information that is sensitive or confidential. Again, this may seem obvious, but as part of the *Project Management Professional Code of Professional Conduct*, you agree not to disclose sensitive or confidential information or use it in any way for personal gain.

Often when you work under contract, you'll be required to sign a non-disclosure agreement. This agreement simply says that you will not share information regarding the project or the organization with anyone, including the organization's competitors, or use the information for your personal gain.

However, you don't have to work on contract to come into contact with sensitive or private information. You may work full time for an organization or a government agency that deals with information regarding its customer base or citizens. For example, if you work for a bank, you may have access to personal account information. If you work for a governmental agency, you may have access to personal tax records or other sensitive material. It would be highly unethical and maybe even illegal to look up the account information of individuals not associated with the project at hand just to satisfy your own curiosity. In my organization, that is grounds for dismissal.

Don't compromise your ethics or your organization's reputation by sharing information that is confidential to the organization or would jeopardize an individual's privacy.

Company Data

While it may seem obvious that you should not use personal information or an organization's trade secrets for personal gain, sometimes the organization has a legitimate need to share information with vendors, governmental agencies, or others. You will need to determine which vendors or organizations are allowed to see sensitive company data. In some cases, you may even need to determine which individuals can have access to the data. When in doubt, ask.

Here are some examples. Maybe the company you're working with has periodic mailings they send to their customer base. If one of your project activities includes finding a new vendor to print the mailing labels, your organization may require the vendor to sign a nondisclosure agreement to guard the contents of the customer lists.

Discovering just who does have access to the information might be tricky. Another example involves data regarding citizens maintained by the government. You might think that because the data belongs to one agency of the government, say the Internal Revenue Service, any other agency of the government can have access to the data. This isn't the case. Some agencies are refused access to the data even though they may have good reason to use it. Others may have restricted access and so on depending on the data and the agency policy regarding it. Don't assume that others should have access to the data because it seems logical.

Most organizations require vendors or other organizations to sign nondisclosure agreements when giving out sensitive company data. It's your responsibility to ensure that the proper nondisclosure agreements are signed prior to releasing the data. This function is often handled by the procurement department.

Intellectual Property

You are likely to come into contact with intellectual property during the course of your project management career. Intellectual property is things developed by an organization that have commercial value but are not tangible. Intellectual property includes copyrighted material such as books, software, and artistic works. It may also include ideas or processes that are patented. Or it might involve an industrial process, business process, or manufacturing process that was developed by the organization for a specific purpose.

Intellectual property is owned by the business or person that created it. You may have to pay royalties or ask for written permission to use the property. Intellectual property should be treated just like sensitive or confidential data. It should not be used for personal gain or shared with others who should not have access to it.

Balancing Stakeholders' Interests

Projects are undertaken at the request of customers, project sponsors, executive managers, and others. Stakeholders are those who have something to gain or lose by implementing the project. As such, stakeholders have different interests and needs, and one of your jobs is to balance the needs of the stakeholders.

Customer satisfaction is probably the primary goal you're striving for in any project. If your customer is satisfied, it means you've met or exceeded their expectations and delivered the product or service they were expecting. You've got a winning combination when the customer is satisfied with the product and you've also provided excellent customer service along the way. Satisfied customers tell others about your success and will most likely use your services in the future.

One of the key ways to assure that customer satisfaction is achieved is to employ appropriate project management techniques to your project. This includes taking the time to discover all the requirements of the project and documenting them in the scope statement. You will find that stakeholders who have a clear understanding of the requirements and have signed off on them won't suffer from faulty memory and pull the ever famous "I thought that *was* included" technique. Take the time to define your requirements and get stakeholder sign-off. You can't forget or fudge what's written down.

Competing Needs

Stakeholders come from all areas of the organization and include your customer as well. Because stakeholders do not all work in the same areas, they have competing needs and interests. One stakeholder's concern might take the form of system security issues, while another stakeholder is concerned about ease of use. As the project manager, you will have situations where stakeholder needs compete with each other and you'll have to decide between them and set priorities. Sometimes you'll be able to accommodate their needs, and sometimes you'll have to choose among them. You will need to examine the needs against the project objectives and then use your negotiation and communication skills to convince the stakeholders of priorities.

Individual stakeholders may or may not have good working relationships with other stakeholders. Because of this, office politics will come into play. I advise you to stay away from the politics game, but get to know your stakeholders. You'll need to understand their business processes and needs in order to make decisions about stakeholder requirements.

Dealing with Issues and Problems

Problems will occur on your project—it's part of the process. We've talked throughout the book about how to deal with problems and risks and how to use conflict resolution techniques in handling problems. Balancing stakeholder needs comes into play here also.

You'll have to determine alternatives that will meet the key requirements of the project without jeopardizing the competing needs of other stakeholders. Once you're into the Executing process of the project and beyond, redefining scope becomes less and less of an option. So your responsibility is to resolve issues and determine alternative solutions to problems as they occur without changing the original objectives of the project. Enlist the help of your project team members and stakeholders during these times. Use some of the techniques we talked about in Chapter 6 like brainstorming and the Delphi technique to find solutions.

Another problem you might find with stakeholders is trying to make them understand your decision or the technical nature of a problem. Again, this is where communication skills help you immensely. Take the case of a technical problem that's cropped up on your project. You should not expect your stakeholder to understand the technical aspects of rocket science if they work in the finance department, for example. It's up to you to keep the explanation at a level they can understand without loading them down with technical jargon and specifications. Keep your explanations simple, yet don't skip important details they'll need to make decisions.

Balancing Constraints

Your toughest issues will almost always center on the triple constraints: time, cost, or quality. Because of the very nature of the constraints, one of these is the primary driver and one is the least important. Keep a close eye on stakeholders who want to switch the priority of the constraints for their own purposes. Let's say the project sponsor already told you that time is the primary constraint. Another stakeholder tells you that a requirement of the project is being overlooked and quality is suffering. Be careful that the stakeholder isn't trying to divert the primary constraint from time to quality to suit their own objectives.

 Real World Scenario

The Geographical Information System

Matt Loveland is a project manager for a multinational company. He's working on a complex software project that involves rewriting the organization's mainframe accounting system to become a browser-based system running on thin-client architecture. A major problem with the existing system occurs when new accounts are entered into the system or account information changes. The accounts are tied to geographic areas, which are assigned to individual sales associates. Sales commissions are paid based on where the account resides. To date, the process of determining which territory an account belongs to has been done manually by looking at a map.

The project sponsor, Victor, requested a geographical information system as part of the requirements of this project. The hope is that errors will be eliminated and commissions will get processed correctly. The sponsor is hoping that Matt's internal team can write the GIS system that will tie to the accounting system. Let's drop in on Matt and Victor's conversation.

"I just don't understand, Matt. I can go onto that Internet site and plug in an address and get directions from my house to anywhere in the country. It seems easy enough to me. Why can't your team write code like that?"

"Victor," Matt replies, "it isn't that we can't write a program to do that. But there are several issues surrounding this request that I'd like to explain to you. I'd like you to understand why I'm asking to purchase a software product from an external vendor that will take care of these functions for us."

"Let's hear it," Victor says.

"One of the first problems is that our sales force is multinational. It would take us months just to obtain address information to populate the program. The second issue is that our sales districts are not divided by any known boundaries. Most GIS systems work off of latitude and longitude or geographic boundaries like county borders or zip code boundaries."

Victor interrupts, "Well here's what we do. You give me a set of maps and I'll hand draw in the sales districts and you can take that and put it into the system."

"Unfortunately, it's just not that easy. Our sales district boundaries are not consistent with known boundaries, and our existing address database is not standardized. For example, some addresses use the word *Street* spelled out; some use the abbreviation *St.* All of the addresses need to be standardized, and then we have to figure out which addresses belong to which territory.

"This process could take a great deal of time. There are vendors that specialize in GIS systems that could have us operational in a matter of weeks. I've already checked on a couple of the top vendors, and there aren't any problems interfacing with our new system. The time we'd save in the long run far outweighs the cost associated with purchasing this system from a vendor. And one last point: If I were to build this system internally, I'd have to take our top programming team off of existing project priorities to put them on this. GIS systems are extremely complicated. We're talking several months, if not a year or more, delay to get our programmers up to speed on GIS techniques and then write the programs."

Victor says, "If we're talking about a major delay in the schedule as you say, we can at least look at what these vendors have to offer. It's important that this system is accurate as well, and I think I hear you saying, 'Why reinvent the wheel.' Let's have a look at the costs."

Respecting Differences in Diverse Cultures

You have probably taken diversity or cultural differences training classes sometime during your career. Most organizations today require diversity training for all employees and contractors. Project managers who work on contract may find themselves taking these classes multiple times as companies want to assure that every employee and contractor has taken their own company's version of the class.

I won't attempt to repeat diversity training here but will point out some of the things you should know about working in other countries and about working with people who have backgrounds and belief systems that are different than yours.

Global Competition

More and more companies compete in the global marketplace. As a result, project managers with multinational experience are increasing in demand. This requires a heightened awareness of cultural influences and customary practices of the country where you're temporarily residing.

One thing I've witnessed when working in foreign countries is U.S. citizens who try to force their own culture or customs on those whom they're visiting or working with. That isn't recommended, and it generally offends those you're trying to impress. Don't expect others to conform to your way of doing things, especially when you're in their country. You know the saying, "When in Rome, do as the Romans do"? While you may not want to take that literally, the intent is good. For example, a quick kiss on both cheeks is a customary greeting in many countries. If that is the case and it's how you're greeted, respond with the same.

Culture Shock

Working in a foreign country can bring about an experience called culture shock. When you've spent years acting certain ways and expecting normal, everyday events to follow a specific course of action, you might find yourself disoriented when things don't go as you expected. This is known as culture shock.

One of the ways you can avoid this is to read about the country you're going to work in before getting there. The Internet is a great resource for information like this. Your local library is another place to research customs and acceptable practices in foreign countries.

When in doubt about a custom or what you should do in a given situation, ask your hosts or a trusted contact from the company you'll be working with to help you out. People are people all over the world, and they love to talk about themselves and their culture. They're also generally helpful and will respect you more for asking what's expected rather than acting as though you know what to do when you clearly do not.

Respecting Your Neighbors

Americans tend to run their lives at high speed and get right down to business when working with vendors or customers. It isn't unusual for a business person to board a plane in the morning, show up at the client site and take care of business, and hop another flight home that night.

You'll find that many other countries are not this way. People in other countries will expect you to take time to get to know them first, building an atmosphere of trust and respect. Some cultures build relationships first and then proceed to business. And don't expect to do that relationship building in a few hours. It could take a day or days depending on the culture. They may even want you to meet their family and spend time getting to know each other. Resist the urge to get right down to business if that's not customary in that culture because you'll likely spoil the deal or damage relationships past the point of repair.

Spend time building relationships with others. Once an atmosphere of mutual trust and cooperation is established, all aspects of project planning and management including negotiating and problem solving are much easier to navigate.

Training

Sometimes you may find yourself working with teams of people from different countries or cultures. Some team members might be from one country and some from another. The best way to assure that cultural or ethical differences do not hinder your project is to provide training for all team members.

Team-building activities are a method of building mutual trust and respect and of bonding team members with differing backgrounds. Choose activities that are nonoffensive and where everyone can participate.

Diversity training makes people aware of differences between cultures and ethnic groups, and it helps them to gain respect and trust for those on their team. Provide training regarding the project objectives and the company culture as well. Project objectives are why you are all together in the first place. They cut across cultural bounds and keep everyone focused on the project and tasks at hand.

Perceiving Experiences

All of us see the world through our own experiences. Your experiences are not someone else's experiences, and therefore what you perceive about a situation might be very different from what others believe. Keep this in mind when it appears that a misunderstanding has occurred or that someone you're working with didn't respond as you expected. This is especially true when you're working with someone from another country. Always give others the benefit of the doubt and ask for clarification if you think there is a problem. Put your feelings in check temporarily and remember that what you think the other person means is not necessarily as it appears due to cultural differences.

Project Case Study: New Kitchen Heaven Retail Store

Jill Overstreet thought you did such a great job of managing this project that she's offered to buy you lunch at one of those upscale, white table cloth–type French restaurants. The iced teas have just been delivered, and you and Jill are chatting about business.

"I'm impressed with your project management skills. This store opening was the best on record. And you really kept Dirk in line—I admire that. He can be headstrong, but you had a way of convincing him what needed doing and then sticking to it."

"Thanks," you reply. "I've got a few years of project management experience, so many of those lessons learned on previous projects helped me out with this project. I enjoy project management and read books and articles on the subject whenever I get the chance. It's nice when you can learn from others' mistakes and avoid making them yourself."

Jill takes a long drink of tea. She glances at you over the top of her glass and pauses before setting it down. The look on her face implies she's sizing you up and deciding whether to tell you what's on her mind.

"You know," Jill starts, "we almost didn't hire anyone for your position. Dirk wanted to do away with the project management role altogether. He had a real distaste for project management after our last project."

"Why is that?"

Jill explains, "The last project manager got involved in a conflict of interest situation. She was working on a project that involved updating and remodeling all the existing stores. Things like new fixtures, signs, shelving, display cases, and such were up for bid. And it was a very sizable bid. Not only did she accept an all-expenses-paid weekend visit to a resort town from one of the vendors bidding on the contract, she also revealed company secrets to them, some of which leaked to our competitors."

Your mouth drops open. "I can't believe she would accept gifts like that from a vendor. And revealing company secrets is almost worse. Conflict of interest situations and not protecting intellectual property violate the code of professional conduct that certified PMPs agree to adhere to. I can understand why Dirk didn't want to hire another project manager. Behavior like that makes all project managers look bad."

"I'm glad you kept things above board and won Dirk back over. The project management role is important to Kitchen Heaven, and I know your skills in this discipline are what made this project such a success."

"Jill, not only would I never compromise my own integrity through a conflict of interest situation, I would report the situation and the vendor to the project sponsor. It's better to be honest and let the project sponsor or key stakeholders know what's happening than to hide the situation or, even worse, compromise your own integrity by getting involved in it in the first place. You have my word that I'll keep business interests above my own personal interests. I'll report anything that even looks like it would call my actions into question just to keep things honest and out in the open."

"That's good to hear," Jill replies. "Congratulations on your new assignment. Dirk and I were discussing the new Home Chef Pro project yesterday. We're venturing into new territory with this project, and I'm confident you'll do an excellent job heading it up. Dirk made a good choice."

Project Case Study Checklist

Ensuring personal and professional integrity

Adhering to the *Project Management Professional Code of Professional Conduct*

Not placing personal gain above business needs

Avoiding conflict of interest situations

Truthfully reporting questionable situations and maintaining honesty

Protecting intellectual property

Summary

Project Management Professionals are responsible for reporting truthful information about their PMP status and project management experience to prospective customers, clients, and employers and to PMI. As a project manager, you're responsible for the integrity of the project management process and the product. In all situations, you are responsible for your own personal integrity.

Personal integrity means adhering to an ethical standard. As a PMP, you'll be required to adhere to the *Project Management Professional Code of Professional Conduct* established by PMI. Part of this code involves avoiding putting your own personal gain above the project objectives.

As a professional, you should strive to maintain honesty in project reporting. You'll be required to abide by laws, rules, and regulations regarding your industry and project management practices. You should also report any instances that might appear to be a conflict of interest. It's always better to inform others of an apparent conflict than to have it discovered by others and your methods called into question after the fact.

You will very likely come across confidential information or intellectual property during your project management experiences. Respect the use of this information and always verify who may have permission to access the information and when disclosures are required.

Stakeholders have competing needs and business issues and as such will sometimes cause conflict on your project. You will be required to balance the needs and interests of the stakeholders with the project objectives.

Many project managers today are working in a global environment. It's important to respect and understand the cultural differences that exist and not try to impose your cultural beliefs onto others. Culture shock is an experience that occurs when you find yourself in a different cultural environment than you're familiar with. Training is a good way to provide project team members with relationship management techniques regarding cultural and ethnic differences.

Exam Essentials

Be able to define integrity.   Adhering to an ethical standard.

Be able to name the ethical standard PMPs are required to adhere to.
Project Management Professional Code of Professional Conduct.

Be able to describe the areas in which PMPs must apply professional knowledge.   Project management practices, industry practices, and technical areas.

Be able to name the key activity that assures customer satisfaction.
Documenting project requirements.

Be able to define how multinational project managers must manage relationships.   By building relationships based on mutual trust and acceptance and recognizing and respecting diverse cultures and ethnic beliefs.

Key Terms

Before you take the exam, be certain you are familiar with the following terms:

conflict of interest

Project Management Professional Code of Professional Conduct

Review Questions

1. As a project manager, you're responsible for maintaining and ensuring integrity for all of the following except:

   A. Personal integrity of others

   B. Project management process

   C. Personal integrity

   D. Product integrity

2. You are a project manager working on contract. You've performed earned value analysis and discovered that the project will be completed on time and under the original estimated amount. This means the profit to your company will decrease as will your personal bonus. Which of the following should you do?

   A. Add activities to the project to increase the cost enough to meet the original estimated amount.

   B. Tell the customer you're adding additional requirements to the project that were originally cut because of cost constraints.

   C. Upon completion inform the customer the project has come in under budget.

   D. Bill the customer for the full amount of the contract as this was the original agreed-upon price.

3. Integrity in the project management field is accomplished through all of the following except:

   A. Training to learn how to manage relationships with others from different cultures

   B. Adhering to an ethical code

   C. Applying established project management processes

   D. Following the *Project Management Professional Code of Professional Conduct*

4. You are a project manager for a manufacturing firm that produces Civil War–era replicas and memorabilia. You discover a design error during a test production run on your latest project. Which of the following is the most likely response to this problem?

   A. Reduce the technical requirements so that the error is no longer valid.

   B. Go forward with production and ignore the error.

   C. Go forward with production but inform the customer of the problem.

   D. Develop alternative solutions to address the error.

5. You are a project manager for a telecommunications firm. You're working on a project that entails upgrading technical hardware and equipment. The estimated cost of the hardware and equipment is $1,725,000. You are reviewing products from three different vendors. One of the vendors invites you to lunch. What is the most appropriate response?

   A. Thank them but let them know this could be a conflict of interest since you haven't made a decision about which vendor you're going to choose.

   B. Thank them and decline. You know this could be considered personal gain, which could call your integrity into question.

   C. Thank them and accept. You don't believe there is a conflict of interest or a personal integrity issue.

   D. Thank them and decline. You believe this could be a conflict of interest on the part of the vendor, and you don't want to encourage that behavior.

6. You are a project manager for a telecommunications firm. You're working on a project that entails upgrading technical hardware and equipment. The estimated cost of the hardware and equipment is $1,725,000. You are reviewing products from three different vendors. One of the vendors offers you and your family the use of the company yacht for the upcoming three-day weekend. What is the most appropriate response?

A. Thank them and accept. You don't believe there is a conflict of interest or an integrity issue at stake.

B. Thank them and decline. You know this could be considered personal gain, which could call your integrity into question.

C. Thank them and accept. Immediately report your actions to the project sponsor so that your motives are not called into question after the fact.

D. Thank them and decline. You know this could be considered an integrity issue on the part of the vendor.

7. You are a project manager working on contract with a company in a foreign country. At the project kick-off meeting, you are given an expensive-looking gift. The person who presented this to you said that it is customary in their country to give their business partners gifts. What is the most appropriate response?

A. Thank them and decline. Explain that this is considered personal gain, which is unacceptable in your country.

B. Thank them and accept. You don't believe there is a conflict of interest or an integrity issue at stake.

C. Thank them and decline. Explain that this is considered a conflict of interest, which is unacceptable in your country.

D. Thank them and accept since you know that it would be considered offensive to decline the gift in their culture. Immediately report the acceptance of the gift to the appropriate parties at your company so that your actions are not called into question later.

8. You are a project manager and are in the Closing processes of the project. Your customer has been presented with a formal acceptance and sign-off document. They refuse to sign, claiming the product does not meet their expectations. You know that this situation could have been prevented by doing all of the following except:

    A. Documenting the requirements

    B. Documenting the customer's refusal to sign

    C. Performing quality inspections during the process

    D. Requesting sign-off at important milestones

9. As a project manager, you know that the most important activity to ensure customer and stakeholder satisfaction is which of the following:

    A. Documenting the requirements

    B. Documenting the performance measurements

    C. Reporting changes and updating the project plan and other project documents where appropriate

    D. Reporting project status timely and regularly

10. As a PMP, you will be required to comply with the *Project Management Professional Code of Professional Conduct*. This code refers to all of the following except:

    A. Reporting conflicts of interest

    B. Reporting experience and PMP status truthfully

    C. Complying with stakeholder requirements

    D. Complying with rules and policies of foreign countries

11. You are a contract project manager working with the State of Bliss. Your latest project involves rewriting the Department of Revenue's income tax system. One of the key stakeholders is a huge movie buff, and she has the power to promote you into a better position at the conclusion of this project. She's discovered that one of her favorite superstars lives in the State of Bliss and therefore must file income tax returns in that state. She asks you to look up the account of this movie star. What is the most appropriate response?

A. Report her to the management team.

B. Refuse to comply with the request, citing conflict of interest and violation of confidential company data.

C. Look up the information she's requested. Since the data is considered part of the project, there is no conflict of interest.

D. You believe that tax records are public information, so you comply with the request.

12. You are a contract project manager working with the State of Bliss. Your latest project involves rewriting the Department of Revenue's income tax system. As project manager, you have taken all the appropriate actions regarding confidentiality of data. One of the key stakeholders is a huge movie buff, and she has the power to promote you into a better position at the conclusion of this project. She's reviewing some report data that just happens to include confidential information regarding one of her favorite movie superstars. What is the most appropriate response?

A. Report her to the management team.

B. Request that she immediately return the information, citing conflict of interest and violation of confidential company data.

C. Do nothing as she has the proper level of access rights to the data and this information showed up unintentionally.

D. Request that she immediately return the information until you can confirm that she has the proper level of access rights to the data.

13. As a PMP, you will be required to comply with the *Project Management Professional Code of Professional Conduct*. Part of your responsibility concerns applying professional knowledge. All of the following are part of applying professional knowledge except:

    A. Developing relationships based on mutual respect

    B. Staying abreast of project management practices

    C. Keeping up with industry trends and new technology

    D. Honestly reporting your project management experience

14. You are a project manager with several years of experience in project management. You've just accepted your first project in a foreign country. You've been in the country a week or two and are experiencing some disoriented feelings. This is known as:

    A. Collocation

    B. Diversity shock

    C. Global culturing

    D. Culture shock

15. You are a project manager for a software manufacturing firm. The project you've just finished created a new software product that is expected to become a number-one seller. A friend of yours is a certified software instructor. They have asked you for a copy of the software prior to the beta release through the marketing department so they can get familiar with it. What is the most appropriate response?

    A. Since your friend is certified to teach your company's brand of software, provide them with a copy of the software.

    B. Ask them to sign a nondisclosure agreement before releasing a copy of the software.

    C. Decline the request since you stand to gain from this transaction by receiving free training.

    D. Decline the request because the software is the intellectual property of the company.

16. Your upcoming project includes project team members from a foreign country. In order to make certain that cultural differences don't interfere with team performance, thereby affecting the success of the project, your first course of action is to do which of the following:

A. Provide diversity training to all the team members.

B. Collocate the project team.

C. Perform team-building exercises.

D. Inform the team members of the organization's rules and standards.

17. You are a project manager for Pizza Direct, which is a retail pizza delivery store. Your company is competing with another retail store for the option of opening two new stores in a foreign country. You have been invited to dinner with the prospective foreign business partners and their spouses upon your arrival. You know that all of the following are generally true except:

A. You should spend time building relationships with your prospective foreign business partners before getting down to business.

B. You should explain your company's rules, standards, and operating policies at your first meeting with the prospective foreign business partners.

C. You should build an atmosphere of mutual trust and cooperation.

D. You should respect the cultural differences you'll encounter when working with your prospective foreign business partners.

18. You are a project manager for Pizza Direct, which is a retail pizza delivery store. Your company is competing with another retail store for the option of opening two new stores in a foreign country. You've been told that it is culturally unacceptable to eat certain foods in this country. You know that one of these foods happens to be a secret ingredient in the pizza sauce. What is the most appropriate response?

    A. Inform the potential partners that your sauce recipe is secret, but you're certain there are no forbidden ingredients in it.

    B. Inform the potential partners that you suspect there might be a forbidden ingredient in the sauce and you'll request an investigation to determine if any of them exist in the sauce.

    C. Inform the potential partners that a forbidden ingredient exists in the sauce and determine to work with them to come up with another ingredient to replace that one.

    D. Don't tell the potential partners about the ingredient because the sauce they'll be using in the stores is shipped to them already prepared in cans. They won't know the ingredient is in the sauce.

19. You are a project manager for Pizza Direct, which is a retail pizza delivery store. Your company is competing with another retail store for the option of opening two new stores in a foreign country. You know, but have not yet informed your company, that you are going to go to work for the competitor, which happens to be bidding for this same opportunity. What is the most appropriate response?

    A. You decline to participate in the initial meetings with the foreign business partners due to conflict of interest.

    B. You've not yet received an official offer from the competing company for your new job opportunity, so you choose to participate in the initial meetings with the foreign business partners.

    C. You decide to participate in the initial meetings with the foreign business partners because any information you gain now will help you when you make the move to the new company.

    D. You inform the foreign business partners that you're going to be working with a new company and that you know the deal they'll receive from the competing company is better than the one this company is proposing.

20. You are the project manager for a new construction project in your city. Your longtime personal friend is bidding on the project. They've asked you to give them an indication of the budget for this project so that they do not overbid and lose the deal. What is the most appropriate response?

    A. Give the information to your friend. You know their character and can trust that they won't tell anyone.

    B. Tell your friend that after all this time, they should know you better than to think you'd put your personal integrity on the line or compromise your job due to a conflict of interest. Decline to give them the information.

    C. Tell your friend you'll give them the information if they'll promise not to tell anyone and if they'll agree to help you out with some materials on your basement-refinishing project.

    D. Give the information to your friend and inform the project sponsor so that the information can be shared with the other bidders as well.

Answers to Review Questions

1. A. You are not responsible for the personal integrity of others, but as project manager you do have influence over others such as your project team members.

2. C. Integrity means you'll honestly report project outcomes and status. Your personal gain should not be placed above the satisfaction of the customer.

3. A. Diversity training is used to help you manage project teams that are made up of people from other countries or cultures. Integrity is accomplished by following an ethical code and applying project management practices.

4. D. The best answer to this problem is to develop alternative solutions to address design error. Reducing technical requirements might be an alternative solution, but it's not one you'd implement without looking at all the alternatives. Ignoring the error and going forward with production would result in an unsatisfactory product for the customer.

5. A. A luncheon date could be considered a conflict of interest prior to awarding a contract to a vendor. Consider what a competitor of this vendor would think if they spotted you having lunch together.

6. B. The best response to this situation is to thank the vendor and decline based on the fact that this could be considered personal gain on your part. Answer D may seem correct, but remember you're not responsible for the integrity of others. And it's often common business practice for vendors to offer gifts to potential customers.

7. D. The best response in this case is to accept the gift because it would cause great offense to the other party if you were to decline. Report the gift and the circumstances as soon as possible to the appropriate parties at your company.

8. B. Documenting the requirements, performing inspections, and requesting acceptance and sign-off at important milestones are all acceptable ways to assure customer satisfaction.

9. A. Documenting the requirements is one of the key things you can do to assure customer satisfaction. The requirements describe what the customer is looking for, and the final product is compared against them to determine if all of the requirements were met.

10. C. Stakeholder requirements are needed to determine if the project is successful and are not a part of the professional code.

11. B. The situation presented here requires you to put the interest of the company and the confidentiality of the data above your own personal interests or those of your stakeholders. Answer D is not the most correct response as it says you believe the information is public. This implies you haven't verified whether the data is private or public. Until you know, treat the data as confidential. In this case, the information is confidential and should be shared only with those who have a valid reason for using it.

12. C. As project manager, it's your responsibility to make sure the people you will be sharing data with have the proper permissions to see the data. In this case, answer D is not correct as it implies you did not verify ahead of time that the stakeholder had the proper level of approvals to use the data.

13. A. Applying professional knowledge involves staying abreast of project management practices, industry trends, and new technology and honestly reporting your experiences.

14. D. Culture shock is the disoriented feeling that people may experience when working in a foreign country.

15. D. The most appropriate response is to deny the request. Software is considered intellectual property and should not be used for personal gain or given to others without prior consent from the organization. This question states that the release of the beta software is handled through the marketing department, so you should not give your friend a copy of the software outside of this process.

16. A. The most correct response is to first provide training to your team members to teach them how to respect and work with others from different cultures. Collocation may not be possible when you're working with team members from two different countries. Team-building exercises are a good idea as well but are not your first course of action.

17. B. Your first meeting with foreign partners should be spent getting to know them. Many cultures like to spend time building relationships first and then talking business. Since you've been invited to dinner upon your arrival and the dinner includes the spouses of your prospective partners, chances are they want to spend some time getting to know you personally first.

18. C. The most appropriate response is to inform the potential partners that an ingredient exists in the sauce that is not acceptable and determine to come up with a solution to the problem. As a professional, you're required to be honest in your reporting. Not telling them, or stalling by promising an investigation, is not an honest response.

19. A. The most appropriate response is to decline to participate due to a conflict of interest.

20. B. This situation is clearly a conflict of interest and should be avoided. Decline to provide your friend this information.

Appendix

A

Practice Exam

Practice Exam

1. You are going to take some performance measurements for your current project. You know that PV = 450, AC = 500, and EV = 375. What is the CV and SV respectively?

   A. CV = 125, and SV = 75.

   B. CV = –75, and SV = –125.

   C. CV = 75, and SV = 125.

   D. CV = –125, and SV = –75.

2. You are the project manager for a software consulting firm that is working on developing a new software program for a customer in another country. Things seem to be progressing well. Recently, your stakeholders examined the work of the project and formally accepted the work results. Which process was just performed?

   A. Scope Verification

   B. Quality Assurance

   C. Performance Reporting

   D. Quality Control

3. You are a project manager for Candy Works candy factory. Your project involves reporting information from the newly installed candy-counting machine to the financial system. This will give executives the ability to see production run counts at any time during the day. The project sponsor has promised you a bonus if you get this project completed two weeks sooner than the scheduled project end date. The bonus will come in handy on your trip to the Bahamas planned for later this spring. You've got a few remaining project activities to wrap up before you can close out the project. Which of the following is the most appropriate response?

   A. You tell the sponsor the project is complete and treat the remaining activities as though they're problems that came up after project closure so that you can still get the bonus.

   B. You tell the sponsor the remaining activities are outside the scope of the project so the project really is completed and collect your bonus.

   C. You tell the sponsor the stakeholders added these requirements after the project was well under way and you never agreed to include them in the project so the project really is complete, and you collect your bonus.

   D. You tell the sponsor you aren't going to make the two-week early completion date as there are remaining activities to finish up.

4. You've reached a state of independence where you're able to express yourself and perform at your peak level of performance. Being the best you can be is the motivator that drives you. Which of the following is true?

   A. This is an example of the Expectancy theory.

   B. You've reached self-actualization in Maslow's Hierarchy.

   C. This is an example of the Hygiene theory.

   D. You've reached the highest level of the Achievement theory.

5. Intellectual property includes all of the following except:

   A. Software

   B. Patents

   C. Hardware

   D. Business processes

6. The project manager, stakeholders, and project team members all have roles and responsibilities throughout the project. As the project manager, you might link the project scope definition to the project roles and indicate which activities each person will participate in. You might display this information in which of the following ways:

   A. PDM

   B. RAM

   C. SOW

   D. RRM

7. During a recent team meeting, you reached a resolution to a problem that's been troubling the team for several weeks. You took responsibility for searching out the facts of this problem and uncovered the right answer to this problem. You presented the facts at the project status meeting, and everyone reached agreement on the recommended solution based on the facts you presented. This is an example of what type of conflict resolution technique?

   A. Compromise

   B. Smoothing

   C. Confrontation

   D. Forcing

8. You are a project manager for Capella Systems. Your company writes custom software for accounting and financial systems for medium- to large-sized corporations. Your recent project has experienced some setbacks, and you've been forced to rework the design of one of the programs because it doesn't match the customer's requirements. Since some parts of the program have already been written, it will have to be rewritten so that it matches the design changes. This rework has increased costs, and you're beginning to notice some signs of poor morale because of the rework. Which of the following is true?

A. The problems occurred because the WBS was not constructed properly.

B. The quality assurance plan was carried out correctly, which is how the design problems were discovered.

C. The problems occurred as a result of poor scope definition.

D. The Risk Management Planning process details these kinds of risks and the responses you should put into place should they occur.

9. You are a project manager for a network cabling project for your organization. Your project team is made up of six full-time employees and three contractors. This is the first time they have all worked together. This project requires accurate information exchange at all times during the life of the project. How many lines of communication exist among the project team members?

A. 36

B. 41

C. 18

D. 34

10. You are a project manager for Candy Works candy factory. Your project involves reporting information from the newly installed candy-counting machine to the financial system. This will give executives the ability to see production run counts at any time during the day. You need to purchase an expensive piece of hardware as part of this project. One of the vendors bidding on the project is a close friend. In order to win the bid, she needs to know how much money the company is willing to spend on the equipment and consulting. Your friend asks you to give her this confidential information and not tell anyone you did. Which of the following is the most appropriate response?

A. Tell your friend that as a PMP, you're required to abide by the *Project Management Professional Code of Professional Conduct* and this would violate the code as it's a conflict of interest.

B. Tell your friend that as a PMP, you're required to abide by the *Project Management Professional Code of Professional Conduct* and this would violate the code as it's a personal gain.

C. Tell your friend that as a PMP, you're required to abide by the *Project Management Professional Standards and Ethics Code* and this would violate the code as it's a conflict of interest.

D. Tell your friend that as a PMP, you're required to abide by the *Project Management Professional Standards and Ethics Code* and this would violate the code as it's an ethics violation.

11. Which of the following describes a unique characteristic of the project Executing and Controlling processes?

   A. The core processes in the Executing and Controlling processes are from the Project Integration knowledge area.

   B. Both the Executing and Controlling processes measure variances in project performance and use corrective action to bring performance back in line with the plan.

   C. Executing is an input to the Controlling processes, and Controlling is an input to Execution.

   D. Executing and Controlling each have only one core process.

12. You are preparing a cash flow analysis for a project the company is considering undertaking. The project's cost is $525,000, and expected cash inflows are $125,000 the first year and then $75,000 per quarter the second year and $100,000 per quarter after that. What is the payback period?

   A. 16 months

   B. 27 months

   C. 32 months

   D. 28 months

13. You are going to take some performance measurements for your current project. You know that PV = 450, AC = 500, and EV = 375. What is the CPI and SPI respectively?

A. CPI = .90, and SPI = 1.2.

B. CPI = .75, and SPI = .83.

C. CPI = 1.2, and SPI = .90.

D. CPI = .83, and SPI = .75.

14. All of the following are true regarding the Executing processes except:

A. Executing has one core process.

B. The majority of the project budget is spent here.

C. The greatest conflicts are schedule conflicts.

D. Project performance is measured to identify variances.

15. You are a project manager for a network cabling project for your organization. Your project team is made up of six full-time employees and three contractors. This is the first time they have all worked together. You know that the team will go through the stages of team development in the following order:

A. Forming, storming, norming, and performing

B. Storming, norming, forming, and performing

C. Norming, storming, forming, and performing

D. Forming, norming, storming, and performing

16. All of the following are tools and techniques of the Quality Control process except:

A. Monte Carlo Analysis

B. Statistical sampling

C. Pareto diagrams

D. Trend analysis

17. You are a project manager working for Mail House King. Your company processes orders for several mail-order catalog companies. Your project is to install new mail-sorting equipment and software. You've had some problems and experienced some variances so far during the project. You do not expect these variances to continue as they're atypical. Your project sponsor has asked for an EAC. You know the following information: PV = 800, BAC = 700, EV = 675, AC = 750, and ETC = 30. Which of the following is the correct EAC given the circumstances?

    A. 25

    B. 760

    C. 775

    D. 833

18. You are working on a project and are in the Quality Planning process. You know that if the customer requirements are not satisfied while the product is still in the control of the organization, it may result in corrective action, rework, scrapping, and downtime. Which of the following is true regarding the cost of quality?

    A. Cost of quality is an output of this process, and this is an internal failure cost.

    B. Cost of quality is a tool and technique of this process, and this is a prevention cost.

    C. Cost of quality is an output of this process, and this is a prevention cost.

    D. Cost of quality is a tool and technique of this process, and this is an internal failure cost.

19. You are the project manager for your company's annual Spring Fling. You've made all the plans and reserved the outdoor grounds for the appropriate day and time. You are now two days away from the big day, and the forecast is calling for light rain showers in the afternoon. You rented tents just in case this risk occurred. This is an example of which Risk Response Planning tool and technique?

A. Passive acceptance

B. Contingency planning

C. Avoidance

D. Transference

20. You are a project manager who believes people will always perform at their best if given the proper expectations and motivation. Which theory do you subscribe to?

A. Theory X

B. Hygiene theory

C. Contingency theory

D. Theory Y

21. The tools and techniques of Source Selection include all of the following except:

A. Contract negotiation

B. Work authorization system

C. Weighting systems

D. Independent estimates

22. You are an international project manager from the United States living in a foreign country. The project you're working on has lasted two-and-a-half years. During that time, you've really gotten to feel comfortable in the foreign country and have enjoyed living in their culture. The project has just ended, and you've returned to the United States. Upon your return, you're surprised to find that you're feeling a little disoriented as you've gotten so used to the foreign culture and its slower pace that you've forgotten what some things are like in the US. This experience is known as:

    A. Diversity shock

    B. Global norming

    C. Culture shock

    D. Culture norming

23. Which performance measurement is the cost of work budgeted for an activity within a certain time frame?

    A. AC

    B. PV

    C. EV

    D. EAC

24. You are a project manager for Uncle Sam's Flag Company. Your company has designed a new line of products featuring the American flag. Due to some unique circumstances, the products are in hot demand and the project sponsor has asked you to do whatever it takes to get this project completed early and make the products available. You regularly check the progress of the project with your team members using which of the following techniques?

    A. E-mail communication

    B. Status review meetings

    C. Project management information systems

    D. Receiver communication model

25. What is the process in the Executing process group that determines if the project satisfies quality standards, identifies lessons learned, and reviews quality management activities to verify the correct quality elements are being examined?

A. Quality Control

B. Quality Monitoring and Control

C. Quality Assurance

D. Scope Verification

26. You are a project manager for Snow Fun, a chain of retail shops specializing in winter sports gear and clothing. You've been working on contract with Snow Fun and are ready to move on to your next assignment. As the project manager, you know all of the following are true regarding the project Closing processes except:

A. Administrative Closure is always required at the close of the project.

B. The Closing processes are the most often skipped processes.

C. Administrative Closure should occur prior to Contract Closeout.

D. Both Closing processes verify that the work and product of the project were completed satisfactorily.

27. You are a project manager for Cashiers Systems. Your company produces cashiering systems and software for the retail industry. Your customer has requested a change that will change the characteristics of the cashiering system. You've described the characteristics of the cashiering system using this tool and technique of the Integrated Change Control process:

A. Product description

B. Product analysis

C. Decomposition

D. Configuration management

28. The lowest level of the WBS is called what?

    A. Code of accounts

    B. Requirement

    C. Milestone

    D. Work package

29. Your organization regularly uses a tool and technique of the Contract Closeout process to identify lessons learned, including the successes and failures, which will benefit future activity on this project and on future projects. Which tool and technique are they using?

    A. Product documentation inspection

    B. Contract process review

    C. Performance measurement review

    D. Procurement audit

30. You are a project manager for Safari Outfitters. Your company is going to offer a new product line in the upcoming spring catalog. Your project team has 10 months to secure contracts with suppliers, finalize the designs, get the product into the catalog, and stock the warehouse. This is an example of:

    A. An assumption because the project team has worked on projects like this before and know they can meet the 10-month deadline

    B. An assumption because the project team has a limited amount of time to complete the project

    C. A constraint because the project team has a limited amount of time to complete the project

    D. A constraint because the project team is working with a new product line that hasn't been developed before

31. What is the name of the unplanned response used to deal with negative risk events in the Risk Monitoring and Control process?

   A. Mitigation

   B. Contingency plans

   C. Workarounds

   D. Corrective action

32. You are ready to perform the Activity Sequencing process for your project. To make your job easier, you're going to use a software tool to help you draw a PDM network diagram. Most software programs use this technique. You know all of the following are true regarding the PDM except:

   A. It shows the activities on arrows and connects them to dependencies usually depicted as circles.

   B. It's also called AON.

   C. It shows the activities in boxes with arrows connecting the dependent activities.

   D. It uses four types of dependency relationships of which finish to start is one.

33. Project managers have the greatest amount of authority in which kind of organizational structure?

   A. Functional

   B. Projectized

   C. Weak matrix

   D. Balanced matrix

34. You are a project manager for Snow Fun, a chain of retail shops specializing in winter sports gear and clothing. You've been working on contract with Snow Fun and are ready to move on to your next assignment. The customer has signed off on the project, formal acceptance notices have been distributed, and project closure procedures have been performed. What type of project ending is this?

    A. Extinction

    B. Starvation

    C. Integration

    D. Addition

35. Brainstorming and the Delphi technique are two types of information-gathering techniques found in which process?

    A. Risk Management Planning

    B. Risk Response Control

    C. Risk Identification

    D. Quantitative Risk Analysis

36. You are a project manager working for Mail House King. Your company processes orders for several mail-order catalog companies. Your project is to install new mail-sorting equipment and software. You've had some problems and experienced some variances so far during the project. You expect these variances to continue throughout the life of the project. Your project sponsor has asked for an EAC. You know the following information: PV = 800, BAC = 700, EV = 675, AC = 750, and ETC = 30. Which of the following is the correct EAC given the circumstances?

    A. 778

    B. 780

    C. 861

    D. 833

37. What is the key activity during Contract Closeout and Administrative Closure?

   A. Documenting lessons learned

   B. Creating project archives

   C. Disseminating information to formalize project closure

   D. Documenting project closure

38. You know that change control systems are important as they describe how to submit change requests and document how to manage the change, track the status, and determine the management impacts of the change. Each of the following processes in the Controlling process group uses a change control system as one of its tools and techniques except:

   A. Integrated Change Control

   B. Quality Control

   C. Scope Change Control

   D. Schedule Control

39. You are in the Planning process of your project, and your project sponsor has requested an accurate cost estimate in two weeks from today. You'll use which of the following techniques to provide her with the most accurate cost estimate?

   A. Bottom-up

   B. Analogous

   C. Top-down

   D. Earned value

40. The Critical Path Method is a mathematical tool and technique of the Schedule Development process. All of the following are true regarding CPM except:

    A. Determines a single early and late start date and a single early and late finish date

    B. Calculates expected value

    C. Focuses on the calculation of float time

    D. Shows the critical path, or the path with the longest duration

41. You are a project manager working in the automotive industry. You are performing quality control and decide to rank order the frequency of problem occurrences over time using which of the following:

    A. Control chart

    B. Pareto diagram

    C. Cause-and-effect diagram

    D. Scatter diagram

42. You are developing your project schedule and have decided to use the PERT method to determine project duration. The estimates you've gathered so far include the following: Most likely is 200 hours, optimistic is 180 hours, and pessimistic is 220 hours. Which of the following is the correct PERT estimate?

    A. 190

    B. 266

    C. 200

    D. 210

43. You are a project manager for Uncle Sam's Flag Company. Your company has designed a new line of products featuring the American flag. Due to some unique circumstances, the products are in hot demand and the project sponsor has asked you to do whatever it takes to get this project completed early and make the products available. You decide to eliminate some of the requirements that are not critical and to add resources to the project. The sponsor agrees to pay the additional costs since time is now a critical factor. Which technique have you used?

   A. Crashing

   B. Resource leveling

   C. Fast tracking

   D. Resource loading

44. You've just accepted a new project management assignment. The project is for a customer in a foreign country. You've requested a business analyst and two other project team members from the country the customer resides in to participate on your team. The remaining team members are from your country. You know that the best way to ensure the project team doesn't get bogged down in cultural differences and hold up project progress is to:

   A. Perform team-building exercises using videoconferencing to allow team members to get to know each other and get to the performing stage of team development as soon as possible.

   B. Provide diversity training for all the team members to make them aware of cultural differences and teach them to function effectively as a team despite these differences.

   C. Establish your role as project manager as the first order of business and require compliance to company policies.

   D. Require project team members to read and sign the organization's diversity policy.

45. You are a project manager for Cashiers Systems. Your company produces cashiering systems and software for the retail industry. Your customer has requested a change to the product. You will handle this change using the scope change control system. All of the following are true except:

    A. Changes to product scope should be reflected in project scope.

    B. Project scope changes may result in adjustments to the performance measurement baselines.

    C. Changes to project scope should be reflected in the product scope.

    D. Scope changes may result in performance improvements.

46. You are the project manager for a nonprofit organization. Your project has come about due to a social need. Your sponsor wants to get right to the Planning process. However, you know that a scope statement should be published prior to proceeding to the Planning processes. All of the following are true regarding scope statements except:

    A. It documents roles and responsibilities.

    B. It can be modified to reflect changes to the scope of the project.

    C. It describes the project deliverables, requirements, and objectives of the project.

    D. It serves as a baseline for future project decisions.

47. Which of the following processes involves receiving bids and proposals and applies evaluation criteria to the proposals to rank order the sequence of award?

    A. Contract Administration

    B. Procurement

    C. Source Selection

    D. Solicitation

48. You are the project manager for a nonprofit organization. Your project has come about due to a social need. Your sponsor wants to get right to the Planning process. However, you know that a project charter should be published prior to proceeding to the Planning processes. All of the following are true regarding project charters except:

   A. Project charters always include cost and time estimates.

   B. B. Project charters always include the product description and business need for the product.

   C. Project charters recognize and acknowledge the existence of the project.

   D. Project charters commit organizational resources to the project.

49. During contract negotiations, your vendor tells you that the equipment originally bid in the RFP is no longer available. They say the best solution is to buy the new equipment they're offering, which is a higher price than the original equipment. You have concerns that the new equipment might not be compatible with existing equipment and try to discuss this with them. They remind you that this decision was already made during the last contract negotiation meeting so there's no need to continue to discuss it. This is an example of which of the following?

   A. Proposal

   B. Compromise

   C. Storming

   D. Fait accompli

50. Lessons learned are used for all of the following except:

   A. To provide historical information that you can review during your next project

   B. To document employee performance

   C. To identify successes and failures on the project

   D. To record the causes of performance variances

Answers to Practice Exam

1. D. CV is calculated as follows: EV – AC. SV is calculated as follows: EV – PV. Therefore, CV is $375 - 500 = -125$, and SV is $375 - 450 = -75$.

2. A. Scope Verification is concerned with acceptance of work results, while Quality Assurance is concerned with the correctness of the work.

3. D. As a PMP, you're required to maintain integrity during the course of the project. This includes honestly reporting on the status of the project. Personal gain should never be a factor in project status reporting or project decisions.

4. B. Self-actualization is a state of independence allowing you to express yourself and perform at your peak. This is the highest level of Maslow's Hierarchy of Needs.

5. C. Intellectual property includes things developed by an organization that have commercial value but are not tangible such as books, software, artistic works, ideas, or processes that are patented, or business processes developed by the company. Hardware is tangible and therefore cannot be intellectual property.

6. B. The Responsibility Assignment Matrix (RAM) links the project roles and responsibilities to the scope definition and WBS elements or activities. The RAM usually has a row and column format showing activities and the roles assigned to those activities.

7. C. Confrontation is also called problem solving and is the best way to resolve conflict. The other conflict resolution technique not shown in this question is withdrawal.

8. C. Poor scope definition can result in increased costs, rework, and poor morale. There is no quality assurance plan. Quality Assurance is a process, and the Risk Management Planning process details how the risk management processes will be identified, managed, and controlled throughout the project.

9. A. The formula to calculate lines of communication for this question is as follows: $[9 \times (9 - 1)] \div 2 = 36$.

10. A. As a PMP, you're required to adhere to the *Project Management Professional Code of Professional Conduct*. Giving your friend confidential information is considered a conflict of interest.

11. C. The Executing and Controlling processes are inputs to each other. Workarounds are unplanned responses to risks that deal with the negative risk event as they occur. Since the project team is not aware of the risk events until it happens, no contingency plan exists to deal with the risk event.

12. B. For the first 12 months, cash flows equal $125,000. In the following year, another $300,000 is received bringing the total to $425,000. The next quarter brings in an additional $100,000, which totals the original $525,000 outflow over a period of 27 months.

13. B. CPI is calculated as follows: $EV \div AC$. SPI is calculated as follows: $EV \div PV$. Therefore, CPI is $375 \div 500 = .75$, and SPI is $375 \div 450 = .83$.

14. D. Project performance measurements are taken during the Controlling processes to identify variances and make adjustments to the project plan if appropriate.

15. A. The stages of team development are as follows: forming, storming, norming, and performing. In the forming stage, team members are formal and reserved. During the storming stage, they become confrontational. In norming, they show affection for each other. And performing is where they're the most productive and effective.

16. A. The tools and techniques of the Quality Control process include inspection, control charts, Pareto diagrams, statistical sampling, flowcharting, and trend analysis.

17. C. The question says that the variances you've experienced to date are atypical. The formula for EAC given these circumstances is as follows: $EAC = (AC + BAC) - EV$. Therefore, our calculation looks like this: $(750 + 700) - 675 = 775$.

18. D. Cost of quality is a tool and technique of Quality Planning. Internal failure costs are a cost of quality that results in rework, scrapping, and downtime. You have the ability to control internal failure costs while the product is still in the control of the organization.

19. B. Contingency planning is a form of active acceptance. Active acceptance involves developing contingency plans that are put into place should the risk event occur. Mitigation might have been an acceptable answer in this case as well, but it didn't appear as an option.

20. D. Theory Y managers believe that people will give you their best if they know what's expected of them and they have proper motivations.

21. B. The work authorization system is a tool and technique of the Project Plan Execution process. The other tool and technique of Source Selection not listed in this question is screening systems.

22. C. Culture shock is a feeling of disorientation experienced by those working in foreign countries. The question describes another scenario where culture shock might be experienced—living in another culture that you get used to and then coming back to your original culture and expecting things to be the way they were in the foreign country.

23. B. Planned value is the cost of work budgeted for an activity during a certain time frame.

24. B. Status review meetings are a way to formally exchange project information. The purpose of the status meeting is to provide updated information regarding the progress of the project. Status review meetings are also held with stakeholders, the management team, users or customers, and others depending on the project.

25. C. Quality Assurance is the process that reviews quality management activities to ensure the correct quality elements are being examined, identifies lessons learned, and makes certain the project is satisfying the quality standards laid out in the quality plan. Scope Verification and Quality Control are in the Controlling process group.

26. C. Contract Closeout should be performed prior to Administrative Closure.

27. D.   Configuration management describes the characteristics of the product of the project and makes sure the description is accurate and complete. Configuration management controls changes to the characteristics of an item, and tracks the changes made or requested and their status. Configuration management is sometimes used as the change control system.

28. D.   The lowest level of the WBS is called the work package level. The work package level is where you create time and cost estimates.

29. D.   Procurement audits review the procurement process from Planning through the Contract Administration process and document the lessons learned so that future procurement activity for this project and other projects is improved.

30. C.   The imposed deadline is a constraint because it restricts the project team's options. Constraints limit what options the project team can put into play.

31. C.   Workarounds are unplanned responses to risks that deal with the negative risk events as they occur. Since the project team is not aware of the risk event until it happens, no contingency plan exists to deal with the risk event.

32. A.   The PDM places activities on nodes, usually shown as boxes or rectangles, and connects the dependencies with arrows. The four dependency relationships used by the PDM are finish to start, finish to finish, start to start, and start to finish.

33. B.   Project managers have the most authority in projectized organizations. They have a great amount of authority in balanced matrix organizations also, but even more authority in a projectized organization.

34. A.   Extinction occurs when the project is completed and the stakeholders have signed off on the project.

35. C.   The Risk Identification process has five tools and techniques: documentation reviews, information-gathering techniques, checklists, assumptions analysis, and diagramming techniques. Brainstorming and the Delphi technique are two types of information-gathering techniques, and interviewing is the third.

36. A. The question says that the variances you've experienced to date are expected to continue throughout the project. The formula for EAC given these circumstances is as follows: EAC = [AC + (BAC − EV) ÷ CPI] . CPI = .9. Therefore, our calculation looks like this: [750 + (700 − 675) ÷ .9] = 777.77, or 778 rounded down.

37. C. The key activity in the Closing process group is concerned with gathering and disseminating information to formalize project closure. Project closure should always include informing stakeholders, customers, management, and team members that the project has been formally accepted and closed.

38. B. Change control systems are documented procedures that describe how to submit change requests. They track the status of the change requests and track the approval status, and they define the level of authority needed to approve changes. All of the following processes in the Controlling process group use change control systems as one of their tools and techniques: Integrated Change Control, Scope Change Control, Schedule Control, and Cost Control.

39. A. Bottom-up estimating allows you to estimate each work item and then roll each of these estimates up to an overall total. This is a time-consuming technique but will give you more accurate estimates than analogous estimating techniques, which are also known as top-down estimating techniques. Earned value is not a cost estimating technique.

40. B. The PERT method calculates the expected value, or weighted average, to determine project duration.

41. B. Pareto diagrams are typically displayed as histograms. They rank order the most important factors by their frequency over time. Cause-and-effect diagrams are a type of flowchart that shows how the causes and effects of problems relate.

42. C. PERT's expected value calculation is as follows: [optimistic + pessimistic + (4 × most likely)] ÷ 6. The calculation for this question looks like this: [180 + 220 + (4 × 200)] ÷ 6 = 200.

43. A. Crashing is a duration compression tool and technique of the Schedule Development process that looks at cost and schedule trade-offs. Crashing can be accomplished by adding more resources to the project and limiting or reducing project requirements.

44. B. Diversity training is the best way to ensure team members will learn to recognize and deal with cultural differences among the members as clashes could impede the project's progress.

45. D. Performance improvements are an output of the Team Development process and aren't related to the change control processes.

46. A. According to the *Guide to the PMBOK*, the scope statement should include all of the following: project justification, project product, project deliverables, and project objectives. It can be modified when approved changes in scope are made and serve as the basis for future project decision making.

47. C. Source Selection uses weighting systems, screening systems, and independent estimates to rank order proposals in sequence, starting with the top scoring proposal.

48. A. Project charters, according to the *Guide to the PMBOK*, must at least include the product description and the business need for the product or service of the project. The purpose of a project charter is to recognize and acknowledge the existence of a project and commit resources to the project. The project charter may contain cost and time estimates but does not always contain this information.

49. D. Fait accompli is used during contract negotiations. One party convinces the other that the particular issue under discussion is no longer relevant or cannot be changed.

50. B. Lessons learned are not used to document employee performance but rather to note the successes and failures that occurred during this project, including information such as the reasons why certain corrective actions were put into place, the causes of performance variances, and so on. If employees feel negative information in the lessons learned file will be used against them, they won't be honest in reporting lessons learned and you'll miss out on the benefit of learning from past mistakes.

Glossary

Activity Definition   This process identifies the activities of the project that need to be performed to produce the product or service of the project.

Activity Duration Estimating   This process assesses the number of work periods needed to complete the project activities. Work periods are usually expressed in hours or days. Large projects might express duration in weeks or months.

activity list   An extension of the WBS that contains all the activities of the project and a description of each activity. It's an output of the Activity Definition process.

activity on arrow (AOA)   A diagramming method that places activities on arrows, which connect to dependent activities using nodes. This is also known as the arrow diagramming method.

activity on node (AON)   A diagramming method that places activities on nodes, which connect to dependent activities using arrows. This is also known as the precedence diagramming method.

Activity Sequencing   This process sequences activities in logical order and determines if dependencies exist among the activities.

actual cost (AC)   The cost of work to date including direct and indirect costs.

Administrative Closure   This process is concerned with gathering and disseminating information to formalize project closure. The completion of each project phase requires administrative closure also.

analogous estimating   This technique uses the actual duration of a similar, completed activity to determine the duration of the current activity. This is also called top-down estimating and is a form of expert judgment.

arrow diagramming method (ADM)   A diagramming method that places activities on arrows, which connect to dependent activities using nodes. This is also known as activity on arrow.

assumption   An event or action believed to be true. Project assumptions should always be documented.

benchmarking   Compares previous similar activities to the current project activities to provide a standard to measure performance against. It's often used to derive ideas for quality improvements for the project.

bottom-up estimating   Every activity or work item is individually estimated and then rolled up, or added together, to come up with a total project estimate. This is a very accurate means of estimating, provided the estimates at the work package level are accurate.

cause-and-effect diagram   Shows the relationship between the effects of problems and their causes. Depicts every potential cause and subcause of a problem and the effect that each proposed solution will have on the problem. This diagram is also called a fishbone diagram or an Ishikawa diagram.

change control system   Documented procedures that describe how to submit change requests and how to manage change requests. It tracks the status of change requests and defines the level of authority needed to approve changes. It describes the management impacts of the changes as they pertain to project performance.

checklist   Provides a way to determine if the required steps in a process have been followed. Also used to help identify risks by compiling historical information from previous projects.

code of accounts   Unique, numeric identifiers assigned to each element of the WBS. Also known as a chart of accounts.

collocation   Team members physically work at the same location or hold project meetings in a common area such as a war room.

communications management plan   Documents the types of information needs the stakeholders have, when the information should be distributed, and how the information will be delivered.

Communications Planning   This Planning process determines the communication needs of the stakeholders, when and how the information will be received, and who will receive the information.

configuration control board (CCB)   A team established by the organization that's given the authority to review all change requests and approve them or deny them. This is also known as a change control board.

configuration management   Describes the characteristics of the product of the project and ensures the description is accurate and complete. Controls changes to the characteristics of an item, and tracks the changes made or requested and their status. It is usually a subset of the change control process in most organizations, or it may serve as the change control system.

conflict of interest   Occurs when personal interests are put above the interests of the project. Also occurs when personal influence is used to cause others to make decisions in favor of the influencer without regard for the project outcome.

constraint   Anything that either restricts the actions of the project team or dictates the actions of the project team.

Contract Administration   This process involves monitoring vendor performance and ensuring all the requirements of the contract are met.

Contract Closeout   This process is concerned with completing and settling the terms of the contract and determines if the work described in the contract was completed accurately and satisfactorily. This process is performed before Administrative Closure.

cost baseline   The expected cost for the project. Cost baselines are produced during the Cost Budgeting process.

Cost Budgeting   This process assigns cost estimates to activities and is used to create the cost baseline, which measures the variance and performance of the project throughout the project's life.

Cost Control   This process manages the changes to project costs using the cost change control system.

Cost Estimating   This process develops an approximation of the cost of resources needed for each project activity.

critical path (CP)   The longest path through the project that's made up of activities with zero float.

Critical Path Method (CPM)   Determines a single early and late start date and early and late finish date for each activity on the project.

culture shock   A disorienting experience that occurs when working in foreign surroundings or cultures that you are not familiar with.

decomposition   The process of breaking project deliverables down into smaller, manageable components so that project tasks and activities can be planned and estimated.

deliverable   An output that must be produced to bring the phase or project to completion. Deliverables are tangible and can be measured and easily proved.

Delphi technique   A Risk Identification technique used to gather information. Similar to brainstorming, only participants don't usually know each other nor do they have to be present at the same location.

discounted cash flow   Compares the value of the future cash flows of the project to today's dollars.

earned value (EV)   A measurement of the project's progress to date, or the value of the work completed to date.

earned value analysis   The most often used performance measurement method. It looks at schedule, cost, and scope project measurements and compares their progress as of the measurement date against what was excepted. The three measurements needed to perform earned value analysis are planned value (PV), actual cost (AC), and earned value (EV).

fast tracking   A schedule compression technique where two activities that were previously scheduled to start sequentially start at the same time. Fast tracking reduces schedule duration.

feasibility study   Undertaken to determine if the project is a viable project, the probability of project success, and the viability of the product of the project.

float time   The amount of time you can delay the early start of a task without delaying the finish date of the project. This is also known as slack time.

flowchart   A diagram that shows the logical steps that must be performed in order to accomplish an objective. It can also show how the individual elements of a system interrelate.

functional organization   A form of organizational structure. Functional organizations are traditional-type organizations with hierarchical reporting structures.

impact scale   Assigns a value to depict the severity of a potential risk impact using a cardinal value, or actual numeric value.

Information Distribution   This process concerns providing stakeholders with information regarding the project in a timely manner via status reports, project meetings, review meetings, e-mail, and so on. The communications management plan is put into action during this process.

Initiation   This is the first process in a project life cycle. It acknowledges that the project, or the next phase in an active project, should begin.

Integrated Change Control   This process is concerned with influencing the things that cause change, determining that change is needed or has happened, and managing change. All other change control processes are integrated with this process.

internal rate of return (IRR)   The discount rate when the present value of the cash inflows equals the original investment. Projects with higher IRR values are generally considered better than projects with lower IRR values. Assumes that cash inflows are reinvested at the IRR value.

iterative   To repeat processes more than once. The five process groups are repeated throughout the project's life due to change requests, responses to change, corrective action, and so on.

logical relationship   Describes the four types of dependencies between activities including finish to start, start to finish, finish to finish, and start to start. These are also known as precedence relationships.

matrix organization   A form of organizational structure. Employees in a matrix organization report to one functional manager and at least one project manager. Functional managers assign employees to projects and carry out administrative duties, while project managers assign tasks associated with the project to team members and execute the project.

milestone   A major deliverable or key event in the project used to measure project progress.

net present value (NPV)   Similar to discounted cash flows. It evaluates the cash inflows using the discounted cash flow technique, which is applied to each period the inflows are expected. The total present value of the cash flows is deducted from the initial investment to determine NPV. NPV assumes that cash inflows are reinvested at the cost of capital.

organizational breakdown structure (OBS)   Relates the WBS elements, or the work package level for very large projects, to the organizational unit responsible for completing the work.

parametric modeling   A mathematical model that uses parameters, or project characteristics, to forecast project costs.

payback period   The length of time it takes the company to recover the initial cost of producing the product or service of the project.

Performance Reporting   This process concerns collecting information regarding project progress and project accomplishments and reporting it to the stakeholders, project team members, management team, and other interested parties. It also makes predictions regarding future project performance.

planned value (PV)   The cost of work that's been budgeted for an activity during a certain time period. (Note: PV also stands for present value.)

precedence diagramming method (PDM)   A diagramming method that places activities on nodes, which connect to dependent activities using arrows. This is also known as activity on node.

present value (PV)   A financial calculation that determines value in today's dollars—not to be confused with planned value (also abbreviated PV).

probability scale   Assigns a value to depict the probability that a risk event will occur and is expressed as a number between 0.0 and 1.0.

procurement management plan   A document that describes how the procurement process will be managed, the type of contract to use, what authority the project team has, if more than one contractor will be used, and how the procurement process will be integrated with other project processes.

Procurement Planning   This process identifies what goods or services will be purchased from outside of the organization. Also uses make or buy analysis to determine if goods or services should be purchased or performed by the organization.

program   A grouping of projects that are managed together. The individual projects are usually part of one bigger project and are therefore related.

Program Evaluation and Review Technique (PERT)   Uses expected value, or weighted average, of critical path tasks to determine project duration by establishing three estimates: most likely, pessimistic, and optimistic. Used when activity duration estimates are highly uncertain.

progressive elaboration   The process of taking incremental steps to examine and refine the characteristics of the product of the project. Processes may be progressively elaborated as well.

project   Projects are temporary in nature, have definite start and end dates, create a unique product or service, and are completed when the goals and objectives of the project have been met and signed off on by the stakeholders.

project charter   An official, written acknowledgment and recognition that a project exists. It's issued by senior management and gives the project manager authority to assign organizational resources to the work of the project.

Project Communications Management   One of the nine knowledge areas of project management. Ensures proper and timely communications and includes these processes: Communications Planning, Information Distribution, Performance Reporting, and Administrative Closure.

Project Cost Management   One of the nine knowledge areas of project management. Ensures proper cost planning, budgets, and controls and includes these processes: Resource Planning, Cost Estimating, Cost Budgeting, and Cost Control.

Project Human Resource Management   One of the nine knowledge areas of project management. Ensures effective use of human resources and includes these processes: Organizational Planning, Staff Acquisition, and Team Development.

Project Integration Management   One of the nine knowledge areas of project management. Involves coordinating all aspects of the project and includes these processes: Project Plan Development, Project Plan Execution, and Integrated Change Control.

project life cycle   The grouping of project phases in a sequential order from the beginning of the project to the close.

project management   The process that's used to initiate, plan, execute, monitor, control, and close out projects by applying skills, knowledge, and project management tools and techniques to fulfill the project requirements.

Project Management Knowledge Areas   These nine project management groupings, or knowledge areas, bring together common or related processes.

project management office (PMO)   Established by organizations to create and maintain procedures and standards for project management methodologies to be used throughout the organization.

Project Management Professional Code of Professional Conduct   An ethical code established by PMI to ensure personal and professional conduct on the part of PMPs.

project manager   The person responsible for applying the skills, knowledge, and project management tools and techniques to the project activities in order to successfully complete the project objectives.

project plan   A document, or assortment of documents, that constitutes what the project is, what the project will deliver, and how all the processes will be managed. Used as the guideline throughout the project Executing and Controlling process groups to track and measure project performance and to make future project decisions. Also used as a communication and information tool for stakeholders, team members, and the management team.

Project Plan Development   This process takes the outputs from all the other Planning processes and brings them together in a concise, logical format as one main document with reference to other pertinent documents, or as several documents organized in a logical fashion. Its output is the project plan.

Project Plan Execution   This process involves carrying out the project plan. Activities are clarified, the work is authorized to begin, resources are committed and assigned to activities, and the product or service of the project is created. The largest portion of the project budget will be spent during this process.

Project Procurement Management One of the nine knowledge areas of project management. Concerns procurement and contract oversight. The processes included in this knowledge area are Procurement Planning, Solicitation Planning, Solicitation, Source Selection, Contract Administration, and Contract Closeout.

Project Quality Management One of the nine knowledge areas of project management. Ensures quality requirements of the project are satisfied. The processes included in this knowledge area are Quality Planning, Quality Assurance, and Quality Control.

project records All information regarding the project including project reports, memos, project schedules, project plans, and other documents.

Project Risk Management One of the nine knowledge areas of project management. Concerned with identifying and planning for potential risks that may impact the project. Its processes include Risk Management Planning, Risk Identification, Qualitative Risk Analysis, Quantitative Risk Analysis, Risk Response Planning, and Risk Monitoring and Control.

project schedule Determines the start and finish dates for project activities and assigns resources to the activities.

Project Scope Management One of the nine knowledge areas of project management. Concerned with the work of the project and only the work that is required to complete the project. Its processes include Initiation, Scope Planning, Scope Definition, Scope Verification, and Scope Change Control.

project sponsor Usually an executive in the organization. Has the authority to assign resources and enforce decisions regarding the project.

Project Time Management One of the nine knowledge areas of project management. Concerned with estimating the duration of the project plan activities, devising a project schedule, and monitoring and controlling deviations from the schedule. Its processes include Activity Definition, Activity Sequencing, Activity Duration Estimating, Schedule Development, and Schedule Control.

projectized organization A type of organizational structure focused on projects. Project managers generally have ultimate authority over the project, and, sometimes, supporting departments like human resources and accounting might report to the project manager. Project managers are responsible for making project decisions and acquiring and assigning resources.

Qualitative Risk Analysis   This process determines what impact the identified risks will have on the project and the probability they'll occur, and puts the risks in priority order according to their effect on the project objectives.

Quality Assurance   This process performs quality audits to determine how the project is proceeding and is concerned with making certain the project will meet and satisfy the quality standards of the project. This process should be repeated throughout the project's remaining life.

Quality Control   This process is concerned with monitoring work results to see if they fulfill the quality standards set out in the quality management plan. It determines if the end product conforms to the requirements and product description defined during the Planning processes.

quality management plan   Describes how the project management team will enact the quality policy and documents the resources needed to carry out the quality plan, the responsibilities of the project team in implementing quality, and all the processes and procedures the project team and organization will use to satisfy quality requirements.

Quality Planning   This process identifies the quality standards applicable for the project and how to fulfill the standards.

Quantitative Risk Analysis   This process assigns numeric probabilities to each identified risk and examines their potential impact to the project objectives.

requirement   The specifications of the goal or deliverable.

resource histogram   Displays resource usage in chart form with project time along the horizontal axis and hours needed along the vertical axis.

resource leveling   Attempts to smooth out the resource assignments so that tasks are completed without overloading the individual and without negatively affecting the project schedule. Some ways to perform resource leveling include delaying the start of a task to match the availability of a key team member, giving more tasks to underallocated team members, and splitting tasks.

Resource Planning   This process defines all the resources needed and the quantity of resources needed to perform project activities.

Responsibility Assignment Matrix (RAM) Ties roles and responsibilities with the WBS elements to ensure that each element has a resource assigned. A RAM is usually displayed in chart form.

Risk Identification This process identifies the potential project risks and documents their characteristics.

risk management plan Details how risk management processes will be implemented, monitored, and controlled throughout the life of the project. It does not define responses to individual risks.

Risk Management Planning This process determines how risks will be managed for a project.

Risk Monitoring and Control This process involves responding to risks as they occur. The risk management plan details how risk is managed, and the risk response plan details how risk response strategies are implemented in the event of an actual risk event. This process implements risk response according to the plan.

Risk Response Planning This process defines what steps to take to reduce threats and take advantage of opportunities and assigns departments or individual staff members the responsibility of carrying out the risk response plans developed in this process.

Schedule Control This process involves documenting and managing changes to the project schedule.

Schedule Development This process calculates and prepares the schedule of project activities, which becomes the schedule baseline. It determines activity start and finish dates, finalizes activity sequences and durations, and assigns resources to activities.

Scope Change Control This process involves documenting and managing changes to project scope. Any modification to the agreed-upon WBS is considered a scope change. Changes in product scope will require changes to project scope.

Scope Definition This process breaks project deliverables down into smaller, manageable components so that project tasks and activities can be planned, estimated, and controlled. This is also known as decomposition, which is the primary purpose of this process.

scope management plan   Analyzes the reliability and stability of the project scope. Documents the process that manages project scope and changes to project scope.

Scope Planning   This process uses progressive elaboration to define the work of the project and culminates in the scope statement, which describes the project deliverables, objectives, and justification.

scope statement   Documents the project goals, deliverables, and requirements, which are used as a baseline for future project decisions. It also includes the project objectives and the business justification for the project.

Scope Verification   This process formalizes the acceptance of the project scope and is primarily concerned with the acceptance of work results.

slack time   The amount of time you can delay the early start of a task without delaying the finish date of the project. This is also known as float time.

Solicitation   This process involves obtaining bids and proposals from vendors in response to RFPs and similar documents prepared during the Solicitation Planning process.

Solicitation Planning   This process involves preparing solicitation materials, such as RFPs, RFIs and RFQs, and reviewing lists of potential qualified vendors.

Source Selection   This process involves the receipt of bids or proposals and choosing a vendor to perform the work or supply the goods or services.

Staff Acquisition   This process involves attaining human resources and assigning them to the project. Human resources may come from inside or outside the organization.

stakeholder   A person or organization who has a vested interest in the project and stands to gain or lose something as a result of the project.

statement of work (SOW)   Contains the details of a procurement item in clear, concise terms and includes the project objectives, a description of the work of the project, concise specifications of the product or services required, and a project schedule. Either buyer or seller may prepare the SOW.

supporting detail   An output of some of the project management processes. Includes constraints, assumptions, and any information not specifically documented during the process.

Team Development   This process concerns creating an open, encouraging environment for stakeholders to contribute as well as developing the project team into an effective, functioning, coordinated group.

work breakdown structure (WBS)   A deliverables-oriented hierarchy that defines the total work of the project. Each level has more detailed information than the previous level.

work package   The lowest level in a WBS. Team assignments, time estimates, and cost estimates can be made when this level represents tasks or activities. On very large projects, this level is handed off to subproject managers who develop their own WBS to fulfill the requirements of the work package deliverable.

Index

Note to the reader: Throughout this index **boldfaced** page numbers indicate primary discussions of a topic. *Italicized* page numbers indicate illustrations.

Z

TELL US WHAT YOU THINK!

Your feedback is critical to our efforts to provide you with the best books and software on the market. Tell us what you think about the products you've purchased. It's simple:

1. Visit the Sybex website
2. Go to the product page
3. Click on **Submit a Review**
4. Fill out the questionnaire and comments
5. Click **Submit**

With your feedback, we can continue to publish the highest quality computer books and software products that today's busy IT professionals deserve.

www.sybex.com

SYBEX Inc. • 1151 Marina Village Parkway, Alameda, CA 94501 • 510-523-8233

PMP®: Project Management Professional Study Guide

Project Management Professional Exam Objectives

OBJECTIVE	CHAPTER
Project Initiation	
Determine Project Goals	2
Determine Deliverables	2
Determine Process Outputs	2
Document Constraints	2
Document Assumptions	2
Define Strategy	3
Identify Performance Criteria	3
Determine Resource Requirements	3
Define Budget	3
Produce Formal Documentation	3
Project Planning	
Refine Project	4
Create WBS	4
Develop Resource Management Plan	5
Refine Time and Cost Estimates	5
Establish Project Controls	6, 7
Develop Project Plan	7
Obtain Plan Approval	7
Project Execution	
Commit Resources	8
Implement Resources	8
Manage Progress	8, 9
Communicate Progress	8
Implement Quality Assurance Procedures	9

SYBEX